THE BONDS OF FREEDOM

JAKE SUBRYAN RICHARDS

The Bonds of Freedom

LIBERATED AFRICANS AND THE END OF THE SLAVE TRADE

Yale UNIVERSITY PRESS NEW HAVEN AND LONDON

Published with assistance from the foundation established in memory of Calvin Chapin of the Class of 1788, Yale College.

Yale University Press books may be purchased in quantity for educational, business, or promotional use. For information, please e-mail sales.press@yale.edu (U.S. office) or sales@yaleup.co.uk (U.K. office).

Set in Scala type by IDS Infotech Ltd.
Printed in the United States of America.

Library of Congress Control Number: 2024949786
ISBN 978-0-300-26320-6 (hardcover)

A catalogue record for this book is available from the British Library.

Authorized Representative in the EU: Easy Access System Europe, Mustamäe tee 50, 10621 Tallinn, Estonia, gpsr.requests@easproject.com

10 9 8 7 6 5 4 3 2 1

For the freedom dreamers, future, present, and past

CONTENTS

ACKNOWLEDGMENTS

While commuting by bicycle along the river routes of South London, I would write these acknowledgments in my mind. The prose flowed far more elegantly on two wheels than it now does on the page. But I hope these acknowledgments still convey the range and depth of my gratitude. Every historian relies on primary sources that exist only because people and institutions conserve them: my first, heartfelt, thank-you is to the people of Sierra Leone, South Africa, Brazil, Cuba, the United Kingdom, and the United States for supporting the archives and libraries that have provided access to documents to me. The ethos of public access to the past is both an achievement to admire and a value to defend, especially as the parlous state of many of the records that I have used testifies to how fragile our collective historical knowledge is.

My thanks to the institutions who have supported my scholarship while writing this book: Durham University and the London School of Economics and Political Science. Grants from the LSE's STICERD Fund and the Department of International History's Research Clusters and RIIF funded research and publication costs. The Martin Lynn Scholarship funded part of my research in Sierra Leone, which is featured in this book. I am grateful to the many archivists who have helped with documents. I would like to thank the team at the Western Cape Archives and Records Service, especially Erika Le Roux and Thembile Ndabeni; the staff of the Sierra Leone Public

Archives, including Abu Koroma and Albert Moore; Fred Ferreira and his colleagues at the Arquivo Histórico do Itamaraty; Helba Mattos and Roberto at the Arquivo Nacional, Rio de Janeiro; Naomi O'Farrill, Juana Martinez, and Niurbis Ferrer Prada at the Archivo Nacional de la República de Cuba; and the staff of the UK National Archives, particularly Greg Cole and Grace Quartey. I am grateful to the Instituto Histórico de Cuba for hosting me during my archival research. Parts of the manuscript use material from my article "The Adjudication of Slave Ship Captures, Coercive Intervention, and Value Exchange in Comparative Atlantic Perspective, ca. 1839–1870," *Comparative Studies in Society and History* 62, no. 4 (2020): 836–67 (under the terms of the Creative Commons Attribution license, https://creativecommons.org/licenses/by/4.0/).

I am grateful to the many scholars who have given me feedback on my work in progress. Lisa Ford, Benedetta Rossi, Margot Finn, Michael Lobban, David Armitage, Camillia Cowling, and Francisco Bethencourt participated in a manuscript workshop at LSE and sent me constructive reports on my draft. Keila Grinberg, Vincent Brown, Roquinaldo Ferreira, Richard Huzzey, Emma Hunter, Peter Mandler, Sarah Balakrishnan, and Catherine Peters participated in a workshop online. Jonathan Connolly, Mark Hannam, Sujit Sivasundaram, Harri Englund, and Molly Richards also read the full draft and provided detailed comments. After I redrafted the manuscript, Samantha Leigh Payne, Emma Hart, Hendrik Hartog, and Andrea Richards commented on it. Each person's feedback has made my book so much better. Kathleen M. Brown provided brilliant insight and encouragement and reworked my introduction beautifully. Paul Halliday spent hours talking with me about legal history at the American Society for Legal History annual conference and made time to discuss the entire manuscript with me. James Sweet responded graciously to my request to meet during the American Historical Association annual meeting when he was still president—"I would be delighted to meet you [but] AHA has me booked almost every waking hour"—and then proceeded to conjure a waking hour in which to talk with me about the book. He then read the manuscript in Accra and parts again in Wisconsin.

I owe special thanks to Margot Finn and Nicholas Guyatt. Margot's intellectual brilliance is matched by her wonderful mentorship. Nicholas not only has read my work diligently but also has championed my scholarship at every turn. Margot and Nick are models of professional integrity whose examples I wish to emulate.

I wish to thank Lauren Benton, Vincent Brown, Kimberly Welch, Sadiah Qureshi, and Fiona Vernal for their feedback in framing my first book project. The same applies to Jean Comaroff and Dane Kennedy for their professional guidance. Each of them has reminded me that "I believe in you, and I believe in this book" when I needed to hear it the most. Many scholars have given me feedback on excerpts of the manuscript. My thanks to Saul Dubow, David Schorr, Simon Newman, Jennifer Pitts, Michelle McKinley, Lauren Benton, Kimberly Welch, Gautham Rao, Sarah Barringer Gordon, Naama Maor, Christine Whyte, Jean Besson, David Seipp, Katherine Paugh, Merry Wiesner-Hanks, Diana Paton, Gabriela Ramos, Jennifer Davis, Pauline Peters, Annie Ruderman, Cherry Leonardi, Jack Parlett, John Comaroff, Jesús Sanjurjo, Abosede George, Nemata Blyden, Andrew Barnes, and Roberto Saba. I would also like to thank participants in the Hurst Summer Institute for Legal History, the Law and Society Association Early Career Workshop, and the Comparative Law Works-in-Progress Workshop for their feedback.

At Durham, Richard Huzzey and Cherry Leonardi gave me feedback on my draft work and have remained advisers and friends ever since. At LSE, Tanya Harmer and Taylor Sherman gave me feedback on parts of the manuscript. My especial thanks to Taylor and to Patrick Wallis for their constructive engagement with my scholarship and for their professional guidance. Charles Stafford has shown his commitment to my career in various ways since I joined LSE. During lectures and seminars, many students at Durham and LSE have pushed me to clarify my own thinking, which has enriched this book.

I would like to thank the organizers and audience members at the following venues for enabling me to try out arguments and for improving them with many questions and comments: the London Group of Historical Geographers and the History of Political Ideas Early Career Seminars at the Institute of Historical Research; the Archives of the Disappeared/Margaret Anstee Centre Lecture at Newnham College, Cambridge; the World History Seminar at the University of Cambridge; the Laboratory for the Economics of Africa's Past at Stellenbosch University; the Caribbean Research Seminar Series in the School of Advanced Study at the University of London; Durham University; the Wilberforce Institute for the Study of Slavery and Emancipation; King's College London; the University of Oxford; the University of Central Lancashire; Brown University; New York University;

the British History Seminar at Northwestern University; plus audiences at annual meetings of the Brazilian Studies Association, American Society for Legal History, the American Historical Association, UK Latin American Historians, and Law and Society Association.

Yale University Press has been the ideal home for this book project. From our first conversation, Adina Popescu has been an author's dream editor: responsive, dedicated, and positive about the project. I also appreciate the work of the wider team on the manuscript—particularly Andrew Katz, Eva Skewes, Erica Hanson, Jonah Miller, and Jeffrey Schier. The two anonymous readers gave me constructive and incisive comments that have greatly improved the book. I warmly thank them both. My thanks to Miles Irving for making the maps.

I am grateful to my friends across the world who have supported my scholarship, particularly when I have been far from home. My thanks to Solange and Antônio Alves Costa, Franci, Maxine Rubin, Josh Platzky Miller, Josephine Dauda, Dennis Michael John, Choi Wong-Muhammad, Kadeem Simmons-Bah, Afolabi Ajibade, Alex Gibbs, Will Jeffs, Yema Tucker, and Taira Miyatake. My parents have always supported my career with great joy, dedication, and intellectual engagement. My sisters, Molly and Evie, have made me laugh more and write better. I am grateful to Aedin and Mark Carlisle for their good cheer and encouragement and to the wider clan of Carlisles and Dormers. Naomi, you have been by my side with this book from conception to delivery. Thank you for critical feedback and steadfast love. Viola brings a joy to my life that knows no bounds. Thank you for your smiles. Deep river, my home is with you both.

A NOTE ON TERMINOLOGY

The term "enslaved person," which centers the individual's fullness of life, thoughts, feelings, and actions, is superior to the reductive term "slave." But many aspects of social norms and legal systems that underpinned slave societies limited recognition of the legal personality of an enslaved person—indeed, some denied that this personality existed at all. For this reason, this study adopts a range of terms. I use "slave" and "enslaved person" as equivalent terms, prioritizing the former when explaining a social attitude or legal position and the latter when discussing a specific person or group of people. I use "captive" and "captivity" to emphasize some aspects of the process of enslavement, such as the condition of being treated as a person held against one's will aboard a slaving ship. The distinction between somebody in this position and somebody on a plantation becomes vital at various points in the book.

When people in positions of power created sources about enslaved and freed people, they created racialized categories about them. In the archives, I frequently encountered people described interchangeably as "black," "slave," or "African," when of course these designations were not coterminous. I have prioritized naming people as "liberated Africans" as the most accurate sociolegal term and the term of description that people most frequently used in petitions. This term refers to people rescued from slaving ships by maritime patrols, as distinct from all other procedures for exiting slavery. Most of the people I discuss were born in Africa and were mostly racialized as Black, but sometimes they could fit into other socially constructed categories such as *pardo*. Homo sapiens originated in Africa, so "people of African descent" is tautologous. Whenever racialized terms are used in the book, they are used as cultural constructions, rather than fixed identities.

I name each person where the sources provide such information. In quoting from primary sources, I have retained original orthography, grammar, and spelling. Following convention, I have modernized the spelling of Brazilian names. Brazil's currency is the real, and in the nineteenth century, it had no subdivision. Lei 59 of 1833 fixed the currency as the mil-réis, written Rs 1$000. Amounts below one thousand réis were written as Rs 999. Amounts above one million réis (called a *conto*) were written as 1:536$300 = 1,536,300 réis.

THE BONDS OF FREEDOM

Introduction

IN SEPTEMBER 1879, SEVERAL YEARS after the final slaving ship crossed the Atlantic, Librada petitioned the governor of Matanzas in Cuba for a freedom letter. Like millions of people, Librada had been trafficked aboard an illegal slaving ship from West Africa to the Americas. But unlike most transatlantic slaving ships in the nineteenth century, the ship that held Librada was captured by authorities as part of efforts to suppress the trade. Despite the growing calls for liberty throughout the Atlantic world, Librada was still working as a bonded laborer long after her "liberation" from a slaving ship. Even the name that the Spanish colonial authorities assigned to her reflected her predicament: *librada* means both "freed" and "issued" like an order.

Librada petitioned amid the Thirty Years' War in Cuba, a period of insurgent warfare against colonialism and slavery. A notary transcribed her spoken words. She explained that in 1863, the Spanish colonial authorities had disembarked her from a slaving vessel and "deposited her in the barracoons at the moat of Havana." Then they assigned her to compulsory service for several years to earn her freedom. The notary did not record Librada's birth name or where she had come from in West Africa. The fact that she was "de nación conga" indicates that she was perhaps born in the Congo-Angola region. Librada called her situation "most sad and regrettable" because she was separated from her seven-year-old son, Alfredo, who was in service in another area, San Juan de los Remedios.[1] In a second

Liberated Africans in Cuba endured bonded labor and the difficulty of gaining official recognition of their children's free status. Aicheta (labeled with the number 2) holds her forty-day-old baby (3), while standing next to her partner (1). Their names were not recorded. The photograph is from a racist pseudoscience publication. (Henri Dumont, "Antropologia y patologia comparada de los negros esclavos" [1876], reprinted in *Revista Bimestre Cubana* 10, no. 4 [July–August 1915]: 268a. Public domain. Reproduction courtesy of the Digital Library of the Caribbean)

petition, Librada explained that "having arrived as a ten-year-old and having spent time on this island in Havana and Puerto Príncipe . . . without seeing any of her shipmates [*compañeros*]," she could not present a deponent who had been trafficked to Cuba on the same slaving ship to corroborate her account.[2] In her petition, Librada cited her own experience of illegal trafficking from Africa to Cuba and signaled the importance of relations between shipmates for claiming freedom for herself and her son.

A legal regime that provided for the rescue of hundreds of thousands of African captives from slaving ships and their assignment into time-limited service was a novel force in nineteenth-century global history. It had profound consequences for the people who gained authority from it and those who were subjected to it. The regime meant that liberated Africans

In this figurative drawing, Lela Harris uses clear lines and precise shading to foreground the faces of Aicheta, her partner, and their baby, thereby giving the family a renewed presence. (Lela Harris, *Aicheta's Family*, pastel and charcoal on paper, private collection. Courtesy of the artist)

like Librada were doubly *diasporic*. Displaced by force in the massive movement of people that constituted the transatlantic slave traffic, they found themselves once again swept up in the legal maneuvers that defined their circumscribed emancipations. The regime comprised a set of legal processes and institutions produced by Atlantic slave traffic prohibitions, international treaties, illegal slaving activities, and liberated Africans' own legal strategies.[3] Political authorities in various Atlantic jurisdictions defined the legal status of individuals like Librada, but this was not the end of their stories. Librada and her liberated counterparts were often left to overcome legal obstacles and reconfigure their status to achieve actual liberty.

People like Librada found that the laws that created the possibility of their liberation from slaving ships did not provide a detailed template for their lives as freedpeople. These same laws also had wide-ranging consequences beyond the end of the slave trade for the societies in which liberated Africans resided. Their stories invite us to crisscross the Atlantic as a region in which a diasporic group navigated their way through a world structured by empires. Uncovering the legal regime that defined the status of liberated Africans requires an approach that focuses on the interaction between top-down imperial and bottom-up diasporic processes.

The capture of slaving ships by anti-slave-trade vessels, with their own strict social hierarchies, subjected the rescued shipboard Africans to a middle passage. This middle passage would end only once the anti-slave-trade captor found a court with jurisdiction to decide on the legality of capture. Three types of court were particularly important: vice-admiralty courts in British colonies, which applied prize law; Mixed Commissions in various Atlantic empires and independent polities, which applied treaty law; and domestic courts in slave societies such as Brazil and Cuba.[4] Once the court had declared the capture lawful, local officials with authority under domestic or treaty law assigned the liberated Africans to compulsory labor. The slippery distinctions between being liberated on the high seas or in coastal waters or being assigned to labor on urban public works or a plantation could be life-changing. The liberated Africans' middle passage, the jurisdiction of the courts, and compulsory labor assignments formed a common pathway for hundreds of thousands of liberated Africans, revealing similarities and differences among them.[5] Liberated Africans confronted multiple stages of captivity during the making of freedom from the transatlantic slave trade.

LIBERATED AFRICANS AND THE ABOLITION OF THE SLAVE TRADE

From the early sixteenth to the late nineteenth centuries, the trade in enslaved African people was foundational to creating the modern world. Enslavers trafficked more than twelve and a half million people in sub-Saharan Africa. They captured some people in warfare. Other people suffered enslavement as criminal punishment. Still other people were detained as collateral for debt, which morphed into sale as a slave. West and Central African elites used each of these processes to enrich themselves, distorting African societies. Societies in sub-Saharan West Africa often had low population densities. Any use of power that members perceived to be unjust could cause mass departures from the society. Legal processes consequently focused on how to resolve a dispute to restore reciprocal relations among members. These processes could involve violence, including punishments such as enslavement or death. But the focus of these processes on reciprocity disrupts a teleology toward modernity that is defined by the jurisdiction of nation-states and institutions such as prisons. The market incentives for slave-trading made it profitable for rulers to reconfigure legal systems to produce slaves.[6] Enslavers marched these captive people to the coast, where there was still the prospect of redemption in exchange for payment. Most captives suffered sale to transatlantic traders, who embarked them on slaving ships.

Slave-trading was always a complex enterprise that operated between multiple polities, and it became even more so during the era of its gradual illegalization. African warriors, Afro-European brokers, European merchants, and polyglot, multiracial slaving-ship crews engaged in transactions. Merchants in European ports extended credit for slaving voyages and devised new financial instruments such as maritime insurance to manage the risk of loss of capital. From 1807 onward, parts of these trading systems became clandestine, yet that did not diminish the scale of trading. Approximately three million people were trafficked across the Atlantic after Britain's Abolition Act of 1807, constituting one-quarter of the entire trade.[7] During the gradual illegalization of the trade, central Cuba and southeastern Brazil, with their large sugar and coffee plantations, together received over 80 percent of all people trafficked from Africa across the Atlantic.[8]

As enslaved laborers, these trafficked Africans and their descendants worked in every economic sector, producing goods and services for global markets at a time of rapid industrialization and population growth. This transoceanic trafficking was unique: aside from being unjust in the victims' eyes, it breached the domestic law of many places in the Americas. The trade also breached emerging international law. One prominent aspect of applying these laws against the trade was the deployment of anti-slave-trade maritime patrols that captured hundreds of slaving ships heading to the Americas. The patrols rescued hundreds of thousands of shipboard captives from these ships. The names for these people included "prize slaves," "captured negroes," "recaptured Africans," "recaptives," "emancipados," and "free Africans." During the era of suppression, the commonest name to emerge was "liberated Africans." Around the Atlantic, courts adjudicated the legality of these maritime captures. Local officials assigned the liberated Africans from these ships into compulsory service, which formally lasted for up to fourteen years but in practice often lasted much longer. After horrific ordeals of maritime captivity and labor that bore many similarities to enslavement, these "liberated Africans" navigated their own path. They confronted political authorities committed to slavery, racialized inequality, and imperial rule. Following their paths helps illuminate illegal enslavement, its protracted abolition, and its troubling afterlives. The liberated African diaspora, which resulted from the most significant intervention against the largest slaving routes, allows us to ask new questions about the role of law, empire, and struggles for freedom in the transition from slavery to emancipation in the nineteenth century.

Following liberated Africans reveals the conflicting aspects of the legal regime as it subjected them to authoritarian control and provided a domain for them to produce their own vision of freedom. The legal regime reorients our conception of Atlantic history by showing extensive connections between north and south. As Britain, the leading global imperial power, began to act against the largest illegal slaving routes to Brazil and Cuba, an anti-slave-trade legal regime emerged through connected processes of maritime capture, court adjudication, compulsory labor, and the ending of compulsory labor in British colonies such as Sierra Leone, the Cape Colony, and Caribbean territories, as well as in Brazil and Cuba.[9] At least two hundred thousand people, from vastly different backgrounds across sub-Saharan Africa, underwent this common legal journey of liberation in the nineteenth century.[10]

Several Atlantic powers declared the abolition of the transatlantic trade in enslaved African people. Throughout the Atlantic world, the Haitian

Revolution inspired people who opposed slavery. Following Haiti's declaration of independence in 1804, the new nation outlawed the slave trade and slavery. The revolution also increased fears among slaveholding powers, including nearby Spanish colonial Cuba, that enslaved and free people of color might launch insurrections against enslavement. Imperial powers began to regulate the trade to control the populations inside their colonial territories. In 1792, Denmark became the first imperial power to abolish the trade. In the United States, Congress passed legislation that prohibited slave-trading to its territories in 1808 after the expiry of a constitutional moratorium on any federal ban. The maritime ban fitted alongside restrictions on the movement of free Black sailors in port towns because state authorities perceived them to encourage resistance movements. The ban related to transoceanic voyages alone. Anti-slave-trade legislation in the United States did not stop the huge interprovincial slave trade from the Upper to Lower South that led to the boom in commodity production there.

Measured by the number of captives liberated from slaving ships and the wide-ranging repercussions on other Atlantic powers, the most significant anti-slave-trade intervention was by the British Empire. According to one estimate, British patrols were responsible for capturing 1,596 of 1,994 slaving ships (80 percent) detained under anti-slave-trade measures in the nineteenth-century Atlantic world, with over 186,000 captive people on board of a total of over 205,000 (91 percent).[11] Such captures revealed how suppression involved an Atlantic composed of many sovereign powers. When a British vessel captured the slaving ship *Amelia* on its way from Cabinda to Brazil in 1811, it brought the interests of British captors, Cabindan enslavers, US shipowners, and Portuguese imperial authorities into conflict. The 1807 Abolition Act is often taken as the transformative piece of legislation for the abolition of the trade. The early enforcement of this act in two theaters of war, the Caribbean and the Upper Guinea Coast, is where the story of liberated Africans begins. Through this act, legislators, naval officers, and judges adapted the common practice of capturing enemy ships in wartime to the capture of slaving ships. Early prohibition thus drew on maritime prize law, which governed the capture of enemy vessels and property in wartime. Chapter 1 traces the act in the vice-admiralty courts located in the tiny plantation colony of Tortola and the colony for people freed from slavery, Sierra Leone. African people liberated from the *Amelia* settled just outside Freetown. Despite the 1807 act, market demand for

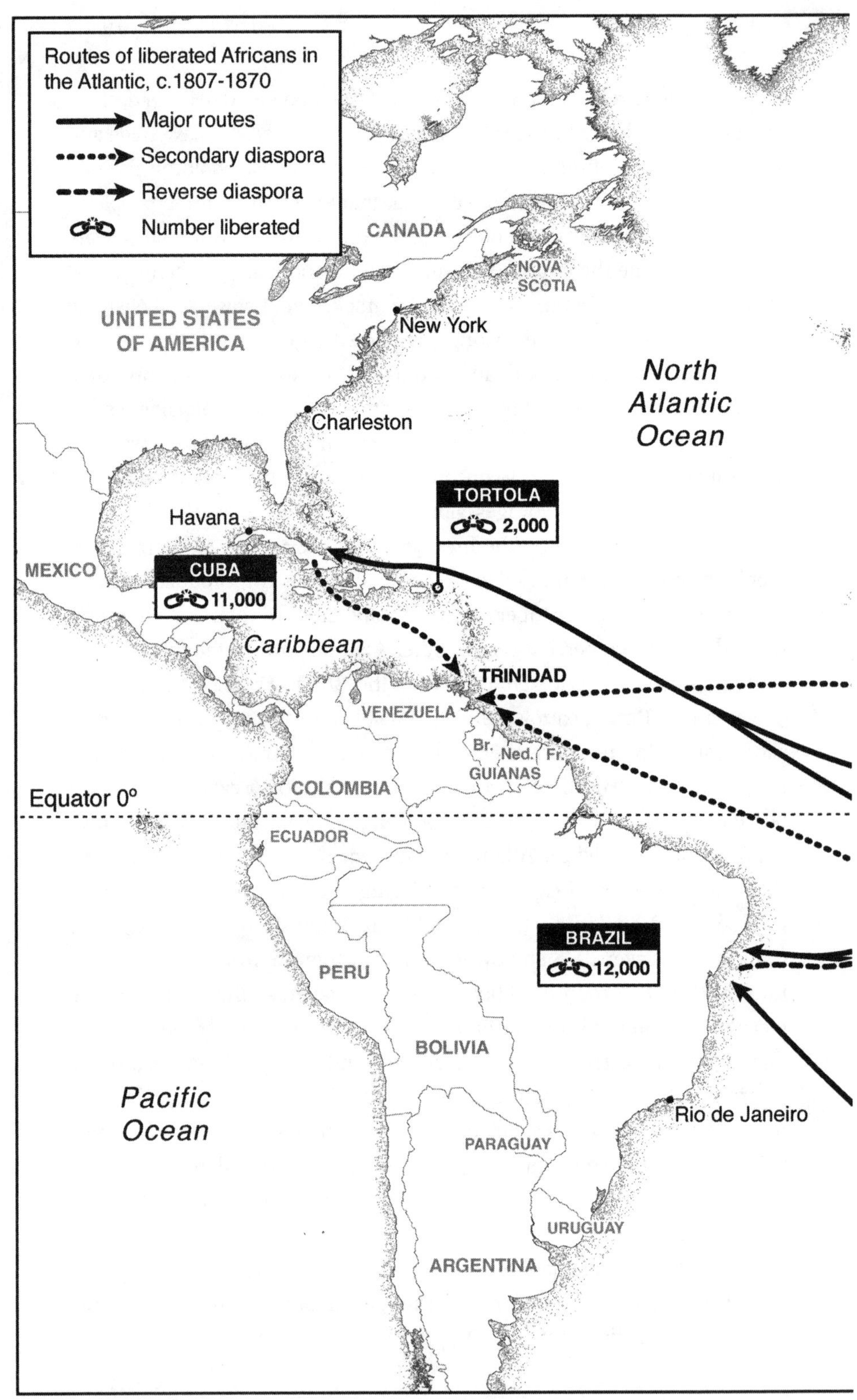

Map of liberated Africans in the Atlantic world, 1807–70. Estimates rounded to the nearest thousand. (Sources: Daniel Domingues da Silva, David Eltis, Philip Misevich, and Olatunji

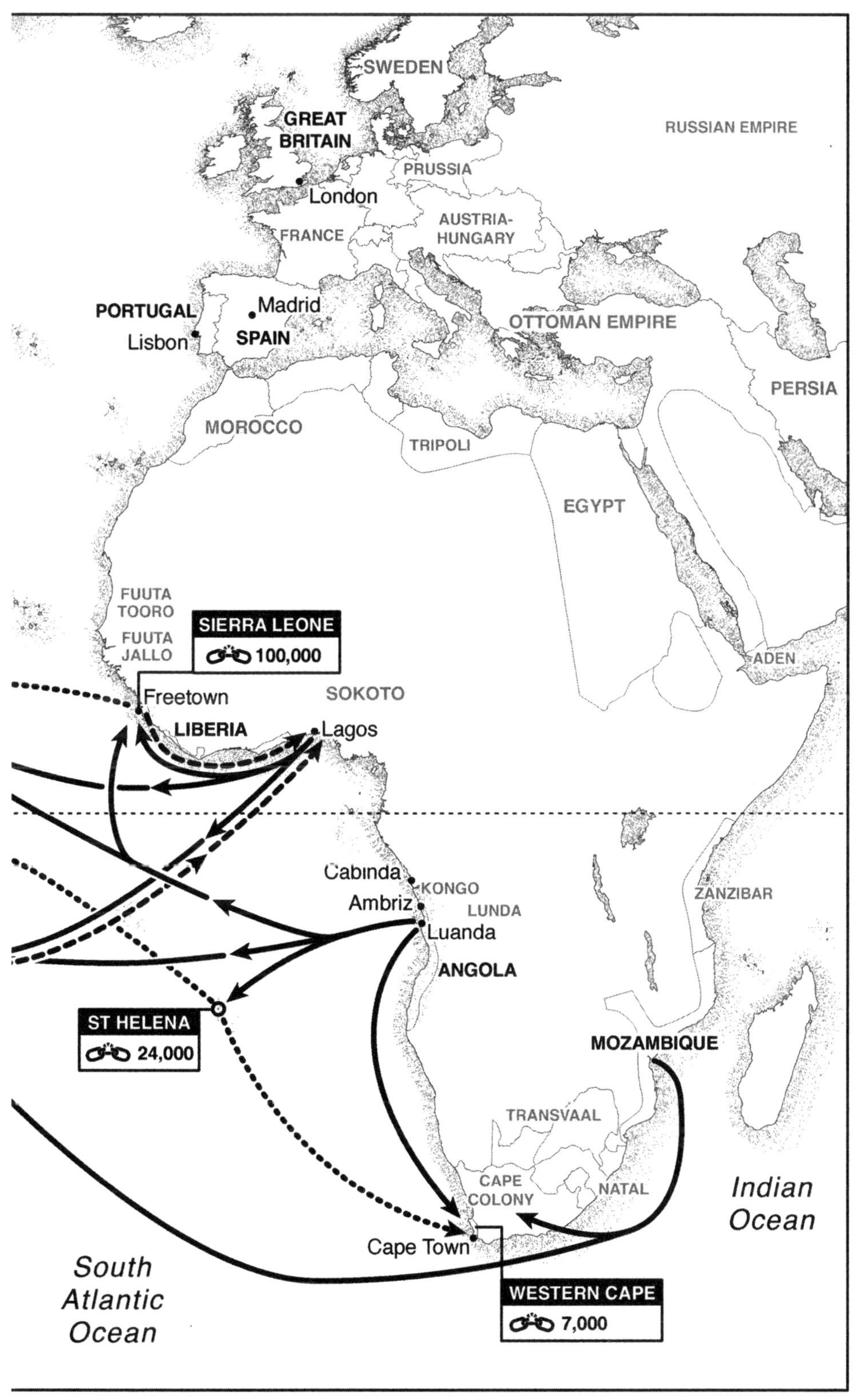

Ojo, "The Diaspora of Africans Liberated from Slave Ships in the Nineteenth Century," *Journal of African History* 55, no. 3 (2014): 347–69; SlaveVoyages; Parliamentary Papers)

slave-produced commodities rose throughout the first half of the nineteenth century. As commissions of inquiry discovered in the 1820s, even in British colonies, liberated Africans faced horrendous work conditions and the risk of reenslavement. The 1807 act neither ended the slave trade nor guaranteed the security of liberated Africans.

After the end of the Napoleonic Wars in 1815, prize law no longer operated under wartime conditions. Unlike Denmark, Haiti, the United States, and Britain, most polities (a term for a political community before the era of nation-states) had not passed laws against the slave trade. Without international agreement that the slave trade violated the law of nations, the High Court of Admiralty decided that only treaties between contracting sovereign powers could authorize their respective navies to search foreign slaving ships on the high seas. Using Britain's considerable postwar military, naval, and financial leverage, negotiators cajoled other polities to sign up to treaties. For instance, they offered debt forgiveness to Portugal as a quid pro quo for an anti-slave-trade treaty with a mutual right of naval search. Britain's former enemy France and the United States had sufficient resources to refuse to participate in the treaty order. From 1815 until the end of the transatlantic trade in around 1870, treaties awarded this mutual right of search among imperial powers. There were additional treaties and agreements between European empires and African polities for the suppression of the trade and further treaties to suppress the slave trade in the Indian Ocean.

The primary focus of these treaties was regulating maritime captures of slaving ships and the adjudication of the legality of these captures. The Mixed Commissions, which had jurisdiction over naval captures effected under treaty law, had one branch in British colonial Freetown and one in the treaty cosignatory's territory. Commissions sat in slave societies, including Brazil, Cuba, and Angola. The Commissions thus established a common set of institutions in the North and South Atlantic. In 1821, the British ship *Morgania* captured the slaver *Emilia* en route from Lagos to Bahia, which became the first capture adjudicated by the Mixed Commission in Brazil. Chapter 2 investigates how anti-slave-trade courts operated in slave societies and the compromises and tensions that they created. The treaties did not create a jurisdiction over the trade's underlying business practices. These practices implicated the very same powers that had introduced anti-slave-trade domestic or treaty law. Merchants exported British manufactured goods to West Africa and Brazil, where slave traders used them to purchase captives on the African coast. Sailors and financial capital from the United States, which refused to join the treaty order until the Civil War, contributed to illegal voyages.[12] Although liberated Africans from the *Emilia* worked alongside enslaved people in Rio de Janeiro, the treaties did not directly affect the status of enslaved people in Brazil or other slave societies.

In the late 1830s, the gaps and loopholes of the treaties became increasingly apparent. In an era of global population growth, industrialization, and urbanization, merchants exported Cuban sugar and Brazilian coffee to markets worldwide. One important destination was the empire that had transformed itself from being a global slaving power to a proponent of anti-slave-trade and antislavery projects: Britain. Importing slave-produced commodities while using diplomatic negotiations, gunboat violence, and secret intelligence to insist Brazil and Spanish colonial Cuba abolish transoceanic trafficking was just one among many contradictions.[13] As explored in chapter 3, the British shifted to authorizing gunboat attacks on the West African coast from the late 1830s. The Royal Navy also attacked the coast of Brazil in 1850 to try to force an end to the trade. In the name of "free trade," in the 1830s to 1850s, Britain's navy shelled ports in Brazil, West Africa, and China. Maritime patrolling to suppress the trade, which constituted as much as 10 percent of all naval deployments, imposed a huge cost on public finances and raised the price of consumables like coffee and raw materials like cotton. Members of Parliament, merchants, and naval and military officers used anti-slave-trade and antislavery arguments to justify the colonization of African lands and peoples. Suppression was therefore not part of a systemic pursuit of maximum economic benefit to Britain. In each of these actions, antislavery sentiment and capitalist interests were interrelated. Even if we could disentangle these threads, what is at stake is explaining how they produced not abolitionism per se, or even abolitionist policy, but rather the specific pathway that composed the process of interdicting the transoceanic slave trade in the nineteenth century.[14] Until the ending of the trade in the late 1860s, British imperial intervention provided both a warning to proslavery interests and a resource to enslaved people, unsettling slave societies on both sides of the Atlantic.

The anti-slave-trade legal regime not only targeted illegal slaving routes but also created something new: an early path toward postemancipation order. The operations of the illegal trade and the diasporic origins of liberated Africans mean that no single site or polity occupies the center of this history. Instead, African people liberated from vessels like the *Emilia* moved through layers of institutions in a multi-imperial world across jurisdictions in Europe, Africa, and the Americas. Their paths cut across prevailing boundaries between international and domestic law, civil and criminal law, or Indigenous and colonial forms of dispute resolution in Africa. This approach builds on studies of anti-slave-trade projects, such as the founding of colonial Sierra Leone, that have focused attention on how abolitionists accumulated and spent their "moral capital."[15] Historians have revealed the practical workings of anti-slave-trade activity, such as the social history of the naval crews that intercepted slaving ships.[16] Britain's anti-slave-trade and antislavery imperial policies propelled a shift from maritime interdiction of transoceanic trafficking to territorial colonization in Africa.[17] British policy makers and merchants exploited economic opportunities in Africa through the so-called legitimate commerce of raw materials such as palm oil that were important in industrial processes. Indeed, liberated Africans worked as interpreters and missionaries on one such venture: the failed Niger expedition to establish an agricultural colony in 1841. The promotion of "legitimate commerce" in goods, which were often produced by enslaved laborers, favored British manufacturing while limiting British moral and financial responsibility to free or protect these enslaved people.

As well as focusing on the imperial ideologies and practices that underpinned British anti-slave-trade projects, scholars have studied "liberated Africans" released from slaving ships like the *Emilia*. In British slave colonies in the North and South Atlantic, colonial administrators used liberated Africans as an indentured labor force, a practice that continued during the era of emancipation.[18] In response to their displacement, liberated Africans engaged in ethnogenesis—the development of new identities—that helped them form coherent communities based on common linguistic and regional backgrounds in West Africa, journeys on the same slaving ship, or a combination of the two.[19] Imperial authorities also settled liberated Africans outside British spaces, including in Angola, Brazil, and Cuba. In slave societies—where enslaved labor underpinned the most important aspects of social, economic, cultural, and political life—liberated Africans illuminated the indistinct boundary between slave and free status.[20]

The African people released from the *Amelia* in Sierra Leone and *Emilia* in Brazil came from different places in West Africa and were liberated in different territories, yet the next step in their journeys was similar. Each liberated African served as a bonded laborer for a private master or institution. In the British Empire, some men were enlisted in the army and navy, whereas other men, women, and children were bound as apprentices. Treaty and local legislation usually stipulated that labor was supposed to take the form of a contractual apprenticeship to learn a skill for a period of up to fourteen years. A typical contract included time off, subsistence, and accommodation. Some arrangements included a wage. For the African people liberated from the *Emilia* under treaty law, the opportunity to learn the "civilizing" tenets of Catholicism was a requirement. Apprenticeship was supposed to be categorically different from slavery, in which the enslaver held property rights in the enslaved person. But state officials and private masters tended to allocate liberated Africans to whichever work they deemed most pressing, often without a contract and sometimes exceeding the time limit. The term "compulsory labor" encapsulates this capacious range of practices.

Chapter 4 investigates how compulsory labor produced a new political economy in urban Atlantic societies. Polities tried to manage the transition from an economy that depended on regular imports of African captive people to one that relied on immigrant or indentured labor. In slave societies, liberated Africans suffered multiple periods of compulsory labor, separation from their families, and even kidnapping into slavery.[21] Liberated Africans had greater personal security in nonslave societies compared to slave societies, yet all forms of compulsory labor rendered them vulnerable to exploitation. Compulsory labor provided authorities with the chance to experiment with authoritarian methods, which favored strict obedience rather than individual liberty.[22] Authorities commodified freed Black people's labor, developed carceral institutions to punish them, and withheld citizenship from them. Across the globe, the authoritarian aspects of anti-slave-trade law helped create a free and propertyless population of color with insecure civil and political rights.

At each stage along this authoritarian pathway of liberation, liberated Africans from ships like the *Amelia* devised their own practices and gave meaning to what they valued. Some of these ventures operated within formal legal processes, such as petitioning political authorities or litigating in courts. Other ventures produced order and value outside the formal law. Liberated Africans joined fugitive communities, acted as insurgents, and turned to belief systems such as Santería, Candomblé, or Islam.[23] Such vernacular ordering practices began aboard slaving ships: the captives aboard the *Amelia* successfully rose up against the slaving crew, thereby precipitating anti-slave-trade interception by a British vessel. Chapter 5 centers these insurgent visions in the 1840s, a pivotal decade of uprisings against plantation slavery in Brazil and Cuba. Those who engaged in vernacular, insurgent ordering practices wished to keep their plans secret, and the only sources about them that remain exist because authorities suppressed such practices with violence. Chapter 5 thus asks a different sort of question, less about how the anti-slave-trade legal regime worked and more about the plausibility of the claim that liberated Africans participated in insurgencies. It investigates the effects that rumors of insurgency had on the legal order of slave societies. These formal and "vernacular" ventures produced liberated Africans' own diasporic visions of freedom and justice, which survived long after the end of compulsory labor and the slave trade in both the North and South Atlantic.

By the late 1850s, the political authorities in the places that were most heavily involved in the illegal trade were under unyielding pressure from the Mixed Commissions, British gunboat violence, and now rumors of internal insurgency. They decided to implement their own limited laws against the slave trade. These powers tried to stop the trade by increasing criminal liability for participation in it. Chapter 6 examines these laws in a context of a powerful culture of property rights in Brazil and Cuba. From the early nineteenth century, slave traffickers had smuggled African captive people into the Americas in violation of anti-slave-trade laws. Enslavers purchased these captives. In so doing, the traffickers and purchasers acted as though they had a legitimate title to property. They even created fake paperwork, such as bills of sale and baptism records, to present themselves as lawful owners. State authorities and social norms favored such a performance over any enslaved person's claim that illegal trafficking constituted grounds for freedom. Domestic anti-slave-trade courts did not investigate any historical cases of trafficking. But when new cases of trafficking into coastal waters came to light, the courts interrogated the trafficked captives. Liberated Africans who had been seized on land testified not only about transoceanic trafficking but also about the forced march overland and enslavers' tactics to hide them among the plantation workforce. This testimony disrupted the default assumption in a slave society that a powerful person who claimed to own a Black person indeed possessed that right. Political authorities had established domestic court jurisdiction to separate slave-trade suppression from British imperial pressure and insurgent violence, thereby preserving slaveholding. Yet liberated African testimony turned domestic courts into fora where judges, slave owners, and state agents debated how far the state should protect a slavery-based social order.

One common research finding has been that liberated Africans who were settled in societies that had outlawed slavery had more opportunities than those settled in slave societies. British colonial Sierra Leone, with its large villages of thousands of liberated Africans who worked the land and the vibrant markets of Freetown, arguably offered the greatest scope for building a life after liberation, albeit one constrained by both imperial and missionary authorities.[24] Still, wherever liberated Africans were settled, imperial authorities treated them as repaying the "debt" of being rescued through compulsory labor in situations of onerous, even carceral, oversight.[25] This research has been vital at centering liberated Africans in histories of the slave trade and its suppression and the development of imperial governance.

This scholarship has also raised unresolved questions regarding the framing of liberated Africans' histories, the nature of change over time, and understandings of what it meant to be a liberated African. First, the emphasis on national and imperial frameworks has marginalized how rescue and settlement under bilateral treaty law made liberated Africans subject to the jurisdiction of two powers. For these African people, and for many others who saw themselves in an analogous situation, this legal order created the possibility of petitioning multiple authorities to advance their interests. The legal status of liberated Africans in any one place was defined through comparison and connection to multiple jurisdictions, rather than within the boundaries of a single state. For instance, liberated Africans from the *Emilia* knew that they were subject to overlapping, inconsistent, and at times conflicting jurisdictions. Nor were any of the authorities who claimed to have jurisdiction interested in defining liberated African status in terms of rights or autonomy. They were instead invested in compelling them to repay the debt of rescue by laboring for private individuals or state organizations. In turn, liberated Africans could not rely on the language of rights to advance their interests. Limiting the focus to a single jurisdiction and to the security or abuse of rights risks missing the complexity of the legal definition of liberated African status, applying a paradigm that lawmakers at the time did not intend to implement, and foreclosing the sheer diversity of liberated Africans' responses to the predicament of liberation.[26]

Second, many studies have focused on how authorities used the labor of liberated Africans for their own purposes, but rarely have they asked if the relationship ever ran the other way. Naval cruisers, Brazilian prisons, and British colonial auctions were all sites where liberated Africans could collaborate on their own visions of freedom, shaping the societies in which they lived. Third, while ethnic identity mattered to the liberated Africans, a more pressing question for them was how they might survive the tortuous journey from maritime interception to the ending of compulsory labor.

Answering these questions of framing, change over time, and collective action requires close attention to the legal politics surrounding each process that composed the liberated Africans' journeys. Chapter 7 investigates the process after compulsory labor: how liberated Africans navigated a path in the absence of guarantees of rights to citizenship or residency. Liberated Africans' formal and vernacular ventures replaced forced labor with self-directed labor in which they could own a stake in what they produced. With little legal assistance and few financial resources, they often relied on their relationships with fellow shipmates to navigate a future path. Shipmate bonds, forged through sharing resources, formed the alternative to national citizenship and the individualizing incentives of an unequal world still structured by enslavement and empire. Formal and vernacular strategies were multiple and not necessarily compatible: some relied on the legal tools of empire to succeed, whereas others rejected imperial structures. And while these strategies were remarkably innovative, they were the result of interacting with legal regimes that enshrined difference rather than citizenship or equality. The legal regimes placed the liberated Africans in deep insecurity. To see both the authoritarian control and diasporic visions of freedom that were fundamental to the history of the end of the transatlantic trade requires a *diasporic Atlantic legal history*.

A DIASPORIC ATLANTIC LEGAL HISTORY

With a focus on the North Atlantic, Atlantic history has usually been bookended by the beginnings of transoceanic trade in the fifteenth century and the age of revolutions in the early nineteenth century.[27] This model does not work for the South Atlantic, whether defined geographically as the zone below the equator or conceptually as the historical antecedents of the Global

South.[28] In the South Atlantic, colonialism and the illegal slave trade endured much longer into the nineteenth century.[29] Many states that gained independence from the Spanish Empire in Central and South America created constitutions that enshrined both emancipation from slavery and greater access to citizenship. But the governing elites in Spanish colonial Cuba and independent Brazil delayed emancipation until 1886 and 1888, respectively.

In West Africa, there was wide-ranging debate about the legality of enslavement, which intensified in the eighteenth century. Fuuta Jallo and Fuuta Tooro formed as Islamic polities that opposed the enslavement of Muslims. Opposition to the transatlantic trade spread to the Bight of Benin. Jihadist expansion and internal uprisings by enslaved people and fellow marginalized groups led to the overthrow of the Ọ̀yọ́ Empire, one of the largest in West Africa.[30] Polities such as the Asante Empire and Dahomey consolidated their position through the gold-mining industry and the illegal slave trade.[31] In Central Africa, maritime suppression was largely ineffective, as exports of captive people to Brazil and Cuba continued into the second half of the nineteenth century. Just as important was the longer-term pattern of gatekeeper states in which elites used access to external markets in captive people and the merchandise of "legitimate commerce" to consolidate their position.[32] For enslavers, maritime suppression resulted in a reallocation of captive people into the domestic production of commodities.[33] Many liberated Africans came from regions where the legality of slave-trading was a tense political issue long before 1807 and where slave-trading would continue long afterward.

At the same time, neither the anti-slave-trade legal regime nor the liberated African diaspora divided neatly into North and South Atlantic zones. For instance, from the 1830s, Brazil's government used liberated Africans to build the first public prison in Brazil: the Casa de Correção. It provoked regular protests from British diplomats, which culminated in 1863 when Brazil broke off diplomatic relations with Britain over disputes regarding liberated Africans.[34] The Casa emerged from slave-trade suppression, which brought two empires into conflict with consequences in both the north and south seas. Building prisons in Brazil, laying the first major railroad in Cuba, and transporting liberated Africans as indentured laborers between British colonies relied on extensive crossings between the North and South Atlantic. Liberated Africans from vessels like the *Emilia* devised ideas and practices of diasporic freedom that also connected the North and South

Atlantic. After serving as apprentices in Brazil for fourteen years, sixty-eight shipmates decided in 1836 to travel to Lagos aboard the British ship *Porcupine*.[35] Most liberated Africans would not return to their birthplace community. Each person had a story of dislocation and bonded labor that stands as a reminder that maritime suppression alone was not sufficient for freedom. There were clear examples of Black freedom after slavery that did not require compulsory labor or imperial control. Alexandre Pétion, president of the Republic of Haiti, used the Constitution of 1816 to offer citizenship to people who had escaped from slavery elsewhere in the Caribbean.[36] As liberated Africans crossed boundaries in the North and South Atlantic, they defined freedom in their own ways, including in ways that transcended any empire or nation-state.

Legal scholars have emphasized that various anti-slave-trade laws banned only specific parts of the trade. One prominent area of debate has been the significance of the Mixed Commissions as either brave new human-rights tribunals or weak limbs of the British Empire.[37] But how exactly the Mixed Commissions related to other layers of anti-slave-trade law, including prize law and domestic law, has remained an open question. The effect of such a layered order on the liberated Africans has also been left unanswered. The fragile peace at the end of the Napoleonic Wars, and the prospect of huge profits from slave-produced commodities, made it hard to agree to a comprehensive suppression system between polities. Several unilateral attempts to rewrite the rules left gaps in the legal order. By approaching different officials, liberated Africans made legal claims to try to protect themselves from being reclassified as property.

Following the liberated Africans requires a method that looks beyond the judge's decision in a case like the capture of the *Emilia* because liberated Africans' legal ordeals continued afterward. The law was the site where different normative orders about life came into conflict, with these conflicts changing over time.[38] When multiple empires aligned to subject liberated Africans to authoritarian control and when liberated Africans crafted legal strategies to advocate their own interests, they cut across different aspects of the legal regime. Empires have thrived on the ability to place heterogeneous populations in "unequal but incorporative" polities.[39] Imperial practices of dividing populations according to racialized or religious status have ongoing effects on the rule of law in postcolonies.[40] In many colonial and postcolonial societies in the hemispheric Americas, enslaved and free Black people devised litigation strategies that forced authorities to grant them standing to make claims.[41] Black legal activism had potent political effects. For instance, enslaved people in the Southern United States who escaped to the North and challenged enslavers' attempts to detain them under the Fugitive Slave Law of 1850 pushed the United States to a national reckoning regarding slavery.[42] In the nineteenth century, each Atlantic empire faced the challenge of incorporating liberated Africans as a new immigrant population into its existing legal structures.

Law mattered for its normative role in describing what social status was and prescribing what it should be. People used imperial legal regimes to make worlds and to maintain them.[43] Studying jurisprudence enables us to see how judges made worlds with law, just as following a litigant's strategy enables us to see how they appealed for justice. To understand the world-making of a diaspora requires additional tools. If the law was the site where multiple normative orders came into conflict, we need to take seriously the many normative orders that liberated Africans generated. Sometimes these forms of social regulation and visions of justice did not enter the written archives of states. At other times, political authorities recorded evidence of these forms and visions only because they had decided to persecute people for believing in them. Liberated Africans often came from societies in sub-Saharan West Africa where legal processes focused on how to restore reciprocal social relations.[44] These alternative ways of ordering society were crucial to liberated Africans, who needed to confront transoceanic displacement. They encountered a legal order that did not ascribe to them a specific postservice status. Liberated Africans crafted new ventures beyond those defined by protracted legal vulnerability. Liberated Africans' visions of freedom stretched beyond the recording practices of imperial regimes, and evidence of them exists only in fragments in state archives.

Liberated Africans devised their diasporic visions of freedom and justice as one group among the many peoples of the African diaspora. Scholars have studied the African diaspora ranging in scale from the microhistory of a single person to the macrohistory of the forced migration of millions of people from certain West African regions to particular destinations in the Americas.[45] Such scholarship has uncovered powerful examples of how people survived displacement, taking with them ideas of freedom, family, and foodways.[46] Scholars have also focused on how enslaved and freed Black people struggled to claim citizenship in the face of gradual emancipation policies that sought to restrict their rights in frontier zones in the Americas.[47]

Together, these scholars have moved the field beyond an older cultural paradigm in which change over time was measured according to how far diasporic African people retained African practices or created creole cultures.[48]

The diaspora of liberated Africans from vessels like the *Amelia* transcended processes of bilateral transatlantic connection or developments on a single frontier. Liberated Africans were often multiply displaced, not only from West Africa to the Americas but also *within* West Africa, such as from Cabinda to Freetown. During compulsory labor, state authorities moved liberated Africans from ports where the anti-slave-trade courts were based to frontier zones. They relocated them from bustling colonial Freetown to the satellite missionary villages and from Rio de Janeiro to factories and foundries in São Paulo. Some liberated Africans even migrated *back* from places of anti-slave-trade liberation to their homelands, especially in the Bight of Benin. Focusing on liberated Africans' journeys along the pathway of liberation foregrounds these secondary and reverse diasporas.

If the legal status of liberated Africans in diaspora was ill defined, it was even less clear for their children, such as Librada's son, Alfredo. For liberated Africans, the common experience of their own middle passage mattered beyond the conventional focus on slaving ships as prototype prisons or as sites for creating creolized cultures.[49] Their middle passage was the incubator of legal strategies among shipmates. Without official recognition, liberated Africans used shipmate bonds to obtain paperwork that gave them residency in the polity where they lived and registered their children as free rather than enslaved. Others sought an onward migration. Relations between shipmates, ranging from giving depositions in court to pooling financial credit, helped liberated Africans navigate toward a more just future for themselves and their children. Liberated Africans developed a new political imaginary that saw rights and duties as flowing not from a nation-state or empire but rather from the shipmate community.

SOURCES

For liberated Africans from ships like the *Amelia* whose diasporic journeys connected the North and South Atlantic, often the only sources that remain are legal records. Authoritarian forms of control and diasporic visions of freedom emerged through the wide range of documents related to anti-slave-trade law. Judges' written decisions developed precedents regarding the legality of maritime capture. A selection of case law, the earliest and last cases in each jurisdiction, and controversial cases provides an emblematic account of how the regime developed over time. Official correspondence between governments reveals how liberated Africans made claims to multiple authorities to pursue their interests. Some archives have classified these documents in particular series, such as "Emancipados," whereas others have gathered them into miscellaneous collections. The documents often contain stories that have no neat beginnings or endings. The year after Librada's petition, the authorities tracked down the man who held her son in service. He agreed to hand Alfredo back to his mother in Havana on 13 May 1880. The final entry in the record is a marginal comment probably made by an assistant to the president of Matanzas. Its hope and urgency are tantalizing: Librada "appeared on 12 May and was so instructed."[50] We do not know whether Librada and Alfredo were reunited.

All historical sources, including Librada's two petitions, have specific conventions regarding form and content. Each producer of these sources was obliged to adopt these conventions even if they sought to undermine them: Librada's petition showed deference to the governor and pleaded for justice. None was created directly by a liberated African. We hear their voices as transcribed by notaries and clerks, and we see them as described by naval officers, diplomats, and state officials, all of whom were following professional and cultural conventions. The producer of a legal record tended to omit any information that was not relevant to the resolution of the dispute at hand. Such omissions could include details that shaped behavior during a court hearing, including the layout of the courtroom, a deponent's gestures, or periods of meaningful silence. The record also did not mention any resolution outside the formal legal process. Like all litigants, when liberated Africans went to law, they did not do so to give a truthful account of their lives but rather to tell a story that advanced their interests in a controlled and ritualized setting.[51]

Paying close attention to how a case involving liberated Africans entered the archive can help us see legal conflict over different normative views about what being a liberated African meant and how that changed over time. Some disputes revolved around how one political authority perceived another to be administering liberated African status wrongly. Liberated Africans, in making their claims, caused indirect changes to the anti-slave-trade legal order. For instance, on the Upper Guinea Coast, liberated Africans requested British naval assistance to free them from illegal detention within African polities. Those claims resulted in British breaches of foreign territorial waters and changes to British legal doctrine about state actions. Other disputes erupted when a liberated African's view about what liberation meant clashed with that of a political authority. Legal records can reveal that liberated Africans developed their own ideas about law, justice, and social order outside the anti-slave-trade legal regime. Unlike later "native courts" in Africa, these cases do not deal with African litigants' strategies in courts that colonial authorities had established to uphold a reified version of custom. Nonetheless, going to court as a liberated African produced a similar transformation as that observed in colonial societies in which courts provided a new forum for people of low social status to further their interests.[52] This is not to reduce law to being a tool either for social control or for subaltern struggles for justice. Instead, it means observing patterns in how different parties engaged with the law as a field that provided an independent standard of justice for ends including authoritarian control and diasporic visions of freedom.

Two intertwined narratives emerge from this approach. The first traces the anti-slave-trade legal regime, as it defined liberated African status and subjected these people to forms of authoritarian control. This regime comprised multiple jurisdictions: it had both domestic and international elements. It also comprised layers of different types of law, including prize, treaty, and criminal law. As the regime developed, it began to affect aspects of domestic law, such as property rights in slaves, and international law, such as sovereignty on sea and on land. The second narrative explores how liberated Africans defined their own visions of freedom. These visions were remarkable acts of creativity in response to coercion. Liberated Africans were not marginal characters on the nineteenth-century stage where issues such as the operations of the slave trade, unequal access to civil rights, and a new international order were played out, but at the center of the action for each.

Liberated African status matters to histories of the transition from slavery to postslavery freedom in the nineteenth-century Atlantic world. Many scholars have examined the "problem of freedom": how political authorities sought to manage the process of legal emancipation. In Jamaica, the British colonial administration tried to replicate the social arrangements and economic modes of production that existed under slavery.[53] Colonial authorities used antivagrancy laws and restrictions on landownership to coerce freedpeople into wage labor. The problem emerged because freedpeople wished to retain neither the social relations of slavery nor its economic means of production. In Jamaica, Brazil, Cuba, and beyond, freedpeople instead engaged in self-sufficient agriculture, independent skilled work, and ecological guardianship in regions where political authorities struggled to exert their power.[54]

Liberated Africans reveal that the problem of freedom had longer roots, and was even more contested, than previous accounts have suggested. The liberation of African captives from slaving ships provided a zone for political authorities to experiment with the problem of freedom long before emancipation legislation in British colonies in the 1830s or in Brazil and Cuba in the 1870s and 1880s. As soon as suppression began, authorities planned for how to replace slave labor. Debates over the authoritarian control of freedom—its continued commodification of Black laborers, its reliance on new carceral institutions, and its prolonged withholding of citizenship from freedpeople—began with liberated Africans. The debates continued across the entire nineteenth century. As liberated Africans sought to ascribe meaning to their status on the basis of their own vision of freedom, the true range of governance measures and the repertoire of freedpeople's strategies for defining freedom become clear.

The story of liberated Africans also reveals that the prevailing chronological narrative about the development of a spectrum of statuses between slavery and freedom presents a conceptual problem. Except for Cuban plantations, indentured labor has been considered as developing after, and as an imperial solution to, shortages in the postslavery labor supply.[55] People liberated from the *Amelia* and *Emilia* knew that indentured labor was part of the protracted suppression of the trade, rather than chronologically distinct from it. Thousands of liberated Africans moved between categories of slavery, captivity, penal servitude, and indentured labor during the era of slavery's ending in British colonies and its expansion in Brazil and Cuba. Sometimes, they moved themselves between the categories to further their interests; at other times, political authorities reclassified them. The anti-slave-trade legal regime subjected people like Librada to new forms of authoritarian control that constrained their freedom long before the era of emancipation, yet it also provided a domain for them to devise their own vision of true freedom. To make liberation meaningful required enduring bonded labor, petitioning multiple authorities by calling on the painful memory of displacement, seeking corroboration from shipmates, and dreaming of freedom.

CHAPTER ONE

War's Crucible

WAR PROVIDES A SEDUCTIVE and violent metaphor for righting a moral wrong. Call it a war, and supporters become foot soldiers. The perpetrators become enemies and the bystanders complicit. Abolitionists in the late eighteenth and early nineteenth centuries harnessed the power of this language. Olaudah Equiano, author of one of the most celebrated slave narratives, asked his readers, "Is not the slave trade entirely at war with the heart of man?"[1] For the 1807 Act for the Abolition of the Slave Trade, the first legislative achievement of the abolitionist campaign in Britain, warfare was not merely a guiding metaphor. With greater significance for the people liberated under the act, war provided the prevailing context and vital mechanism of early suppression.

Following cases of anti-slave-trade maritime capture and their aftermath in global perspective reveals how the 1807 act operated in practice. The legal category of "liberated African" originated during the early history of British slave-trade suppression in the Napoleonic Wars. Imperial authorities used analogous terms, such as "prize slave," and devised practices of liberating groups of enslaved people in the eighteenth century. A study of case law and lesser-known cases from the archives of vice-admiralty courts reveals how the term and practices took on new meanings with the 1807 act. Naval squadrons and privateers (private vessels with an official commission to attack enemy ships) captured slaving ships as part of maritime suppression. People subjected to liberated African status raised new problems regarding the procedure of maritime capture and the subsequent process of "liberation."

Early prize cases in British colonial Tortola developed important precedents in international law and practices in the apprenticeship and enlistment of liberated Africans. As a case from another booming theater of prize war, the Upper Guinea Coast, reveals, anti-slave-trade maritime captures often prolonged the privations of slaving voyages. The liberated Africans were subjected to a "recaptive middle passage." British efforts to adapt prize law to abolishing the slave trade would wane after the peace of 1815. In 1817, William Scott at the High Court of Admiralty ruled that without agreement among polities that the slave trade was against the law of nations, only treaties could grant the mutual right to search foreign slaving ships. Treaty-making soon superseded prize law as the leading edge of anti-slave-trade law. Liberated Africans released during wartime saw their ordeals continue beyond the rise of treaty law. Into the 1820s, the vague terms of apprenticeship and enlistment under the Abolition Act produced global scandals about liberated Africans, which Parliament appointed commissions of inquiry to investigate.

Early anti-slave-trade law as the wartime outgrowth of prize law began processes that informed the long history of suppression. British naval practices had important repercussions for liberated Africans at the point of maritime capture and long thereafter. The emerging legal regime commodified the slaving ship and its cargo—including captive people—as exchangeable for monetary compensation. It positioned rescued captives as people indebted to their liberators, who must repay their debt through labor. Implementing the law prompted new bureaucratic methods to manage liberated Africans long after the moment of rescue. The debt of labor and new governing techniques constituted the early authoritarian aspects of anti-slave-trade law. Maritime warfare and postwar commissions of inquiry provided liberated Africans with a domain to articulate their own vision of freedom through shipboard insurgencies, petitions to Crown officials, and establishing new settlements.

A WORLD AT WAR

Between 1701 and 1815, frequent wars erupted between the major Atlantic empires. One key reason for these imperial wars was competition for lucrative colonial economies with large enslaved populations, access to raw materials, and new consumer markets. Warfare entrenched Atlantic slave systems. It strengthened victorious states' capacities to protect private property rights, including in people. Naval fleets protected long-distance shipping that brought new captives to the colonies and slave-produced commodities to the metropole. Warfare bolstered the military infrastructure and manpower for the territorial defense of colonial plantations. Eighteenth-century writers as varied as John Locke and Olaudah Equiano understood slavery as a modified state of war.[2] But the relationship extended beyond that: warfare intensified slaveholding.

Proslavery warfare occupied two major antagonists, Britain and France, in the global revolutionary and Napoleonic Wars that have been called "perhaps the most powerful agents of social change between the Reformation and World War I."[3] Both empires attempted to overturn the revolution by enslaved people in Saint-Domingue. Each empire sought to conquer the territory and reintroduce slavery there, despite the French colonial abolition law of 1794. Toussaint Louverture's superior military tactics, combined with the high mortality rate of invading troops from yellow fever, defeated the British invasion in 1798.[4] Napoleon sought to reconquer Saint-Domingue as part of his global strategy against Britain. In 1802, the Napoleonic regime restored slavery throughout most of the empire but was defeated two years later in the Haitian War of Independence. Despite the setback in Haiti, British forces conquered Martinique and Guadeloupe and annexed many territories as colonies, including Trinidad, Demerara, Berbice, Essequibo, Mauritius, and the Cape. Slave labor was crucial in all these conquered territories. After the loss of North America, Britain became the preeminent global empire and a global slaveholder through warfare on land and sea.

During these wars, naval vessels and privateers seized enemy ships in battle and followed well-established legal procedures to turn captured ships and cargoes into financial capital, known as prize money. European monarchs and governments offered prize as an incentive to the army, navy, and privateers to fight. The jurisdiction of England's admiralty courts to decide prize cases was widely respected both within England and by other European polities. When a naval vessel or a privateer captured an enemy ship, it took the case to a vice-admiralty court to decide whether the maritime capture was lawful under its prize jurisdiction.[5] If the court found that an enemy owned the ship, it condemned the vessel and cargo as a lawful prize to the captor. The captor was then able to sell the ship and cargo for profit. If the court found that the capture was unlawful, it returned the ship and cargo to its rightful owner with costs for delay and damage. By one calculation, between 15 and 45 percent of eighteenth-century British-flagged slaving ships were foreign vessels seized as enemy ships in wartime.[6] Vice-admiralty courts were effective ways to convert the capture of enemy property into prize money and the capture of enslaved and free sailors of color on enemy ships into coerced seamen on British vessels.[7]

Alongside prize law, warfare provided the impetus for British colonial officials to develop another significant imperial procedure: the management of freed slaves. In 1775, the British governor of Virginia, Lord Dunmore, declared "all indented Servants, Negroes, or others, (appertaining to Rebels,) free that are able and willing to bear Arms, they joining His MAJESTY'S Troops as soon as may be, for the more speedily reducing this Colony to a proper Sense of their Duty, to His MAJESTY'S Crown and Dignity."[8] Thousands of "Black Loyalists" consequently fought for Britain during the American War of Independence. After the war, these Loyalists and their families went into exile in Nova Scotia and London. Suffering from deprivation and without the land promised to them by Britain, over one thousand Black Loyalists subsequently migrated to Sierra Leone, a colony run by a private company on the Upper Guinea Coast.[9] In the 1790s, they were joined by another free Black group: Maroon people from British colonial Jamaica. The Maroons were descended from people who had escaped from slavery and formed self-governing martial communities on the mountains and in the limestone caves of Jamaica. In 1795–96, when they rebelled against a colonial officer's punishment of their people, a brief war with British colonial authorities resulted in their deportation to Sierra Leone. Their martial skills were useful to the colonial authorities, who deployed Maroon soldiers to suppress a Nova Scotian movement to establish an independent settlement in 1800.[10] Military recruitment and transoceanic deportation were crucial British imperial strategies for managing the exit of small groups of people from slavery.

Wartime prize law, military and naval recruitment, and transoceanic deportation came together in the Abolition Act of 1807. The legal arm of the abolitionist movement in Britain, led by the lawyer James Stephen, sought to harness state power to prohibit the slave trade. Prior to his conversion to the abolitionist cause, Stephen had worked as an admiralty lawyer in the

British Caribbean. Since 1788, the sole regulation of British slave-trading related to conditions aboard the slaving ship, such as the number of captives on board. Regulation increased in 1805, when the King-in-Council introduced an order that licensed slave-trading to recently conquered territories in the Americas at a rate of three captives for every one hundred enslaved people already resident in each territory.[11] Crown agents had the authority to seize any unlicensed captives.[12] Building on the Order-in-Council, Stephen masterminded the Foreign Slave Trade Act of 1806.[13] The act banned British subjects from trading in slaves from Africa or from any British territory to a foreign jurisdiction. Under the 1806 act, captives would now be "seized, forfeited, and prosecuted," rather than sold.[14] This provision "created [the category of "liberated African"] in substance, if not in name." The category emerged on both sides of the Atlantic: in 1800, the US sloop *Ganges* captured two slaving ships as prizes under the 1794 Slave Trade Act. A US district court in Philadelphia declared the capture lawful and assigned the liberated Africans to the Pennsylvania Abolition Society, which indentured them.[15] Indenture, rather than immediate liberty, characterized early definitions of liberated African status.

Stephen also sought to harness abolition legislation for stopping neutral ships that enabled enemy powers to continue their colonial trade in defiance of British naval blockades.[16] Stephen advocated a return to the practice from earlier wars, when English admiralty courts had condemned these neutral vessels as enemy vessels.[17] For Stephen, a major risk of unconstrained neutral shipping was an expanding slave trade to enemy territories, helping their economic growth. Stephen's project to strengthen the Crown's power to reassign property rights and combat neutral shipping culminated in the 1807 Abolition Act. An early bill in 1807 sought to ban the trade in general terms. Its first clause outlawed the trade from any place in "*Africa* or *The West Indies* or in any other part of *America*, not being in the Dominion, Possession, or Occupation of His Majesty."[18] As its language suggests, the bill outlawed the traffic of slaves both across the Atlantic and within the Americas. It did not limit this ban to British subjects. Its reference to "dominion, possession, or occupation" envisaged abolition in a wide range of territories, including colonies and those occupied during warfare. The bill declared that offenses against the act would be "misdemeanours" and contained no details about what should happen to shipboard captives.[19]

The final bill, as amended by committee, specified that the ban applied to British subjects. A clause added by the committee became article 7 of the act passed by Parliament. It stipulated that shipboard captives seized from slaving ships as prizes of war and those seized under any act of Parliament, including the 1807 act, should be treated the same. All such shipboard captives "shall be condemned as Prize of War, or as forfeited to the sole use of His Majesty . . . for the purpose only of divesting and barring all other Property, Right, Title, or Interest whatever, which before existed, or might afterwards be set up or claimed in or to such Slaves or Natives of Africa so seized, prosecuted, and condemned."[20] The term "condemnation" referred to the practice of treating the captives as prize property, but instead of arranging their sale, the court would remove property rights from them.

A Crown officer would have authority to "receive, protect, and provide for such Natives of Africa as shall be so condemned, either to enter and enlist the same, or any of them, into His Majesty's Land or Sea Service, as Soldiers, Seamen, or Marines, or to bind the same, or any of them, whether of full Age or not, as Apprentices, for any Term not exceeding Fourteen Years, to such Person or Persons, in such Place or Places, and upon such Terms and Conditions, and subject to such Regulations, as to His Majesty shall seem meet." Each enlisted and apprenticed African "shall be considered, treated, and dealt with in all respects as if he had voluntarily so enlisted or entered himself."[21] This phrasing experimented with the concept of status. It attributed to each liberated African the limited legal capacity to enlist or become apprenticed, for the sole purpose of assigning them to such labor without their personal consent. The enlisted or apprenticed African would acquire the legal capacity to make their own arrangements at the end of the period of bonded labor.

After the initial period of service, Crown officers possessed the authority to order any African person apprenticed under the act to continue working to prevent them "from becoming at any Time chargeable upon the Island." Imperial officials could assign additional work to ensure that the economic value of the liberated Africans' labor outweighed any cost involved in accommodating them in a British colony.[22] Black soldiers, unlike their white counterparts, had no right to receive a pension for service.[23] Warships and privateers at sea and Crown agents on land had authority to seize slaves. Article 8 stipulated that these "captors" were entitled to head money of up to forty pounds for every man, thirty pounds for every woman, and ten pounds for every child whom they captured.[24] Article 11 specified that the governor of a British colony received a lower tariff of head money.[25] In fact, the act's prize money provisions were inconsistent regarding who counted as a child. Article 8 declared a child to be "not above Fourteen Years old," that is, including those aged fourteen, whereas article 11 defined a child as "under the Age of Fourteen Years," excluding those aged fourteen. In England, parents organized apprenticeships for their children to learn a trade at the age of fourteen, which may explain its use in article 8.[26] As we shall see, such ambiguity over the status of fourteen-year-olds would have major ramifications for liberated Africans after rescue. In the 1807 act, legislators used prize law incentives and removed property rights in African captives to bind them to labor in a transitional process to a limited freedom.

THE 1807 ACT IN PRACTICE: THE VICE-ADMIRALTY COURT

The vice-admiralty court in the Caribbean island of Tortola appears to have adjudicated the first case of a maritime capture of a slaving ship under the new Abolition Act. Tortola was a small British colony in the Leeward Islands, where British, French, Spanish, Dutch, and Danish empires competed for trade and territory. Its sugar and cotton plantation economy had declined since the late eighteenth century.[27] The vice-admiralty court in Tortola was active in prize adjudication. After the capture of a slaving ship, the captors needed to find a competent court to declare the capture lawful and realize the prize money. Prize adjudication and provisioning warships and privateers provided lucrative, and much-needed, business in Tortola. These prize cases developed a legal status in which rescued captives had no standing in court and were required to labor to repay the debt of rescue.

In late 1807, the American slave ship *Nancy* attempted one final venture before the federal ban on slave-trading to the United States came into force on 1 January 1808. Chartered out of Charleston, the major slave-trading port of the early nineteenth-century United States, the *Nancy* involved influential proslavery political elites. Phillips & Gardner, a prominent slave-trading firm, owned the vessel. Between 1805 and 1807, the firm had organized at least six other slaving voyages to the United States with a partner firm.[28] Phillips & Gardner had purchased the *Nancy* in a deal brokered by Christian & De Wolfe, a Charleston-based firm. The De Wolfe family patriarch, James, had dodged charges for murdering an enslaved girl aboard a ship. He grew wealthy from offering credit and insurance to slave traders and from his

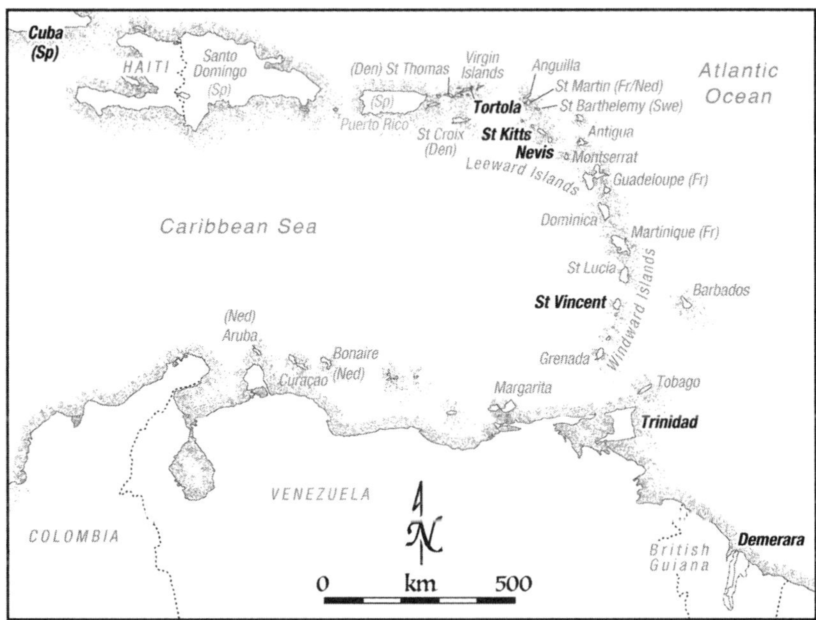

The Caribbean after the end of the Napoleonic Wars, 1815. Locations in bold are mentioned in the text.

plantations in Cuba. The *Nancy*'s master, Joshua Viall, previously completed a voyage from Senegal to Charleston on the same vessel in 1806 with "about fifty Slaves" on board. In separate transactions, Phillips & Gardner and Christian & De Wolfe sold the captives.[29] The *Nancy* formed part of a huge transatlantic political and commercial network that connected Senegal, Cuba, and the United States.

In September 1807, the *Nancy*'s crew purchased around eighty captives from Senegambia and began its voyage to Charleston. The crew probably knew that the slaving venture was risky but could not anticipate how the manifold risks might converge. First, Atlantic warfare had produced several naval blockades. The British blockade in the Caribbean encompassed free ports, such as St. Thomas, and enemy colonies, such as Cuba. These blockades reduced access to neutral and enemy territories that offered alternative markets to the United States for selling captives. Second, the *Nancy* had embarked captives from Senegambia, who were notorious for shipboard rebellions. As slave markets in the Americas grew, so too did slaving raids across Senegambia. These raids made people who were previously protected from sale to outsiders, including warriors and enslaved laborers in the gum industry, vulnerable to transshipment. These people had suffered recent displacement to the Southern Rivers region and were forced to farm plantations to supply rice and millet to slaving ships. They knew that the risk of sale into the transatlantic trade was pervasive.[30] Their leadership, martial training, and memory of lost honor inspired them to revolt.

A passenger aboard the *Nancy* later testified that "he frequently on the Passage heard the Master and crew say, they were apprehensive the slaves would break out."[31] Warfare, sickness, and shipboard rebellion led to the capture of the *Nancy* in November 1807. As crewmembers fell sick, the captives launched three uprisings. Such was the distress caused by their failure that one captive took his own life. Viall, fearful and with his crew reduced to just two healthy members, tried to navigate the ship to neutral St. Thomas. He fell in with the British naval ships *Cerberus* and *Venus*, which were blockading the region. With his ship in distress, Viall did not resist capture.

In court, the crucial issue was the ownership of the captives, as determined by the ship's papers and the captain's testimony. Prize proceedings followed a strict protocol. The captured ship's crew answered formulaic "interrogatories" to establish the ship's itinerary, the ownership of the vessel and cargo, and the circumstances of capture. Viall initially testified that all the captives, excluding three bought by crewmembers, were the property of Phillips & Gardner. A day later, pleading ill health, Viall amended his testimony to state that ten out of eighty captives were being shipped by "one La Coste a French man, on freight at forty dollars a head, to be sold for the account of the said La Coste."[32] The King's Counsel, acting for the captors, seized on this piece of evidence. In wartime, the King-in-Council ordered general reprisals against French ships and subjects. Naval officers received commissions from the High Court of Admiralty to capture and seize French property for adjudication by the vice-admiralty courts. The King's Counsel, George Clarke Forbes—who will return in our story—argued that the *Nancy* was a prize of war and the captives were prize slaves under the Abolition Act.[33] Warfare provided a context for adjudging *all* the captives to be enemy property and subject to Crown forfeiture. Viall countered that there was no enemy subject aboard at the time of capture or of adjudication.[34] Viall did not make much of his earlier points that the vessel had been in distress and that his alleged intention was to reach neutral territory. His feeble claim made it easy for the judge, James Robertson, to declare the capture lawful. In late November, Robertson pronounced the vessel, its fittings, tackle, furniture, and all the surviving captives to have belonged to enemies of the Crown at the time of capture.[35]

In December 1807, the Tortola vice-admiralty court heard a second major case, of the *Amedie*, a US-flagged ship bound from Bonny to Charleston. Fearful of missing the window before the federal ban, the acting master had diverted the vessel to the burgeoning market of Matanzas, Cuba. A British vessel captured the *Amedie* on its voyage to this enemy port. Under examination, the master admitted this plan: "he believes that the reason of the capture was owing to the Vessels being bound to Matanzas in the Island of Cuba."[36] Judge Robertson declared the vessel and its cargo to belong to an enemy and thus the capture lawful. As with the *Nancy*, the ship was a prize of war to the captor, and the captives were prizes of war forfeited to the Crown.[37]

Both the *Nancy* and *Amedie* decisions reached the appeals court, the High Court of Appeals for Prizes in London. The judge, Sir William Grant, heard the *Amedie* case first. The ship's owners were the appellants, known as claimants, who argued that the intention was to sail to Charleston, with Matanzas a mere contingency plan. The captors of the *Amedie*, known as respondents, defended the case. They claimed that the voyage dates suggested that the slave traders never planned to arrive in the US before the federal ban: Cuba was the intended destination. The King-in-Council had exempted neutral subjects from a wartime ban on trading with enemy colonies. But this exemption did not apply to trades that the neutral state itself—the United States—had prohibited. From this basis, Grant took an expansive view of the court's jurisdiction. He argued that positive law was required for a neutral subject to trade in slaves and that the burden of proof lay on the claimant "to shew that by the particular law of his own country he is entitled to carry on this traffic."[38] In the case of the *Nancy*, Grant held that a neutral ship trading in enemy property to an enemy port made it liable for condemnation.[39] For Grant, the captives from both the *Nancy* and *Amedie* were lawful prizes. Determining the property rights in shipboard captives established the legality of prize capture in early international law.

The proceedings in the cases of the *Nancy* and *Amedie* also helped define "liberated African" status. Under the 1807 act, the vice-admiralty court converted shipboard captives into bonded laborers. The liberated

Africans thereby gained limited legal capacity. The court did not give the Africans standing to testify in court about the horrors of the crossing, the circumstances of prize capture, or their perspective on enlistment and apprenticeship. The vice-admiralty court adjudicated both captures after the passage of the Abolition Act but *before* an important Order-in-Council of 16 March 1808. This order stipulated that the colonial collector of customs was responsible for registering the Africans rescued from a slaving ship. Commanding officers of the land and sea forces had, respectively, first and second choice of enlisting the men. The collector of customs would bind the rest as apprentices, ensuring that the women "shall not be employed in the labours of agriculture, but in domestic service."[40] The order also modified article 8 of the Abolition Act, to apply the head money tariff on children under fourteen years old.[41] But without this order, Crown agents in Tortola were required to devise their own procedure.

Tortola's small political and commercial elite controlled the early enlistment and apprenticeship process. In the cases of the *Nancy* and *Amedie*, the captor's agent distributed the liberated Africans in collaboration with Judge Robertson and the president of Tortola, William Turnbull. The local naval commander, Alexander Cochrane, requested that the adult men serve in the Royal Navy and the remaining liberated Africans be assigned to his plantation in Trinidad. "In the present state of that property," Robertson and Turnbull decided, "we can have no objections to assenting to the terms of Sir Alexander's requisition."[42] Considering trafficked people as seized property, the Crown officers assigned them a financial value and then indentured eleven women, twenty girls, thirty-two men, and nineteen boys to labor on Cochrane's Northumberland and Good Hope Plantation in Trinidad without oversight or support.[43] This decision exposed the liberated Africans to the risk of plantation slavery. From 1813 until 1828, Northumberland and Good Hope had between 153 and 213 enslaved people bound there.[44] John Jervis, a vice-admiral who benefited from wartime prize money, labeled the Cochranes "not to be trusted out of sight, they are all mad, romantic, money-getting and not truth-telling—and there is not a single exception in any part of the family."[45] On Cochrane's plantation, the distinction between being an unwaged apprentice and enslaved laborer threatened to disappear. Like thousands of fellow liberated Africans, those who were enlisted on warships and apprenticed on Cochrane's plantation would repay the debt of rescue by working for up to fourteen years.

THE RECAPTIVE MIDDLE PASSAGE

Just as much as the Caribbean, British naval officers saw West Africa as a region that offered lucrative opportunities for anti-slave-trade prize warfare. The West African coast, particularly between Senegambia and Sierra Leone, was an intensive theater of war. Slave ships were vulnerable to seizure. In 1808, the Crown took control of the Sierra Leone Colony from the Sierra Leone Company, which had been headed by metropolitan abolitionists and was facing bankruptcy. Sierra Leone now became a site where official policy directed anti-slave-trade activities. The colony was a convenient solution to the human consequences of the developing anti-slave-trade regime. As with Liberia, which was established as a colony by the American Colonization Society with the support of the US government, official policy sought to manage large freed Black populations by settling them outside the metropole.[46] Tensions over whether colonization in Liberia was supposed to preserve slavery in the United States by removing free Black people or provide a precedent for emancipation characterized the scheme. Unlike Liberia, Sierra Leone remained firmly an anti-slave-trade colonial project. The project would involve fateful compromises with regimes of bonded labor and conflict with Indigenous people, as Liberia would also face in later years. Under Crown control, naval officers found Sierra Leone to be a welcome base for prize warfare.

With regard to the number of captures, the West Africa Squadron was the most significant anti-slave-trade force in the Atlantic world. British naval squadrons stationed at the Cape and South America also captured slaving ships. The Portuguese, Brazilian, United States, French, and other navies made smaller contributions to international suppression. By the late 1840s, critics in Britain were complaining that such patrols were financially costly to the Treasury, caused traders to adopt riskier embarkation tactics that worsened the conditions for the captives, and had little effect on the overall volume of the slave trade.[47] One landmark study concluded that maritime suppression had a small effect on the seaborne trade: the price of captives in the Americas would probably have been 8–11 percent lower without pressure from squadrons, diplomats, and antislavery campaign groups. This pressure prevented at most a further 290,000 captives being transported to the Americas between 1807 and 1850.[48] Still, British cross-party political support for naval suppression overcame the criticisms of a select committee in the 1840s. Political support endured until the end of the transatlantic trade and continued for the navy's redeployment in the Indian Ocean to interdict slaving routes later in the century.

Despite this widespread domestic acclaim, anti-slave-trade patrols replicated many horrors of Atlantic crossings. Slaving ships, anti-slave-trade naval vessels, and privateers were all highly disciplined spaces, in which the captain had ultimate authority to act to preserve the ship and the people on board. Maritime patrolling was onerous and often dangerous work for the crew. A "prize crew" from the captor boarded the captured slaving ship to navigate it to a nearby port for adjudication. The desperate conditions aboard slaving ships, caused by malnutrition, disease, and violence, meant that there was often little that prize crews could do to relieve suffering after maritime capture.[49] Far from a triumphant liberation, prize capture continued the conditions of the middle passage.

The most compelling picture of the similar conditions aboard slaving ships before and after maritime capture comes from Sierra Leone. Between 1808 and 1864, over nine hundred captured slaving ships docked at Freetown. The median length of time between departure from the African coast and the disembarkation of captives at Freetown was 40.1 days. This period was only slightly shorter than the median middle passage for a completed transoceanic slaving voyage between 1807 and 1866, which was 46 days. The average mortality on captured slave ships docking at Sierra Leone was 10.8 percent of all shipboard captive people. That percentage was in fact higher than the average mortality of 10.2 percent of captives aboard slaving voyages that completed the crossing to the Americas.[50] This finding is corroborated by data on 136 captures adjudicated in Sierra Leone between 1837 and 1865, which reveal that the mean length of time between the date of capture and the date of the court verdict was 45 days and the median was 33 days.[51] For millions of African captives, malnutrition, communicable disease, spatial confinement, physical violence, and psychological trauma characterized seaborne captivity.[52] Captives responded by forming kin bonds with fellow captives and engaging in insurgent protest and cultural creation.[53] Indeed, rebellions occurred on 8–10 percent of slaving voyages, prompting slave traders to use additional crewmembers to reduce the risk of revolt.[54] Facing the same structural conditions, liberated Africans responded in similar ways. The maritime prize capture of slaving ships created a recaptive middle passage.

The prize capture of the *Amelia* by the British privateer *Kitty* illuminates the recaptive middle passage. The *Amelia* was a slaving ship whose crew had embarked 275 captives at Cabinda in northern Angola in December 1810. Across the nineteenth century, drought and slave-raiding by warlords displaced people from eastern areas of Central Africa. Those who were unfortunate enough to suffer war captivity, severe hunger, or indebtedness were transported by enslavers to ports in the Congo-Angola region for shipment to Brazil.[55] Until 1810, the port of Luanda, controlled by Portugal, was the most prominent port for exporting captives to Brazil. That year, Portugal imposed new taxes on imports of Brazilian merchandise, prompting Brazilian and Luso-African slave traders to leave Luanda and head northward to establish new clandestine slaving ports at Ambriz, the River Congo, and Cabinda.[56] The captives forced on board the *Amelia* were some of the earliest to suffer from this transformation in the illegal slaving business. As a man documented only by his Anglophone name Ned Brown recalled, these ordeals forced families into desperate decisions. Ned "was put on board the brig *Amelia*, as a slave, by Prince Conzee, his father. It is the custom of his country for a man, when in want of money, &c. if he has three or four children, to sell one or more of them, and keep the others. His father sold him and his sister together."[57] Pushed to the margins of their birth society by drought and debt, Ned and his sister were exiled.

The two siblings must have feared the crew, yet as elite Cabindans, perhaps they found that they could communicate with some crewmembers who spoke Portuguese.[58] The Portuguese owner, Teófilo de Melo, and Portuguese captain, Jose Carlos de Almeida, were a front. Francis Depau, a merchant based in Charleston, and Alexander Campbell, a British ship captain, owned the vessel.[59] They had chartered the ship, which was originally called *Agent*, to sail from Philadelphia to Salvador da Bahia in May 1810. There, Campbell sold the vessel to Melo. On 24 October, Melo wrote to Campbell, informing him, "after leaving this Port, your destination is that of Cabinda where you must make a cargo of slaves and other goods that shall suit my interests."[60] A day later, Melo granted a power of attorney to Campbell to use the vessel as he saw fit. The US vice-consul in Salvador, Patrick Toole, witnessed the power of attorney. He was also probably a partner in the firm Sealy, Roach & Toole, which answered a bill of £4,000 drawn on a Charleston firm by Depau, via an intermediary in Liverpool, to supply the *Amelia* with goods for the slaving voyage.[61] After purchasing Ned and his fellow captives at Cabinda, Campbell probably intended to sail to Havana.[62] As with the *Nancy* and *Amedie*, credit and maritime laborers from the United States were vital to the illegal slave trade that linked Central Africa with Brazil and Cuba. Depau and Campbell devised a voyage that was illegal under Britain's 1806 Foreign Slave Trade Act and 1807 Abolition Act and Portuguese imperial tax law.

Depau and Campbell's insidious planning that transformed the American *Agent* into the Portuguese *Amelia* could not account for how the 275 captives would respond to transoceanic separation from their homes. Ned, who spoke English, became acquainted with Jack White, an enslaved man owned by Campbell, who was working aboard the ship. According to Ned, "White took off his clothes and shewed the slaves his back, saying, 'See how my master has flogged me: when he has taken you to white man's country, he will flog you the same.' When the brig got to sea, White urged the slaves to rise."[63] The shipboard captives had painful experiences of social dislocation and enslavement in Central Africa but not racial chattel slavery. White's body, as corporeal evidence of the brutality of slavery in the Americas, must have shocked the captive people.

The vessel departed Cabinda on 1 January 1811, and after several days at sea, the captain instructed the crew to unchain the captives, who lay belowdecks. This was a common practice by slaving crews, who ordered the captives to exercise on deck and then returned the men belowdecks overnight.[64] On the morning of 20 January, Jack White opened the hatches and allowed the captives up onto deck. Together, they besieged the *barricado* that separated them from the crew. Jack attacked the *barricado* with a hammer. "The mate saw him," Ned recalled, "and shot him through the jaw: the ball cut away his tongue; and when he fell down, he seized hold of the cable with his teeth, and died in that posture."[65] White's actions nonetheless were decisive. In the ensuing battle, the insurgents overpowered the crew, losing thirty of their number in the process.[66] The insurgents saw all crewmembers as complicit: they injured an enslaved man from Cabinda who worked as a cabin attendant aboard.[67] Most crewmembers were forced to flee on a boat.

Ned wanted to go with the fleeing crewmembers, perhaps because he had thought that the captain would treat him well thanks to his linguistic skills. Perhaps Ned thought the odds of survival were better aboard the boat with an experienced captain. But Campbell refused to take Ned, who then dissuaded the rebels from killing the remaining three crewmembers and the boatswain. He told the rebels, "For if you kill them, where will you take the vessel? You do not know how to make sail."[68] Aboard the African-controlled *Amelia*, the rebels must have quickly formed a new social order to distribute rations and collaborate on sailing the ship. After four months, the rebels had navigated the ship to Cape Mount on the Upper Guinea Coast, over eighteen hundred miles north of Cabinda. Ned recalled the desperation on landing, when the self-emancipated shipmates tried to trade for food. They had "sent everything they had on board, even their knives, for rice, and only received one krew [nearly half a bushel] of rice, and a small basket of cassada [cassava]."[69] The owners of the *Amelia* had chartered it to sail from the North Atlantic to the South for a slaving voyage; now the insurgents had navigated it the other way for freedom.

In May 1811, the British privateer *Kitty* encountered the *Amelia* at Cape Mount. The crew, commanded by John Roach, was initially unsure about who commanded the vessel or why it was there. Roach was a former Liverpool slave trader, who, after the 1807 act, redirected his maritime expertise toward taking reprisals against British enemies.[70] Roach's crew searched the *Amelia*, where they found that "the greater part of [the survivors were] not able to move for want of meat."[71] Using an armed boat, Roach took possession of the *Amelia*, though he never explained his authority for capturing a ship that carried the flag of Portugal, an ally. The precedent in the *Amedie* may have helped. The hidden US ownership of the vessel suggested that the burden was on the *Amelia*'s owners to prove that positive law permitted a neutral ship to trade in slaves. During the preceding five months, shipboard resistance created social bonds between the insurgents and now the circumstances for prize capture.

Roach's account of what happened at Cape Mount diverged from Ned Brown's. Roach claimed that he had found so many people in distress due to hunger that he decided to send the weakest survivors on shore. He then tried—and failed—to purchase provisions. On 20 May, he ordered his crew to sail the *Amelia* to Sierra Leone in company with the *Kitty*.[72] According to Brown, Roach abandoned twenty-eight vulnerable self-emancipated people to an English slave trader, one Mr. Thomas, at Cape Mount.[73] On 24 May, with assistance from HMS *Tigress*, the *Kitty* and *Amelia* arrived at Freetown. The vice-admiralty court at Sierra Leone condemned the *Amelia* as lawful prize to the *Tigress*. After almost five months at sea, only 85 of 275 shipboard African people survived the ordeal to be designated liberated Africans at

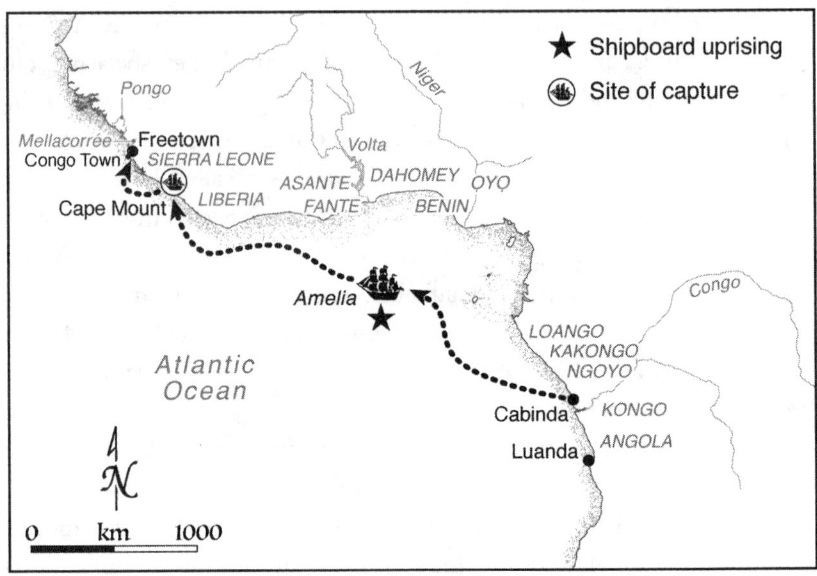

The voyage of the *Amelia* between Cabinda and Freetown.

Freetown.[74] Yet the horrific mortality belies the fact that all the shipmates, not just those who survived, had chosen to take control of their fate.

Upon the arrival of these liberated Africans at Freetown, the colonial authorities applied a new governing technique to them that subjected them to an emergent form of control. The authorities registered each person's name, sex, age, height, and "description" of distinguishing features such as scarification. Invasive physical examination exacerbated the trauma of captivity. In many cases, British colonial officials assigned the liberated Africans an Anglophone name alongside recording the person's original name.[75] Through this naming ritual, officials marked the transformation from shipboard captive to bonded laborer. The registers were part of colonial writing techniques that constituted legal procedure, defining who counted as a liberated African and what that status entailed.[76] Eventually, authorities in Brazil, Cuba, the Cape, and elsewhere would devise similar registration rituals. The register for the *Amelia* included men named Ned Brown, Jack, Doomba, and Loobella alongside women such as Selou, Zeela, and Chingayo.[77] In line with the Order-in-Council of 1808, the clerk classified those who were aged fourteen or over as adults. It is probably impossible to discern how these liberated Africans understood their age during their lives in their birth societies. But the relationship between elders and young

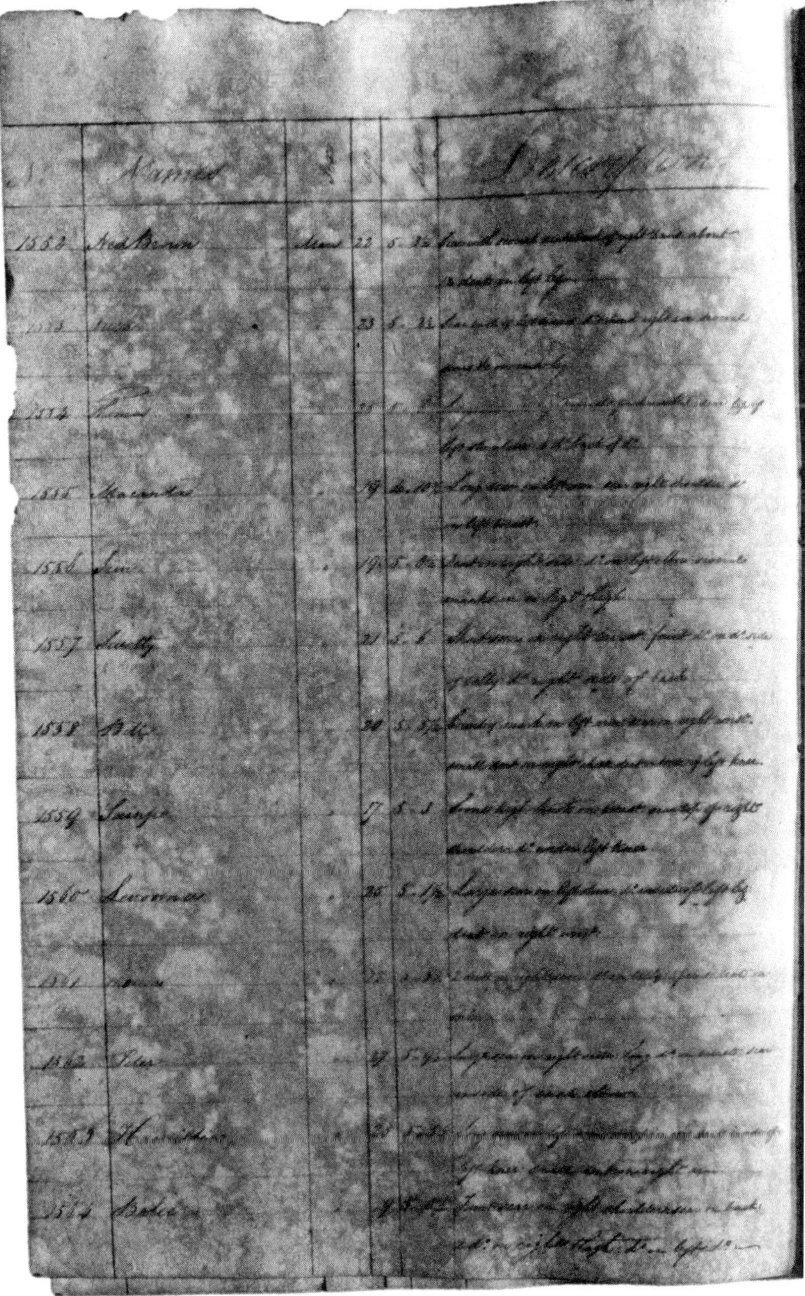

Ned Brown's details featured in the top row on this page of a new technology, the register of liberated Africans: Liberated African Register [1808–1812], Public Archives of Sierra Leone. (Image courtesy of the British Library, EAP443/1/17/20, https://eap.bl.uk/archive-file/EAP443-1-17-20)

people that shaped how the latter advanced through stages of rights and obligations to become a full person was probably a significant factor for them, perhaps more so than chronological age or biological maturation.[78] Such nuanced understandings of how age shaped personhood were lost when the clerk recorded age through a visual interpretation of physical attributes. The clerk classified Frank, Chinkocolo, Bononghee, and Sonna as fourteen years old. Colonial registration based on a cursory assessment of age assigned these four fourteen-year-olds from the *Amelia* and thousands more besides into apprenticeship or enlistment as adults.

The clerk recorded an Anglophone name for men but not for women, boys, or girls. Such names could suggest their willingness to convert to Christianity, but there is no reason to suppose that men would be the sole converts. A more convincing explanation is that the army or navy had already targeted these men for enlistment. During the Napoleonic Wars, prize capture and enlistment stretched from the North Atlantic to the South. The newly conquered Cape Colony also became a prominent site in slave-trade interdiction and the recruitment of liberated Africans.[79] The *Amelia* paperwork formed part of the earliest register in Freetown, which began a new authoritarian technique to control liberated Africans throughout the Atlantic world.

Roach's agents successfully appealed against the vice-admiralty court verdict: in 1814, the Lords Commissioners of Appeals in the High Court of Admiralty ruled that the *Kitty*, rather than HMS *Tigress*, was the lawful captor.[80] In 1816, Roach's proctor (representative in the court), now acting for Constance Roach after her husband's murder by a slaving crew during a subsequent attempted capture, appealed to the Lords. Roach requested that the Crown cover the *Kitty*'s costs in salvaging the *Amelia*. These included the delay to the *Kitty*'s intended voyage and the costs of clothing, food, and materials for the *Amelia*'s rebels and crew. The Lords had previously directed that the expenses should be paid out of sale proceeds of the *Amelia*, its fittings, and its cargo. But Constance Roach claimed that widowhood had left her in financial hardship; she needed as much of the proceeds as possible.[81] In response to the petition, the Lords "directed the matter to stand over for the present."[82] The captors, including Roach's widow, would receive nothing additional for the time being. The insurgents had raised the question of who should bear financial responsibility for the cost of the voyage between capture and adjudication—one that the appeals court struggled to answer.

The Africans' ordeal did not end with registration in Freetown, but their maritime insurgency created new bonds between them that enabled them to devise their own vision of freedom. The colonial authorities settled the surviving self-emancipated people on a hillside near the signal station and called the settlement "New Cabenda," after the port where they had been embarked. By 1816, the New Cabenda settlers had renamed their settlement Congo Town and become a population of four hundred people.[83] A missionary's letter suggested their willingness to engage with Christian missionaries while maintaining "country fashions," by which he meant Indigenous spiritual practices.[84] Eventually, the settlers purchased new land on the waterfront. Over forty years later, over four thousand liberated Africans released at Liberia would undergo a similar journey. Having been enslaved in different parts of Central Africa, they were recaptured by US patrols and settled in Liberia. These liberated Africans also survived brutal apprenticeship labor, and some of the survivors formed their own Congo Town.[85] In the Sierra Leone case, the length of their recaptive middle passage to Freetown probably made them an unusual group compared with the many liberated Africans from Sherbro, Mende, Temne, and Vai regions who had suffered enslavement within sixty miles of the Sierra Leone coastline.[86] The liberated Africans' insistence on a new settlement and willingness to navigate colonial land policies and missionary activities were significant. Their creative practices indicated not a fixed ethnic identity but rather a determination to innovate regarding how they wished the colonial authorities to recognize them.

The *Amelia* case held different meanings depending on perspective. For British colonial officials at Sierra Leone, the vice-admiralty court, and Roach, it represented the workings of the prize system. Prize money gave naval and privateer vessels incentives to capture slaving ships. Settled near the environs of Freetown, African laborers could be commodified and managed. For illegal slave traders in the South Atlantic, the case was a rare exception to their operations that cloaked North American capital and labor in a foreign guise to slip around national prohibitions. For the African people liberated from the *Amelia*, at each stage from shipboard insurgency to labor in Sierra Leone, the line between slavery and freedom remained thin and porous. With few material resources, they turned to the one thing on which they could rely—the bond between shipmates—to establish their new settlement at Congo Town.

Almost one hundred years after the insurgents aboard the *Amelia* established Congo Town, W. S. Johnston photographed market activities in the town. Photograph taken before 1915. (Library of Congress)

A RIGHT OF WAR IN PEACETIME

So lucrative was prize warfare that naval squadrons and privateers like the *Kitty* looked beyond the high seas or territorial waters of British colonies to capture slaving ships. Several early colonial governors of Sierra Leone were military or naval officers who had fought imperial enemies. In 1814, one such governor, Charles Maxwell, authorized a joint military and naval expedition to Fouricaria in a Mandinka polity north of Sierra Leone. Maxwell had demanded that the local chief, King Amurah (or Amra), bring to justice the killer of a British trader who resided in Fouricaria. When Amurah refused, Maxwell accused him of being beholden to American and European slave traders residing along Rio Pongo within Fouricaria who saw Sierra Leone as a threat to their business interests.[87] In March 1814, Maxwell ordered 150 troops of the Royal African Company to embark on the *Princess Charlotte* and *Doris* to the Rio Pongo and "destroy every factory belonging to the Europeans and Americans."[88]

At Rio Pongo, two months previously, traders had forced 148 captives aboard the Spanish slave ship *Ysavel*. In January 1814, five or six days into the Atlantic crossing, the captives aboard the *Ysavel* "killed . . . Felix de Pusadas the Master and also the Mate and every other white Person on board. . . . The said Slaves then took possession of the said Ship and put back into the Rio Pongo."[89] They hoped to find freedom. By March, the merchant who had first sold the captives managed to seize them again, for the benefit of their Havana-based purchasers. Fearing an imminent attack on his slaving factories by Maxwell's expedition, the merchant sent 64 captives northward to a trader at Rio Nunez. Despite Spain now being a British ally in the Napoleonic Wars, the *Princess Charlotte* captured the *Ysavel* with 148 captives aboard.

In a single process, the Pongo expedition attacked a rival polity, seized African captives and slave ships for financial reward, and arrested slave traders. The expedition seized 240 captives for liberation in Sierra Leone and three schooners as prizes. Maxwell said the expedition "succeeded in this service beyond my most sanguine hopes."[90] The force also seized four English slave traders. The Sierra Leone court of quarter sessions sentenced three of them to fourteen years' transportation and the remaining man to three years' hard labor. The capture of the *Ysavel* was declared lawful at Sierra Leone's vice-admiralty court. One of the agents who collected the prize money for the captors was Zachary Macaulay, a member of the Clapham Sect and former governor of Sierra Leone.[91] Anti-slave-trade expeditions against an allied ship and inside African territory provided an opportunity for some insurgent captives aboard the *Ysavel* to gain liberation at Sierra Leone. The Havana merchants appealed at the High Court in London. Such an extraterritorial attack far exceeded the bounds of lawful prize capture. It thereby damaged relations between polities and raised the risk of appeals for compensation. Naval violence against foreign polities as a strategy to suppress the trade and protect liberated Africans, all while furthering British imperial interests, would continue into the 1850s.

Cases such as the *Ysavel* attracted the attention of critics of the Clapham Sect in Britain. A former vice-admiralty court judge, Robert Thorpe, criticized the Pongo raid as illegal. He saw it as evidence of the undue influence that the African Institution, an organization led by the Clapham Sect, wielded over both abolition policy and colonial administration. Maxwell had abused his power in authorizing the arrest of slave traders and the liberation of the captives: "The white men were caught, carried in irons to Sierra Leone, and condemned by an illegal power to transportation, while the black natives thus seized were condemned to our Sovereign, and instantly turned into soldiers for life, or placed as the Governor thought fit."[92] Thorpe may have been melodramatic, but he highlighted an important point. The African Institution saw liberated Africans as integral to British colonial "civilizing" projects in Africa to achieve comprehensive suppression. Three of the four Englishmen convicted for slave-trading were pardoned for being tried in the wrong court.[93] In 1818, the slave-owning member of Parliament (MP) Joseph Marryat took the argument even further. Rather than preventing slaving ships from entering Rio Pongo and Rio Nunez, he alleged, British officers waited until slave traders had put "the victims on board whose condemnation entitled the captors to bounty-money."[94] The proslavery lobby cast abolitionists as hypocritical for putting the liberated Africans at risk and endangering diplomatic relations with African polities.

In 1815, Britain, Prussia, Russia, and Austria signed the Treaty of Vienna that committed them to fighting Napoleon until his comprehensive defeat. The treaty included a declaration against the slave trade as repugnant to humanity and morality. After Napoleon's defeat, in 1816 plenipotentiary ministers for each allied power met for a conference in London to cement their opposition to France. Led by the British minister, Lord Castlereagh, the conference ended with a memorandum against alleged piracy by the Barbary powers of the Mediterranean and against the slave trade. The memorandum envisaged an extensive anti-slave-trade system to be confirmed in a future treaty. The powers would agree to the right to visit and detain slave ships off the African coast and to establish a central treaty court to adjudicate these captures. "To take away excessive temptation to detain property," stated the memorandum, only a small share of the prize proceeds would go to the captor. The expense of providing for the liberated Africans would fall on the allied powers, and the "mode of disposing of them [was] to be settled by common consent." Such a system would not "affect general rights or principles," but it left open whether it would change the law of nations.[95]

Into 1816, British ships continued to capture slave ships according to prize warfare practices. In January, the French ship *Le Louis* tried to purchase twelve African captives at Cape Mesurado for transshipment to Martinique. Before the crew embarked the captives, the British ship *Queen Charlotte* tried to visit, search, and capture *Le Louis*. The *Princess Charlotte*, the same vessel that participated in the Rio Pongo raid, assisted the *Queen Charlotte*. The French ship's crew resisted this attempt, killing twelve crewmembers of the *Queen Charlotte* and losing three of its own crew in the battle. Thomas

Boyland, a West African soldier, and Jack Brown, a Kru sailor, died trying to suppress the slave trade.[96] After overpowering the crew, the *Queen Charlotte* sent the *Le Louis* to the vice-admiralty court at Sierra Leone for adjudication as a prize. Was killing potential naval captors to preserve a slaving voyage an act of piracy or a defense of property?

The vice-admiralty court in Freetown declared the capture lawful based on the violation of French anti-slave-trade law and the piratical resistance to the lawful search of the vessel.[97] The owners of *Le Louis* appealed to the High Court of Admiralty, where the judge was William Scott. Scott's comments on historical cases suggested that the only time when it was legitimate for one nation to interfere with another's shipping was in wartime.[98] Scott understood maritime property rights as flowing from the "rules of Civil Law chiefly founded on the nature and right of possession."[99] Unlike Grant, Scott was conservative in his interpretation of jurisdiction.

In 1817, William Scott ruled that the crew of *Le Louis* had legitimately defended their property on the high seas when they resisted the attempted seizure.[100] They were not guilty of piracy or murder. In fact, the British captors owed compensation to the French crew for an unlawful attack on the high seas in peacetime. In a fragile postwar peace, widespread British searches of ships would produce "gigantic mischiefs." Scott emphasized that "if this right of war is imported into peace by [treaty] convention," it must be limited by time, place, and circumstance.[101] The case marked the end of prize capture of foreign ships. Only treaties could grant the mutual right of visit and search between polities and create anti-slave-trade courts to adjudicate captures made under treaty law.

Scott's decision in *Le Louis* had no immediate impact on liberated Africans, but it meant that treaties were a precondition of future British maritime captures of foreign slave ships. His decision also made previous British captures vulnerable to compensation claims on appeal. To calculate Spanish claims for compensation, in 1816 a royal order tasked the Real Consulado to estimate the financial losses incurred by individuals based in Cuba whose ships the British had seized. The Consulado was the body that represented mercantile and landowner interests and sought to improve agricultural output through population growth and infrastructure development in roads, canals, and ports.[102] In July, the Consulado published a request for all prospective claimants to lodge their case with the office. It took until the end of 1817 for the Consulado to record every claim, corroborate the crucial details such as dates of departure and arrival and registered cargo with the Real Hacienda (the tax office), and check the status of appeals with the claimants' lawyers at London's High Court of Admiralty.[103] The result was a list of twenty-eight major claimants in relation to forty-eight seizures, who sought compensation of $1,476,790 (in Spanish American dollars) for the loss of ships and cargo and $1,869,000 (in Spanish American dollars) for the loss of slaves.[104] These included a claim by Antonio Escoto for the *Ysavel* that totaled $18,934. The London Slave Trade Commission, established to distribute compensation for cases of unlawful capture, subsequently awarded payment to the *Ysavel*'s owners.[105] Several claimants referred to slaves "abandoned" on the West African coast because of the capture of a slaving ship and its adjudication at Sierra Leone.[106]

GLOBAL INQUIRY INTO LIBERATED AFRICANS

Peacetime prompted profound investigations not only into the legal basis of maritime captures of slaving ships but also into the status of liberated Africans in British colonies. Wartime prize captures released thousands of liberated Africans into enlistment and apprenticeship across Britain's global empire, from the Caribbean to Sierra Leone, the Cape, and Mauritius. In the 1820s, this vast regime came under parliamentary scrutiny as abolitionists continued their campaign to abolish colonial slavery and as the governance of recently conquered territories produced scandals. These pressures led to commissions of inquiry in many British territories, each with distinct origins and different instructions from the colonial secretary, Lord Bathurst.[107] The Commission of Eastern Inquiry investigated the legislative and executive functions in the Cape, Mauritius, and Ceylon (Sri Lanka). The commission into the "state of Africans liberated from slavery in the West Indies and South America" focused on liberated Africans. The commission into the state of the West African settlements inquired into the administration of civil government at Sierra Leone and its dependencies on the Gold Coast and the Gambia.

The three commissions shared a directive to investigate liberated Africans. The Commissioners of Eastern Inquiry were required to analyze "the condition of the Government slaves, and of that of the apprenticed Africans, their present manner of employment, and the means of their future emancipation and maintenance."[108] The commission to the Caribbean and South America should "ascertain the actual condition of all Negroes, who

[have] been condemned to His Majesty, under any of the Acts passed for the abolition of the Slave Trade." They would "report how far those Negroes are now capable of providing for their own wants, if released from the state of apprenticeship or subjection in which they have hitherto been retained."[109] The mandate of the Commission in West Africa included a "review of the arrangements which were originally adopted for the settlement of those individuals [liberated Africans], of the causes which may appear to [the commissioners] to have rendered those arrangements successful, as it is understood in some instances, but ineffectual in others; whether these causes of success or failure be referable to circumstances of mismanagement, to any marked defect in the disposition or habits or people of so many different nations, or to the sudden increase [in people]."[110] The three commissions used apprenticeship to measure both the efficacy of colonial governance and the readiness of liberated Africans for a postslavery labor regime.

The commissioners had varying levels of experience with the law regarding the slave trade. John Dougan, a commissioner in Tortola, had previously acted as a prize agent in anti-slave-trade cases, whereas J. P. Gannon traveled from Europe to act as commissioner.[111] The commissions could be fraught with disagreement. Commissioners Dougan and Moody failed to agree on their findings for Tortola and so submitted separate reports. In Nevis, commissioners Gannon and Bowles fell out over Bowles's proposal to interview apprentices separately. Eventually, the Colonial Office made clear that the commissioners only had authority to interview apprentices together.[112] The commissioners of inquiry interviewed liberated Africans about apprenticeship. They offered a new forum for liberated Africans to make claims, in ways that the vice-admiralty courts rarely did. Yet the commissions also operated within a paradigm that envisaged bonded labor as necessary for antislavery, rather than as antithetical to it, thereby constraining the kinds of claim that they would approve.

Nelson and Argus, two men liberated from the *Amedie*, typified how liberated Africans used the commission in Tortola to claim freedom from apprenticeship. They were interviewed by the commission about their indentures as a domestic servant and cooper, respectively. Nelson's case illustrated the inconsistent regulation of apprenticeship: although he was still apprenticed, there was no corresponding indenture in the customs house or entry for him in the parliamentary returns consulted by the commissioners.[113] Far from a contractual arrangement, early anti-slave-trade indentures operated more like labor assignments to fulfill contingent needs, with little official documentation or oversight. Would, the commissioners asked, Argus and Nelson like to rent land from a white overseer in the burgeoning sugar colony of Trinidad? Argus answered that "he can manage himself now. . . . He does not wish to go." Nelson said that "he would not like to go to Trinidad, he could make out hire between Tortola and St Johns."[114] Both men knew of the special legal status attributed to them under the 1807 act. They acquired this knowledge despite the absence of Nelson's indenture and the fact that neither man had been "taught to read."[115]

The report illustrated that becoming literate depended on a master's willingness to provide such an opportunity rather than any official effort or formal structure. Direct evidence of communication among liberated Africans in Tortola about the law is elusive, but enslaved people throughout the Leeward Islands provided a precedent. Some enslaved people exerted considerable control over their work by selling their produce from provision grounds to the crews of warships and mercantile ships.[116] In 1788, the legislature at Tortola outlawed the practice of slaves living by themselves after discovering that skilled enslaved workers at Road Town were living independently as housekeepers and traders.[117] These practices suggested that legal knowledge about trading and accommodation could circulate through oral networks. Liberated Africans like Argus and Nelson built on these precedents to exit apprenticeship in favor of laboring under their own terms. They preferred itinerant self-sufficiency between the various colonial jurisdictions of the Leeward Islands to plantation labor.[118] In Tortola, liberated Africans also became tenants at an agricultural settlement, King's Town, without any formal land rights.[119] Tortola's elite perpetuated the vulnerable, propertyless position of the liberated Africans after the end of apprenticeship, which many of them sought to overcome through itinerant maritime work.[120]

Repaying the debt of labor, a key authoritarian feature of early anti-slave-trade law, could involve migration from Tortola to other colonies. The liberated African Inyounge, also known by her English name, Caroline, had been apprenticed for ten years, in Tortola and then St. Kitt's. When the commissioners interviewed her, she was working in the house of a Mr. Watson and had one year remaining on her indenture. In abbreviated form, the commissioners recorded Inyounge's answers to their questions: "She now subsists herself by selling small goods for Mr. Watson, who allows her 1 bit (4 1/2 d.)

This small watercolor on a map provides a vital clue about liberated Africans' strategies after the end of apprenticeship: they used small vessels to travel between islands as fishers and hawkers. (The National Archives, ref. CO700/VIRGINISLANDS7)

per dollar for what she sells; sometimes sells but very little. Would wish to remain at St. Kitt's if there was any person who would take care of her in case of sickness or want. Lives with a reputed husband, a boatman."[121] In her testimony, Inyounge proved that she was already self-sufficient. She also gained some official recognition of her family to prevent a further indenture or transfer to another colony. Argus, Nelson, and Inyounge challenged the bureaucratic category of apprenticeship imposed on them by finding self-directed work. Liberated Africans asserted their own priorities as independent producers of goods and services long before freedpeople developed similar strategies in postemancipation societies, including in the British Caribbean and United States.[122]

The poor oversight of apprentices led to labor assignments in breach of anti-slave-trade legislation. Twenty-eight of the thirty-one liberated Africans in Nevis were apprenticed to George Clarke Forbes, a plantation owner who had acted as King's Counsel in the case of the *Nancy*. Forbes transferred some apprentices from Tortola, including Sally, Jane, Bessy, Maria, Davy, and Nicholas, all liberated from the *Amedie*. He also transferred two children born to Sally and Jane in Tortola.[123] In breach of the 1808 order, Forbes assigned many women apprentices to agricultural work on his sugar plantation until they were "withdrawn from the negro gang, in consequence of the arrival of the Commission at Nevis."[124] Many of these apprentices used the chance to testify to the commission to highlight the brutality of plantation work. For instance, Adenon (given the English name Coma) "had always worked in the field with the Gang until the last month. When too late was beaten (*got banged*). . . . Driver has often banged her for not working hard enough." The commissioners observed, "She has marks of the Cart whip on the arm and she was ready to prove that she has abundant tokens of the same instrument on other parts of the body."[125] Forbes promised that he would no longer subject Adenon to agricultural work or corporal punishment: "she has been employed in the field in crop time, but shall not be sent there any more, she shall be employed as a sick nurse."[126] Called before the commissioners multiple times to respond to the apprentices' allegations, Forbes did not contest any of them.

Legal activism by liberated Africans involved not only countering unlawful labor assignments but also preventing illegal trafficking. In around 1820, Sally Sibley, an enslaved woman from St. Kitt's, began working for a Mrs. Cleary, first in St. Vincent and then in Demerara. Sibley told the commissioners, "When Mrs Cleary and the person with whom she cohabited were concerned in an attempt to export slaves to Surinam she gave information to Major Staple Comptroller of Customs."[127] Suriname was a Dutch colony in which slavery was lawful until 1863. Sibley's testimony ensured that Crown officers judged her to have been illegally imported to Demerara—and thus designated her to be a liberated African—to prevent reenslavement in Suriname. Joan was another enslaved woman from St. Kitt's whom Cleary brought to Demerara. As Joan testified, she "was brought to Demerara by Mrs Cleary who wanted to take her to Surinam and she gave information." In Demerara, Joan had had a son, Jerome, who was born in 1822 or 1823. Her child gave her added impetus to seek freedom. In the Americas, the legal status of the child followed that of the mother, and so Jerome was born enslaved. Not only was Cleary's attempt to sell them in Suriname a breach of the Abolition Act, but for Joan, it also meant possible separation from her son in a foreign colony. Going to the collector of customs was therefore brave and life-changing. As the commissioners noted, "Her son, altho' born subsequently to the date of her importation, was condemned as above with his mother."[128] Testimony to the collector of customs had enabled Joan to free herself and her son as liberated Africans. The commissioners reported that one of the illegal traffickers was caught and sentenced to two years in prison, and another escaped at Nickarie in Suriname. Sibley and Joan successfully petitioned the collector of customs to prevent criminal trafficking and ensured that their testimony entered the commissioners' report to further guarantee freedom for themselves and Jerome.

In the Cape, the Commission of Eastern Inquiry considered the assignment of liberated Africans in response to an allegation that the collector of customs had assigned liberated Africans to labor on estates in which he had an interest to increase their sale price.[129] The commissioners interviewed Samboo and Malamo, both apprenticed to William Wilberforce Bird, the comptroller of customs whom the commissioners found to be implicated in the corrupt dealings.[130] They asked the apprentices if they had any complaints. Samboo replied, "I have no complaints to make, except that my children are all apprenticed out, and I wish the one which is with Mr Moore, a baker at Wynberg, should be returned to his mother. . . . I further wish, that the Commissioner would find out how long I have to serve, as I do not know." Malamo complained that Wilberforce Bird "beats [him] for very little cause."[131] Liberated Africans also testified to the protector of slaves, an office established to ameliorate slaves' living conditions in Crown colonies. In August 1826, five former and current apprentices testified on behalf of Present, an enslaved man who claimed that he had been illegally trafficked from Mozambique into slavery at the Cape. Present asked the authorities to recognize him as a liberated African. July stated that he "knows Present, who came in the same vessel with him."[132] Eventually, the protector freed Present and another man on the grounds of illegal importation.

The commissioners also unwittingly exposed the limitations of the register as a key authoritarian tool of early anti-slave-trade law that constructed legal truth. Liberated Africans like Bull in Demerara defied continued surveillance by escaping.[133] Others presented borderline cases or said that they had names that varied from official records, making it difficult to establish whether they had been enlisted or apprenticed under the act. For instance, Canara was captured by a British warship in the Indian Ocean and brought to Île de Bourbon (Réunion) in around 1811. He was then enlisted in the Bourbon Corps and transferred to the First West India Regiment. As the commissioners noted, neither the parliamentary returns of liberated Africans nor the War Office records accounted for such recruits. They were "therefore unable to decide whether this person (Canara) was taken as prize of war, or as forfeited under the acts for abolishing the Slave Trade. But, from the account he gave, it was evident that he had been carried from his own Country as a slave, and that he was not free until he entered the army. He consequently belongs to the class of persons who come under the Inquiry of this commission."[134] Canara's oral testimony led the commissioners to classify him as a liberated African. He worked alongside other liberated Africans at the fort at Brimstone Hill on St. Kitt's. The actions of these petitioners both exposed the extensive coercion to which anti-slave-trade legislation subjected liberated Africans and challenged the limited legal capacity inherent in their status, an early example of the importance of law in antislavery struggles across the British Empire.[135] Throughout the empire, liberated Africans used the gaps in the legal regime to gain official recognition of their self-directed labor and freedom from illegal enslavement.

Sierra Leone also came under commissioners' scrutiny as a colony transformed by the Napoleonic Wars. Unlike the Caribbean colonies and the Cape, it was not a slave society. Moreover, the colony had accommodated a far greater number of liberated Africans. These distinctive features meant that commissioners and Parliament assessed the outcomes of liberated African settlement as indicative of the success of anti-slave-trade policies, rather than as a population that exposed slave owners' despotism or officials' corruption as in the Caribbean and the Cape.[136] Liberated Africans gained access to land, either in districts close to Freetown such as Congo Town or in villages that missionaries managed. They faced a lower threat of kidnapping into slavery. Liberated Africans were expected to grow crops to help the colony transition from being a net importer of foodstuffs from neighboring

African polities to agricultural self-sufficiency. The report contained little direct testimony from liberated Africans. Overall, the commissioners doubted that the colonial administration would become fiscally self-sufficient, not least because liberated Africans arrived in the colony in poor health and then contended with a troubling disease environment.[137]

These commissions of inquiry revealed that the problem of defining postslave labor emerged through the attempted management of liberated Africans in slave and nonslave colonies after the Napoleonic Wars. A new Order-in-Council in 1825 sought to address many of the gaps in the early anti-slave-trade regime. It authorized collectors of customs to apprentice liberated Africans to themselves with all the powers that a master could exercise over an apprentice in England.[138] In 1828, the colonial secretary ordered colonial governors to distribute freedom papers to all liberated Africans whom they deemed to be capable of looking after themselves and who had either finished apprenticeship terms or not been assigned. By 1832, 1,982 liberated Africans had received freedom papers.[139] For a period of over two decades before general emancipation legislation came into force in 1834, liberated Africans served as a precedent for how the state could free people from captivity while retaining strict control over them. Colonial officials recognized liberated Africans' free status without compensating them for their labor or redistributing any assets to them, thereby leaving them in a precarious position.

The politics of liberated Africans' legal status reveals that the "problem of freedom" emerged in a postwar global context rather than in a postemancipation national setting. For the commissioners, the answer to the problem was simple. The King-in-Parliament should subject liberated Africans and freedpeople of color more generally to regimes that would acculturate them to wage work and military service to white employers and masters. Christian conversion would ideally accompany such labor. Within the constraints imposed by the 1807 act and the structure of the commissions, liberated Africans' legal activism pushed the legal regime in directions not anticipated by legislators or commissioners. Liberated Africans demonstrated that their own vision of freedom included self-directed labor and protection against illegal enslavement.

During the Napoleonic Wars, the legal status of liberated Africans emerged through the adaptation of prize law to interdicting the slave trade. The legal order commodified the slaving ship and its cargo—including captive people—as exchangeable for prize money. It positioned rescued captives as people indebted to their liberators, who must repay their debt through labor. Implementing the law prompted new governing techniques to manage liberated Africans long after the moment of rescue. This transitional process from slave-ship rescue to compulsory labor would be common to every major attempt at maritime suppression over the next sixty years.

After the Napoleonic Wars, British maritime prize captures produced scandal and reform both inside and outside the British Empire. Inside the empire, official commissions of inquiry were tasked with investigating the situation of liberated Africans in the Caribbean, Sierra Leone, and the Cape. In each case, the merits of liberation were assessed in relation to how far liberated Africans had become acculturated to wage work and the administrative cost of rescue. Liberated Africans used whatever resources were available, including a new legal forum and the relations forged by shipboard insurgency, to craft strategies to exit apprenticeship and protect their freedoms. The commissions of inquiry mirrored tensions in the metropole over the rule of law. During the revolutionary and Napoleonic Wars, the government regularly suspended habeas corpus, the writ that prevented unlawful detention, to detain political opponents without trial. Rising inequality in an industrializing society produced political unrest against such repressive measures.[140] The commissions of inquiry fed into a broader politics about whether slaveholding could be reformed through ameliorative measures or required complete abolition.

Still, the legislative line from the 1807 act to the Act for the Abolition of Slavery in 1833 was crooked. The most straightforward connection was personal: James Stephen's son, also called James, drafted the act as counsel in the Colonial Office.[141] And both Acts were gradualist: they created a stage during which the bonded workforce would reproduce, thereby ensuring the labor supply required for imperial political economy.[142] Unlike the 1807 act, the 1833 act defined enslavement in British colonies rather than maritime trafficking as unlawful. The 1833 act classified people as praedial attached, praedial unattached, or nonpraedial workers; the first two categories referred to agricultural work. Public funds, rather than prize auctions, paid compensation to the slave owner, rather than to the maritime captor. But each step—defining a population to emancipate gradually, creating a legal category of bonded labor, and paying compensation—drew on the precedent set by the anti-slave-trade regime that affected Stephen's work in the Colonial Office on a regular basis, as his minutes on governor's dispatches reveal. Compared with smaller deportation and recruitment schemes in the eighteenth century, the anti-slave-trade regime showed that it was possible for a global empire to release large groups of slaves into bonded labor with new mechanisms to manage them. Liberated Africans released after 1807 prefigured and endured every subsequent legal change regarding slavery—amelioration, emancipation, apprenticeship, and indenture—in the nineteenth-century British Empire.

In the British Empire's external relations, Scott's decision in *Le Louis* opened the path toward fraught negotiations over compensation and the mutual right of search. Britain would try to use its leverage over other powers, particularly as a creditor to Portugal and Spain, to agree to comprehensive anti-slave-trade treaties. Such treaties often dovetailed with British interests to reduce or remove tariffs on British manufactures entering foreign markets. But these rival empires had their own reasons to prolong the slave trade as an integral part of the commodity export industries that led their economic growth. They also had their own law of slavery that shaped the place of liberated Africans in the slave societies of Brazil and Cuba. The emergence of a treaty anti-slave-trade regime, and the continuities and changes that it imposed on liberated Africans' legal status, lay ahead.

CHAPTER TWO

A Narrow Window

THE LARGO DO PAÇO IN central Rio de Janeiro was a square of four sides and two faces. One face looked outward to the world of seaborne trade on the Atlantic Ocean. The other face looked inward at a sprawling urban slave society. In the nineteenth century, Rio's residents—known as "cariocas"—knew the connections between these two faces. So did visiting artists, who depicted enslaved and free Afro-Brazilian people unloading vessels, cutting the hair of officers and sailors, and hawking their wares. It was here that the Portuguese emperor, Dom João, established his royal court in 1808, soon after fleeing from Napoleon's march on Lisbon with British naval protection. Eleven years later, on the same square, in the conference room of the Real Junta do Comércio, Agricultura, Fábricas e Navegação, a fateful meeting took place. Two commissary judges and two commissioners of arbitration, one of each to represent the Portuguese Empire and the British Empire, came together. They met "with the view of opening . . . the Mixed Commission, which, in conformity with the Convention of the 28th July 1817, annexed to the Treaty of the 22nd January 1815, was to be established in this kingdom of Brazil."[1] Under new treaty law, the Mixed Commission would adjudicate the capture of slaving ships and assign the rescued captives to the local Portuguese authorities to become liberated Africans.

The founding act was symbolic, not least because it took place within a Portuguese institution that promoted the interests of merchants, including those involved in slaving.[2] The slave traders even managed to install one of their own as an interpreter in the Mixed Commission. In January 1822, when João's son, Pedro, decided to stay in Brazil as regent rather than return to Portugal, he widened the split between the imperial metropole and colony. Some prominent Bahian residents in Rio presented a congratulatory address to Pedro. One of the signatories was familiar: Teófilo de Melo, the straw buyer of the *Amelia*, who signed as "Interpreter of the Mixed Commission, and Curador of the Libertos Minas."[3] Such was the power of slave traders: even an anti-slave-trade commission conducted its business under their watchful gaze.

The Mixed Commissions as a new binational anti-slave-trade jurisdiction defined by treaty law have been extensively studied. The commissions were sites of debate about the protocols of international law, including the procedure for the search of suspected slaving vessels and definitions of nationality based on evidence such as a vessel's flag and registration papers.[4] After adjudication of the capture and registration by the Mixed Commissions, the liberated Africans entered apprenticeships in urban slave societies. They were a jurisdiction that attempted some monitoring of liberated Africans.[5] Over time, the commissions as sites of slave-trade suppression and monitoring became compromised by the limitations of the treaty order. The Mixed Commissions had jurisdiction to adjudicate the capture of slave ships on the high seas alone, and they recognized as liberated Africans only those rescued from the high seas. These limitations excluded the far-larger number of African people trafficked into territorial waters (within three nautical miles of the coast, as defined by the range of cannon fire) or onto land. Accordingly, the Mixed Commissions have been characterized as flawed steps in British anti-slave-trade diplomacy on the protracted path toward final suppression.[6]

The Mixed Commissions, and the liberated Africans processed by them, raised a fundamental issue: What exactly did "liberated African" legal status mean in an urban slave society? This issue provoked tense debate. British commissioners sought to encompass captures beyond the high seas under the Mixed Commission jurisdiction. Their Portuguese and Spanish counterparts and local officials wished to restrict who was eligible to be a liberated African and constrain them regarding work and mobility. The liberated Africans sought to increase and protect their individual and collective freedoms. Their status also illuminated the case of illegally trafficked captives who had reached territorial waters or land and were therefore outside anti-slave-trade law and could no longer be freed. The Mixed Commissions' origins lay in the anti-slave-trade treaty negotiations after 1815. Treaty ratification made imperative domestic laws that placed liberated Africans within the Spanish and Portuguese slaveholding empires. The Mixed Commissions and domestic legislation shaped their legal status by mandating time-limited compulsory labor and some oversight mechanism, yet they left the definition of "full freedom" vague. Liberated Africans used legal paperwork to try to exit apprenticeship early. They petitioned local courts, the Mixed Commission, and British diplomats for freedom. Through fugitivity, liberated Africans also looked beyond the formal law to create their own visions of justice and practices of social regulation.

The Mixed Commission was a flexible domain at the threshold between nominal liberation and illegal enslavement that meant different things to different parties. For British commissioners and diplomats, it promised to be a vehicle of British anti-slave-trade imperialism. For the domestic authorities in slave societies, the Mixed Commission was a threat to the slave trade that required mitigation. They made legal changes to render the illegal trade socially permissible. These changes included designating the liberated Africans to be an exceptional population who were vulnerable to expulsion. For the liberated Africans, the court offered a new, albeit narrow, window for claiming freedom, on the streets that stretched out from sites like Largo do Paço.

TREATY NEGOTIATIONS

Treaty law introduced a new layer to defining the status of Africans liberated from slaving ships throughout the Atlantic world from 1815 onward. The aftermath of the Napoleonic Wars and Scott's ruling in *Le Louis* shaped the treaty negotiations. The United States and France (though defeated) had sufficient naval and military power to refuse to agree to treaties that would permit British naval searches of their vessels. The two other leading slave-trading and slaveholding empires were Portugal and Spain, and neither was committed to abolition. In the early nineteenth century, Portugal had no notable abolitionist movement.[7] In the Spanish Empire, leaders of anticolonial uprisings, including in Venezuela and Mexico, had proposed slave-trade suppression. Spain's Cortes of Cádiz, which claimed Spanish sovereignty in the wake of Napoleon's invasion and sought to establish constitutional government, debated slave-trade prohibition in 1811.[8] But these were fragmented rather than sustained imperial movements. Both empires came to negotiate anti-slave-trade treaties because they had relied on Britain to overturn Napoleonic occupation of their metropoles and owed large debts to Britain.

The Treaty of 1815 with Portugal declared a joint aim to ban the slave trade, but it applied only north of the equator. It thereby excluded most of the trade, which the traders organized to the south. Britain agreed to end all repayments on a loan of £600,000, plus a separate agreement for compensation of £300,000 for British captures of Portuguese ships alleged to be involved in the slave trade up to 1 June 1814.[9] The Convention of 1817 established the mutual right of search and a court—the Mixed Commission—with jurisdiction to adjudicate any capture made under treaty law. The Britain-Spain Treaty of 1817 had similar clauses that protected the South Atlantic slave trade, provided compensation of £400,000 for historical captures, and avoided the introduction of a Spanish criminal anti-slave-trade law.[10] This stance was consistent with Spanish imperial political economy that sought to prolong the slave trade and indentured labor immigration while minimizing the risk of disorder: in 1817, a royal order imposed a tax on slaving ships to fund increased white immigration to Cuba as a demographic defense against enslaved insurrection.[11] In the short term, Britain gained the right of search in exchange for forgiving loan repayments and committing funds to a compensation scheme for historical unlawful captures. The London Slave Trade Commission was established to adjudicate compensation claims. Two judges, one representative of each treaty party, judged each case. If they failed to agree, two commissioners of arbitration would draw lots for the chance to form a three-person panel with the judges. By the time of its closure in 1824, the commission had paid out £225,000.[12]

The anti-slave-trade treaties adopted the same model of two judges and two commissioners for the new courts, called Mixed Commissions. Established with one branch in British colonial Sierra Leone and one in the dominion of the other party, these commissions formed a new bilateral anti-slave-trade jurisdiction around the Atlantic world that would eventually adjudicate over six hundred cases of maritime capture.[13] Compared with the millions of people trafficked to Brazil and Cuba after 1817, the number of liberated Africans was tiny: in total, approximately eleven thousand people in Cuba and a similar number in Brazil, of whom some were liberated by the Mixed Commission and others by domestic courts.[14] But how each empire sought to regulate liberated African status was crucial for protecting the illegal trade. The sources about liberated Africans, created by Mixed Commissions and by the political authorities of the territories in which they were situated, provide vital insight into both anti-slave-trade law and the illegal trade. The treaties established the right of each contracting party to use naval vessels to visit and search ships belonging to the other party that the patrol suspected of carrying captives. The treaties gave the Mixed Commission jurisdiction to adjudicate the capture. They also stipulated that lawfully captured ships and cargo, except the shipboard captives, would be sold at public auction. The Mixed Commission's running costs had first claim on the net proceeds from this sale. Unlike the 1807 act, the treaties did not specify head money tariffs for each liberated African. Any remaining proceeds would be divided equally, with half going to the government of each party to the bilateral treaty. If the vessel was condemned by the Mixed Commission for an unlawful voyage, the liberated Africans "shall receive from the Mixed Commission a certificate of emancipation, and shall be delivered over to the Government on whose territory the Commission, which shall have so judged them, shall be established, to be employed as servants or free labourers. Each of the two Governments binds itself to guarantee the liberty of such portion of these individuals as shall be respectively consigned to it."[15]

The treaties were novel in establishing bilateral jurisdiction and protocols surrounding liberated Africans, but they contained telling limitations. The Mixed Commissions did not have criminal jurisdiction over slave-ship crews or any other party who had an interest in a slaving voyage. In a complex, illegal business, these complicit parties included shipowners, insurers, and the purchasers of captive people. Nor did the treaties cover the supply of goods, including British manufactures, that merchants used to purchase captives in coastal sub-Saharan Africa. It took until 1843 for Parliament to ban Britons from participation in a comprehensive range of slave-trading activities, such as providing goods or credit for slaving ventures.[16] Such limitations revealed the paradox inherent in British abolitionism. British anti-slave-trade naval patrols in South America suited commercial imperatives of securing preferential access for manufactured goods and for financial credit, such as through a commercial treaty with Brazil in 1827. Local merchants used British manufactures and credit to organize slaving voyages, mechanize their plantations, and finance railway transportation in Brazil and Cuba. In West Africa, naval patrols helped Britain's policy of "legitimate commerce" in promoting African exports of groundnuts, cotton, and palm oil rather than shipments of enslaved people. These goods were vital for industrial processes in Britain. As industrialization gathered pace, increasing British demand meant that enslavers forced more enslaved people into commodity production in Africa.[17] In these treaty negotiations, each party's pursuit of short- and long-term commercial and geopolitical objectives compromised any plan for comprehensive suppression.

The treaties also changed British domestic legislation regarding slave-trade suppression. In 1821, a British parliamentary act established that the Crown would allocate its half of the net proceeds to the naval captors.[18] This financial structure would mean less chance of payment, and lower payments, for naval captors than under the expansive wartime regime. Now naval cruisers patrolled a smaller geographic zone and without the prospect of large wartime prize profits. In 1824, a parliamentary act consolidated British abolition laws, including the provision that slaves "seized or taken as prizes of war or liable to forfeiture under this Act [shall] be considered, treated, taken, and adjudged as slaves and property, in the same manner as negro slaves have been therefore considered, treated, taken, and adjudged, when seized as prize of war, or as forfeited for any offence against the laws of trade and navigation respectively."[19] This provision created a common regime for liberated Africans captured under wartime prize law and those captured under peacetime treaty law who were settled in British territories.[20] It also introduced bounty payments of ten pounds for every liberated man, woman, and child in cases adjudicated by either vice-admiralty courts or the Mixed Commissions.[21] The treaties continued the trend of positioning rescued captives as people who must repay the debt of liberation through labor.

LIBERATED AFRICANS IN THE LAW OF SLAVE SOCIETIES

In the Spanish Empire, the Real Cédula (Royal Charter) of 19 December 1817 brought the Treaty of 1817 into Spanish law. It defined the place of Africans liberated by the Mixed Commission. Article 1 banned vassals of the Spanish king from purchasing captives in Africa north of the equator: "The blacks [*negros*] who were purchased on the said coasts will be declared free [*libres*] in the first port of my dominions at which the vessel in which they are transported arrives: this vessel with the remaining cargo shall be confiscated for my Royal Treasury, and the purchaser, captain, master and pilot shall be irredeemably condemned to ten years in prison in the Philippines."[22] The remaining articles defined other elements of the prohibition. The ban extended to the South Atlantic from 30 May 1820 onward, with a five-month window after this date to complete slaving voyages. The number of captives per ton would be regulated. The punishment of Spanish vassals for slave-trading would also apply to foreign ships trading in slaves to Spanish dominions. The Cédula stipulated that royal authority made shipboard captives "free" in Spanish dominions without specifying the precise mechanisms for doing so or what free status entailed.

The word "libre" offered one clue about how the liberated Africans would fit into the Spanish colonial legal order. Early nineteenth-century Cuba was a slave society: slavery was fundamental to the major aspects of economic, political, and civil life. The Cédula's preamble mentioned that in the Americas "the number of indigenous blacks has grown prodigiously, and even the number of free blacks [*los libres*], because of the mild regulation of Government, and of the Christian and humane conduct of the Spanish owners."[23] The Spanish code Las Siete Partidas, which became the main source of civil law in Spanish colonies, included various mechanisms to exit slavery. The Siete Partidas, published under royal authority in the thirteenth century, was composed when Spanish Christian rulers contended with rival Islamic polities in the peninsula. They wanted the Partidas to provide Christian subjects held captive by these rival polities with legal means to escape slavery. The Partidas drew on the Roman Law doctrine that slavery was against the law of nature. If a slave owner sells or gives a slave to another person "under an agreement that he will be emancipated by a certain day," this agreement cannot be altered.[24] This constraint on the slave owner's power over the slave would eventually inform the development of the customary right of *coartación* (self-purchase by installments). The Partidas also granted official recognition of freedom to slaves who escaped from their masters and lived as free people for a specified time.[25] Knowledge of the law and the Spanish language were prerequisites for negotiating any type of manumission, including *coartación*. Spanish colonial authorities devised additional mechanisms for manumission based on the imperatives of imperial rule. Some gained freedom by fighting in the imperial forces. In 1800, the enslaved people in the mining region of El Cobre in eastern Cuba secured their freedom by petitioning the Spanish emperor.[26] As freedpeople went on to have children who were born free, a significant free population of color emerged in Spanish colonies, including Cuba. When disputes erupted over the terms of manumission, enslaved people went to the *síndico procurador*, the public official who represented an enslaved litigant's interests. In the nineteenth century, about 1 percent of the enslaved population in Cuba gained manumission each year.[27] Manumission procedures did not disrupt the development of a slavery-based economy that was as brutal for enslaved people as any other in the Americas.

The Cédula referred to both manumitted people and liberated Africans as "libres," but they occupied distinct positions under the law. On the one hand, liberated Africans had more formal recognition of their existing freedom than manumitted people did. The authorities declared them free upon arrival in a Spanish territory rather than as becoming free through wage-earning or loyal service. Moreover, the Mixed Commission, rather than a slave owner, had jurisdiction to bestow this freedom on liberated Africans. The Spanish Crown then recognized this freedom. In at least two previous cases unrelated to anti-slave-trade law, the Crown had declared free the shipboard captives from slaving vessels captured and brought to Cuba. In 1800 and 1817, the Spanish king decreed the captives who had arrived on the vessels *Nuestra Señora del Carmen* and *Dos Hermanos* to be free; the latter case involved serial petitioning by the African people to receive freedom papers.[28] On the other hand, liberated Africans did not have access to the structures and practices that regulated manumission, such as the office of *síndico* or the options of *coartación* and *papel* (the request to transfer from one owner to another).[29] The Cédula both acknowledged the sui generis nature of liberated Africans' freedom and left it unregulated regarding labor, rights, or duties.

Compared with the Spanish Empire, Portuguese imperial legislation offered more detail regarding liberated African legal status. In Brazil, the imperial Alvará (Order) of 26 January 1818 brought the Treaties of 1815 and 1817 into Portuguese law. The Alvará imposed the criminal punishment of exile to Mozambique on anybody who fitted out or prepared a ship for a slaving voyage north of the equator. Prize money from auctioning the captured ship would be split equally between any informant and the Real Fazenda (Royal Treasury). Section 5 of the Alvará placed the liberated

Africans under the jurisdiction of a *juiz da ouvidoria da comarca* (district judge) or, in their absence, the Conservatory of Indians. They would "serve there as freed people [*libertos*] for a period of 14 years, or in another public service in the admiralty, forts, agriculture and trade crafts, as most suitable, being for this enlisted in their respective Roles; or leased to established private individuals of known probity, assigning these individuals to feed, clothe, religiously instruct, and teach them the trade or work that suits them."[30] Such service mirrored the treatment of *escravos da nação* (national slaves), a category that encompassed abandoned and unclaimed slaves as well as those confiscated from the Jesuits. These enslaved people were generally assigned into public service.[31]

Diligent "service and good manners" could reduce the fourteen-year term. At the end of service, the liberated Africans would enjoy "the full right of their freedom." During the period of service, the liberated Africans "will have a Curador, a person of known probity, whose training will be proposed by the Judge, and approved by the Court of Justice in the Imperial Court [Mesa do Desembargo do Paço desta Corte], or by the Governor or Captain General of the respective Province; and his office will involve claiming everything that is in the interest of the *libertos*, monitor abuses, ensure that service ends at the appropriate time, and in general promote what in his judgement and observation is prescribed by the law for orphans."[32] As defined by the crucial civil code, the Ordenações Filipinas, the role of a *curador* was to promote the interests of those who were assigned to his guardianship. A *curador* represented the interests of those, such as orphans, who were unable to act as full legal persons. The Juiz d'Orfaos "will take care to give Tutors and Curadors to all Orphans and minors, who do not have them, within one month of their being orphaned; the Juiz will bring to these Tutors and Curadors all moveable and immoveable goods, and money of the said orphans and minors for a description and inventory to be made by the clerk."[33] The *curador* must be financially independent and of good character to ensure that he acted in his ward's interests.

The legal status of liberated Africans thus drew on the emperor's subjection of groups such as Indigenous people, *escravos da nação*, and orphans to state authorities. Individuals in each of these categories were persons with limited legal capacities. As a freedperson, legal personhood was limited in telling ways. Liberated Africans did not have the right to change to whom they hired their labor. They had no clear property rights. Neither the right to a family life nor the right to residency was confirmed by the Spanish Cédula or Portuguese Alvará. For people with limited legal capacities, the horizon of when "training" would be complete, and what constituted the "full right of their freedom," was indistinct. Both Spanish and Portuguese imperial authorities located liberated African status within their legal structures resentfully, fearing that ceding the power to free African captives to an external institution would create a dangerous precedent.

THE WINDOW OPENS

In 1821, the capture of the *Emilia* was the first case adjudicated by the Mixed Commission in Rio de Janeiro and the only one before Brazilian independence.[34] The Africans liberated from the vessel confronted the severe constraints and occasional opportunities of an expanding slave society. The Mixed Commission decided that the capture was lawful and declared the captives to be liberated Africans on 31 July. It took several months to organize apprenticeships for most of the liberated Africans. A municipal judge organized a bidding process for creditworthy individuals to compete to hire approximately three hundred apprentices. Henry Hayne, one of the commissioners at the opening of the Mixed Commission at Largo do Paço, reported that the remaining fifty apprentices entered government service.[35] These apprentices lit streetlamps, tended the public gardens, and maintained a public fountain.[36] Africans apprenticed to private households and public institutions spread throughout a city with vibrant Afro-Brazilian communities. The gridded street structure and topographical landmarks of churches, squares, and fountains connected the parishes and created patterns for labor, worship, and social activities.

At the northern limit of the parish of Santa Anna lay the Valongo wharf, where hundreds of thousands of enslaved captives were illegally disembarked in Brazil. An uninhabited zone to the south kept the newly arrived slaves in quarantine. Across Campo de Santa Anna lay a series of streets where many liberated Africans served apprenticeships to private masters. Rua do Conde, Rua do Senado, and Rua dos Inválidos connected Santa Anna to Sacramento parish. In Sacramento, a fifteen-minute walk northeast would take a carioca to Nossa Senhora do Rosário e São Benedito, one of the major churches for enslaved and *liberto* people. Here, they were equidistant between the coastal Largo do Paço (now Praça XV) in Candelaria parish and Campo de Santa Anna. Liberated Africans were already familiar with the

The city of Rio de Janeiro with key sites for liberated Africans, 1831–50. (Map based on Farès el-Dahdah, Alida Metcalf, Axis Maps. imagineRio [Spatial Studies Lab, Rice University, 2014], https://doi.org/10.25613/Y1A2-CM40)

Mixed Commission in the former. The latter was the site of ritual by slave owners, including parades and public whippings. But the squares were also sites of social gatherings, gossiping while collecting water, and, at Santa Anna, dancing.[37] On these squares and the surrounding streets, enslaved and freed people held processions where they crowned "kings" and "queens" to represent their interests.[38]

Northward along the coast from Largo do Paço lay the parish of Santa Rita, which contained the Arsenal da Marinha. From the early nineteenth century, the arsenal held enslaved and free Afro-Brazilian people and Indigenous people and, later, liberated Africans as bonded laborers.[39] A carceral, semimilitarized institution like the arsenal was a laboratory for experimenting with forms of indentured and apprenticed labor long before legal emancipation in the later nineteenth century. Throughout these parishes, enslaved people often worked for wages (*ao ganho*) to earn money for self-purchase. Only a small number of people ever achieved

At the public fountain in Rio de Janeiro, Afro-Brazilian women talked, free from enslavers' oversight. Visiting artist Thomas Ender drew and painted many closely observed scenes of Afro-Brazilian life. (Thomas Ender, *Gruppe am Brunnen im öffentlichen Garten,* watercolor and pencil, HZ 13691, Graphic Collection of the Academy of Fine Arts Vienna)

self-purchase. But their independent work, which often resulted in purchasing the freedom of enslaved family members or slaves for their own profitable hiring out, produced dynamic urban African diasporic laboring groups. Over the next fourteen years, the liberated Africans from the *Emilia* worked as apprentices in these parishes. The apprentices interacted with both the institutions that sought to control the liberation process and the spaces of urban Afro-Brazilian world-making.

In the case of the *Emilia,* the proceedings during capture, adjudication, and apprenticeship caused disputes between Britain and Portugal. The Portuguese commissioner objected to the naval captor's detention of the slave-ship crew aboard a British vessel of war. The commissioners refused to allow the claimant to the slaver to see the evidence before condemnation. The King's Advocate, Christopher Robinson, criticized both the detention and the refusal in his review for the Foreign Office. For Robinson, the Portuguese Chancery was wrong for objecting to the Mixed Commission's form of proceeding because such interference was not authorized by the Treaty of 1815 or the Additional Convention of 1817.[40] Finally, Robinson stated that the liberated Africans "should not be detained, as in this case, a month after the condemnation, in a worse situation, than if their state of slavery had continued."[41] Another official criticized the commissary judges for citing law beyond the treaty in their verdict, such as the Alvará of 1818.[42] Even a seemingly straightforward case of naval capture resulted in Portuguese accusations of British imperial high-handedness and British counteraccusations of failing to respect treaty law.

After independence, Brazil's new constitution of 1824 declared citizens to include "those who were born in Brazil, whether they are freeborn or freed from slavery [*libertos*]."[43] This clause included *libertos* born in Brazil and excluded *libertos* born in Africa, whom authorities perceived to be likelier to rebel. It also excluded liberated Africans, which could have signified that Brazil was committed to suppression and so no further enslaved Africans would enter its territory. Perhaps the constitutional delegates hoped that such a signal would increase the prospects of British recognition of Brazilian independence, which was necessary for standing as a sovereign power.[44] But the exclusion from citizenship was perhaps also motivated by concern about the activities of people freed by an external power. From 1824, the "full right of freedom" for liberated Africans did not include citizenship. Indeed, the 1832 Naturalization Law gave foreign soldiers who had fought for Brazil an easier path to citizenship than it did African-born free people.[45] The exclusion from the constitutional right to citizenship probably gave some of the surviving liberated Africans from the *Emilia* an additional reason to leave Brazil. At the end of apprenticeship, they set sail on a British vessel to Lagos in 1836.[46] Like over ten thousand people who would come after them in Brazil, the people liberated from the *Emilia* had limited legal capacities as bonded laborers under the jurisdiction of a local judge and *curador*. The first liberated Africans in Brazil turned to their family and shipmate connections to remove the constraints imposed by an expansive slave society.

In Havana, the release of liberated Africans from the Mixed Commissions was even more politically charged than in Rio. Court proceedings created new social networks and paperwork for liberated Africans that the local proslavery political and economic elite saw as a threat. In 1822, a Spanish slaver originally named *Piragua* sailed to Baltimore, a major site for the building and outfitting of nineteenth-century slave ships.[47] In 1824, the British naval ship *Lion* captured the vessel, now renamed the *Relámpago*, and brought it to Havana. The *Relámpago*'s voyages cut across momentous changes in Spain and colonial Cuba. The vessel had first set sail when Spain was still under constitutional rule, but by the time of adjudication, Ferdinand VII had restored his absolutist regime. The Mixed Commission arranged for interpreters to interview each captive to record their key biographical details. Like registration practices in Freetown, the procedure was invasive. Staff reduced a captive person's prior life in Africa to the category of "African name" and "nación" and exacerbated the trauma of captivity by inspecting brand marks. Each person must have found the routines of inspection and the long days of waiting in confinement very similar to the barracoon and ship's hold.

Registration also brought the liberated Africans into conversation with enslaved and free Black people in Havana.[48] Four key interpreters were Juan de la Holla, Tomas Villa, Salvador Aguilar, and Francisco de Paula Martinez. Unlike most enslaved people, these interpreters had surnames recorded by the authorities. Other than de la Holla, each had his enslaver's surname—which indicated likely birth in Cuba and a position of privilege within the master's household. Their Spanish-language skills suggested that they were *ladinos*, distinguished from captives who had recently arrived from Africa, known as *bozales*.[49] *Ladinos*, who were either born locally or had spent sufficient time in the colony to become fluent with its language and customs, tended to have greater opportunity than *bozales* to earn an income from urban work.[50] These four interpreters helped the commission's secretary, Juan Francisco Cascales, to record family relationships between some of the captives: Soró and Qüeje were cousins, Goña was Yongó's mother, Guayeró and Manyá were sisters, six-month-old Naré was the daughter of Bamanyá.[51] Most shipboard captive people probably did not know each other prior to embarkation, but the *Relámpago* register reminds us that some of them developed relationships that built on preexisting ties.[52] The interpreters then told the liberated Africans that they would be assigned to compulsory labor. In a subsequent case, the liberated Africans "were instructed, it being repeated many times, that they were no longer in the class of slaves here, but rather as free men [*sic*], albeit subject for a certain time to the voice and obedience of the persons in whose care the government will place them."[53]

Each person received a letter of emancipation and a tin ticket with a registration number that corresponded to that on the letter. During apprenticeship, these letters and tickets functioned more like identity documents than guarantors of liberty. The liberated Africans then entered apprenticeship in Havana, for which there are few extant records. Captain General

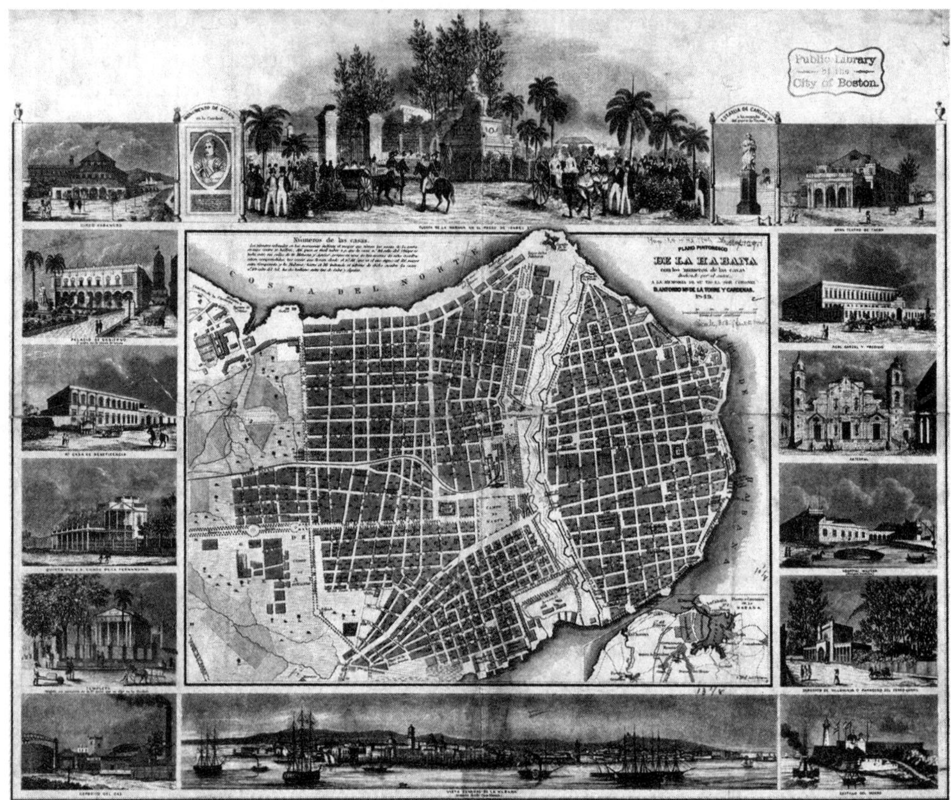

Liberated Africans in Havana encountered a city dominated by its gridded streets and imposing city walls. *Plano pintoresco de la Habana: Con los numeros de las casas* (1849). (Map reproduction courtesy of the Norman B. Leventhal Map & Education Center at the Boston Public Library)

Francisco Vives issued regulations stating that he and his officers, such as the *comisarios de barrios* (neighborhood deputies), had authority over the apprentices. They could assign the liberated Africans to apprenticeship terms of five years for adults and seven years for children, set maintenance rates, inspect their treatment during apprenticeship, and issue fines for noncompliance.[54] The treaty regulations provided for Catholic instruction of apprentices. For instance, some apprentices were baptized at a church in central Havana, Santo Cristo Buen Viaje.[55] On 1 June 1827, the priest baptized Quebé, who was liberated from the *Relámpago* and named Donato by the Mixed Commission.[56] The priest named him Donato Guirola; his master during apprenticeship, Angel Guirola, stood as godfather.[57] Some godparents may have helped the new arrivals understand the prospects for social advancement through colonial institutions: the godfather of Higino José Avilés, baptized at the same church, was Ramon Rodriguez, a lieutenant in the Battalion of Loyal Morenos, a militia composed of free people of color.[58] At the end of the apprenticeship period, the captain general was required to distribute new letters of emancipation.[59] Social networks that spanned enslaved people and commission officials, and paperwork that registered "liberation," distinguished the liberated Africans as a population in Havana.

After the verdict of condemnation in the *Relámpago* case, political opposition to the release of liberated Africans into Cuba grew. Two powerful bodies, the Consulado and Ayuntamiento, petitioned the Spanish king. They were natural bedfellows: the Consulado consisted of landowners and merchants who promoted economic growth, and the Ayuntamiento was the Havana town council, which was dominated by rich landowners. Both organizations favored a sugar economy based on importing captive labor. The petition urged the king to agree to terms with Britain for deporting the liberated Africans from Cuba. According to the petitioners, the liberated Africans set "a most injurious example to the Slaves, and otherwise [are] prejudicial to the Island."[60] By May 1825, even the Spanish commissioners in the Mixed Commission agreed. They recommended that Britain and Spain agree "to convey such negroes again to their own Country; or to any other place out of this island."[61] Vives's assertiveness over apprenticing the *Relámpago* captives and the Spanish commissioners' advocacy of deportation indicated the growing authoritarianism of colonial rule. On 25 May, this trend culminated in the notorious *facultades omnímodas*, the authority granted by the king to the captain general to banish people, confiscate property, and suspend judicial sentences. In a climate of increasing authoritarianism, the liberated Africans' free status became a threat to urban colonial governance and the expanding sugar industry.

The legal politics between British imperial officials and their Spanish and Portuguese counterparts shaped the Mixed Commission as a narrow window with a significant and arbitrary opening for liberation. Only people rescued from slave ships on the high seas, rather than in barracoons, on the city streets, or on plantations, could gain liberated African status. The situation changed fatefully once the crew began disembarking the captives. Those who purchased and held the captives acted as though they lawfully owned them—and through bills of sale, mortgages, and wills, a legal title began to form.[62] Just as important was cultural performance, with enslavers acting in public as if the legal title had always existed. Illegal trafficking could thus become legally regulated enslavement, beyond the scope of treaty law. Restricting the capture of slaving ships to the high seas was vital to the Spanish and Portuguese regimes, given the enormous number of illegally imported Africans undergirding their slave societies. If captures extended into territorial waters and land, the entire system could fall apart. Such captures were rare: in the period 1819–26, the British commissioners reported one single case in which the colonial police force removed captive African people from a barracoon on Cuban soil.[63] British commissioners complained that local political authorities failed to investigate illegal slaving and to protect liberated Africans, and their counterparts saw any such effort as a threat to slave society. The limitations of the Mixed Commissions in Rio and Havana were becoming ever more apparent.

PAPER LIBERATION

The prevalence of slavery in Rio de Janeiro and Havana made the apprentices vulnerable to exploitation and forced disappearance into enslavement. For prospective masters, the hiring fees and overheads involved in housing, feeding, and paying apprentices terminated with the apprentice's death. Commissioner Hayne thought that this termination made apprentice labor potentially cheaper than the ongoing costs of owning enslaved people and the "loss of capital in the event of death or desertion."[64] Hayne's concerns regarding apprenticeship would lead to stronger oversight in another slave society, Angola, in the 1840s. In Brazil and Cuba, many apprentices survived tough working and living conditions to gain full freedom. But hirers of apprentices, known as "masters," also smuggled many apprentices into slavery. They purchased death certificates to confect evidence of a liberated African apprentice's death. They also purchased the corpses of other Black people, "a practice which, as there is no want of subjects for all anatomical purposes, can only, it would seem, have for its object to carry off into slavery the Africans so hired out, by alleging them to have died."[65] Masters then smuggled the person out of the city and onto a plantation. A mortuary economy helped turn legally free people into slaves with little prospect of recourse. The result was that the Mixed Commission's jurisdiction extended radially in both time and space. The farther that the liberated Africans moved from the court both in time since naval capture and in distance from the court building, the weaker the protection that anti-slave-trade law afforded them.

The movement of legal papers through the Mixed Commission and local government offices shaped the liberation process. In June 1831, Casemiro, who was working in the Passeio Público, a prominent public park in Rio, petitioned the municipal judge for his freedom. Casemiro claimed that he was a "black man of the Nagô nation and a freed man by the Convention of 28 July 1817 in addition to the Treaty of 22 January 1815 and the Alvará of 28 [*sic*] January 1818."[66] He alleged that during his "obligatory service . . . he did not receive a wage or other remuneration in all that time."[67] Casemiro's petition was an early case of petitioning from the *Emilia* that raised the question of how the Portuguese authorities would distribute emancipation letters.[68] Casemiro's petition contained a small clue that he or his legal representative may have visited the court to formulate his case. He had served for only ten years. The Alvará provided for a term shorter than fourteen years in cases of good service. As we have seen, the commissioners had cited the Alvará as grounds for condemning the vessel, much to the chagrin of the Foreign Office. Perhaps Casemiro or his representative had read the Mixed Commission records to know which laws to cite in his case for freedom. Within a month, Casemiro decided to submit another petition, this time with three fellow liberated Africans.[69] All petitioners sought to exit apprenticeship before the end of the fourteen-year term. They worked in the Passeio Público, which suggests that sites of apprenticeship offered liberated Africans the chance to build alliances for a life in exile. The outcomes of the two petitions are unknown. Nonetheless, the petitioners combined evidence from the Mixed Commission regarding ship capture with Brazilian legal conventions that protected the freedom of *libertos*. Liberated Africans in Rio devised innovative legal strategies to construct a possible path out of apprenticeship.

Despite the provisions of the 1818 Alvará, diligent service did not guarantee that liberated Africans could get liberty. The legal process tended to privilege any evidence that could justify extending the period of bonded labor. In 1843, Helena petitioned the *juiz d'orfaos* to ask whether she still needed to serve. Helena had been apprenticed since 22 April 1831 to Anna Joaquim Rosa, "to whom the petitioner has provided her services for more than ten years until she died." She wished to know "if there is or not a new contract relative to her services." Helena thought her loyal service justified her freedom. A police deputy in the São José parish swore, "I am not aware that the petitioner has been disobedient" during her apprenticeship.[70] The judge asked the *curador*, Jose Baptista Lisboa, to decide Helena's case. In his judgment, Lisboa argued that the fourteen-year term referred to serving not just the original master but also their heirs: "therefore to release the African from their service without their consent, or without proving the fulfillment of conditions [of service], is a violation of the faith of contracts."[71] The liberated Africans' labor was inheritable. A year after Helena's petition, a master who had hired Domingos complained that "he has become perverse, and incorrigible, to the point of arming himself with a knife against her son for which he was sent to the Casa de Correção on the orders of the Deputy of the Parish of S. José, who also established a criminal charge against him."[72] Although the outcome for Domingos is unknown, liberated Africans in the Casa became forced laborers in the service of the state, something that Spanish colonial authorities in Cuba also practiced.[73] The police officers' actions in regulating Helena's and Domingos's behavior revealed that the surveillance of liberated Africans as bonded laborers expanded urban policing.[74]

Newspaper advertisements revealed that liberated Africans also escaped from compulsory labor. Even prominent anti-slave-trade locations, like the British naval base and the Mixed Commission, were not immune to escapes or disappearances: "Disappeared from the warehouses of the English squadron, on the Ilha das Cobras, a . . . liberated African, of the Cabinda nation, appears to be twelve years old, and responds to the name Thomaz, he wore a shirt of blue baize, he has hair missing from the top part of his head; there will be a good reward for whoever brings him to the said warehouses or to rua Direita No. 8."[75] Rua Direita (now Rua Primeiro de Março) ran along one side of Largo do Paço, where the Mixed Commission was originally located. A ten-year-old boy, known as Claro, wearing a "jacket with red stripes, already faded," escaped from the home of Eusébio de Queirós, Rio's chief of police.[76] Claro's worn clothes indicated the brutal work conditions that the liberated Africans escaped. Lisboa's and Queirós's roles in addressing liberated Africans' freedom strategies in the 1830s would shape their participation in the final suppression of the trade to Brazil in the 1850s.

Like they had with the commissions of inquiry in British colonies, people used liberated African legal status to further their interests when addressing the authorities. The African men Alexandre and Antonio "say they are liberated Africans," according to police officers who detained them in the Calabouço prison.[77] The offenses that merited detention were unspecified. Perhaps they were liberated Africans who had escaped from compulsory service. If they were illegally trafficked people, it meant that they had heard about the protections owed to liberated Africans. They had ample opportunity to hear such news. People of unfree status like Alexandre and Antonio, including convict laborers and enslaved people whose enslavers had rented out their labor or punished them with assignments, were a significant workforce. Unfree people worked alongside liberated Africans on most public works projects in urban Rio.[78] Liberated Africans who escaped may have communicated with these groups to find new roles in the Afro-Brazilian urban economy.

Such communities were not legible to the authorities, but the occasional advertisement hints at them. In January 1839, the captain Feliciano Firmo Monteiro placed an ad, which appeared under the "Fugitive Slaves" section of the *Diário do Rio de Janeiro,* about the apprentice Felicio. The description of Felicio revealed how the register and letters of emancipation functioned like identification documents. Monteiro surely drew on such sources to describe Felicio with such precision: "of the Congo nation, branded with a V on the left breast, round-faced, quite black, beardless, and missing one or more teeth at the front." Felicio "has been learning the trade of carpentry with Senhor Antonio de Padua in an open house on rua S. Francisco de Paula: he disappeared on Saturday, 29 of the previous month, between 8 and 9 o'clock in the morning." Monteiro "protests against the person who has sheltered him."[79] With his new trade, Felicio could easily work for himself. He had escaped on a street next to Nossa Senhora do Rosário e São Benedito, a church where Afro-Brazilian people regularly met to pray, organize as a brotherhood, and trade. Beyond the city, enslaved African people escaped to *quilombos* that developed along the rivers of provincial Rio.[80] Yet many of the liberated Africans who disappeared were probably captured by enslavers. Alexandre, Antonio, and Felicio made talk about freedom for liberated Africans public. Escapes and protests rejected not only the terms of compulsory labor but also the underlying assumption that liberated Africans needed to be "trained" to be responsible with their freedom.

Liberated Africans also made claims to multiple authorities to get a favorable judgment—"forum shopping"—to gain freedom from

At Nossa Senhora do Rosario, near where Felicio made his escape, Afro-Brazilian people worshiped, traded, and socialized. (Thomas Ender, *Pfarre de Nossa Senhor[a] do Rosario*, watercolor and pencil, HZ 13651, Graphic Collection of the Academy of Fine Arts Vienna)

apprenticeship. In Havana, the liberated African Gavino Pinedo petitioned both the Mixed Commission and captain general for freedom. Scholars have carefully analyzed Gavino's case to explore enslavement in the Galinhas region of the Upper Guinea Coast, the gap-ridden agency that he had as an apprentice, and British antislavery agents' attempts to free him.[81] Focusing on the structure and language of his petition complements their approaches to reveal how Gavino fought attempts by his masters and the colonial state to force him into slavery.

Gavino was liberated from the Spanish slave ship *Fingal* in 1826 and was then apprenticed to Luisa Aper de la Paz.[82] A fellow Black person taught him to be a water carrier in Havana. Gavino served for three consecutive five-year periods, paying his wages to Aper de la Paz and then, after her death, to her son, Felix Pinedo. In 1841, Gavino sought the help of David Turnbull, the British consul and superintendent of liberated Africans and a notoriously radical antislavery agent. Gavino's first petition to the Mixed Commission reflected Turnbull's priorities of criticizing the commission for its weak oversight over liberated Africans, including the withholding of Gavino's wages.[83] In Gavino's second petition, a declaration to Turnbull, he narrated how the five-year term of service was renewed not once but twice, at the captain general's "house." On the expiry of the third term, he was not brought to the captain general, and "nothing was said to him on the subject of his being still in the services of a master; but he has continued as before to pay over his earnings to Don Felix Pinedo."[84] Gavino explained that competition in the water-carrying sector had reduced the amount that he paid Pinedo from one dollar per day to ten dollars every four weeks. But his most serious complaint was far more alarming. Pinedo had refused permission for Gavino to marry his partner, the enslaved woman Candelaria, even though Candelaria's mistress had given her consent to the marriage. Candelaria and Gavino had a seven-year-old daughter. According to the main source of colonial civil law, the Siete Partidas, an enslaved person had the right to marry even against the will of their master, let alone the will of the master of an apprentice.[85]

Gavino ended his declaration with two direct requests to the consul: "to take measures to procure him his liberty and to enable him to marry the mother of his child."[86] Gavino aimed to bring his family together and to protect them with more emancipation papers and a marriage certificate—an armor of legal papers against illegal enslavement. The captain general, Valdés, issued an emancipation certificate. But he also decided to make an example of a liberated African who had invited additional British anti-slave-trade intervention into Cuba. Valdés accused Gavino of fomenting an uprising and, in October 1841, deported him to the penal colony of Ceuta in North Africa.[87] In November, Gavino landed in Cádiz, ill and unable to continue his journey. He died in the city in August 1842. Whether Candelaria or their daughter ever found out about Gavino's fate, or what happened to them, remains unknown. Liberated Africans could engage in forum shopping to get freedom from apprenticeship, but that strategy carried the risk of removal by local authorities who remained committed to the illegal trade.

As in Rio, liberated Africans in Cuba turned away from the formal law to achieve their goals. In January 1828, the director of Havana's Botanical Garden complained about the apprentices working there. According to him, these "slaves of the Garden were completely abandoned, they tended to all vices, some were involved in nocturnal scandals."[88] There was no further detail about these nighttime incidents, probably because officials had no access to them. Perhaps the events included ancestor worship or drumming: these "nocturnal scandals" came after a prolonged period of festivities by *cabildos de nación* (mutual-aid societies run by people of color) for worshiping saints and orishas that included authorized parades within the city walls.[89] Such rituals among enslaved and freed people around the Atlantic helped build reciprocal relations. The Real Consulado refused the director's request for additional liberated African laborers because it claimed that the Consulado's public works projects were "much more intensive," which required more labor, than those of the Garden.[90]

In 1844, Captain General Leopoldo O'Donnell asked the president of the Junta de Fomento, which had taken over infrastructure projects from the Real Consulado, whether the *emancipada* Bueí, given the Spanish name Paula, was living and working in the Depósito de Cimarrones (the Deposit of Runaway Slaves).[91] The Deposit functioned like a prison. In 1835, eleven-year-old Bueí had been rescued from the slaving ship *Joven Reyna* and disembarked in Cuba. She "fled in the same year during transit from this City to the Countryside, during this time she was a *bozal* and for this reason she will have changed her Christian name."[92] The Real Consulado reported that it could not identify her among the Deposit's residents.[93] Over the past nine years, Bueí had remained hidden from the authorities. Perhaps she joined a *palenque*, a fugitive community of self-liberated people in urban and rural areas. Another possibility is that an enslaver captured her and put her to work on a plantation. Although there seems to be no further trace of her, Bueí's decision shows that even a liberated African child could escape from bonded labor that she found oppressive. The constraints imposed by the treaties, 1817 Cédula, and 1818 Alvará prompted some liberated Africans to turn away from formal anti-slave-trade laws to vernacular sources of social regulation. Fugitive communities provided one such alternative. Liberated Africans' visions of freedom refused the terms of compulsory labor and demanded early exit from it by forum shopping, which political authorities sought to restrict with new policing and deportation measures.

LEGAL CHANGES FOR THE ILLEGAL TRADE

Suppression actions authorized by treaty law aimed not only to rescue shipboard captives but also to stop transoceanic trafficking. Yet suppression had a limited effect on transatlantic slave-trading. Naval patrols and diplomatic protests imposed small transaction costs on slaving businesses. This cost was significant enough to push some traders out of the market and to prompt others to change their business methods.[94] In the 1840s, three large firms—José Bernardino de Sá, the Pinto da Fonseca brothers, and Joaquim

Pereira Marinho—were responsible for 24 percent of all voyages to Brazil by named owners. Small groups of major merchants and land proprietors were also responsible for the slave trade to Cuba. The first group was made up of men born in Spain, including Catalonia, or in Cuba, who dominated the trade from the 1790s until the 1840s and continued to participate in the trade into the 1860s.[95] The second group comprised Portuguese merchants who had been expelled from Brazil, and it became prominent in the 1850s.[96] In Brazil and Cuba, a small group of merchants consolidated their control of the illegal trade, which would have important implications for final suppression in the 1850s and 1860s.

Brazil's anti-slave-trade criminal law of 1831, the Lei Feijó, isolated liberated Africans to protect private property rights in newly trafficked slaves. Introducing a criminal law was a requirement of the British-Brazil Treaty of 1826, which adapted the 1817 treaty with Portugal to the new independent Brazilian Empire. The Liberal administration introduced the bill at a time of political turmoil. The emperor, Dom Pedro I, had responded to Brazilian military opposition and a political crisis in Portugal by abdicating the Brazilian throne. A regent would rule until Pedro's son, who was a minor, came of age. Named after the Liberal minister of justice, Diogo Antônio Feijó, the bill sought to criminalize the importation and purchase of captives. Although the legislature passed the bill, the bitter debate over the scope of the criminal law resulted in a consequential political stalemate. The law specified the crime of importing slaves to Brazil as one of "reducing free people to slavery" and defined "importers" widely. But the law made no mention of whether it applied retrospectively. Tens of thousands of people who were trafficked unlawfully between the first applicable treaty with Portugal in 1817 and the criminal law of 1831 should have been liberated but languished in bondage. In remaining silent about whether the Lei Feijó would liberate these people, the senators rejected the radical possibility, proposed by senator Luiz José de Oliveira Mendes, of declaring that "all black people, who have been enslaved after the period laid down by the treaty, are *livres*."[97] The senators decided not to make "africano livre" (liberated African) status open to all people trafficked illegally to Brazil and advocated the deportation of liberated Africans at the cost of the illegal importers.[98]

The management of a small number of liberated Africans was crucial to the regulatory transformation of illegally trafficked people into lawful property under Lei Feijó. The legislation conceived of a thin yet impenetrable line between the category of liberated African and that of being an illegally trafficked slave. The first article declared "all slaves, who enter the territory or ports of Brazil from outside it, are free," except for certain enslaved sailors and fugitives.[99] The article used the same term that referred to liberated Africans: "livre." Yet the law made no provision for what should happen to captives who were smuggled into Brazil undetected. It specified no mechanism for how captive people could bring a case of illegal importation to the attention of the authorities. The authorities avoided treating all captive people who were illegally trafficked by these traders to their territories as *potential* liberated Africans entitled to freedom. Immediately after disembarkation, the possible outcomes for illegally trafficked people starkened: either the authorities seized them to declare them to be liberated Africans, or the traffickers sold them to purchasers who would act as if they owned lawfully held slaves. Political authorities recognized this performance of ownership by regulating it as a property right rather than reclassifying these trafficked people as liberated Africans.

The executive and the courts enforced the Lei Feijó briefly, but several changes in the early 1830s rolled back such enforcement. The United States reduced the tariff on coffee in 1830 and removed it entirely in 1832, leading to a doubling of coffee imports to the US. The US market accounted for almost half of Brazil's total coffee exports. By 1835, each American was drinking on average almost two hundred cups of coffee per year.[100] Coffee-plantation owners demanded a reopening of the slave trade to provide the labor for this expanding market. Protecting a major industry that depended on human trafficking became a more urgent priority than adhering to anti-slave-trade treaty and domestic law. Second, domestic political conflict raged over Brazil's new constitution, especially the Ato Adicional of 1834 that limited the central government's power. The uncertain role of the future emperor made the political support of major merchants and landowners even more vital. Third, in 1835, one of the largest rebellions by enslaved and free people, the Malê Revolt, erupted in Salvador, prompting the provincial legislative assembly to petition the national legislature for the removal of subversive African-born people.[101] The combination of economic, constitutional, and insurgency pressures prompted the Liberal administration to disavow the anti-slave-trade law that it had championed.

In 1837, the Marquis of Barbacena proposed a new bill that would strengthen the surveillance of ships, including those equipped for the slave trade. To increase political support for the bill, Barbacena planned to legalize the enslavement of all African captives brought to Brazil prior to the bill's passage. All these captive people could—indeed, *should*—have been liberated Africans, yet in a grave betrayal, they would now become legally held property. The Barbacena bill was the most notorious legislative attempt to convert the *performance* of ownership in an African person into a formal property right. The Senate passed the bill, but the Chamber remained divided on it until the end of its session.[102] The bill's stagnation marked the downfall of Feijó's Liberal administration and the rise of a new cabinet led by the Regresso, whose leading members formed the Conservative Party. The new Conservative administration, allied with major proslavery interests in southeastern Brazil, abandoned the enforcement of the Lei Feijó, providing the political conditions for the criminal trafficking of over half a million people to Brazil by 1850.[103] Enslavers used registration documents to turn illegally trafficked people into lawfully held slaves rather than into liberated Africans. For instance, in 1861, the priest Francisco Pereira de Sousa obtained registration papers and paid the required costs in provincial Bahia to transfer thirteen enslaved people to his new college in Rio de Janeiro.[104] Among the thirteen people, Jorge and José were both born in Africa and transported to Brazil after the Lei Feijó came into effect. Thirty-year-old Gaspar may also have been trafficked illegally. The Lei Feijó had become an anti-slave-trade mirage, there *para inglês ver*: "for only the English to see." Parliamentary consolidation and state-building depended on legislative support for the illegal trade. Legislative support relied on defining the liberated Africans as an exceptional and limited population rather than a status to which all illegally trafficked people who were held in slavery were entitled.

In the Spanish Empire, the imperial administration in Madrid and captain general delayed any criminal anti-slave-trade law until 1845. Ten years previously, Spain had signed a new anti-slave-trade treaty with Britain that covered the South Atlantic as well as the North Atlantic. The treaty contained an equipment clause, which enabled naval patrols to capture slaving ships that were fitted out for the trade but that did not have captives aboard.[105] The treaty obliged Spain to introduce a criminal law.[106] The delay provided the traffickers with a long period for continuing the trade. Enslavers used official registration procedures to re-present illegally trafficked people as lawfully owned slaves. For instance, an heir might claim that a testator's death caused them to misplace a certificate of ownership, prompting the colonial administration to replace it.[107] By the 1830s, Spanish policy had shifted against free Black people in Cuba, whom the administration saw as a threat. In Cuba, the number of free people of color closely matched the number of white people. The authorities introduced regulations that detained free Black sailors in port until their ships had left Cuba. An earlier measure in South Carolina in 1822 targeted free Black seamen as potential insurgents after the crushing of the plot led by Denmark Vesey. The Spanish colonial authorities also dissolved the Black militias, such as the one in which the *emancipado* Higino José Avilés's godfather served. The legal repression of free Black people was a common strategy to preserve slaveholding in the Western Hemisphere.[108]

Colonial repression of the free population of color also operated through a treaty clause that enabled British naval captors to transport liberated Africans from Cuba to British colonies in the Caribbean.[109] Throughout the 1830s, British ships transported thousands of liberated Africans out of Cuba to colonies including Jamaica, British Guiana (Guyana), and Trinidad.[110] The 1830s were also the most important decade for the relocation to the Bahamas of captives en route to Cuba.[111] As part of the clampdown on free Black people in Cuba, the captain general also objected to the presence of Black soldiers from the West India Regiments on Cuban soil during their service aboard HMS *Romney*, a British holding ship for liberated Africans in Havana's harbor.[112] Spanish colonial slavery depended on expelling liberated Africans as impediments on the narrow path of allowing the slave trade without openly condoning it.

The exclusion of liberated Africans from the body politic in Brazil and Cuba began to affect the status of liberated Africans within the British Caribbean in the 1830s. Alongside transfers from Cuba, British authorities transferred around twenty-five hundred liberated Africans from Brazil to the British Caribbean at the end of their apprenticeship terms.[113] In colonies like Trinidad and British Guiana, these liberated Africans were a crucial labor source. British forces conquered both colonies in the Napoleonic Wars. Landowners converted their relatively fertile soil to sugar production and demanded immigrant labor for their plantations. The recruitment of liberated Africans served British interests of supplying agricultural laborers and soldiers to colonies during the gradual emancipation of the resident enslaved population between 1834 and 1838. Liberated African labor migration provided a precedent for the political economy of indentured labor throughout the nineteenth century.

For the Spanish, Brazilian, and British authorities, these transfers were of "uncivilized" Africans who would obey official instructions. Yet even Africans who had been recently liberated had their own understandings of captivity and expectations for the future. In June 1837, Dâaga, a liberated African enlisted in the First West India Regiment, launched a mutiny at St. Joseph's Barracks in Trinidad. Dâaga was from the Great Popo region of Dahomey and had worked as a slave dealer before being tricked by a Portuguese trader who embarked him on a slaving vessel. British forces captured the slaving ship in the Caribbean, gave Dâaga the English name Donald Stewart, and enlisted him in the army. Chanting a war song in the early hours of 18 June, between 60 and 280 recruits seized weapons and attacked their officers. Dâaga killed Charles Dixon, a soldier, and fired on his commanding officer, Colonel Bushe, before the militia and police began a counteroffensive. The mutineers dispersed, with some heading to the eastern town of Arima. The authorities captured Dâaga, killed twelve mutineers, and rounded up the survivors; six had taken their own lives rather than be captured.

The authorities were quick to reestablish order on Trinidad by court-martialing Dâaga and four other alleged leaders. At Dâaga's trial, in which two interpreters translated testimony for him, he offered no defense. His reasons for mutinying were not a line pursued by the prosecution, which focused on his responsibility for mutinying, setting fire to buildings, and murdering Dixon. Lieutenant Charles Bentley deposed that he had heard the regimental sergeant major tell Colonel Bushe that "the Recruits had seized on the arms, and intended to fight their way back to Africa."[114] The mutineers probably had varying motives. Some sought to reclaim honor that they had lost in captivity: one alleged leader, Mawee (alias Maurice Ogston), in his defense "states through his Interpreter that in his own Country he was a governors [*sic*] son."[115] Others protested the heavy manual labor and routine corporal punishment inflicted on the recruits.[116] Still others may have desired to escape military discipline for a life of self-sufficient foraging and fishing along the coast and at sea.[117] The court-martial sentenced Dâaga and Mawee to death. The outcome of the mutiny was a transition from blanket to targeted recruitment of liberated Africans into the West India Regiment.[118] Still, the colonial secretary ordered the end of apprenticeship for all liberated Africans in the British Caribbean, including those transferred from Havana, in May 1838. The end of apprenticeship for liberated Africans predated the end of apprenticeship for the resident formerly enslaved population, which occurred in August.[119]

Even after 1838, British officials experimented with the legal status of liberated Africans to reshape imperial political economy. In 1841, the new colonial secretary, Lord John Russell, told the governor, "we are not bound to maintain in the colony of Sierra Leone all the captured negroes who are sent thither; and . . . Africans landed there in future should, at the expiration of three months, be bound, 1st, to show that they are in a state to maintain themselves on the spot; or 2dly, to signify their consent to emigrate [*sic*] to the West Indies; or 3dly, to leave the colony."[120] This structured choice produced a new legal mechanism for emigration. In theory, these liberated Africans were free to choose their work arrangements; in practice, they faced constraints. The requirement to prove the capacity for self-sufficiency or face being contracted for labor by the stipendiary magistrate obligated most liberated Africans to serve as indentured laborers in plantation agriculture.[121] Between 1841 and 1860, approximately forty thousand liberated Africans migrated from British naval bases at Sierra Leone and St. Helena to Jamaica, Trinidad, and British Guiana. Indentured liberated Africans arrived in the British Caribbean at the same time as tens of thousands of indentured laborers from the Indian subcontinent, China, Madeira, and elsewhere.

Rival powers were quick to point out the apparent hypocrisy of Britain's official demands for international slave-trade suppression while recruiting liberated Africans as contract laborers. Spain and France criticized the migration scheme even while France recruited African laborers as *engagés*.[122] In 1846, the president of the United States, James Polk, also criticized the migration scheme in a debate about the expansion of slavery during the Mexican-American War. Historians have highlighted the divisions in political parties over whether to permit slavery in the territories acquired in the war as a turning point in making slavery a sectional issue.[123] For Polk, expansion was necessary. The relocation of liberated Africans proved that all Atlantic powers depended on slave labor. Polk was scathing: "The plan appears to be to carry the captured blacks to the English settlements in Africa, and then the naked savage . . . is *asked* to emigrate [*sic*] to the English West Indies, where they are *hired* by planters *as voluntary* immigrants, on plans of the most improved philanthropy."[124] Consent was a pretense.

Rather than a new slave trade in which the traders commodified the person, the scheme was a form of poorly regulated contract labor to expand imperial cash-crop production.[125] After the end of apprenticeship in 1838, resident freedpeople left the estates in droves. The removal of protective tariffs on sugar imports to Britain in 1846 was a further blow to British colonial sugar production.[126] Imperial officials and private merchants were desperate to relieve these pressures. The labor supply to British colonial estates became more fragile just as the supply of cash crops produced by slaves on plantations in Brazil and Cuba increased. The use of African immigrant laborers became an attractive solution. To tie the laborers to the estates, imperial authorities shifted from specifying liberated Africans' right to barter for employment terms in the 1840s to subjecting them to compulsory taxation and three-year contracts in the 1850s.[127] The structured choice made indenture part of suppression rather than subsequent to it, deploying African labor as part of the imperial solution to the problem of freedom. While the slave trade continued, the imperial state found in liberated Africans a welcome supply of laborers who worked in the postemancipation economy under increasingly severe terms.

The Mixed Commission was a flexible domain that meant different things to different parties, and it satisfied none of them. The treaties were limited by geographic restrictions to slaving vessels on the high seas rather than territorial waters. The jurisdiction of Mixed Commissions applied to captures in the North Atlantic, yet most transoceanic slaving occurred in the South Atlantic. Throughout the 1820s and 1830s, British commissioners and diplomats pushed their counterparts in Brazil and Cuba to extend the Mixed Commission's jurisdiction, provoking counteraccusations of imperialist interference. Portuguese, Brazilian, and Spanish authorities developed delaying and evasion tactics to ensure that the illegal trade could continue. When enslavers performed ownership of illegally trafficked people, the authorities recognized the performance as a property right. Liberated Africans found themselves subject to domestic legislation that ascribed to them limited legal personhood. They frequently looked beyond the vague rights attributed to them by the Spanish Cédula and Portuguese Alvará to advance their interests. Some, like Gavino, went forum shopping to the Mixed Commission as a jurisdiction outside a single empire or to British diplomats. Others escaped from apprenticeship, seeking freedom in diasporic African and Afro-Latin American communities in Havana and Rio. These petitioning and fugitive strategies provoked official responses that intensified policing, deportation, and denials of citizenship.

African people liberated by the Mixed Commissions in Brazil and Cuba in the 1820s–1830s enable us to see these slave societies differently. Unlike the law of slavery, the law of anti-slave-trade liberation was not defined by any single jurisdiction. Instead, it emerged through legal disputes about clashing and overlapping jurisdictions, particularly between the Mixed Commission, the host government, and British imperial authorities. Domestic authorities worked hard to contain any notion of an analogy between liberated Africans and all African people trafficked into unlawful enslavement. Accordingly, when disputes arose, they took the form of jurisdictional politics rather than as a surge of illegally trafficked people claiming freedom. British diplomats complained about the lack of treaty jurisdiction over voyages that had reached territorial waters or lands. They tended to interpret these cases as individual scandals rather than as evidence of endemic problems with the laws of suppression. Domestic authorities insisted that they had no basis to question the private property rights that enslavers claimed to have in illegally trafficked people. Liberated Africans could try to convert the documentary proof of liberation into social relationships that would protect them from reenslavement or look beyond the law altogether. These parties' rival interpretations of anti-slave-trade law raised the question of whether the future of slave societies hinged on preventing the problem of maritime suppression from becoming the problem of freedom.

The limitations of anti-slave-trade treaties did not stop polities signing them throughout the nineteenth century. Yet by the late 1830s, widespread dissatisfaction provoked a rupture from them. Brazil's Conservative administration made clear that it would no longer enforce the 1831 Lei Feijó, reneging on a key treaty commitment. The Spanish Empire violated the spirit of the 1835 treaty by protecting the illegal trade and deporting liberated Africans to British colonies. Shaped by frustrations about how existing treaty law and parliamentary legislation restricted anti-slave-trade captures to the high seas, a new generation of aggressive anti-slave-trade agents emerged. These naval officers and diplomats advocated unilateral action, sending shockwaves across the oceans, along the coastlines, and into the plantations of the Atlantic world. The Palmerston Act of 1839 and Aberdeen Act of 1845 would authorize captures in the South Atlantic. The leading edge of suppression, and the legal status of liberated Africans, began to form along the coasts of Atlantic West Africa, far away from the Largo do Paço.

CHAPTER THREE

Gunboat Regulation in Atlantic Africa

FROM A BIRD'S-EYE VIEW, look down, for a moment, on the Atlantic Ocean. Imagine each slaving ship was a red light heading from sub-Saharan Africa to the Americas. The light turned yellow whenever an anti-slave-trade patrol captured the vessel and took it to a port to have the capture declared lawful. During the Napoleonic Wars in Atlantic Africa, the lights pulsed yellow mainly around Sierra Leone, with some cases around the Cape. Between 1815 and 1839, under treaty law, the yellow lights almost vanished from the South Atlantic and clustered around Sierra Leone, with a few notable cases in Brazil and Cuba. From 1839, the yellow lights increased in frequency and geographic range. They illuminated both the North and South Atlantic. They pulsed on the high seas, in coastal waters, and even at barracoons on the African coast. The pattern of suppression had changed. Suppression was no longer confined by treaty law. The Palmerston Act of 1839 granted British naval vessels unilateral authority to capture vessels in the South Atlantic, including vessels whose nationality did not correspond to a treaty cosignatory.

The Palmerston Act changed how political authorities interacted with each other regarding naval patrols and protections for liberated Africans in their respective dominions. It changed the incentives for British naval patrols as they hunted Portuguese slaving ships in the South and North Atlantic. The act preceded new treaties between British delegates and

African powers. In the early-modern era, agreements afforded individual European and Eurafrican traders the status of being mercantile "strangers" to a specific African "landlord."[1] Anti-slave-trade treaties marked a transformation. In the 1840s, the Foreign Office used a standard agreement template for all African powers to ban the slave trade. A revised template from 1843 stipulated that any breach by the African parties would incur the "displeasure" of Queen Victoria.[2] The new agreements may have recognized a British right to use force, but the frequent use of force in coastal raids dated to the earlier Palmerston Act.

These shifting practices had one major unintended consequence: they opened new legal measures for people in detention to claim to be liberated Africans. Having been limited to the high seas by treaty law, naval cruisers now began to patrol in territorial waters again. The usual story is that gunboat violence changed the British state by generating the "act of state" doctrine. Under this doctrine, Crown agents were (and are) not liable for acts committed against foreign subjects in foreign jurisdictions. One interpretation of this doctrine suggests that acts of state are nonjusticiable in English courts: not only are Crown agents immune from liability, but the courts have no jurisdiction to order the Crown to compensate injured parties. But this story obscures the fact that liberated Africans often took the initiative in these cases, not because they wanted to develop the "act of state" but rather because they wanted to advance their own interests, particularly in protecting themselves from reenslavement. Patrols in territorial waters produced conditions for people to claim protection as liberated Africans. They prompted the development of new forms of dispute resolution between British colonial authorities at Sierra Leone and Indigenous African political rulers. These patterns of legal regulation were the unpredictable outgrowths of proliferating gunboat interventions in the wake of the Palmerston Act.

ABANDONING THE TREATIES

In the late 1830s, as the initial term of the British-Portuguese Treaty approached its end, the Portuguese government signaled that it was unlikely to agree to a new treaty. British naval officers were growing increasingly frustrated with treaty regulations, including the geographical restrictions to the Northern Hemisphere. The earliest treaties prevented squadrons from capturing suspect ships fitted out for the trade but with no captives aboard.

They also prevented the capture of ships whose nationality did not correspond to a treaty party. Slaving crews promptly disguised the nationality of the vessel by flying decoy flags or carrying decoy papers. Those frustrations dovetailed with an imperial pivot toward gunboat attacks as a cheap way of opening foreign markets. These markets could import British manufactures and export raw materials that were crucial to Britain's industrial revolution.[3] Naval officers' frustrations with treaty law and parliamentary support for the free-trade imperialism of the laissez-faire state formed a happy union in 1839 in the Palmerston Act.

In targeting Portuguese slaving ships, the Palmerston Act authorized naval captures south of the equator. It included an equipment clause: any ship that had numerous decks, open gratings, shackles, or other features commonly associated with slaving was now liable to capture. Although the Palmerston Act identified Portuguese vessels as the target, three weeks after its passage, naval officers were instructed to capture any vessel of indeterminate nationality.[4] The act abandoned William Scott's judgment in *Le Louis* that positive treaty law was required to visit, search, and detain foreign ships in peacetime. The act was not a continuation of the international law of the sea; it was a repudiation of it.[5] Under the act, naval captures would now be adjudicated by vice-admiralty courts with appeals to the High Court of Admiralty. The act revived prize jurisdiction and highlighted the limitations of the Mixed Commission. The Palmerston Act incorporated three other acts. One of these acts reduced the bounties payable to naval captors from £10 per captive to £5.[6] Another act stipulated that the Royal Navy would receive £1 10s per ton for a lawfully captured ship, plus £4 per ton if the ship were empty of captives. Considering that the tonnage tended to be smaller than the number of captives, capturing empty ships was less financially rewarding. But empty ships also carried much-lower risk than ships loaded with captives, where the dangers of disease, mortality, and uprising were ever present. Death reduced the prize bounty payable for a liberated African person by half. This is not to say that naval squadrons were unprofessional or solely interested in prize money. But anti-slave-trade parliamentary legislation created incentives to capture large, empty ships.

Cruisers focused on the major routes of the illegal trade to Brazil, including from Mozambique. From the early sixteenth century, Portuguese authorities and landowners enslaved Indigenous Africans in southern and central Mozambique for agricultural labor and military service. From the late eighteenth century, the enslavers developed an export trade. The opening of ports to Brazilian traders in 1811 and the growing Portuguese *prazeiro* estates along the Zambezi River demanded ever more enslaved labor from the interior. Nguni warlords and drought made people vulnerable to war captivity and indebtedness, leading to sale to the Lusophone transoceanic traders.[7] Widespread drought in Mozambique between 1823 and 1831 made more people vulnerable to enslavement, and demand in Brazil for captive labor rose, thereby causing the trafficking of enslaved people to grow rapidly in the 1820s.[8] These factors undermined customary protections against export afforded by Portuguese slave owners to enslaved *achikunda* soldiers and domestic servants. Insecurity led to accusations of witchcraft against people to attribute blame for social disorder. Enslavement was a frequent punishment: by one estimate, one-quarter of embarked captives were exported as criminal punishment for witchcraft convictions.[9]

In 1843, the *Progresso*, a Brazilian slaver, left Quelimane and entered the Mozambique Channel, triggering a capture that revealed how unilateral suppression could sharpen the racialized control of liberated Africans. On 12 April at 6 a.m., the crew of HMS *Cleopatra* spotted the *Progresso* and chased it for six hours, firing shots to bring it to.[10] The captors decided to navigate the prize to the vice-admiralty court in British colonial Cape Town.[11] The prize crew was unprepared for managing 447 captives for the journey to the Cape. The captain, Christopher Wyvill, sent Lieutenant W. C. Alexander and eleven men on board the *Progresso* to navigate it, but no crewmember spoke the same languages as the captives. Only one crewmember, George Brown, had a background that suggested that he might have spoken Portuguese.[12] This shortfall of linguists probably explains why the captain sent Brown and the chaplain, Pascoe Grenfell Hill, on board the *Progresso* as potential interpreters.

The prize crew boarded a ship that was in disarray. Excrement and urine had seeped through the planks in the hold, spreading dysentery rapidly in a "pestilential atmosphere."[13] Most of the captives were children, whose parents had probably lived through famine and the terror of witchcraft accusations. The naval crew did not know how to care for them. As soon as the *Cleopatra* had fired on the *Progresso*, the captive children began to protest the conditions on board. In Hill's published account, "having broken through all control, [the slaves] had seized everything to which they had a fancy in the vessel." After boarding the vessel, the seventeen-strong prize crew were required to take a head count, registering twenty-five captives as sick. They were also supposed to send the *Progresso*'s crew to the *Cleopatra* for detention. In fact, the prize crew retained four slave-ship crewmembers "to assist in superintending and managing the negroes."[14] The following evening, the *Progresso* was sailing into a squall. The liberated Africans lay around the ship's deck, enjoying their newfound freedom. However, the prize crew felt that they were impeding attempts to navigate through the bad weather. The crew ordered the liberated Africans to go beneath the deck. Perhaps the naval crew was collaborating with the slaver's crew. Detention in the hold was yet another punishment, on top of political exile, social exclusion, and malnourishment.

Soon after being ordered under, the liberated Africans began pressing against the hatch, begging to be let out. The shouting and distress increased the temperature in the hold. As the night air cooled, a deathly vapor covered the deck: it was steam from people's bodies. Fifty-four recaptives died during the uprising against forced detention. They had risen once against the slaver's crew and now once against the prize crew. For the rest of the journey, the prize crew treated the liberated Africans with contempt. They flogged the liberated Africans fifteen to twenty times for stealing water during the night. The prize crew laughed at the hierarchy among them, especially the *capitões marinheiros* (maritime captains), who wore canvas frocks as a mark of authority. These *capitões* had responsibility for pulling ropes to help sail the ship. "Even the most considerate," Hill claimed, "seem prone to look on this unhappy race as an inferior order of beings." The prize crew depersonalized the recaptured people even during death, remarking " '*It* will die, '*that* is dying.' "[15] By the time the *Progresso* docked at Simon's Town in the Cape Colony, 177 liberated Africans (39.6 percent of the total) had died.

There was no immediate investigation into this tragedy. By February 1844, the foreign secretary heard of Hill's publication, and Hill himself had sent copies to the Lord Commissioners of the Admiralty. An official investigation now began. The Lords instructed the commander in chief of the Cape of Good Hope, Admiral Joscelin Percy, to investigate the case.[16] Percy's report in May 1844 favored the explanation for the high incidence of mortality and morbidity provided by Captain Wyvill, Lieutenant Alexander, and the surgeon, all of whom served aboard the *Cleopatra*. Percy blamed the deaths on the first night on the captives' "having become intoxicated from drinking ardent Spirits; & eating raw meat, and to their sickly and diseased condition when taken possession of by the Captors; and that it became necessary to take strong measures to keep them quiet during the bad weather."[17] Alexander, the senior officer aboard the prize, claimed that the slave-ship crew had released the captives from all restraint just before naval capture. The captives "devoured incredible quantities of Salt Beef, breached, and drank a large cask, of the most fiery Spirits."[18] Such excess meant that many other liberated Africans, who were not put belowdecks, also died. Captain Wyvill noted that the captives in fact had had more room than usual in the hold because "the Brazilians on board said that the vessel was not full by one hundred." Up to two-thirds of the captives were children.[19] The surgeon claimed that he had in fact registered one hundred slaves as sick rather than only twenty-five. The high sick count was due, he suggested, to the long time that the captives had spent in the barracoon in Mozambique.[20]

Yet if two-thirds of the liberated Africans were children, they were hardly a credible threat to the crew's management of the ship while on deck. Their young age, hunger, and thirst probably made alcohol a low priority. Under standard capture procedure, the *Cleopatra* should have sent additional casks of water to the *Progresso*, but there is no evidence that the crew did so. This lack of water probably explains why, later in the voyage, the captives were punished for dipping rags into casks of water to extract extra drinking supplies. In the absence of the order and additional resources that the prize crew should have provided, the liberated Africans had established their own practices of justice. Hill observed their "fair dealing" of food among themselves when eating out of communal cooking pots.[21] Such a ritual became a social norm among them, a way to formulate values to distribute the few resources they had. While belowdecks, some liberated Africans had "forced one end of the grating up, and the other fell down into the hold," allowing approximately twelve people to escape through the opening.[22] At another time, some people who were shackled in pairs used a spare nail to release themselves.[23] It did not seem to occur to any crewmember that the liberated Africans were desperate to escape the hold.

The *Progresso* was an exceptionally awful case that demonstrated some key characteristics of the anti-slave-trade legal regime after the Palmerston Act. In common with maritime captures during the Napoleonic Wars, the regime created incentives for naval crews to treat African captives as prizes with a financial exchange value rather than as people. Precisely the same number of captives who had died aboard the *Progresso*—177—survived to become apprentices in the Cape. They were probably distributed among the garrisons, public works, farm labor, and domestic service in the homes of the Capetonian elite. In a rapid transformation of scale since the Napoleonic era, the regime now sprawled throughout the vast South Atlantic. The Palmerston Act permitted naval squadrons to be more aggressive. In bypassing treaty cosignatories, the act reduced official scrutiny of naval actions.

The unilateral attempt to rewrite anti-slave-trade rules by capturing ships under the Palmerston Act rather than treaty law came under English judicial scrutiny when slaving crews resisted naval capture. In 1845, HMS *Wasp* captured the slave ship *Felicidade* north of the equator near Lagos. Sixteen naval crewmembers, led by Lieutenant Robert Stupard, took command of the slaver. While commanding the *Felicidade* as a prize, they chased another suspicious ship that was trading at Lagos, the *Echo*, for two days and nights. Stupard captured the *Echo* with 434 captives on board on 2 March. He placed the *Echo*'s captain, Francisco Ferreira de Santos Serva, and eleven crew on the *Felicidade* under the charge of ten naval crewmembers. Stupard attended to the prize captives aboard the *Echo*. Probably unbeknownst to Stupard or his crew, Serva in fact had bitter experience of naval capture. In 1839, he had been the master aboard the *Carolina*, a Brazilian ship captured by the British ship *Electra* in the South Atlantic. The Mixed Commission in Rio declared the capture lawful, and Serva lost 214 captives.[24] Now, six years later, Serva was again separated from a valuable cargo of captive people. He sensed that the *Felicidade*'s naval crew was relatively weak. Serva and his comrades killed the entire British crew and set sail. Was Serva now a pirate, or, like the crew aboard *Le Louis*, had he legitimately resisted unlawful violence by a British cruiser?

Serva's murderous freedom did not last long: on 6 March 1845, the British ship *Star* recaptured the *Felicidade*. After transfer to England, seven of the twelve slaving crewmembers were tried and convicted of murder by a jury in Devon. The Twelve Judges, an advisory panel of senior judges, recommended that this decision be overturned. Stupard did not have naval instructions to capture slave ships while aboard the *Felicidade*. He therefore could not be considered to have been in "lawful possession" of it when capturing Serva's ship, the *Echo*. The judges also doubted that "lawful possession" would confer English court jurisdiction over any offense committed aboard the *Felicidade*.[25] This advice meant that British courts were unlikely to treat slave-ship crewmembers as pirates who could be subject to British criminal jurisdiction, even when they violently resisted naval capture at sea.[26]

In two subsequent cases of resistance, slaving crews successfully pleaded that they should be exempt from vice-admiralty court jurisdiction on St. Helena, with "their national character as a ground of defense." John Dodson, the Queen's Advocate who had represented the Crown in *R v. Serva,* made the implications clear. British courts would not find that "firing at, and killing British subjects under the circumstances stated in this case [being chased by a naval cruiser], would be held to amount to Piracy by the General Law of Nations."[27] British courts would probably decline to hear such cases in the future. Nonetheless, parliamentarians remained committed to the view that legislation could authorize naval captures of slaving ships in the South Atlantic. The same year as the Serva case, Parliament passed the Aberdeen Act, which authorized naval captures of Brazilian slaving ships. This authorization would supersede the Treaty of 1826 between Britain and Brazil, which expired in 1845 after Brazil had refused to negotiate terms for a new treaty. The act extended vice-admiralty courts' jurisdiction over these captures, but such legal regulations did not punish slaving crews or improve conditions for prize captives in the South Atlantic.

British unilateral suppression under the Palmerston Act in the South Atlantic prompted Portugal to sign a new treaty in 1842. Portugal agreed to a treaty, signed on the same day as a free-trade treaty between the two empires, after widespread British captures.[28] The treaty involved new regulations for liberated Africans in Portuguese colonial Angola, a large slave society in the mid-nineteenth century. A Junta would be responsible for the care of the liberated Africans during apprenticeship, including appointing a *curador* to register and protect them.[29] This stronger oversight of apprenticeship drew on a proposal by Henry Hayne, who had criticized apprenticeship practices during his time as a commissary judge in Rio de Janeiro.[30] Even this treaty applied a diminished concept of freedom in Angola. After registration, each liberated African "shall then be marked on the upper part of the right arm with a small silver instrument, bearing for its device a symbol of freedom."[31] The liberated Africans became an experimental population for Portuguese imperial governance, in projects as varied as training in crafts and smallpox vaccination.[32] The two hundred liberated Africans freed by the Mixed Commission received protection from the Junta from reenslavement, but at the personal cost of being branded and subjected to medical experiments.

Local judges and the Tribunal das Presas also liberated captives from ships and barracoons, meaning that there were between two and three thousand liberated Africans in total in Angola. Treaty and domestic law subjected these liberated Africans to new methods of control. Liberated Africans were apprenticed, and the *curador* did not necessarily act in their interests. Some were transported to São Tomé for work, while others were required to work on coffee plantations in Mossamedes. In 1875, legislation abolished "escravo" and "liberto" as legal categories, and required liberated Africans to offer their services for hire.[33] Even an assemblage of new treaty and domestic law as an alternative to the Palmerston Act in the South Atlantic placed authoritarian limitations on liberated Africans' labor and mobility.

DISPUTE RESOLUTION: VIOLENCE AND EXCHANGE

British warships not only captured slaving ships in South Atlantic waters but also liberated captives from barracoons along the African coast in the North Atlantic. Along the Upper Guinea Coast outside the Sierra Leone Colony, naval patrols sought redress from African leaders for the captivity of liberated Africans who resided in their jurisdictions. The consequent patterns in settling disputes over anti-slave-trade regulation formed part of a longer history of intensified slaving and resistance. From the 1720s, revolutionary Islamic resistance to slaving had produced Fuuta Jallo and Fuuta Tooro, two new expansionist polities that were north of Sierra Leone. The revolutions destabilized incumbent slaving elites. Islamic leaders promised to protect Muslim subjects from slaving. They also enslaved non-Muslim people for labor. On the Upper Guinea Coast, captives boarded onto ships, and their allies on land were among the likeliest across West Africa to resist transshipment: such incidents were almost three times likelier there than at the Bight of Benin.[34] At the end of the eighteenth century, sustained resistance and the prospect of British maritime interdiction meant that the market for sale to coastal transatlantic slave traders contracted. The contraction produced a "glut" of captives along the trade routes. Enslavers among the Fula, Susu, and Mandinka were required to find other uses for the people they had captured or bought.[35] They forced the captives to cultivate rice on plantations and housed them in towns separated from the free population, called *runde* in Fula.[36]

These changes in slaveholding brought changes in modes of resistance. Uprisings by captives were rejections of plantation labor and the ideological justifications for enslavement. In 1785, those who were enslaved by the Mandinka allied with Susu warriors, who were fighting their masters, and together they took over the town of Yangakori. The town became a "counter to the *runde*."[37] It took the Mandinka ten years to recapture the town and destroy the fugitive settlement.[38] In 1838, the slave Bilali, the son of an enslaved woman and a Susu king, led an uprising after the king's heirs reneged on a promise to manumit him. He successfully established an independent settlement among the Limba, at Laminyah, that became a refuge for fugitives until 1870.[39]

Intensified slaving and resistance to enslavement converged with an increasing British imperial presence on the Upper Guinea Coast. British colonial Sierra Leone depended on neighboring African polities to supply rice, which was cultivated by enslaved people, for subsistence.[40] British agents were thus reluctant to start conflicts with African polities. But the rapid changes in these neighboring polities made visible several instances of slaveholding of doubtful legality. These doubts arose within the legal framework of African polities and within anti-slave-trade treaty regulations regarding liberated Africans. African political authorities were focused on furthering their own interests in an era of widespread political revolutions like Bilali's and viewed British colonial Sierra Leone as just one among many potential trading allies or wartime enemies.[41]

In the late rainy season of 1840, the naval officer Joseph Denman raided Spanish slave traders at Galinhas, south of Sherbro, disrupting these delicate African-British diplomatic relations. Denman's mission aimed to resolve two cases related to anti-slave-trade law. First, King Siaka of Gendema had protested the British Navy's blockade of the Galinhas ports, which prevented the chiefs from trading for subsistence grains with Sherbro and the Plantain Islands. From the 1810s, Siaka collaborated with US merchants to supply captives to Cuba to build his predatory polity.[42] In a letter to Governor Richard Doherty, signed by Siaka and the powerful Rogers family and possibly assisted by Spanish slave traders, the rulers stated that "although we are Africans," the "law of Nations" still applied. The British governor should command the blockading ships to "take up there [*sic*] anchor out of [the] Port and to take these Lawbreakers 3 leagues from the Land and no nearer."[43] Second, in September 1840, a liberated African from Sierra Leone, Fry Norman, was detained in Gendema, along with her child.[44]

Norman was a washerwoman who had tracked her employer, a Mr. Lewis, to the Galinhas for repayment of a debt. But her former master during her apprenticeship owed money to King Siaka's son, Prince Manna. As Norman wrote to her former master, "[Manna] has catched [*sic*] me on your account."[45] From captivity, she wrote to her husband, "I did try to make my escape but I was overtaken and brought back to Gendema and confined."[46] Norman was no longer simply a liberated African but also detained as collateral on a debt.

Since the home government did not attribute British subjecthood to liberated Africans in Sierra Leone until 1853, the governor had no formal obligation to negotiate Norman's release. But in October 1840, Governor Doherty ordered Denman to rescue Norman, using force if necessary. Denman rescued Norman, burned the barracoons of a Spanish slave trader named Burón, and liberated 841 captives in Freetown. He also negotiated anti-slave-trade treaties with Siaka and Manna, even though neither Doherty nor the Foreign Office had authorized him to do so. The foreign secretary and Britain's Parliament praised Denman's actions and awarded £4,000 to him and his crew. Norman was back safe in Sierra Leone, and Denman's coercion had extended anti-slave-trade treaty law, but at the cost of heightened tensions with the Galinhas chiefs.

Other naval officers followed in Denman's wake, raiding barracoons in the South Atlantic. In 1842, Henry Matson, a naval captain, sacked barracoons at Cabinda and Ambriz in yet more violence against the traders plying the illegal routes to Brazil and Cuba. He also signed treaties with local chiefs.[47] These raids sat alongside increasing use of standard agreements. British delegates and African political authorities agreed to end the slave trade and shift toward "legitimate commerce" in raw materials or cash crops. These agreements often featured free-trade provisions and compensation to African rulers for the loss of income from slave exports.[48] Burón sued Denman for trespass, as part of a wave of tort actions in English courts brought by slave traders against British agents. In 1848, the Court of Exchequer ruled for the defendant, stating that the Crown's praise for Denman's actions had turned it into a new act: an act of state.[49] Naval patrols that responded to the claims of liberated Africans like Fry Norman for protection against captivity inside Indigenous African jurisdictions resulted in a redefined British state that limited its legal liabilities for violent actions.[50]

In 1844–45, the case of three liberated Africans, Tom Peters, William Mering, and John Sharp, further developed the pattern of violent intervention in the North Atlantic. The three men swore before the police magistrate in Freetown, Sierra Leone, that they had recently been captured and sold into the transatlantic trade—for the second time in their lives. Years earlier, after serving apprenticeships, Peters and Mering had headed southward outside the colony. In Sherbro and the Galinhas River region, they worked in the extensive canoe trade of the Upper Guinea Coast. Sharp had migrated eastward, to work on a farm in Soamah, in the Mende country. But kidnappers and rulers had captured them: they traded Peters for ivory, detained Mering on the pretext of damaging property, and held Sharp as compensation for the crimes of an acquaintance, who "took" another man's wife.[51]

By November 1844, Louis, a Spanish slave trader operating in the Sherbro region, had bought all three men and "plenty other slaves." He dismissed their protests that they were "Her Majesty's subjects." In the nineteenth century, the claim to be a British subject could be a powerful call for protection from harm. British naval patrols invariably responded with violent intervention against Indigenous people.[52] But before 1853, this option was unavailable to Peters, Mering, and Sharp. Louis flogged and chained them in barracoons, the holding facilities from which slave traders would embark the three men on canoes and then oceangoing ships. Another person from Sierra Leone, Elizabeth Eastman, had tried to help Tom Peters escape. Louis punished her by flogging her so severely that he allegedly caused the miscarriage of her pregnancy and possibly even killed her.[53] Unjust detention had morphed into sale to transatlantic traders and fatal violence. The prospect of redemption was fading fast.

Louis embarked Peters, Mering, Sharp, and 345 other captives on the Spanish ship *Engañador*. But early in the voyage, a British ship captured the *Engañador* and brought it north to Freetown. The Anglo-Spanish Mixed Commission then released the captives, as liberated Africans, into apprenticeship. Now Peters, Mering, and Sharp stood before the magistrate, Thomas McFoy, a man of color from the Caribbean, hoping for freedom. When the three men approached McFoy, they probably knew that their future was uncertain. Perhaps they hoped that McFoy as an authority figure with a similar diasporic background would sympathize with their plight. On the basis of three men's depositions, the lieutenant-governor of Sierra Leone, William Fergusson, determined that the slave trader Louis had detained the three men inside Harry Tucker's jurisdiction. Tucker was the Sherbro chief of Little Boom River. Fergusson wrote to Tucker to demand "reparation for the gross outrages committed upon Her Majesty's subjects by a person who enjoys the privileges of your countenance and support."[54] The governor sent a naval expedition to seek restitution. When the three men had made their statements, they could not have foreseen British warships sailing southward with such a mandate. But now, violence was on the horizon.

Fergusson had forged a career out of anti-slave-trade imperialism, serving as staff surgeon in the Royal African Colonial Corps in 1825 and attending to liberated Africans from the slaver *Perpetuo Defensor* a year later.[55] Having worked as a civilian surgeon for the Liberated African Department, he was commissioned as lieutenant-governor in 1841. When communicating with Chief Tucker, Fergusson applied the same combination of anti-slave-trade zeal, practical knowledge, and willingness to use military force. Fergusson decided that Tucker's response to his demands for explanations and redress were insufficient. On 20 January 1845, he wrote to naval commodore William Jones, explaining that the three men were enslaved while pursuing an "innocent and lawful calling" and that Louis had willfully ignored their protests. As in his letter to Tucker, Fergusson erroneously claimed that liberated Africans were British subjects. "The legitimate trade of this neighborhood, and the personal safety of Her Majesty's subjects," Fergusson remonstrated, "are in a state of constant jeopardy by those very outrageous and illegal practices."[56] Fergusson authorized Jones to intervene violently against the chiefs. Commodore Jones went to Galinhas to demand redress and promises from the chiefs about the future good treatment of liberated Africans. On 4 February, Jones entered Galinhas with 286 men. They burned the barracoon of the slave trader Angel Jimenez, who had admitted to branding Peters before putting him on the slave ship *Engañador*. Jones ordered the destruction of the towns Tindes, Taillah, and Minah to teach the ruling Rogers family a lesson. Three locals were killed and fourteen wounded. Over the next three weeks, Jones negotiated with, cajoled, and threatened the Galinhas chiefs until they made reparations and pledges. The interaction was an extended, multifaceted debate about competing understandings of anti-slave-trade law.

The African chiefs initially denied that the treaties that they had signed with Denman in 1840 obliged them to expel all Spanish slave traders from their jurisdictions. The chiefs even claimed that Denman had compelled them to sign the treaties at gunpoint, thereby voiding them.[57] Next, Jones and the chiefs disagreed about the boundaries between, and mutual intelligibility of, British and chiefly jurisdiction. Regarding the punishment of Elizabeth Eastman, who had tried to save Tom Peters from the slave traders, Chief Harry Tucker insisted that "country laws," which applied to all residents of his chiefdom, authorized the flogging.[58] Prince Manna, accused by Mering of selling him as a slave, asked Jones for what he described as a "jury" trial, namely, that Mering accuse him in person in Gendema.[59] Finally, Jones and the chiefs disagreed over the process of redress. When the chiefs asked if they should seek payment from the Spanish slave traders to pay compensation to Jones, the commodore refused. The Lord Commissioners of the Admiralty had previously demanded an explanation from Denman for a similar strategy. Perhaps transferring goods from a slave trader to the chiefs exposed the navy to an accusation of perpetuating the commercial relationships of the slave trade. Extrajudicial violence, the normativity of treaties, mutual respect of domestic jurisdiction, and the use of goods to compensate unlawful detention informed how African and British authorities debated what the law meant. Anti-slave-trade jurisdiction emerged from a bundle of interpolity norms and practices.

On 24 February 1845, the chiefs refused to sign a new treaty but agreed in principle to pay compensation. Jones spared Gendema from being razed to the ground to remind the chiefs that they had something to lose. A compensation payment equivalent to the sale price of ten slaves, half of the value paid in muskets, powder, a cutlass, tobacco, and cloth, was unacceptable because the British government "cannot regard human beings as the subject or the representation of pecuniary value; as such, therefore, those goods and those five persons cannot be received."[60] When it came to placing financial value on human life, there was one rule for the Palmerston Act and another for African-British diplomatic negotiations. By June, Harry Tucker had paid compensation to Eastman, who in fact had survived her ordeal. Compensation, which was subject to the approval of the navy and governor, took the form of iron bars, cloth, and the liberation of five captives who were sent to Freetown.[61] Peters, Mering, and Sharp reentered Freetown, perhaps to be apprenticed yet again, though it seems that their lives went unrecorded in the archives.

The legal strategies of Peters, Mering, and Sharp both mobilized and transcended anti-slave-trade law. First, the three men emigrated from Sierra Leone to remove themselves from the constraints of British colonial rule.

Next, when faced with reenslavement, they testified to the magistrate to turn their oral evidence into paper trails that could protect their freedom. Each action sought to remedy displacement and detention with security through the paperwork and collective bonds forged as liberated Africans. Whatever Fergusson may have said, they did not rely on British imperial subjecthood. Instigated by liberated Africans' testimony, naval violence against riverine chiefs produced compensation in the shape of freeing more enslaved people. The price of compensation was intensified legal conflict between the colony and neighboring chiefs over the boundaries of anti-slave-trade law.

Jones's actions also revealed the limits of British imperial authority on the Upper Guinea Coast at midcentury. Naval authorities may have made performative incursions, but Indigenous polity formation, the disease environment, and the complex terrain prevented any attempt at colonization. Low population densities meant that political authority extended over people rather than land demarcated by borders. There was no guarantee that African polities would recognize Britain's claims to colonial sovereignty over particular spaces. In 1832, the settlement of Cobolo, including liberated Africans who had left the colony, made clear the limits of British imperial power. The colonial governor at Freetown sent a force of armed volunteers to take reprisals against Cobolo for robberies allegedly committed by its members. Cobolo rebuffed the expedition. When the governor then sent regular troops to attack Cobolo, they found the settlement deserted. According to Elizabeth Melville, the wife of a judge in the Mixed Commission in Freetown, "There was much discussion as to whether Kobloo was within the bounds of the colony or not, and consequently of the right of the local authorities to try parties for the murder of British subjects not upon British territory; and at last it was decided that Kobloo was *without* the colony's jurisdiction, and therefore no cognizance could be taken of the matter."[62]

Britain's forces received another reminder that such recognition was never self-evident in May 1855, when a military and naval expedition of 150 men went to Malaghea on the Mellacori River. The expedition sought compensation for damage to the property of French and British traders from the king of Malaghea, Bamba Mina Lahai, and the chiefs of the Mooriah country. It ended in disaster.[63] Although the troops burned most of the town, thirty men drowned, and a further thirty-two were killed, missing, or taken prisoner. The expedition also violated the king's flag of truce.[64] The governor of Sierra Leone, Robert Dougan, was forced to abandon the claim to

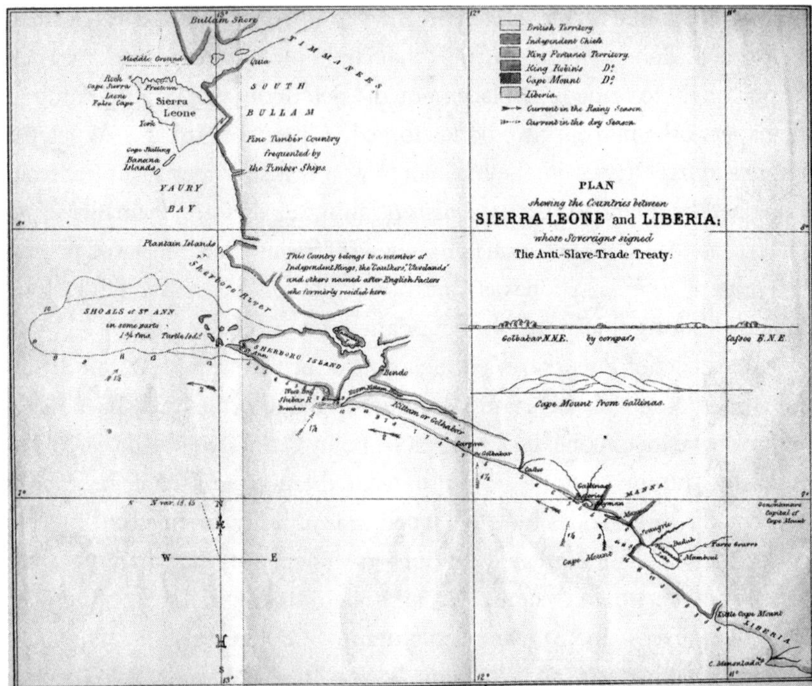

In 1849, Lieutenant Frederick Edwyn Forbes made a map that labeled the heads of polities in West Africa "sovereigns": "Plan shewing the Countries between SIERRA LEONE and LIBERIA; whose Sovereigns signed The Anti-Slave-Trade Treaty." (Image granted by The Afriterra Cartographic Library, www.afriterra.org)

compensation in exchange for the return of prisoners. A peace treaty with the king opened roads and rivers to British and French traders, but it was a humiliating retreat. Dougan was dismissed from office.

Gunboat regulation had severe limitations, and liberated Africans were still being detained inside Indigenous jurisdictions. How else could British and Indigenous African authorities resolve disputes about the protection of liberated Africans? The local letter books of the colonial governor, deposited in the Public Archives of Sierra Leone, contain an unexpected answer. These letters record local negotiations that were rarely disclosed to the metropolitan authorities in London. The negotiations culminated in a very different pattern of resolution from gunboat violence. Between 1845 and 1862, the governor wrote dozens of letters to African chiefs about liberated Africans who were reenslaved or held captive in their jurisdictions. There were at least forty negotiations between the governor and chiefs, which resulted in the return of at least 120 liberated Africans or other British subjects in total.[65]

During these negotiations inside Indigenous African jurisdictions, British officials were required to comply with norms imposed by chiefs. One major normative institution was the "Poro," a society for initiates that connected gods, spirits, and the living. A Poro society advised chiefly political authority and dispensed justice.[66] The institution could also declare a "Poro," forbidding white travelers and other outsiders from entering certain regions. In 1836, the traveler F. Harrison Rankin noted that the Temne declared a Poro that forbade outsiders from venturing farther east than Magbelly on the Rokel River, on pain of capital punishment.[67] To comply with Poro, Sierra Leone's Black police constables traveled outside the colony to conduct diplomacy and rescue liberated Africans from detention. Black emissaries were crucial for interpolity communication on the Upper Guinea Coast.

When governors and chiefs negotiated over reenslaved liberated Africans, they engaged in gift exchanges. In a commodity economy, persons and things assume the social form of things. In a gift economy, things assume the form of persons.[68] For example, in Malaghea, somebody enslaved the liberated African John McFoy. During his thirty years of reenslavement, he had married and had five children. In January 1860, McFoy managed to escape and travel to Freetown, where he asked the governor to request the freedom of his family, too. In March, the king and *alimamy* of Malaghea, Sanasee Famah, sent the children to Freetown. Afterward, the governor sent the king £10.[69] In other interactions, governors sent gifts that included baft fabric, rum, tobacco, arms, and cash. As liberated Africans migrated into Indigenous African dominions, they sought protection from detention from British naval and colonial officials. Liberated Africans' demands for protection prompted the development of measures to resolve disputes between British officials and Indigenous African political rulers.

These exchanges were not commercial, because the parties were political authorities who were trying to resolve problems regarding interpolity mobility. From the chiefs' point of view, to send a reenslaved liberated African to another political authority was to give a gift. It imposed an obligation on the governor to send a gift of equivalent significance, thereby building diplomatic norms, respecting mutual jurisdictions, and consolidating commercial relationships. The local letter books, and cases like McFoy's, tell an important story for the period from 1839 until the late 1850s, one that diverges from the conventional argument that Britain signed anti-slave-trade treaties according to a civilizational hierarchy, with African polities offered the worst terms.[70] Gifting is not necessarily an exchange between equals; it could be competitive or overbearing. But in these cases, there are good reasons to emphasize reciprocity rather than domination. After all, if British officials wished to frame the interactions with the chiefs as imperial, they could have withheld gifts or resorted to violence. And if the chiefs perceived the gifts to be inadequate, they could have continued the detention of the liberated African or written a complaint to the governor. Gifting resolved detention without violence.

In the 1860s, gifting, treaty-making, and annexation overlapped. In 1861, the Sierra Leone Colony annexed Sherbro and Koya.[71] Even under formal treaty law, the return of liberated Africans could take the form of gifting. Indeed, the governor admitted that treaties alone were not sufficient to guarantee the return of British subjects. In 1865, the Reverend J. H. Dufort asked the colonial administration to intercede with chiefs of independent polities in the Rio Pongo area who had signed a treaty with the governor. Dufort complained that a boy had been enslaved, yet the governor's secretary replied, "The colonial government cannot undertake to pay for the liberation of the boy. . . . You should apply to the proper chief for the boy in question." If the chief acceded to the request, the government could "perhaps reward him in some shape." The secretary did not suggest that violent intervention was an alternative. In fact, the boy would have to take the initiative and "make his escape on board some British vessel where he would receive protection."[72] Indigenous chiefs resolved disputes through gift exchanges, which formed part of the hidden history of how anti-slave-trade regulation became international law in the nineteenth-century Upper Guinea Coast.

By 1845, British unilateral naval patrolling had added new layers to the anti-slave-trade legal order. In addition to prize and treaty law, the Palmerston and Aberdeen Acts inserted parliamentary legislation into anti-slave-trade regulation. This legislation defied the law of nations regarding the freedom of the high seas: slaving ships of all nationalities and none became vulnerable to capture. It also violated sovereignty over territorial waters, as Siaka and the Rogers family complained in their letter. British imperial agents claimed a right to violent intervention and denied any liability for its consequences, culminating in the "act of state" doctrine. Liberated Africans' claims for freedom instigated patterns of gunboat violence and value exchange as techniques for dispute resolution. Their claims were infinitely more complex than those envisaged by treaty and parliamentary law that treated liberated Africans as a static cargo to be exchanged for monetary reward.

Rather than being driven by the imperial metropole, regulatory patterns for interpolity law between British and African political authorities developed more often through local engagements. The conjuncture of local factors was vital. Liberated Africans seized the initiative to make their cases visible to British agents. Colonial governors responded to crises. Indigenous political authorities wished to resolve detention in ways that compelled British recognition of their jurisdiction. Conflict among polities over naval patrolling in the Atlantic in the 1840s ran parallel to developments inside polities where anti-slave-trade law applied. Disputes erupted between liberated Africans and host political authorities. In British colonies, Brazil, and Cuba, these battles were particularly acute over the meaning and operation of compulsory labor.

CHAPTER FOUR

Compulsory Labor

THE EMERGENCE OF THE MODERN state and the emancipation of servile populations intersected worldwide in the decades between the Napoleonic Wars and First World War. Early-modern slave societies did not need the bells and whistles of modern statecraft. The monopoly on legitimate violence enacted through the armed forces, police, and prisons mattered little in early-modern empires. Bureaucratic techniques like the census and the "biopolitical" management of subjects' health and education were not priorities for enslavers or officials in early-modern slave societies. Indeed, slaveholders jealously guarded their jurisdiction over the life and death of slaves against any encroachment by state power.

The situation for polities began to change in the nineteenth century. The financial demands of warfare grew during the global Napoleonic Wars. The press and mass political mobilizations in meetings and petitions, along with several other causes, helped the public sphere emerge as a factor in domestic and international politics. Public debate about many emancipations—of slaves, serfs, women, oppressed religious groups, and nations—became commonplace. Emancipation itself was a flexible term: those who promised personal and political transformation could use their power to assert new forms of control over oppressed people through systems of removal.[1] The prospect of emancipating servile peoples to reassign their labor and recruit them as soldiers became a common strategy of transformation in Europe,

North America, and Russia.[2] Many places were unaffected by talk of emancipation: slaveholding continued in many parts of the Americas, Africa, and Asia. More clearly than any other group of people, the compulsory labor of liberated Africans wove together the histories of state formation with the tensions and contradictions of emancipation. Their labor was crucial for the first public prison in Brazil, the major railway in Cuba, and infrastructure projects alongside domestic service and agricultural labor in British colonies. Throughout the Atlantic world, liberated Africans built states.

Under anti-slave-trade law, political authorities freed people from slaving ships and then detained them in public institutions that they were forced to help build. In 1841, a group of African women laborers in Rio de Janeiro's Casa de Correção, Brazil's first public prison, sent a startling petition to the Brazilian emperor. They "implore His Imperial Majesty, must they live, oppressed, in such a way that they live locked inside every day; may His Imperial Majesty order for us to move to the Arsenal." The "administrator treats . . . his slaves with as much barbarity as he treats the Africans." The petitioners complained about how officials treated free Africans like slaves and requested a transfer to a different state institution. These elements suggest that many of the petitioners were liberated Africans who had been rescued from slaving ships and assigned into apprenticeship. Apprentices were not fully free: under treaty and domestic laws, they were required to work for private "masters" or state institutions for up to fourteen years. The precise tasks of the women laboring in the Casa were unclear, but the Casa's paperwork included tables of occupations such as carpentry and domestic service and reports on penal labor in a press gang.[3]

The petitioners complained about the "abuses practiced by the administration that rules over [them]," including the removal of the privilege to do their own work on Sundays and saints' days. According to treaty and domestic law, these privileges were fundamental to liberated African status. They gave the apprentices time to work for their own benefit, to rest, to learn the "civilizing" tenets of Catholicism, and to build a support network in Rio de Janeiro. Violating these privileges, the administrators inflicted corporal punishment on the apprentices. They had beaten one woman so badly that "her clothing looked like a sieve."[4] The administrators also embezzled public funding that they should have spent on food and skilled work opportunities. The emperor did not respond to the petition, but that may not have disheartened the petitioners, who might have hoped to force the emperor's officers to resolve the problems informally.

The petition revealed some important techniques for protesting the inequities of compulsory labor. The petitioners went forum shopping by appealing to a higher power that might be willing to hear their case. They articulated the reciprocal relationship of loyalty to the emperor in exchange for protection from him. Finally, they focused on the most visceral evidence of the injustice committed by an imperial official. With a particular focus on men's service in imperial armies, scholars have demonstrated that in several Latin American colonies, enslaved people used loyal service to claim manumission, obtain official recognition of kinship bonds, and protect their group interests.[5] Freedpeople of color used similar strategies, and these strategies continued after the colonies gained independence.[6] Far from being premodern or antirevolutionary, these strategies enabled marginalized men to create plural visions of citizen-subjecthood and political community. In a wider Atlantic context, enslaved women devised routes to freedom and political belonging through petitioning for manumission, accumulating property, fugitivity, controlling pregnancy, and engaging in bodily performances of freedom through dance and dress. Scholars have revealed these strategies even while foregrounding how imperial administrators and enslavers erased women's resistance from the written records that have entered the archives.[7]

Liberated Africans came into conflict with household masters and institutional hirers in navigating their way through apprenticeship. The risk of persistent unfreedom, even kidnapping into slavery, was inherent in the apprenticeship system. This risk emerged because treaty and domestic laws conceived apprenticeship to be a voluntary labor agreement to which the apprentice was obliged to commit. As state authorities in Brazil and Cuba sought to manage apprentices to protect the slavery-based economy, this risk grew more acute. British diplomats encountered practical limitations in monitoring thousands of liberated Africans. Both inside and outside British jurisdictions, apprenticeship was rarely contractual. Scholars who have focused on British colonial jurisdictions have emphasized that apprenticeship for liberated Africans was gap-ridden. There was limited state oversight of apprentices, who were vulnerable to abuse from unscrupulous masters, in a context of successive failures to reform apprenticeship regulations.[8] Apprenticeship throughout the Atlantic world was compromised, and the principal sources used to produce this finding were commissioned reports and registers of apprentices. Yet these sources yield little historical insight into the relationships between apprentices and household masters or institutions.

A wider source base of scattered petitions, magistrate cases, and official correspondence provides new insight into how apprenticeship worked in the urban Atlantic world.[9] Three principal features of apprenticeship emerge from this approach. First, masters exploited many apprentices, including through attempted sale into slavery, physical or sexual abuse, and the failure to provide any of the promised training. Instead, masters assigned the apprentices to work in whichever way they saw fit. Second, apprentices strategized to exit apprenticeship by complaining to magistrates, appealing to higher political authorities, and flight. Third, political economy developed through apprenticeship, with officials using apprentices to build modern state institutions in a major departure from early-modern apprenticeship practices. Many of these trends began with apprenticeship in the early nineteenth century and continued into the late nineteenth century. Still, in Sierra Leone, the Cape, Brazil, and Cuba, exploitation by masters, apprentices' exit strategies, and the transformation of political economy crystallized in the 1840s to 1850s. During the recaptive middle passage and adjudication in the Mixed Commission, liberated Africans' interactions with legal authorities were similar throughout the Atlantic world. Apprenticeship was the practice in which differences in treatment and expectations became apparent due to the differences between slave and nonslave societies.

COLONIAL CONTROL OVER APPRENTICES IN SUB-SAHARAN AFRICA

In early-modern England, apprenticeship law defined the master as a head of household who was obliged to teach and maintain the apprentice. The law defined the apprentice as a subordinate member of the household who was dutybound to serve the master for a specific term. Apprenticeships were usually for a seven-year term begun at the age of fourteen and with the aim of learning a specific trade.[10] The 1563 Statute of Artificers created a nationwide system of apprenticeship, regulated by magistrates in cases of misconduct by apprentices.[11] In such cases, the magistrate had authority to punish and to order the apprentice to serve the required time. An apprentice could bring a civil suit to the Lord Mayor's Court in London (or an equivalent local court) to terminate their apprenticeship early on certain grounds. From 1747, apprentices whose families had paid less than five pounds to the master as a premium for the apprenticeship could complain to a local justice of the peace regarding ill-usage or refusal to provide necessary provision.[12] Challenging an older paradigm that emphasized the constraints imposed on apprentices, more recent research has revealed that apprenticeship in early-modern England was a relatively open and flexible system of improving human capital that provided favorable conditions for the industrial revolution.[13] Alongside these apprenticeships, under the Poor Law, parish officials had authority to apprentice poor children to reduce the parish's liability for maintaining them. In London, pauper apprentices entered a wide range of sectors: the number who participated in large-scale manufacturing increased during industrialization, while other apprentices entered smaller-scale craft manufacturing and domestic service.[14]

During the 1830s, apprenticeship schemes proliferated. Employers in England increasingly apprenticed children in factories and sweated labor. Parliament applied a different apprenticeship model to all adults and children in British Crown colonies in the Caribbean, the Cape, and Mauritius as part of the emancipation process. Postemancipation apprenticeship required freedpeople to work for former enslavers for up to six years without compensation, but the term was shortened to four years after mass protests.[15] Apprenticeship for African people liberated from slaving ships applied to adults and children. Adults were bound to serve in households and public works, and children served in households. Some young and adult men were enlisted (rather than apprenticed) in the armed or naval forces. Whereas apprenticeship for freed slaves attempted to ensure the supply of a postslavery Black agricultural workforce, the apprenticeship of liberated Africans was far more varied and contingent. Liberated African apprentices often fulfilled immediate needs in infrastructure projects, including in urban areas. In England, apprentices were subordinate members of the master's household and forbidden to marry. But in the Atlantic world, the signatories of anti-slave-trade treaties committed to a vision of creating households of apprentices who had converted to Christianity headed by a paterfamilias in a monogamous marriage.

This vision did not necessarily come to fruition: unlike statute law in the metropole, colonial apprenticeship for liberated Africans was vaguely defined. Neither prize law nor treaty law defined the process for adjudicating disputes between masters and apprentices. Nor did they specify the fate of apprentices' children. These problems were partly the result of poor design: early prize and treaty law focused more on the right to capture slaving ships than on what to do with the captives aboard them. But they also resulted from the influx of an unpredictable number of liberated Africans into polities with limited resources to register and monitor them. This process unfolded most clearly in Sierra Leone. By 1816, the number of captured slave ships produced a population of apprentices that the households of Freetown could no longer accommodate. Governor Charles MacCarthy decided on a new policy of settling liberated Africans in villages run by missionaries and focused on agricultural production.[16] The colonial administration hoped that these villages could help secure the colony's food supply, which depended on neighboring Fulani polities, and provide a defensive bulwark against any nearby military threats.[17]

By the late 1830s, colonial policy prioritized reducing the cost of apprenticeship in Freetown and the surrounding missionary villages. The Liberated African Department, with its headquarters in Freetown and managers in each major village, had authority to assign apprentices. Most Africans liberated in the colony were now apprenticed under treaty law, and there was a small group of officers responsible for thousands of apprentices. To reduce the costs involved in settlement in Sierra Leone, from 1840 the metropolitan government authorized migration schemes from Sierra Leone to British Guiana, Jamaica, and other British colonies.[18] The rapid increase in the maritime rescue of African captives in the South Atlantic under the Palmerston Act dovetailed with the reassignment of the liberated Africans into contract labor in the British Caribbean.

Emigration agents visited Sierra Leone to encourage liberated Africans to migrate to the British Caribbean. Young liberated Africans, who had begun to develop their own culture in Sierra Leone, were reluctant to leave. In 1841, a commissioned report found that the number of children who were "receiving religious education and elementary instruction in the Colony amount to about 8,000," one-fifth of the total colonial population.[19] These children had strong personal, educational, and economic incentives to remain in Sierra Leone. Even recent arrivals could discover enough information to dissuade them from emigration. In 1844, six men and two women, who were recovering in hospital from the trauma of shipment on a slaver, made friends with some fellow "country people." Upon their discharge, a department official reported, "Some of their country people come with them as far as [the] Department gate. From this I believe their minds is [*sic*] already decided against anything like emigration."[20] Although later groups had little choice over emigration, liberated Africans who had communicated with previous settlers or had spent time in the villages tended to reject intensive administrative pressure to migrate. Liberated Africans insisted that they had the right to choose where they worked and lived.

Liberated Africans who remained in Sierra Leone nonetheless faced problems during their apprenticeship. Masters and apprentices went to the Freetown magistrate to resolve conflicts. The magistrate was the most important legal officer for regulating apprenticeship, and the magistrate's books of proceedings contain the most comprehensive set of sources on apprenticeship in households.[21] The proceedings related to the breakdown of household relations and were adversarial in format, with the magistrate questioning the complainant, witnesses, and defendant in turn. The magistrate did not document problems resolved outside the court. The magistracy was the most accessible forum for apprentices to explain the problems that they faced in their own words.

Throughout the 1840s, the magistrate was Thomas McFoy. McFoy had an extensive career in colonial governance. In the 1820s, he was the superintendent of Wellington, a village established for liberated African settlement.[22] McFoy was the magistrate who took the depositions of Tom Peters, William Mering, and John Sharp regarding their reenslavement, which generated intensive debates over dispute resolution in Atlantic West Africa. In the 1840s and 1850s, he also worked as harbor master in Freetown, where he surveyed captured ships suspected of slave-trading for the anti-slave-trade courts.[23] In 1851, the Governor's Council chose him to be mayor of Freetown.[24] McFoy's background as a man of color from the Caribbean did not necessarily imply a commitment to racial equality or to greater political rights for liberated Africans.[25] Nonetheless, McFoy was an officeholder versed in resolving disputes about apprenticeship and enslavement. The commonest cases involved theft, for which McFoy committed the defendant to trial. McFoy punished other offenses, such as absconding from service, with short sentences in the house of correction.

The magistrate also adjudicated cases of defendants charged with detaining liberated Africans in their homes. In 1840, McFoy heard the case of John Butcher, a private in the Royal African Corps, accused by the apprentice Maria South of detaining her in his home against her will. South testified, "she went to the Town to sell something when she saw Prisoner who told her he wanted her[;] he afterwards went to her Master's house who told him if he wanted her he must pay for her, after that she went several times to [the] Defendant's house but always of her own free will."[26] South's master, and two other witnesses, corroborated that she had often run away to Butcher's household. Either the magistrate asked Butcher whether he had sexually assaulted South or Butcher interpreted South's accusation to imply that he had, for Butcher denied that he had "entered the girl[;] whenever she came to him he carried her back to her master."[27] The magistrate did not record South's age, but Butcher's reference to her as a "girl" indicates that she was probably a child or young adult. The magistrate punished Butcher with six weeks in the house of correction. In another case, McFoy sentenced Susannah Langley to one month in the house of correction for detaining an apprentice, despite her defense that the complainant, the apprentice's master, had "turned the girl out of door."[28] The case marked another divergence from early-modern English apprenticeship, in which the contract ended if the master ejected the apprentice. In nineteenth-century Sierra Leone, a magistrate could punish a free person for sheltering an abandoned apprentice.

Informal arrangements in which a master extracted financial payment from a third party for sexual access to an apprentice without their consent could also result in disputes. In June 1841, the police brought John Sawyer and Nancy Macarthy before the magistrate court over Sawyer's treatment of Nancy Best, who was apprenticed to Macarthy. Sawyer had requested Macarthy's permission to marry Best. Macarthy told Sawyer that she "had paid money for her in the Queen's Yard and must have something on her head provided the Girl liked him."[29] Sawyer paid Macarthy twenty shillings. For Macarthy, a marriage offer was a financial transaction that offset the cost of apprenticeship. She might have learned such an approach from the colonial administration: in 1808, the governor stipulated a twenty-dollar payment to receive an apprentice from the *Derwent*, a captured slaver. The scheme caused uproar when his successor branded the arrangements "illegal" and voided them.[30] For Sawyer, marriage involved a payment to the apprentice's head of household so that he could form his own patriarchal household. He too might have learned this precedent from the colonial administration. In the 1830s and 1840s, the Liberated African Department encouraged prospective husbands to give gifts to women to agree to marriages, including to women recently disembarked from a slaving ship who were living in the asylum yard.[31]

Nancy Best was not passive: after six weeks with Sawyer, she ran away. Perhaps she had never wanted to marry him, or perhaps he became abusive. In the hearing, nobody mentioned sexual assault, but Sawyer's methods in getting Best into his household make it a possibility. Perhaps Best had always refused Macarthy and Sawyer's attempts to commodify her body and labor and was waiting for the opportune moment to escape. Best was probably aware of the alternatives to domesticity. Women who worked as market traders regularly walked from the missionary village of Regent to downtown Freetown just after sunrise to sell cassava, fufu, and fruit.[32] In the nineteenth century, some sub-Saharan West African societies were matrilineal, in which married women owned property. Sawyer was of Yoruba heritage, an ethnolinguistic group that constituted a large diasporic population in Sierra Leone, where they were known as "Akus." Different Yoruba communities in their homelands practiced either patrilineal or bilineal descent systems. In both systems, a Yoruba woman upon marriage retained property that she held within her descent group.[33] Such property ownership was rare in Victorian Britain before the Married Women's Property Act of 1870. British colonial administrators in Sierra Leone did not anticipate that women would seek to engage in economic activity outside the household.

By escaping, Best evaded patriarchal household norms. Best's case was exceptionally well documented, but her experiences were common. Throughout the Atlantic world, masters abused apprentices. In the 1850s, liberated Africans transferred from the United States to Liberia suffered abuse. Even in an independent Black republic, the apprentices were subjected to a racialized hierarchy in which being born in Africa and worshiping Indigenous African deities were grounds for Americo-Liberian masters to discriminate against them.[34] In Liberia, such abuse demonstrates not so much that Americo-Liberian administration failed without white oversight but rather the corrupting influence of near-total power over another person. When Sawyer tried to drag Best back to his home, his "country people" (i.e., fellow "Aku" people) intervened to stop him. Like Best, they refused to allow patriarchal violence to become a normative feature of households. The police arrested Sawyer. The magistrate bound Sawyer and Macarthy over to appear at the next quarter session for a criminal trial. Best was now free, but the magistrate did not record what happened to her after the hearing.[35] Best's case reveals the systemic reliance on forced labor in the nineteenth-century Atlantic household, even in free-soil jurisdictions like Sierra Leone and Liberia.

The magistrate took such interest in apprentices' complaints against exploitation because they were a vital part of household social organization and the labor force in Sierra Leone. The magistrate was not the sole arbiter of household relations: apprentices could also call on headmen who were mercantile leaders and liaised with the colonial state. Muslim leaders, societies such as Poro, and mutual-aid societies also offered fora to resolve disputes.[36] Yet, more than any other legal office, the magistrate's jurisdiction covered all households within the colony. Scholars have shown how commerce in Freetown and the creation of missionary villages created a British colonial society in Sierra Leone.[37] Magisterial jurisdiction extends this research by demonstrating that dispute resolution was vital to governing labor in Sierra Leone's colonial political economy.

As well as complaining about exploitation in households, apprentices protested apprenticeships in the missionary villages through forum shopping. The Liberated African Department, the colonial body that registered and monitored liberated Africans from 1808 onward, recorded many such protests. These included individual acts of escape. In 1843, a senior department official, W. G. Terry, wrote a letter to Henry Vincent, the village manager of Waterloo. Terry wrote, "The Bearer Judy has been twice to my house and complains that her master and mistress have beaten her four times pray examine into the truth of that and other allegations such as having been sent to Freetown with foofoo to sell and the people with whom she has been located only gave her 1d to keep her 3 days." Terry told Vincent, "if you find that the statements are founded you will immediately give her to some better Guardian [and] if they have beaten her as the Girl states may bind them over to keep the peace as well, for they are sure to beat this child in revenge for reporting."[38]

Liberated Africans also collaborated to complain about treatment in the villages. In 1844, the department informed Vincent by letter that a group of "twenty two Boys belonging to the Model farm at Waterloo has appeared before [the colonial governor] with some complaints against [him]" and that he must "immediately on the receipt of this come to Town so that the matter may be investigated."[39] Young liberated Africans were prepared to make the daylong journey to Freetown to complain about labor conditions. By petitioning the Liberated African Department, each of these complainants challenged the master's assumed authority to decide what counted as fair labor arrangements. Throughout the 1840s, the use of apprenticeship in Sierra Leone declined as the administration assigned newly recaptured people to serve as indentured laborers in the postemancipation Caribbean. In 1848, the governor and Colonial Office decided to stop assigning liberated Africans into apprenticeship in Sierra Leone, but some of the problems of abuse and lack of oversight continued regarding the apprenticeship of Indigenous African children inside the colony.[40]

Compulsory labor in apprenticeship systems also affected the legal politics of the transition from slave to "free labor" in the Cape. Liberated Africans featured prominently in legislative and public discussions about this transition. In 1840, the colonial governor, George Napier, sought to introduce a Master and Servants Ordinance that brought labor law into line with the postemancipation Order-in-Council of 30 July 1838. The draft ordinance limited contracts of service to three years. If there were insufficient proof of the contract term, service was limited to one month.[41] Members of the Legislative Council, an advisory body to the governor composed of Crown appointees and those elected by large property owners, objected to the draft. Five elected members, including the merchants J. B. Ebden and Hamilton Ross, alleged that the order was "totally inapplicable to the wants, and injurious to the best interests of this Colony," considering "the present depressed state of Agriculture from want of labor."[42] Instead, they wished for informal contracts of three months. Eventually, the Colonial Office ordered the governor to bring the entire ordinance in line with a more recent order of 7 September 1838, which included a limit on contracts for Indigenous workers of one year rather than three.[43]

A year later, 1,049 inhabitants signed a petition demanding that the Cape and imperial government subsidize the migration of laborers from Britain to the Cape. The petitioners, led by leading merchants and landowners, observed that "the Sovereign holds the waste or unappropriated land in the Colonies in trust for the public good."[44] Far from being waste or unappropriated, for centuries San and Khoikhoi people practiced forms of community guardianship to use these lands for hunting and herding. More recently, people freed from slavery used such lands for subsistence agriculture. If the Crown were to sell these lands, claimed the colonists, it could pay for migrants' passages to the Cape. This was one of the largest political protests in the Cape since the advent of British rule in 1803. It surpassed the most recent widespread dissent in 1830, when a couple of hundred slave owners refused to comply with measures to "ameliorate" the conditions of slaves. Such a petition ran counter to the metropolitan government's policy of instructing colonial governments to be financially self-sufficient and the ban on indentured labor migration in the British Empire between 1839 and 1843.[45] The colonial secretary responded by affirming Governor George Napier's position that neither the colonial nor metropolitan government had funding for migration schemes.

Dissatisfied with the response, landowners again pressurized Napier to endorse immigration schemes in early 1842, again in the Legislative Council. In March 1842, Ebden proposed several resolutions. He urged Napier to appoint land and emigration commissioners to encourage immigration and appropriate "wasteland" and rental taxes to provide the "free passage" of British migrants. Ebden's proposals were explicitly racialized: he deplored the continued introduction of liberated Africans, who would "perpetuate the evils of a degenerate race."[46] Politically influential merchants and landowners sought to commodify land at the expense of Indigenous people and freedpeople to fund the immigration of British laborers. Crown appointees to the council opposed the elected members like Ebden. They argued that liberated Africans provided a convenient solution to the labor shortage. African labor may be better suited to the Cape economy, and naval captures provided a fortuitous supply of such laborers. The split in the council was not just over the racialized "capacity" of different immigrant laborers but also over whether private capital, local government appropriations of land, or metropolitan government grants should fund immigration schemes. Most councilors supported Napier's position.

Some councilors, such as Hamilton Ross, were already funding a private scheme to introduce liberated Africans from St. Helena as apprentices from 1842. St. Helena was a tiny British colony in the South Atlantic that functioned primarily as a naval base. Naval officers brought several slaving ships there for adjudication at the vice-admiralty court, but it was a perilous place for African people liberated from these vessels.[47] The lack of adequate institutions and economic opportunities was troubling. The colonial authorities subjected tens of thousands of liberated Africans to prolonged detention at a holding site in Rupert's Valley until they could organize voyages elsewhere, usually the British Caribbean. The governor of St. Helena, Hamelin Trelawny, was keen to approve Ross's plans. But when the first migrant ship organized by Ross and five fellow merchants planned to set sail in early February, it provoked controversy. A doctor in St. Helena objected to the embarkation of the liberated Africans without prior survey.[48] In the Colonial Office, undersecretary James Stephen, son of the abolitionist lawyer and author of the 1833 Act for the Abolition of Slavery, was puzzled by the fact that the vessel's passengers consisted entirely of men and boys. He was concerned that families might have "been broken up" by the agents in St. Helena. "I suspect," Stephen wrote, "that the Slaves had no family ties among them, and that they must have formed the part of a whole of a cargo in which there were no Females." In the colonial secretary's reply to the governor in June 1842, he informed him that future migrant voyages must not exclude women or girls.[49]

In fact, liberated African pressure predated this new directive from the metropolitan government in stopping those who were running the St. Helena–Cape migration scheme from breaking up families. Three weeks after the first vessel set sail, Governor Trelawny tried to organize another migrant ship. He reported, "I had intended only to have sent 40 Females, but there appear to have been formed amongst themselves a determination not to embark if a certain number, namely 27 men, 49 women, and 57 children were separated, *nay* if one of that lot were kept back, the others positively refused to embark."[50] The liberated Africans forced the colonial authorities to recognize their capacity to choose whether to emigrate by insisting on keeping families together. The exact relationship between the men, women, and children and their conceptions of kin are impossible to determine. But familial bonds between liberated Africans existed on St. Helena. In 1850–51, the Anglican Church on St. Helena recorded thirty baptisms of the children of liberated Africans. Many unbaptized parents wished to have their names recorded in the baptism record. For example, Mary had her son George baptized in 1851 with sponsorship by a Robert May and Mungo Park.[51] Besides the religious significance of the baptism ritual, it provided liberated Africans with the opportunity to inscribe relationships between parents and children in official paperwork. In the case of migration to the Cape in 1842, such family relations meant that the Africans refused to board the ship, until eventually the number of women and girls almost tripled. Eventually, the 400 liberated African migrants comprised 290 males and 110 females. Trelawny was so frustrated by the liberated Africans' resistance that he wrote to the colonial secretary requesting that he remove the clause that required migrants "to be embarked with their own free will and consent" from the regulations.[52] By the end of 1842, 1,332 liberated Africans from St. Helena were working in the Cape. By 1847, Ross and his business partners, as well as parallel schemes that established a "Negro Fund," paid for the immigration of over 1,400 liberated Africans from St. Helena to the Cape.[53] Overall, British imperial authorities and merchants transferred over 17,000 liberated Africans from St. Helena to other British colonies, including Trinidad and Guyana, where they worked as contract laborers alongside South Asian and Chinese indentured laborers on the same plantations.[54]

In the Cape, the key legislation that regulated apprenticeship was the Master and Servants Ordinance. The ordinance stipulated that contracts must state the apprentice's tasks, pay, and benefits including time off, clothing, subsistence, and accommodation. In any case of breach of contract, the master or servant was permitted to take the case to the local magistrate for adjudication. If the master breached the contract, they received a civil penalty, usually a fine. If the servant breached the contract, they received a criminal penalty, such as flogging or imprisonment on spare diet. Of 167 cases heard by Cape Town's Police Magistrate Court between 1844 and 1846 that related to liberated African apprentices, all featured the apprentice as the defendant.[55] Only one case featured an apprentice who complained about a master; the magistrate dismissed the suit as "groundless" and punished the apprentice with eighteen lashes.[56] Absences from work accounted for eighty-three of the offenses. Apprentices probably used these temporary absences to work on their own behalf for additional income, to alleviate the drudgery of working for an unreasonable master, or to participate in emancipation celebrations that other freedpeople held in December and January of each year.[57] The magistrate worked alongside a Treasury official, the collector of customs, to register apprentices. William Field, the collector in the period 1843–61, kept a register of over twelve hundred liberated Africans from twelve ships. He assigned these liberated Africans into apprenticeship, including some of those transferred from St. Helena. Field assigned almost all the adult men into farmwork and the women and children into domestic service. A small number became apprenticed in trades such as blacksmithing, tanning, cobbling, and book binding.[58] The register is the one surviving book of perhaps three compiled by the collector. Field's pencil marginalia in the document recorded the hire and wage rates of the liberated Africans. These data suggest that liberated Africans earned more than the Khoi laborers in rural areas did but less than the skilled, English-speaking freedpeople in Cape Town did.[59] Liberated Africans became part of the laboring population of color of the Western Cape.

Field used the register to work out which masters were obliged to present their apprentices to local magistrates in particular months and publicized this information in the *Government Gazette*. In theory, magistrates applied the same rules in every jurisdiction regarding relations between masters and servants. In practice, by 1849, magistrates in different parts of the Cape had divergent attitudes toward liberated Africans and laborers of color in general. Their replies to a survey of the functions of the Master and Servants Ordinances reveal this divergence. Between 1846 and 1849, the resident magistrate in Cape Town had heard no cases of masters complaining against servants, whereas his counterparts in Paarl, Simon's Town, and Stellenbosch (for 1845–48) had heard 38, 25, and 123, respectively.[60] Of complaints by servants against masters, the magistrate in Cape Town had heard 43 cases (mainly regarding unpaid wages), Paarl had heard 10, Stellenbosch 53, and Simon's Town none.[61] Although these cases could involve all types of servant—European migrant, Khoi, San, and liberated African—some magistrates identified "late slaves," "prize negroes," and "negro apprentices" as complainants.[62] Servants complained more readily to the magistrate in Cape Town than to those in other districts, where they were likelier to be subject to proceedings initiated by the master for absconding or indolence.

Most notably, magistrates diverged in their attitude to whether the Master and Servants Ordinance was sufficiently stringent on masters and servants. Nineteen of twenty-five magistrates wished to reform the system to increase the punishments meted out on servants. The magistrates of Albert, Cradock, Paarl, and Tulbagh recommended reinstating corporal punishment.[63] Again, Cape Town's magistrate found himself in the minority in recommending stronger laws in favor of *servants*, rather than masters—specifically, recommending "clearly defined and explained" contracts and medical treatment at the master's expense if the servant suffered injury at work.[64]

Alongside household labor, liberated Africans served in institutions including public works and the military. Liberated Africans responded to this labor with flight and protest. For instance, newspapers carried several advertisements of liberated Africans who had escaped from their masters in the 1840s. On 19 June 1840, Field advertised that "sixteen . . . non-distributed captured negroes, broke out, and made their escape."[65] Collective acts of work stoppage and fugitivity defied the terms of compulsory service. In other cases, liberated Africans chose loyalty rather than flight. In 1846, war broke out between the Xhosa and the Cape Colony due to the breakdown of treaty relations, settlers' resentment at what they perceived to be "pro-Xhosa" government policy, and incidents of cattle theft by Xhosa people.[66] In Cape Town, the colonial government imposed military conscription on burghers by random ballot drawn by a civil commissioner. In addition to the burgher force, Field arranged for 137 liberated Africans to form a volunteer corps.[67] The captain and three lieutenants were British, but the sergeants—Chaveera, John Cezar, Mannigo, and Domingo—were liberated Africans. So too were the corporals—George, Thom, Fortuna, Lavoo, Kannomi, Lavor, Charles, and Makako—and 105 rank-and-file soldiers.[68] They served between May 1846 and January 1847, during which "their efficiency, discipline, and good conduct, were borne favourable testimony to by the Officers in command."[69] After their service, they returned to Cape Town, though it is unclear if they continued as apprentices in other institutions. Military service enabled liberated African men to acquire honor and enabled sergeants and corporals to accumulate followers.

In Sierra Leone and the Cape, British colonial authorities subjected apprentices to authoritarian control by applying criminal punishments whenever they tried to exit compulsory labor before the contract ended. Liberated Africans protested these inequities by demanding their right to choose where to work and live. Because of relationships forged with "country people" and kin, they refused to migrate for labor. Apprentices also went forum shopping to complain about abuse. For them, fairness in work emerged not from a British civilizing mission but rather through reciprocal relationships.

INSTITUTIONAL CONFINEMENT AND PROTEST IN BRAZIL AND CUBA

Alongside the many apprentices assigned in Sierra Leone and the Cape were thousands of people apprenticed under the same treaties in locations outside the British Empire. The Portuguese and Brazilian authorities used the 1818

Alvará, and the Spanish authorities used the 1817 Cédula, to define apprenticeship for liberated Africans settled in Brazil and Cuba. In Brazil, labor schemes involved the *curador*, a state guardian figure appointed to protect the apprentice's interests. The Ministério da Justiça had oversight of apprentices. In Cuba, the Spanish colonial captain general performed a similar role. As with Sierra Leone's Liberated African Department officials, these figures had authority to manage apprentices. Neither British consuls in Brazil and Cuba nor British commissioners in the Mixed Commissions had jurisdiction over them. At most, British officials could monitor apprenticeship conditions, record complaints, and raise problems with the host government and with the Foreign Office in London.

In Cuba, apprentices clashed with state institutions over the ownership of labor and residency rights. One prominent site of these conflicts was the Real Junta de Fomento, the institution responsible for economic development policy. In the early nineteenth century, the Junta owned slaves, which it assigned to ad hoc work such as porterage. The adjudication of captured slaving ships enabled an immediate increase in its workforce. The captain general offered the Junta up to 150 liberated Africans from the *Relámpago* in December 1824.[70] Using the terminology for enslaved boys and men, the Junta responded by requesting as many "in the classes of *mulecones* and *piezas*" as possible.[71] Soon the captain general was asking the Junta to receive additional apprentices, such as Ramona, whose household master no longer wished to employ her. Ramona had made "repeated escapes, thefts, and other excesses."[72] Such behavior undermined the master's patriarchal authority within the household, which was crucial to maintaining social order in a slave society.[73] The Junta agreed to assign Ramona to public works "as a forced laborer."[74] Apprentices also spent time in the Junta's Depósito de Cimarrones, the state depot for enslaved people who ran away from enslavers and had been subsequently detained. Enslaved people were forced to work for the Junta until the enslavers reclaimed them. The Depósito became a vital place where apprentices could meet and talk with these fugitives from slavery and convicts. By 1832, the Junta de Fomento had become the most politically powerful institution that used compulsory labor. Its apprentice labor supply was protected by a guarantee from the captain general that household masters would not be able to reclaim apprentices from its works projects.[75] The Junta combined penal labor and tutelary apprenticeship to build the transportation infrastructure required for industrial sugar production.

The dispersal of apprentices beyond Havana revealed the paradox between material vulnerability and contractual possibility at the heart of apprenticeship. A rare surviving example of an apprenticeship contract template stated that the liberated African "has contracted freely and spontaneously with the Government for a [stipulated] period of years to work in the customary hours, subjecting [herself] to the person to whom this contract is transferred."[76] The contract created rights and obligations for the apprentice and master. Although apprentices acquired rights to a wage, days off, subsistence, and health care, they did not have the right to specify or renegotiate the terms of labor. Apprentices also remained vulnerable to proslavery interests. Public officials sold apprentices into slavery for gold, and the buyer could use falsified registration documents to present a liberated African as a purchased slave.[77]

In response to this threat, in 1841 the British consul and abolitionist David Turnbull proposed a radical redefinition of anti-slave-trade law. He wished to expand the jurisdiction of the Mixed Commission to cover not just the capture of flagged vessels on the high seas but also any case of disembarkation in Cuba, even if the captives had entered plantations.[78] Accordingly, all enslaved people transported to Cuba in violation of treaty law since 1820 would become apprentices. Such a transformation would pose an unprecedented legal challenge to the authority of slave owners and the captain general and disrupt the captive labor supply to the Cuban sugar industry. Many influential individuals and institutions in Cuba objected to Turnbull's proposal. The Audiencia Pretorial of Havana (the appeals court) argued that the scheme would put "in doubt the property rights in slaves currently in the hands of third-party owners." Those "third-party owners" were those who had purchased illegally trafficked captives. The Audiencia warned that the scheme might provoke a revolution against colonial slavery.[79] The Junta de Fomento predicted that implementing the proposal would lead to general emancipation. Jamaica was a warning to Cuba: emancipation would cause the sugar industry to decline spectacularly. The proposal undermined colonial loyalty, which "involves the tacit condition that [the people] will never obey any law that risks their survival."[80] The captain general opposed the project and continued with the deportation of liberated Africans to British colonies once they had finished apprenticeship.[81]

Upon becoming captain general in 1843, Leopoldo O'Donnell was determined to establish policies that were more favorable to slave-trading interests. He was prepared to risk conflict with the Mixed Commission and the British government. O'Donnell reduced the number of certificates of emancipation from apprenticeship that were distributed: the British commissioners observed that in 1842, 1,215 liberated Africans and their children had received certificates from the captain general, which fell to 347 in 1843.[82] O'Donnell justified this reduction by claiming that apprentices had not yet demonstrated their fitness for freedom and assigned these apprentices to the Junta de Fomento instead. For the British commissioners, O'Donnell's scheme was carceral apprenticeship: many apprentices wore "heavier or lighter chains or bolts round their legs" while laying roads.[83] It was also probably corrupt, with O'Donnell receiving six doubloons (equivalent to twenty pounds) for each new apprenticeship contract.[84] The Junta used apprentices on its signature project: the new railway from Guïnes to Havana that had opened in 1837, which enabled unprecedented economies of scale in sugar production and export.[85] In 1844, the Junta received permission from Madrid, despite British protests, to assign 150 liberated Africans as apprentices to extend the railway southward to Batabanó.[86]

For liberated Africans who were looking to exit apprenticeship without British assistance, the Junta de Fomento was both an institution of confinement and one that offered opportunities. In 1835, Fendá, also known as Luisa Mandinga Sosó, fled from serving Maria Pezuela de Frigo in Havana.[87] Fendá arrived in Cuba on the captured slaver *Gallito* in 1829; she might have been working for Pezuela since then. Perhaps Pezuela had exploited Fendá, or perhaps she had heard from fellow liberated Africans or from enslaved people of better opportunities elsewhere. Fendá decided to go to the Junta de Fomento and work in laying roads. In 1844, Captain General O'Donnell must have received a request from Pezuela to track down Fendá. He wrote to the Junta asking if they had enlisted a woman named Fendá/Luisa, who in 1835 was "thirty-two years old, scarred by smallpox, with wide feet and open hands, marked with the number 117."[88] The captain general probably gathered these details from the register in the Mixed Commission.

Three weeks later, the Junta's administrator examined all the *cimarrones* in the Depósito house and identified one woman named Luisa Mandinga who had entered the Depósito in October 1835. He reported that Luisa, "although she expressly denies that she is the *emancipada* from the schooner *Gallito*, . . . does in some respects match the description."[89] Fendá had pulled off a double subversion of the legal ordering of apprenticeship. First, she took advantage of the porous gap between being an *emancipada* and a *cimarrón*. Fendá presented herself as a worker suited to public works projects to subvert the Junta's gendering of such work as masculine. Second, she denied the accuracy of the Mixed Commission register for identifying her. Her strategy mirrored the doctrine in the Siete Partidas that a slave who lived as a free person for ten years in good faith should become free: her work in the Junta continued her prior apprenticeship, entitling her to a freedom letter.[90] O'Donnell instructed the Junta to send Fendá to his office to receive the freedom letter—even if she had not completed the apprenticeship with the master to whom the captain general had originally assigned her.[91]

Other liberated Africans went forum shopping by going above the Junta to the captain general for a freedom letter. In 1843, Basilisa left her apprenticeship assignment in Matanzas to visit Havana, bringing her son, José Lorenzo, with her. Basilisa informed the captain general in Havana that she had "served the time for which she was consigned" and was entitled to a letter of freedom.[92] Although José was probably born in Cuba and thus not liberated under treaty law like his mother, he too was subjected to apprenticeship. He was working for a colonel. By presenting her son to the captain general at the same time as she requested her freedom papers, Basilisa sought to regularize both their statuses as freedpeople in Cuba. Entering the Depósito de Cimarrones and petitioning the captain general directly were ways for women to demonstrate their faithful service as grounds for a freedom letter.

Faced with the captain general's labor assignments and the tightening restrictions on free people of color in the 1840s, liberated Africans found it hard to gain meaningful residency rights. The default position was to deport freed apprentices from Cuba to a British colony. For the liberated Africans, the personal connections that they had made during apprenticeship gave them strong reasons to remain in Cuba. In rare cases, shipmate bonds helped provide proof of the right to freedom. In 1843, the Spanish authorities investigated the case of Pedro Alejandrito. Pedro's master was suspected of registering his death and selling him as a slave with a false certificate of sale. The authorities found that a fraudulent stamp had been used on the certificate. A legal officer, the *asesor general*, also interviewed three shipmates of Pedro's, who "recognized him as a *compañero* and countryman brought from Africa" on the same vessel. O'Donnell agreed with the officer's recommendation to punish the enslavers with fines.[93] Like many punishments for illegal enslavement in Cuba, whether these fines were ever enforced is unknown. In 1849, the captain general informed the superintendent of the Real Hacienda that the apprentice Jeremias was entitled to his freedom letter, probably as a prelude to ordering his removal from Cuba as a free man of color.[94] The Hacienda's officials noted that Jeremias "is very useful on the aqueduct where he is assigned through the intelligence and experience that he has with the pipelines."[95] The Hacienda asked the captain general to grant a freedom letter that would allow Jeremias to remain in Cuba to work for the department rather than being expelled, to which the captain general agreed.[96] The skilled labor needs of Jeremias's employers, as an influential state institution, provided him with rare additional contractual and residency rights at the end of apprenticeship.

In Cuba, apprentices petitioned multiple authorities to claim ownership of their labor, choose their work arrangements, and obtain freedom letters, but their petitions were subject to tight restriction. The state was invested in expanding the colonial slavery economy. The Junta de Fomento shaped the terms of compulsory labor by placing liberated Africans alongside *cimarrones* in public works projects. Liberated Africans also changed institutions such as the Junta. Their labor enabled these state institutions to shift away from the eighteenth-century focus on military defense. Through compulsory labor, the institutions developed the plural functions necessary for a political economy based on the expansion of industrial sugar production to supply world markets. These multiplying activities included policing the internal population, developing transportation infrastructure, and building the carceral state.[97] These same processes enabled early experimentation with indentureship to replace slave labor, which would accelerate in Cuba in the second half of the nineteenth century.

As with Cuba's Junta de Fomento, in Brazil, the Casa de Correção became a major site of conflict between state officials and liberated Africans over the meaning of apprenticeship. Scholars have carefully shown how compulsory labor under apprenticeship was one way that unfree labor systems expanded to replace slave labor in sites like the Casa in nineteenth-century Brazil.[98] Unlike Cuba or the British Caribbean, unfree internal labor rather than indentured immigration facilitated this transition. The Casa's construction fell squarely within the epoch of illegal trafficking. The site was purchased in 1831, the year of the Lei Feijó, the first criminal anti-slave-trade law. The first wing of the panoptic building opened in July 1850, the same month that the Brazilian legislature resumed secret discussions for a new anti-slave-trade criminal law. Liberated African apprentices were vital to the carceral project: they made up 40 percent of its workforce in 1835, falling to 25.5 percent in 1841, and continued to reside in or work at the Casa into the 1860s.[99] The petition by the laborers in 1841 proposed a clear solution to abuse: transfer to the Navy Arsenal, where conditions were better. The petition was just one thread in a pattern of conflict at state institutions in which different parties proposed various solutions to problems with apprenticeship.

Complaints were common because liberated Africans rarely received proper contractual benefits, let alone a stake in what they had produced. Liberated Africans typically did not receive a wage directly. In 1834, British commissioners estimated that the 381 hired-out liberated Africans in Rio had received at most "Rs 3 732$800, whereas the Sum due . . . amounts to no less . . . than Rs 57 063$620."[100] Instead, the wages were paid into a central Fundo Africanos Livres, which eventually the National Treasury recorded as an income stream.[101] When employers were obligated to pay liberated Africans directly, they sometimes objected. In 1840, one employer in Bahia complained that he was obliged to provide a night guard and days off on the weekend and on holy days in addition to a wage to the nine liberated Africans indentured on a public works project, unlike "other servants" such as *libertos* and slaves.[102]

In November 1843, the British commissioners alleged that administrators treated apprentices with "cruelty" inside the Casa de Correção.[103] The Anglo-Brazilian treaty did not specify sanctions against either party for abusing liberated Africans. The only option for commissioners was to notify British diplomats, who might then exert pressure on the Brazilian government. By the time the Foreign Office raised the allegation with Brazil, the court was due to close because the Brazilian government had refused to sign a new anti-slave-trade treaty with Britain, which allowed officials to delay responding to the commissioner's complaint.[104] Brazilian officials responded in October 1845. The Casa's administrator of public works, Thomé Joaquim Torres, wrote to the minister of justice flatly denying all allegations. According to Torres, the liberated Africans did not suffer regarding diet, illness, or overwork. Probably in full knowledge that the Mixed Commission had been disbanded and so could not verify his report, he theatrically asserted that "this Casa, and all its accommodation, are open to anybody who might like to visit them."[105] Indeed, "the Africans have demonstrated great enjoyment in the occupations to which they have been assigned," both inside the Casa and working for private masters. Torres also enclosed two tables as proof. The first described the daily diet of the liberated Africans: dried meat, beans, farinha, rice, and bacon.[106] The second laid out the occupations of the liberated Africans, including stonemasonry, construction, carpentry, and blacksmithing. Professed transparency and schematic tables were scripted responses to complaints about the Casa.

British officials had no way of verifying Torres's report. As an alternative way to sustain pressure on Brazil to end the illegal trade, Parliament passed the Aberdeen Act in August 1845. By replacing the mediating effect of the Mixed Commission with aggressive unilateral action, British politicians replicated the gunboat violence that they had authorized on the West African coast. British diplomats also began paying bribes to a secret informant in Rio's Customs office, alias Alcoforado, to provide intelligence on the movements of slave ships plying routes from Africa to Brazil.[107] Using this intelligence, Britain's navy captured slave ships and navigated them northward to British colonies in the Caribbean. This practice bypassed the need to agree on the legality of capture with the Brazilian government. It also provided additional indentured African laborers to British colonies. To try to win over Brazilian public opinion, British diplomats used secret service money to fund the Rio-based newspaper *O Philantropo* from 1849. They subsidized articles in the *Correio Mercantil*, the leading newspaper to oppose the pro-slave-trade Conservative government.[108] These secret coercive measures failed to curb the trade, which in fact increased in 1848 and 1849, but served to heighten tensions between Britain and Brazil.

In August 1850, several liberated Africans in the Casa wrote to the British consul at Rio, Robert Hesketh, begging him to facilitate their release. They complained of their "disgrace" at having served nineteen years as apprentices rather than the stipulated fourteen.[109] In November, they wrote again, raising the tempo: "in the hand of Your Excellency we hope to reach some hope, that we are disregarded and therefore we seek and ask Your Excellency to send us with all certainty to Your Excellency to know well we are slaves until death in this House of Correction if like this we wish to know we bless the hand of Your Excellency as father of humanity."[110] The apprentices had no way to hold the administrators of the Casa to account but knew that British diplomats might criticize them. This lack of power but access to authority led to the double qualification: "we hope to reach some hope." The petitioners ended their address by praising Hesketh as fictive kin, as a "father" who represented "humanity." This term translated their material and political objectives into a moral register, above the level of interimperial diplomacy.[111] The Africans combined the precedent of Casa protest, as developed by the women petitioners of 1841, with the language of moral obligation and their unusual interpolity leverage. Yet British diplomats did not answer the petition: throughout 1849 and 1850, they focused on British naval attacks on the Brazilian coast instead.

Apprentices also went to local courts to devise an escape route from compulsory labor. In Rio, in 1843, Anna argued that her master treated her like a slave. Anna had arrived in Brazil "eight years ago, more or less," and had been apprenticed to a colonel. She had learned what was necessary to "to live independently" and to "acquire the means of maintaining herself in the status of being free, which at the moment she truly was not." She requested the end of her apprenticeship even if that resulted in being deported to Africa. Anna did not claim that being enslaved necessarily involved *cruel* treatment; rather, it was the denial of the opportunity to live independently ("viver sobre si").[112] Anna's case looked similar to a freedom suit. Enslaved people often initiated suits against their enslavers to enforce manumission agreements. Some people who had been partially manumitted went to court to protect their right to earn money on their own account to accrue capital with which to purchase their full freedom—a right that remained customary in Brazil until 1871 but had become formally recognized in statute in Cuba by the 1840s.[113] Other enslaved people went to court to enforce particular work conditions, such as the types of service required under conditional manumission agreements. As well as to define these legitimate expectations, enslaved people looked to courts to manage the customary credit and community obligations that they had incurred in funding their bid for freedom.[114]

Liberated Africans accelerated the role of the state in arbitrating labor relations. Cases launched by liberated Africans such as Anna were distinct from manumission suits, whether understood as individual actions or as community-led initiatives under customary law. They developed several techniques in a short space of time, including forum shopping by appealing to state, treaty, and British consular authorities to enforce apprenticeship as a contractual relationship. Legal mobilization began to shift the terms of apprenticeship in favor of recognizing some liberated Africans' entitlements. Some apprentices became wage earners, enabling them to present themselves as property owners. They argued that they should be exempt from the post-apprenticeship deportation measures applied by domestic anti-slave-trade law. An indicator of this precedent was the registration of the children of liberated Africans born in Brazil as "ingenûo"—freeborn—rather than as "African" and thus likelier to be able to settle there.[115] Yet enslavers managed to transport other apprentices into enslavement. The trends in labor protest that liberated Africans developed would inform proposals for legal emancipation in the 1860s.

Outside the institutions, many women were apprenticed in the households of Brazil's political elite, which produced different conditions and opportunities for exit. In 1849, the British chargé d'affaires in Brazil, James Hudson, realized that some apprenticeships had expired. Hudson ordered Hesketh to compile a report on all the liberated Africans whom he could trace. Hudson hoped to use the report to agree on a protocol with the Brazilian government to transport liberated Africans to a British colony or to Liberia as a neutral polity. It took Hesketh over two years to compile the data on 856 liberated Africans who had been apprenticed under treaty law. He listed their occupations and workplaces and commented on their lives or work conditions. The protocol ultimately failed, but Hesketh's report became an important source on the labor of liberated Africans in households.

In Hesketh's survey, 48 percent of women apprentices had opportunities to earn additional income. The survey recorded this opportunity either directly, with terms like "hired out," or indirectly, through reference to the multiple occupations that the women had.[116] If the apprentice performed multiple roles such as cooking, hawking food, and working as a seamstress, it suggested the possibility of doing piecework for their own benefit. In Rio, enslaved domestic servants hired out their services as *jornaleros* (day laborers) to earn additional income, especially for self-purchase. A similar opportunity probably existed for liberated Africans.[117] Hesketh did not observe how much income the women apprentices earned from such activities. He recorded the specific hire rates of men alone, who paid some or all of these earnings to their master. Only 13 percent of the men either had multiple occupations or were hired out in ways that suggested that they might keep some of the proceeds. Apprenticed men did intensive manual work as masons, carpenters, and porters. They earned similar wages to hired-out enslaved laborers but less than the most skilled, who probably had spent a longer time in Brazil. The women even told Hesketh how they registered their children as *ingenûo*: Florencia explained that her children Verginia and Joaquim were "both baptized free."[118] The postmortem inventories of enslavers who hired apprentices revealed that they considered women capable of earning more money from *jornalero* work than men could.[119] The fact that wills enumerated liberated African apprentices suggests that masters saw them as transferable to their heirs, underscoring their precarious position. Liberated African women entered households where enslaved and freedwomen were often highly skilled, earned an income, and had developed customs for negotiating with masters and legal authorities. Women had greater negotiating room than men did yet also remained vulnerable to abuse.

Once apprentices had negotiated with the master to end the term of service, they needed to find a way to provide for themselves. One option for Afro-Brazilian freedwomen in Rio was to become a small business owner. In 1841, the same year that the women in the Casa petitioned the emperor, a municipal survey revealed that African women owned over one hundred grocery businesses and food stalls.[120] The many enslaved and free people who moved in and out of the Casa, including shipmates, could also have provided information to the Casa petitioners about their options. Beyond the expansion of unfree labor that replaced slave labor, centering liberated Africans reveals the importance of their labor to building the militarized and carceral institutions of the modern state. Their precarious position generated widespread resistance, ranging from petitioning to fugitivity. These strategies arranged time and work in alternative ways from institutional labor or plantation agriculture. The corollary to state-building using liberated Africans was that these same laborers used state institutions to build their own communities that petitioned for freedom and shared resources.

In both colonial Africa and the Americas, imperial authorities conceived of the apprenticeship of liberated Africans as training for full freedom through labor in households and institutions. This conception quickly broke down as the gaps in apprenticeship became apparent. Telling problems emerged regarding who had the authority to assign apprentices and to resolve disputes between apprentices and masters. Apprentices had greater personal security in nonslave societies such as Sierra Leone and the Cape Colony than in slave societies such as Cuba and Brazil. In nonslave societies, apprentices sought to navigate routes into itinerant urban labor that enabled them to earn income outside the constraints imposed by formal apprenticeship. They were nonetheless in a persistently precarious position, which masters exploited for their own gain. In slave societies, apprentices became the crucial labor supply in state-building, as political authorities built a liberation-to-prison pathway. The authorities hoped that this pathway would both prevent political mobilization by liberated Africans and bolster the productivity of plantations by improving infrastructure. Apprentices were always vulnerable to enslavers' attempts to kidnap them and force them into labor alongside enslaved people. Within each polity, there was variation, with liberated Africans having greater opportunities to petition for freedom or escape into fugitive communities in port cities than in rural areas. Yet no political authority provided space for liberated Africans to develop their own capabilities. Throughout the Atlantic world, liberated Africans faced persistent precarity because political authorities were committed to using their labor for industrial growth and maritime trade in a highly unequal global economy.

In these gaps, several processes emerged in compulsory labor arrangements. Household masters and institutional employers exploited apprentices by assigning them to contingent projects or abusing them rather than providing meaningful training. Women apprentices used loyalty to make legal claims in more varied ways than did enslaved and freed Black men who served in the military in colonial and postcolonial Latin America. In Cuba, Fendá called attention to her labor on public works, and Basilisa emphasized her and her son's completed service. In Brazil, Anna explained that she had earned sufficient wages to maintain herself. Transportation networks and carceral infrastructure were integral to the expansion of the slavery-based economy in Brazil and Cuba. This infrastructure depended on officials' harnessing of the labor released under anti-slave-trade law rather than on people purchased by enslavers in the market. The labor of liberated Africans as compulsory state-builders is still inscribed on the landscape of many Atlantic societies. All that remains of the Casa de Correção in Rio is the entrance gate, which stands on Rua Frei Caneca in front of the prison buildings that the authorities demolished between 2006 and 2010. Nothing speaks of the power of the modern state quite like building a prison complex and then blowing it up.

Only the gate remains: the Casa de Correção. (Photograph by Donatas Dabravolskas; public domain)

Compulsory labor assignments accelerated the development of the authoritarian aspects of anti-slave-trade law, resulting in state formation through a compromised emancipation process. In the 1810s and 1820s, authoritarian measures included precarious work assignments and urban surveillance through policing. By the 1840s, such control was far more wide-ranging. It encompassed penal state institutions and major infrastructure projects that facilitated expanding plantation economies in the Cape, Cuba, and Brazil. Political authorities developed ways to remove apprentices as an unwelcome financial burden and as disruptive to the preexisting domestic law of slavery. The authorities segregated the apprentices by moving them to enclosed institutions, such as nunneries, in some cases even separating parents from their young children.[121] Liberated Africans in all slave societies endured brutal work conditions and carceral oversight, while private individuals profited from their labor. In the United States, for instance, liberated Africans worked on a cotton plantation in Georgia.[122] Following apprentices in Brazil and Cuba adds a new perspective by revealing the extensive role that liberated Africans played in the evolving political economy of slave societies. Compulsory labor assignments would continue under new Brazilian and Spanish colonial anti-slave-trade regulations in the 1850s and 1860s.

Perhaps the final apprentices to petition for freedom were Juan Congo and Coleto Lucumi in Matanzas in 1884, just two years before the legal ending of slavery in Cuba; the outcome is unrecorded.[123]

The framers of anti-slave-trade law expected that liberated African women would be subordinate to their husbands in forming post-apprenticeship Christian households. Women defied these expectations by petitioning for freedom from apprenticeship, possessing property, and forming kin relations with shipmates and apprentices outside the household. Households provided a favorable context for developing these strategies through negotiation with masters. Apprentices in institutions relied more on forging collective strategies with fellow laborers. Liberated Africans proposed solutions to a novel predicament not of their own making: transoceanic displacement followed by compulsory labor to repay the "debt" of capture. In labor arrangements inside households and institutions, liberated Africans emphasized the importance of reciprocity between master and laborer. These plural strategies for subverting the constraints of anti-slave-trade law were visible to the state officials who created paper trails about them. In a context of asymmetric power relations that have structured the archival sources, these examples of women's resistance have endured.

At the same time, there were alliances between liberated Africans and enslaved people that did not usually enter state documentation. A rare insight came when the police arrested Gavino Congo, in Havana, in 1853. A police *capitan pedáneo* "extracted from a tango dance of blacks the Emancipado of the Real Junta Gavino Congo having observed that he was dancing with a knife belted at the waist."[124] For this transgressive dance with his fellow Afro-Cubans, the captain general punished Gavino with six months in shackles.[125] Gavino's tango alluded to a significant shift. Liberated Africans began to affect how authorities thought about issues beyond slave-trade suppression, not least the future of slavery and empire across the Atlantic world. In the years before Gavino's tango, the Brazilian and Spanish colonial authorities' anxieties about liberated Africans' possible collective organizing would combine with official fear of British imperial violence. Rumor would provoke panic and policing inside the secretive world of the plantation.

CHAPTER FIVE

Insurgent Abolition

THE CANE WAS BURNING, and nobody could say why. In March 1844, on the Labotina estate in Yumurí, Cuba, a soldier reported that a plantation was ablaze. It was the height of the harvest, and the authorities feared that the slaves in Matanzas were rising up. It was not the first time that fire had consumed the land. In the early eighteenth century, forests covered much of Cuba, and the Spanish colony was a net exporter of wood to the Caribbean and North American shipbuilding industry. Landowners burned so many trees to clear the land for sugar planting that Cuba was importing wood by the 1790s.[1] Every year, between December and May, slaves worked up to twenty hours per day to harvest the cane that constituted a fifth of the world's total sugar production.[2] But now the land was burning again, and as the flames spread, so too did rumors of slave resistance.[3] The authorities were already investigating an alleged insurrection that had engulfed over 230 sugar and coffee estates in early 1844. According to investigators, the insurgents aimed to abolish the slave trade and slavery and to achieve Cuban independence. The resulting mass imprisonment, expulsions, and executions became known as "La Escalera," after the ladder used to bind and torture suspects. Some people claimed that the Labotina fires were signs that the insurrection was still alive. Others suspected that they were protests against its brutal repression. Some plantation owners insisted, with one eye on protecting their property in persons from further state violence, that the fires were merely an unfortunate accident. If enslaved people knew anything about the fires, they were keeping it to themselves.

Four years later, in southeastern Brazil, rumors swept through the coffee estates that enslaved people were planning an insurrection. The slaves in the Vale do Paraíba between Rio de Janeiro and São Paulo, as well as in Campo and Espirito Santo, were planning to rise up in June 1848. "Brazil is the Vale" became a saying because the Paraíba coffee estates produced the country's leading export, which amounted to half of the world's total coffee exports by 1850.[4] Before the insurrection began, state authorities repressed the movement with violence. Slave-owning land proprietors in Matanzas and the Vale do Paraíba expanded production in coffee and sugar in the first four decades of the nineteenth century. To do so, they relied on the transoceanic trade in captive people that contravened treaty law and domestic legislation. Alongside the Cotton Kingdom, Brazil and Cuba were the most lucrative slave economies in the Western Hemisphere.

Throughout the 1840s, insurrections and rumors of insurrections threatened the status quo in which the Spanish colonial administration and Brazilian postcolonial government protected plantation production. The insurrection of 1844 and thwarted insurrection of 1848 were two of the most widespread movements in two of the most entrenched slave societies in the Americas. The insurrections disturbed the delicate political position of permitting the illegal trades and protesting British anti-slave-trade imperialism. The insurrection of 1844 in Cuba raised the stakes in the tug-of-war between Spain, Britain, and the United States for control. The failed insurrection of 1848 in Brazil lurched the empire closer to war with Britain. The movements threatened the political integrity of the two polities.

Scholars have connected these uprisings with the causal pathway toward final suppression. Some have cast the uprisings as the product of official paranoia rather than extensive insurgent planning. Other scholars have interpreted the movements as radical antislavery projects.[5] The major basis for such studies is the inquisitorial documents that the Spanish colonial and Brazilian authorities made to identify and punish suspected insurgents. These sources cannot reveal the multiple causes behind suppression between the 1840s and 1860s. Nor can these documents answer whether inquisitors or suspects believed what they said or decided. When enslavers produced written records about the enslaved, they either ignored their hopes and perspectives or recorded them only to the extent that it suited their own interests.[6] This power in shaping documentation is doubly significant when dealing with an inquisitorial archive in which the authorities tortured suspects to extract confessions.

These sources invite a different kind of question from one about the causes or operations of suppression. The archival records call attention to their surface-level structure and language.[7] Here, the authorities conceived of possible links between liberated Africans, British anti-slave-trade agents, and plantation insurgents in the rumors that spread throughout Brazil and Cuba. The sources reveal how authorities understood rumors of insurrection and acted to repress them. The covert and flexible nature of rumormongering made it a powerful political tool for oppressed people in societies of steep inequality and domination.[8] In Brazil and Cuba, rumor enabled shifting groups of enslaved and freed people to combine talk about the end of the illegal trade with African diasporic political worldviews. Official investigators ascribed insurgent intentions to activities that contributed to suppression. They alleged that the insurgents created new institutions against state power and formed alliances between rural and urban areas. The interplay between the inquisitors' cognitive frames and the insurgents' strategies, which were often illegible to those same inquisitors, shaped the course and understanding of events in the 1840s.

The authorities accused British diplomats and liberated Africans of conspiring with the insurgents. With or without this alleged help, the insurgents launched their own political projects. The countermeasures to rumors of insurrections would have consequences for the role of state power in the final suppression of the illegal trade to Brazil and Cuba. Insurgency and counterinsurgency would also shape how both state authorities and liberated Africans approached the position of liberated Africans in the social order that emerged after the end of the trade. Insurgency promised a political transformation in which anti-slave-trade law and African authority could unite to forge a future—or in which counterinsurgency could build new state powers to preserve slavery.

EXPANDING PLANTATION ZONES

Alongside the US South, Cuba and Brazil underwent an expansion in slavery in the early nineteenth century. Commodity production on plantations fed growing demand in industrializing North America and Britain. New technology, such as railroads and steamships, enabled the transportation of slave-produced goods on an unprecedented scale.[9] In Cuba, from the late eighteenth century onward, land proprietors envisaged importing large numbers of African captives to work as slaves on sugar plantations in the central region of Matanzas. Led by the proprietor and politician Francisco Arango y Parreño, they adopted new mechanized equipment, including steam-powered grinding mills, vacuum pans, and centrifuges. These techniques improved the quantity and quality of sugar extracted from cane. Arango, who later served as a Mixed Commission judge, was a consummate negotiator. He persuaded Madrid to exempt Cuba from a royal *cédula* of 1789, which granted greater legal protection and rights to slaves. He ensured that the Junta de Fomento had control over infrastructure projects and the customs and tolls to fund them. Cuba now had three major economic zones: the port of Havana in the northwest, sugar production in Matanzas, and coffee production in the southeast. French exiles from Haiti and plantation owners fleeing abolition and emancipation in the British Caribbean participated in the coffee industry.[10] Railway construction continued into the 1840s and 1850s, prioritizing sugar transportation to ports for world markets. The mechanization of production and transport increased enslavers' demands for captive laborers who could harvest crops and work on infrastructure projects. In a wider Atlantic context of constitutional abolition and anticolonial revolution, Cuba's elite was high on a sugar rush fueled by the illegal slave trade, innovative technology, and Spanish military government.

The illegal trade continued at a high rate after it became clear to merchants that the revised treaty of 1835 between Spain and Britain would not stop ships registered as American from transporting captives to Cuba.[11] The vast slave trade increased the African population in Cuba, prompting the government and proprietors to devise new techniques of racial terror. The *libres de color* (people born free or who had acquired freedom from slavery) were not prepared to suffer tightening state control in silence. In 1812, the authorities captured and executed José Aponte, a free Black carpenter, artist, and militia veteran. The authorities alleged that he had planned an island-wide uprising of slaves and *libres de color* and used his book of *pinturas* as evidence. These *pinturas*, probably now lost, depicted Black sovereignty in many settings. The Haitian Revolution, biblical references to Ethiopian kings, and British naval prohibition of the slave trade inspired the images. In the repressions of 1844, the authorities would return to Aponte's *pinturas* for clues about the slaves' plans. Historians disagree about whether the events of 1812 were a conspiracy or outright sedition, how far the plans had spread, and to what extent Aponte was the leader.[12] What mattered at the time was that the authorities continued to fear the ideological dimensions of Aponte's project, which threatened to breach extensive public censorship and restrictions on slaves' movements.

As well as political activities by *libres de color*, resistance by enslaved people changed in response to plantation expansion in the early nineteenth century. Many of the newly imported captives came from the Bight of Benin, where they had fought in wars and suffered captivity in battle.[13] These martial backgrounds prompted the authorities to increase patrols around the plantations. The intensive transshipment of captives—especially Yoruba captives—from the Bight in the early nineteenth century contrasted with the more sporadic, longer-term transshipment of captives from West Central Africa. In secret, Yoruba captives worshiped orisha gods, whereas Central African captives worshiped gods and ancestors through *nganga sacra*.[14] These beliefs were not incompatible, and indeed African people from both the Bight of Benin and West Central Africa played prominent roles in Abakuá secret societies that enslaved laborers from a third African region, Cross River, had introduced.[15] Nonetheless, Lucumí, Congo, and Carabalí people—as each dislocated group became known in Cuba—were subject to racialized management by Cuban enslavers and authorities. The potential for alliance between these three displaced groups became a major concern among enslavers.

The legal politics surrounding resistance movements by enslaved people intensified throughout the first half of the nineteenth century, resulting in new institutional powers and attempted reforms to manumission practices. In 1824, the colonial authorities established the Comisión Militar, a permanent military tribunal, as part of implementing the Spanish king's absolutist rule that replaced the Constitution of Cádiz.[16] In 1825, around two hundred enslaved people in Matanzas engaged in the most sustained uprising yet, killing fifteen white residents and damaging twenty-four estates. After the uprising, the Comisión gained new inquisitorial powers. It now had authority to interrogate, prosecute, and punish suspected insurgents, including by execution. Cuba's governing captain general realized that greater regulation of manumission could incentivize enslaved people to stay loyal to their owners. The authorities increased the prospect of manumission while tightening restrictions on people who achieved freedom.[17] In 1842, Captain General Geronimo Valdés launched an ambitious reform of *coartación*. It had hitherto been a customary practice, with enslaved people and enslavers negotiating over the purchase price of freedom; enslavers were able to withdraw from any agreement. The 1842 regulation compelled owners to honor the *coartación* agreement if an enslaved person had paid at least fifty pesos toward their purchase price.[18]

In the same year as the authorities introduced the new manumission regulation, they expelled David Turnbull, the British consul and superintendent of liberated Africans. His attempts to help Gavino petition and to apply liberated African status to all illegally trafficked slaves in Cuba were not his only abolitionist activities. Colonial administrators now accused him of collaborating with white elites and *libres de color* to foment an insurrection for anticolonial independence and slave emancipation. The conspiracy involved a Jamaican secret society, an expeditionary force led by an exiled Venezuelan general, and correspondence with Henri Boyer, a former president of Haiti.[19] Although Turnbull denied any involvement, at the very least he knew about a plot and perhaps promised arms to some plotters. They visited his successor, Joseph Crawford, in March–April 1843 to claim the weapons. Rapid plantation expansion and the illegal slave trade made Cuba in the 1840s a noticeably unstable place. Alongside resistance, colonial authorities feared that breakaway groups of proprietors sought independence or annexation by the United States, as preferable to rule by the declining Spanish Empire.

Throughout the 1840s, the colonial government remained concerned that liberated Africans' petitioning of multiple authorities would incite the enslaved population to make their own demands for freedom. In 1841, "a *moreno* who said he is an *emancipado*," Felix Lucumí, approached the captain general's secretary, with a horse, to claim a freedom letter. He said that his African name was Dari, he had arrived in Cuba on a slaving ship "long before the latest cholera outbreak," and he had been working on a sugar plantation.[20] The captain general ordered an investigation into whether Felix was a fugitive slave. Diego Fernandez Herrera approached a neighborhood deputy who was tasked with investigating the case to claim ownership of Felix. One José Joaquín Carrera said that the horse belonged to him.[21] In fact, Felix Lucumí had recently gone to the *síndico* to sue both Fernández Herrera and Carrera. Felix claimed that his previous owner had promised to free him in his will. The defendants argued that they were the deceased owner's creditors and claimed Felix as collateral on the debt.[22] With the case dragging on, Felix decided to go forum shopping, presenting himself as an *emancipado* to claim his freedom. The authorities returned Felix Lucumí to those who claimed him as property, but the prospect of enslaved people drawing on liberated Africans' legal strategies would endure into 1843–44. Although liberated Africans' strategies on their own behalf were not necessarily emancipatory, they created a precedent that enslaved people could use for their own insurgent projects.

As in Cuba, plantation production in Brazil depended on an extensive illegal trade in captive people. The absence of cost-effective technology for weeding or harvesting in coffee production prompted proprietors to devise a labor-intensive mode of production. They consequently relied on new imports of captives. Such was this reliance on the trade and the brutality of the work that between 1800 and 1850, 90 percent of the enslaved population in coffee-growing regions was African-born.[23] Credit from British intermediaries and Rio-based merchants, advanced against future crop yields, facilitated purchases of land and captives. Infrastructure investment helped proprietors transport coffee from the valley to downtown Rio for shipment before the advent of the railroad in the 1860s. From the 1840s, laborers constructed the Estrada Nova de Estrella, which ran from northern urban Rio through the imperial seat at Petrópolis to the most important regions of the Vale do Paraíba, including Vassouras and Valença.[24] The Brazilian strategy of economic development involved proprietors and merchants consolidating their wealth in land, labor, and capital at the expense of Indigenous people and African captives.

Proprietors produced coffee according to a strict seasonal schedule. In August, they burned newly acquired land for planting. September and October were dedicated to weeding, which was repeated in March and April. In May, the slaves harvested the coffee berries.[25] Laboring needs were lower during harvest than during cultivation, and so some of the enslaved were reassigned to other tasks including food production and work on provision grounds.[26] Unlike Cuban sugar production, coffee production in the Vale do Paraíba was profitable on small- and medium-sized estates, which were common because of the irregular *sesmaria* (colonial land-grant) system.[27] Individual plantations often had visitors, including itinerant laborers who hewed wood or did skilled piecework. Sometimes fugitives from slavery living under the guise of being free laborers did such work. At a time of increasing production, the infrastructure and porous plantations produced a fragmented landscape in which the enslaved developed knowledge of political power.

Accelerating cycles of commodity production increased the stakes of resistance in the 1830s and 1840s. Slaves who resisted their slave owners' demands were often punished with labor on public works. Penal work included building the roadways that linked the plantations to Rio. In the 1840s, infrastructure projects often used the labor of liberated Africans alongside convict slave labor. For example, in 1845, the authorities ordered up to twelve liberated Africans from the Casa de Correção to the Casa Imperial at Petrópolis, a key site on the Estrella roadway.[28] As porters, carpenters, and masons, liberated Africans and enslaved convicts worked alongside each other on the infrastructure of the exploitative system to which they were subjected. Insurrection and manumission related to how the enslaved understood hierarchies of power. Each route exposed the structural tension in slave societies between seeking freedom within the boundaries of the state-supported plantation economy and transgressing those boundaries. As commodity production increased in Brazil and Cuba in the 1840s, so too did the tension.

"IDEAS OF INSURRECTION" IN CUBA

Using careful planning around gender roles and Atlantic-wide connections, the insurgents burned estates across central Cuba.[29] Orchestrating the insurgency was a junta led by free people of color that connected white pro-independence activists with enslaved insurgents. The junta's president was the poet Gabriel de la Concepción Valdes, known as Plácido. Andres Dodge, a dentist who had trained in London, was the ambassador because he could speak English and French.[30] The insurgents struck at the height of the harvest. The initial response by the authorities reflected the economic value they sought to protect and their frustrations at failing to uncover all suspected participants. In January–February 1844, the governor of Matanzas, Antonio García Oña, and the Comisión Militar president, Fulgencio Salas, led the investigation. They reported their difficulties in finding culprits in Sabanilla, central Matanzas. The vague definition of insurrection in criminal law meant that the authorities and proprietors found a wide range of behavior suspicious: royal *cédulas* and colonial regulations established that district police officers must inform slave owners of insubordination or uprisings to coordinate suppression with them.[31] The Comisión Militar had the authority to investigate and punish "conspiracies against the established order."[32] Regulations presupposed a consensus between state institutions and slave-owning land proprietors at the very same time as some proprietors were advocating US annexation of Cuba. When investigators probed the insurgents' activities on the sugar estate La Andrea and a coffee estate in Limonar, they were concerned by their potential international communication. Papers written in foreign languages were as disturbing to them as stashes of guns, knives, and ammunition. The tone of García Oña's early correspondence reflected paranoia about identifying insurgents when he wrote about the "uprising that ~~the slaves blacks~~ those of the ingenio La Andrea concocted."[33] By late February, the police were urging García Oña to restrict slaves' movements to stop subversive speech and alliances with foreigners. The markets, streets, paddocks, and even pigsties were where the enslaved met "to communicate with each other and try to go ahead with their ideas of insurrection."[34]

One liberated African's actions during the insurrection revealed just how far those who were subject to anti-slave-trade law could insert themselves into Cuban antislavery politics. Mauricio Reyes, also known by the surnames García and Orré, gave several striking statements to the Comisión Militar. The Comisión prosecuted him for having "spoken alarming words about white people in the City of Matanzas." In the initial interrogation, Reyes said that he "is called Mauricio Reyes, from Africa of the Arara Nation, thirty years old, single, a dock worker, an *emancipado libre*, registered as a *vecino* in the City of Matanzas, and is Catholic."[35] Reyes's answer connected his African homeland and liberated African legal status to his claim to be a *vecino*. In Spanish law, a *vecino* was a subject as distinct from a foreigner, vassal, or individuals of otherwise limited legal personhood.[36] The *fiscal* (prosecutor) who interrogated Reyes questioned whether he was an *emancipado*, but the captain general confirmed his account. Reyes was liberated from the Spanish slaving ship *Negrito*, which was captured in 1832 with nearly five hundred people aboard. The captain general gave him his letter of emancipation in 1842.[37] Reyes's subsequent employment in dock work gave him access to foreign ships, which were vital sources of news in a colony that censored speech and the press. Reyes was similar to insurgents throughout the Atlantic world, who used international connections to formulate political projects inspired by the Haitian Revolution and British emancipation in the Caribbean.[38]

Reyes stood accused of participating in the insurrection through his prediction that "soon white people would have to be equal and that white people would be slaves of the black people."[39] The Comisión Militar accused him of saying these words in another person's home in the company of his partner, Isabel, an enslaved woman. Perhaps Reyes had learned these contrasting ideas of racial equality and white subjugation from his knowledge of anti-slave-trade law or from his dock work. Just as plausibly, Isabel could have been his inspiration. Reyes's profile, of having both additional resources as a free man and a direct personal link to slavery, was common to many leaders of antislavery insurrections.[40] There was no freedom of expression in Spanish colonial Cuba, and the Comisión Militar interpreted such speech as insurrectionary. The Comisión sentenced another person, Rita Dominguez, to a year in compulsory service in a hospital for "expressing the desires that animated her that all white people would be shot four times just like what was happening to people of her own color."[41] Faced with such a severe accusation, Reyes denied that he had said such words. The Comisión probably tortured him. He alleged that one accuser, the *comisario* (neighborhood magistrate with policing powers) Manuel Lara, owed him money and that Lara and another *comisario*, Perfecto Fernandez, bore him ill will for denouncing the insurrection to the governor of Matanzas.[42] The *comisarios* were the colonial agents most involved in people's daily lives in Cuba.[43] Reyes described how a wider circle connected to Lara and Fernandez had practiced witchcraft and hidden firearms and machetes in select locations throughout Matanzas.[44]

The authorities were particularly concerned by the prospect of a liberated African having the revolutionary ideas and financial resources to recruit a large group of people. How had Reyes acquired the money to lend to Lara? He answered that "in 1843 . . . he had won a prize of 500 pesos in the Lottery with which he bought some clothes and paid the *jornal* [daily wage] of his partner Isabel, the slave of Carlos Lucumí and the rest he saved with which he lent 240 pesos [to Lara] and the rest he saved in his bank to meet his needs."[45] Reyes used the money to set up an independent life and to fund his partner to have more of her own time. Perhaps she planned to pay *coartación* installments for self-purchase. By making counteraccusations about Lara and Fernandez and explaining how he used his money, Reyes seemed to be explaining his actions in a noninsurrectionary way. Earlier, in May 1844, the Comisión had prosecuted Joseph Kelly, a free Black man from the British colonial Bahamas, for seeking donations from slaves to help buy arms.[46] Free Black people like Reyes and Kelly had the knowledge and financial means to participate in the insurrection; the colonial authorities refused to believe their denials.

The authorities became obsessed with how the antislavery movement connected African spiritual practices to the interimperial legal politics of slave-trade suppression. Such a link risked uniting slaves and *libres de color* in a widespread insurgency. A *fiscal*, Carlos Ghersi, interrogated the enslaved man Tomas Lucumi. Lucumi revealed that free Black people led the insurgency and acquired "brujerías"—witchcraft techniques—and weaponry.[47] Considering that many enslaved Africans came from the Bight of Benin, "brujería" might have referred to spiritual beliefs in orishas. These gods related to the ancestors and polities in Benin. Regional practices of pooling money among group members to enable credit (*osusu*) could also explain the authorities' concern with the insurgents' alleged fund-raising activities. Regardless of specific ethnic backgrounds, many West African belief systems explained enslavement as the result of unjust interpersonal relations.[48] A malefactor seized power or wealth illegitimately through supernatural forces. The victims understood enslavement as a loss of honor and transoceanic shipment as a journey to another realm. Consequently, it would make sense to turn to spiritual practices to navigate the new world of the plantation. West African beliefs anchored people among the instability of daily life.[49]

Cabildos and churches also provided institutions and rituals to ensure loyalty in the face of political differences among the enslaved.[50] In Bainoa, west of Matanzas, a group of insurgents including Lucumí, Congo, and Carabalí people, and led by a "mulatto" freeman, sought to recruit enslaved people. They offered them emancipation, marriage to white women, and landownership if they promised to kill their enslavers. Belying contemporary reports of slaves' ignorance of Roman Catholicism, the insurgents secured these promises by removing the Eucharist from a church.[51] They forced one enslaved man to kiss it "to make him swear his loyalty to the exterminating party."[52] At its most basic, this coercive ritual was an oath of military loyalty. The insurgents may also have understood it as cementing a spiritual alliance that combined the human-divine relationship of orisha worship with the human-ancestor relationship of *nganga* worship. The ritual inverted the holy sacrament's function: instead of facilitating the flow of grace from God to human, it recruited divine power to human ends. The insurgents coerced specific enslaved men and women to join the cause or hold their tongues. The insurgents sought to enforce secrecy, marshal fighting forces, and spread psychological terror among the enemy.

Asked why people had joined the movement, Tomas Lucumi replied that the enslaved people on the plantation were "well treated and fed but they were invited to join the rising the aim of which was . . . to make themselves into the owners [*dueños*] of the Island and be free."[53] Together, West African spiritual practices and weapons would make insurgents into *dueños*, a significant term that often referred to owners of both plantation land and enslaved people. These insurgents either had direct experience or indirect experience through their parents of how an invading group in West Africa could claim land and incorporate a defeated enemy through enslavement. Conquerors also punished the defiant with outside sale or banishment. The insurgents thus had effective strategies of how to deal with defeated white enslavers and become *dueños*. Lucumi expressed the insurrection's aim as the logical response to enslaved status: regardless of how enslavers treated the slaves, they would wish to become free *dueños*.

In an illuminating letter to García Oña, Ghersi combined Lucumi's evidence with his perception of the threat posed by British maritime interdiction. Ghersi alleged that the principal insurgents were *libres de color* who "with witchcraft and promises amazed the slaves," thereby recruiting them as insurgents. The insurgents planned to burn the estates. The *libres de color* were "propagating among [the slaves] the idea, that they were waiting for English Ships, which must arrive on the Coast with Arms and Black men, to assist the rebels, to make themselves *dueños* of the island and distribute it among them."[54] The image harked back to the Black abolitionist sovereign republic in Aponte's *pinturas* and perhaps offers one reason why the authorities reexamined the legal case against him in 1844. Beyond Aponte, the image of maritime liberation alluded to anti-slave-trade activity. Eighteen months before the insurrection, Spanish authorities seized eighty captives from a recent landing near Yumurí and designated them as liberated Africans in Matanzas, probably sparking talk about how maritime suppression could produce a pathway to emancipation.[55] The reference to Black sailors on British vessels alluded to HMS *Romney*, the holding vessel of liberated Africans. HMS *Romney* also had soldiers of color from the West India Regiments serving on board.[56] Whenever these Black men under arms ventured on shore, they defied a law of 1839 that expelled foreign-born free people of color. The *Romney* also accommodated Turnbull after his banishment from Cuba. Perhaps the insurgents hoped that British ships would attack Cuban ports rather than limit their help to liberated Africans. A British attack might destroy the railway that was crucial for sugar exports. Some insurgents had occupied the railway in Matanzas the previous year.[57] By cutting off bureaucracy, credit, and the railway at Havana, ships could help overcome the institutions such as the Junta de Fomento.

The authorities—and subsequent historians—often assumed that the British recruited the slaves and *libres de color* to their abolition project.[58] But the inverse seems just as plausible. The insurgents used West African beliefs to supersede the limitations of British maritime prohibition and Spanish colonial manumission protocols. They remolded institutions to produce their own legal geography of insurgent sovereignty. Throughout late 1843 and 1844, the insurgents hid their projects from the state. The insurgents had over one hundred leaders in rural areas, including overseers and many women designated as "queens."[59] The authorities feared that this mobile and anonymous vanguard was behind the unexplained plantation burnings across Matanzas, including at Labotina, in March and April 1844.[60] Several investigations into fires ended inconclusively, with reports such as "a quietness met its extermination."[61] Although culprits were difficult to identify, so many fires on different plantations in a short space of time seemed likely to be a coordinated attack, and the silence a deliberate withholding of information.

THE COLONIAL COUNTERINSURGENCY

As well as burnings and stashes of weapons, the Comisión Militar alleged that insurgents sought to poison owners.[62] At the end of his interrogation, Mauricio Reyes denied that he knew the various Black people whom the Comisión Militar put to him as potential insurgents. Perhaps he regretted his denunciation and was trying to protect other people, or perhaps he was simply telling the truth. The Comisión sentenced him to four years in prison abroad and banned him from returning to Cuba; he probably never saw Isabel again.[63] His case gave the Comisión a lesson in how to suppress an antislavery insurrection by interrogating suspects and punishing them using mass imprisonment and penal deportation. The Comisión Militar sentenced Joseph Kelly, the man from the Bahamas accused of seeking funds to buy arms, to ten years' exile at Ceuta, the Spanish penal colony in North Africa.[64] The capacious insurgency plans—connecting men and women, plantations and towns, foreign sympathizers and Cuba-born freedpeople, *libres de color* and slaves—created a transformative countersovereignty that had a structural weakness. The police and Comisión Militar repressed the insurrection by dismantling any institution with alleged links to the enslaved or *libres de color*. The repression included organizations that were historically loyal to the Spanish regime, such as the militias. They punished any action, such as insubordination on a plantation, as though it were necessarily in support of insurrection. By late 1844, the counterinsurgency had triumphed.

Enslaved people suffered even more than the *libres de color* from the counterinsurgency. Scholars have emphasized the repression that *libres de color* faced.[65] Of 1,836 people sentenced by the Matanzas branch of the Comisión Militar, two-thirds were *libres de color*.[66] The authorities executed leading *libres de color* like Plácido, confiscated their property, and disbanded their militias. They also subjected liberated Africans to shipment to the British Caribbean. These measures targeted populations whose legal status undermined the connection between Blackness and enslavement. But enslaved people suffered the worst mortality and morbidity. Between 1841 and 1846, plantation labor conditions, the counterinsurgency, and the effect of a major hurricane that struck Matanzas caused the enslaved population to decline by 25 percent, even as the sugar plantation owners continued their aggressive expansion.[67] Three hurricanes in the 1840s prompted enslavers to reallocate enslaved laborers from coffee estates to sugar plantations to accelerate sugar production.[68]

The authorities and landowning elite used the counterinsurgency to recalibrate the risks involved in the slave economy. In the immediate aftermath, they considered newly imported captives to be the likeliest to rebel: the total number of disembarked captives fell to fourteen thousand between 1846 and 1850. This figure was the lowest for any five-year period since 1806–10 and the lowest until conclusive abolition in the late 1860s.[69] Enslavers focused their sinister energies on reproduction. Market prices reflected reproductive priorities: enslaved women became more valuable than men in the market between 1844 and 1846.[70]

As part of this recalibration, Spanish colonial law favored enslavers' claims to property rights in illegally trafficked captives. In 1844, a government-appointed commission proposed a criminal law that punished shipowners and outfitters with imprisonment. Punishments for complicit parties included imprisonment or loss of office.[71] Institutions and landowners in Cuba vigorously opposed the bill. According to Captain General O'Donnell, a comprehensive anti-slave-trade criminal ban "was against [Cuba's] prosperity and would produce . . . the deterioration of its commerce with direct harm to the country and to the positive interests of the Metropolis."[72] The result was a watered-down Ley Penal, which criminalized participation in a maritime slave-trading voyage but not any other complicit action, such as purchasing an illegally trafficked captive. The penal law also forbade official investigations on estates and inquiries into an enslaved person's origins. This narrow scope allowed the colonial administration to comply with treaty law and imperial orders while avoiding the complete prohibition of the trade. With such clear loopholes, in the 1850s merchants reopened the illegal slave trade. The trade to Brazil had ceased, and Cuba became the last substantial market for transatlantic trafficking. Slave-owning land proprietors viewed the trade, led by Portuguese merchants, with a mixture of pragmatism and suspicion. The trade both enabled them to expand their commercial operations and undermined their capacity to build an independence movement free from foreign commercial interference. The illegal trade helped shape the choice for enslavers between continued Spanish colonial rule, US annexation, and political independence as possible political futures.

At the same time, the counterinsurgency strengthened the role of state institutions in the slave economy. The Junta de Fomento demanded that the escape hatches from slavery that were opened by the 1842 Reglamento be nailed shut. As Felix Lucumí had shown, one such tactic was to claim status as a liberated African. The Junta sought to reduce this risk by demanding that future apprentices be segregated on public works projects. After the end of their service, the authorities intended to deport liberated Africans. The Junta also had authority to assign maroon people who had been arrested to compulsory labor.[73] The Junta asked for a ban on public gatherings by the *cabildos* and brotherhoods of *libres de color*. The captain general modified this proposal to a requirement for them to seek permission from the local authority to meet.[74] The Junta combined penal labor and infrastructure development to advance a counterinsurgent slave economy.

INSURGENT AFRO-BRAZILIAN POLITIES

Throughout the province of Rio de Janeiro during the presidency of Aureliano de Sousa e Oliveira Coutinho, rumors of an insurgent movement proliferated. From 1844 to 1848, talk of insurgency spread across Vassouras and Valença in the Vale do Paraíba and further south in Angra dos Reis. All were regions of intensive coffee production. Having benefited from the removal of US tariffs on Brazilian coffee exports, in the 1840s land proprietors took advantage of declining Cuban coffee production after the hurricanes to increase their own output. The insurgents planned to strike in late June 1848, during the harvest and when proprietors were under most pressure to pay off accumulated debts. On 7 June 1848, Aureliano Coutinho's successor as provincial president wrote an emergency report to his incoming replacement, the Visconde de Barbacena, about the planned uprising. "Manifesting itself even during the time of my predecessor, with some light symptoms," he explained, "it has lately assumed a character so pronounced that I judge it to be my duty to call your attention specifically to it."[75] The president was referring to an "insurrection" against slavery, as a special commission's confidential report a month later termed the threat.

According to the report, the insurrection was the master plan of a society, whose members had organized themselves into subunits of fifty enslaved people that were called "circles." Leading each circle was "a chief called a Tate who has six others as deputies, called Cambondos; three or more Black women, with the title of Mocambas do Anjo; and the rest are called Filhos do Terreiro."[76] These titles probably referred to the spiritual and political worlds of Africans captured in Kimbundu- and Ovimbundu-speaking areas of West Central Africa. "Cambondo" referred to a priest's assistant in what was probably a cult of affliction (*kimpasi*), a spiritual system that united knowledge of local ancestral spirits who have died a second death (*bisimbi*) with the Catholic Saint Anthony.[77] The enslaved identified both *bisimbi* and Saint Anthony as helping to cure illnesses, including collective misfortune. A reference in the report to iron may suggest that at least one Tate was a blacksmith, a skilled occupation for an enslaved person and one that featured in the origin stories of polities in West Central Africa.

The society agreed that "on the Day of São João this year all the chiefs must meet, to receive orders and instructions and proceed in the massacre mainly through poisoning administered to the *senhores* by the Mocambas do Anjo."[78] Considering the extensive provision grounds in the Vale do Paraíba, the insurgents had plenty of opportunities to grow the "large quantities of mineral and vegetable poisons" that the authorities found in the hands of some Tates and Mocambas.[79] The provision grounds where insurgents were most likely to have grown these poisons were liminal spaces. In Central Africa, such spaces were where people discussed hidden causes and their effects and where *bisimbi* dwelled.[80] Considering that some enslaved Africans understood transshipment as death, the insurgents may well have been consulting their fellow captives who had died a second death on the plantation. As *bisimbi*, these captives could guide an insurrection. For the enslaved, these were spirits with a "public" function in resolving collective misfortune.[81]

The insurgent rank-and-file adopted a name that connoted public space, *filhos do terreiro*, sons and daughters of the earth. Their name was a double entendre, referring both to the central square that dominated plantation space and to Brazilian territory more generally. The term also implied a spiritual alliance. *Terreiro* was the place of Candomblé worship. As a blacksmith, the Tate would have also been an honorable figure in Yoruba belief systems, related to Ogún, the god who animated agricultural tools and weapons.[82] As in Cuba, a coalition between Yoruba and West Central African enslaved people was crucial to the insurrection. The insurgents were not simply poisoning slave owners and fleeing slavery; they were claiming Brazilian land on their own terms.

As the *mocambas do anjo* suggested, leadership in such a polity included women. Atlantic slave revolts featured many men as prominent leaders, such as Tacky of Jamaica and Nat Turner in Virginia. Enslaved men could look to dominate women through revolt. Yet enslaved women from Central Africa had plenty of scope to advance themselves as leaders endowed with specialist knowledge. Two years after the planned insurgency, and further south in Rio Grande do Sul, a freed Afro-Brazilian woman, Maria José, obtained a license to parade through the streets in the role of Queen Njinga. As queen of the Ndongo (in present-day Angola) in the seventeenth century, Njinga sold slaves but also resisted Portuguese imperial expansion. Maria José's parade sought to raise donations for health-care and funeral costs.[83] Of course, the insurgents may not have thought Njinga worthy of emulation because of her slave-trading, but her example of Central African queenship was probably available to them.

Throughout the Vale, rumors of insurrection swirled with revolutionary ideas. In Lorena, in 1848, a *liberto*, Agostinho, led a movement in which

The *terreiro* was where the enslaved workforce assembled and where they dried the coffee. Marc Ferrez's idealized photographs from the 1880s erased the violence inherent in plantation agriculture. (Marc Ferrez/Coleção Gilberto Ferrez/Acervo Instituto Moreira Salles)

enslaved people planned to revolt on the festival of São João for the "abolition of slavery in Brazil." As in the insurrection organized by the "circles," a secret society organized the movement in Lorena. Interrogators described the movement as "a timely plan combined with enough premeditation, from what is understood by the relevant legal Process, and the interrogations of the blacks, when they declare that they have met to gather firearms to achieve their freedom by means of force, for which the English will help them given that Brazil finds itself sufficiently beholden to the English Nation, and so much more for having ended the traffic in slaves, and other propositions of this nature."[84] Agostinho knew how to read and write, and he met a Frenchman, Jacob Troller, who discussed newspaper reports with him. In these conversations, Troller made "observations about the current state of Brazil, disapproving of slavery, and pondering about its consequences, that it could lead to similar ones to those on the Island of Saint Domingue."[85] The same year that Agostinho and Troller deliberated antislavery, one illegally enslaved young man, Luis Gama, escaped from his enslaver in Lorena and joined the military.[86] Gama would go on to play an important role in legal activism against slavery.

Liberated Africans served as apprentices on projects that connected the Vale with Rio. As well as labor at the Imperial Palace, liberated Africans worked in a gunpowder factory on the Rua da Estrella that ran from Rio to the Vale do Paraíba.[87] On the other side of the provincial border with São Paulo, liberated Africans worked in an iron foundry at Ipanema alongside slaves and convicts. In 1846, liberated Africans became the single largest workforce there, and the director frequently reported issues with discipline and flight.[88] The rumors of mass uprising against the illegal trade featured visions of Afro-Brazilian political formation that drew on African, British imperial, and revolutionary Haitian precedents. The rumors of Afro-Brazilian insurgency affected the southern regions that were most transformed by illegal trafficking.

An insurrection was a specific crime in Brazil's Código Criminal, a code coauthored by the proslavery politician Bernardo Pereira de Vasconcelos. Vasconcelos celebrated the slave trade because it had "civilized" Brazil by producing economic growth.[89] A section of "Crimes against internal security and public tranquility" specified conspiracy, rebellion, and sedition as crimes, with insurrection the most severe. Unlike the other crimes, insurrection involved twenty or more slaves trying to "gain freedom by means of force."[90] Freedom must be the intention and force the means. An insurrection targeted the landowning enslavers, who were advised by one influential manual to see themselves as "having the attributes of legislator, magistrate, commander, judge, and sometimes executioner."[91] In February 1848, the proprietors played this role with even greater enthusiasm because the emperor made an extended visit to the Vale do Paraíba.[92] During his stay on plantations, enslaved people would have cleaned the estate house, swept the *terreiro*, and prepared the food that the emperor ate. Enslaved people were at once intimate with and distant from the emperor's body. The timing and scale of the insurrection suggested a strike not just against the odd slave owner but against the alliance of state power with plantation capital.

Insurgent rumors in the Vale add to prevailing explanations of slave resistance in nineteenth-century Brazil. Scholars have carefully examined fugitivity to *quilombos* (settlements of self-liberated peoples), popular monarchism, and revolts as calculated attempts to exit slavery. Such activities could also aim to achieve postmanumission inclusion as citizens.[93] The projected insurrections of 1848 aimed neither to flee from the state nor to work within its confines. Instead, the insurgents' "circles" and conversations about Haiti were forms of public deliberation about a political future that aimed to transcend the state. The insurgents wanted to create Afro-Brazilian polities. Afro-Brazilian polity formation depended on developing connections beyond the plantation. Here, the special commission referred explicitly to the liberated Africans (*os africanos livres*). As the report self-pityingly put it, "the Government did a great disservice to the Country when it improvidently poured into the interior millions of Africans, whom it declared to be *livres*, to whom a Curador was appointed, obliged always to repeat to them this proposition [of freedom], and to take care of how those who bought the services of these Africans treated them."[94] The report exaggerated: in fact, there were around ten thousand liberated Africans in Brazil, rather than millions. In anti-slave-trade regulations, the *curador* provided liberated Africans with an advocate regarding their labor and any future property in a foreign country. This legal protection was unavailable to most enslaved people. The commission provided no further identifying details about how the liberated Africans and *curador* may have been involved in the planned insurrection.

Perhaps the most startling connection between liberated Africans and the insurrection lay elsewhere. There is an intriguing lead in the survey of over 850 liberated Africans conducted by the British diplomat Robert

Hesketh in Rio two years after the insurrection. Hesketh interviewed fourteen people apprenticed by Senator Aureliano de Sousa e Oliveira Coutinho, during whose provincial presidency the insurrection plans allegedly began. Interviewing the liberated Africans at Aureliano Coutinho's home on Rua do Lavradio in central Rio, Hesketh never asked whether they had been insurgents. Yet their answers to questions about their welfare pointed to the possible communications between liberated Africans and enslaved people in Rio. The apprentices Francisco and Pedro had itinerant jobs as a hawker and muleteer, respectively, enabling them to handle cash and equipment. They could move around the city with few restrictions. Other apprentices were not so fortunate. Some told Hesketh that they did not know how long they had been in Aureliano Coutinho's service or even how much they earned. They were subject to his whims in moving between the townhouse and a *fazenda* out of town. One interviewee, Luzia, told Hesketh that Aureliano Coutinho "had many more [apprentices] at one time but several are now dead."[95]

Further down the same street, Generosa, apprenticed to a different master, complained about the kidnapping of fellow liberated Africans. Probably using the term *companheiros* (shipmates), Generosa told Hesketh that "she was one of the Africans deposited at Armação & [has] never seen any of her companions who were stolen from thence."[96] The threat of illegal enslavement pervaded life for liberated Africans. Could these Africans have communicated Aureliano Coutinho's movements to the insurgents in the Vale do Paraíba over the past four years? Did the two groups find solace in a shared frustration about the limitations of British maritime interdiction and the fear of the spiraling labor demands in coffee production? Placing the confidential report's surface meaning within this social context reveals the possible connections between the *curador*, liberated Africans, and enslaved people. But if these connections did exist, as the inquisitors feared, the insurgents never revealed them, and Hesketh did not uncover them. The special commission claimed that the "emissaries of the Chiefs of the Corte [the city of Rio] were hawkers" who traveled between plantations with insurgent instructions. The hawkers "animated the Blacks saying that so many blacks should not be subject to so few Whites."[97] Hawking was typical labor for enslaved men and women looking to earn cash for self-purchase, as well as for freedpeople and liberated Africans. They were also prominent fixtures in Rio's *quitandas*: licensed food stalls or shops in markets. In the 1840s in

Santa Anna, the same parish where one commissioner, Jose Alves Carneiro, first practiced as a judge, 30 of 348 businesses (8.6 percent), including *quitandas,* had African owners. These *quitandeiras* knew how to obtain legal recognition from the state and to establish financial credit relationships. Women market stallholders could have offered legal and financial literacy to the insurgents.[98]

SECRECY AND POLICING IN THE BRAZILIAN COUNTERINSURGENCY

Even if the insurgent polities existed only in rumor, they had political consequences, as the special commission well knew. Assigned by the provincial legislative assembly, the commission's three members had personal experience in the law and governance of a slave society. Francisco Gê Acaiaba de Montezuma was the commission's most experienced member. He was a veteran of the independence struggle who adopted a name to reflect the political heritage of the Indigenous Americas. Montezuma was the founding president of the Instituto de Advogados Brasileiros (Institute of Brazilian Lawyers) in 1843. He was also a former minister of justice and a committed abolitionist. The second member was Francisco Dias da Motta, an established administrator who was director of provincial Rio's school system from 1846.[99] The third member had the most relevant local political experience: Jose Alves Carneiro, who began his career as a municipal judge in Rio. In 1840, he advertised his legal services from his home, including dispute resolution, swift criminal justice, and resolutions to minor breaches of municipal regulations.[100] This was not necessarily surprising, as judges offered mediation between slave owners and the enslaved outside formal court settings.[101] By June 1848, Carneiro was president of the legislative assembly.[102] Montezuma, Dias da Motta, and Carneiro were all members of the provincial assembly. As a commission, they were an inquisitorial body that combined judicial and legislative functions. The elder statesman, the bureaucrat, and the assembly president interrogated captured insurgents and informants to produce a secret report, which became the most important source for understanding the insurrection of 1848.

From the archival sources that remain, it is impossible to analyze the polity that the insurgents envisaged regarding its constitutional arrangements, representative institutions, or terms of inclusion and exclusion. The insurgents' ultimate vision was allegedly to massacre the white population and install "as king of these places a Tate Corongo."[103] The society had members who communicated between plantations and even foreign agents who connected the insurrection to downtown Rio. "These places" could therefore refer to the region encompassing urban Rio and the Vale do Paraíba. If membership were to range from enslaved agricultural laborers in Vassouras to agents in Rio, the polity's arrangements would need to accommodate political differences regarding urban and rural representation and priorities. According to the commission, the society's actions constituted the crime of insurrection: gaining freedom by means of force.

Surrounded by news and rumors from the market and port, the *quitandeiras* could provide intelligence to the inland insurgents. After months, possibly years, in the planning, why wait until June 1848 to strike? Perhaps the hawkers had told the plantation insurgents about reports of revolutions in Europe. If political turmoil caused European demand for coffee to fall, landowners would be weakened, and the provincial government would have reduced tax revenue.[104] A financial crisis would exacerbate an unstable police force, which Aureliano Coutinho had criticized in his final presidential address as being in "almost total disorganization."[105] With potentially fewer police officers patrolling the plantations, the insurrection would have a higher chance of success. The commission denied the possibility of this astute planning, instead insisting with racial stereotypes that Afro-Brazilian people required a "superior intelligence" to direct them.[106] As in Cuba, state authorities attributed radical politics to white outsiders rather than enslaved and freed people, even as they punished insurgents.

In the aftermath of the suppression of the thwarted insurrection, Montezuma, Dias da Motta, and Carneiro recommended increased policing of plantations. The commission urged the provincial government to employ three hundred new police officers to patrol the plantations in proportion to the enslaved population. They argued that the Guarda Nacional was insufficient. The revolutions in Europe had reduced demand for coffee and thus government revenues from exports. The commission recommended funding the additional police force by cutting expenditure elsewhere, including reducing the number of regular police *soldados* by 40 percent. Defunding other state projects would increase funding for the police. The assembly supported the commission's proposal and passed the amended police budget.[107] The special commission also recommended deporting foreigners "judged to be dangerous to public order and in this category the liberated Africans are included."[108] Although that proposal failed, the commission's recommendations generally dovetailed with the slave-owning land proprietors' postinsurrection plans. Launching a Comissão Permanente for mutual defense in Vassouras in 1854, the proprietors labeled the slaves "our uncompromising enemy," a ritual declaration to bind the proprietors into a collective force.[109] The Comissão rejected the long-standing customary practice of assigning provision grounds to slaves. They sacrificed the benefits of provision grounds, such as an increased food supply and crop diversity, in favor of extra coffee and less chance of poison.

The consequences of an insurgent polity spread into the realm of interimperial politics about slave-trade suppression. In all the published provincial reports and assembly debates, Brazilian statesmen avoided acknowledging that the rumors of insurrection in the Vale existed. The commissioned report survived only because the British chargé d'affaires in Rio, James Hudson, sent a copy to the foreign secretary, Lord Palmerston, on 20 February 1850. Hudson had an extensive network of informants in Brazil and conceivably knew about the insurrection before that date. Yet he waited until almost two years after the insurrection to send the report. The most plausible explanation is that Hudson wanted to use the report publicly to push Brazil's reluctant politicians into legislating for suppression. In 1848, after news of the insurrection broke, the imperial parliament resumed debate on the Barbacena Bill. The bill proposed new criminal penalties for slave-trading but declared that all Africans shipped to Brazil between the dead-letter Lei Feijó of 1831 and the new act would become lawfully held slaves. Despite its failure to pass in the Câmara in 1837, the Barbacena Bill now looked like a promising option to stop imports of African captives. Comprehensive slave-trade prohibition would reduce the number of African immigrants, whom the authorities perceived as posing a risk of insurrection.

In January 1850, Hudson spied an opportunity to pressurize the Brazilian government to pass a new anti-slave-trade law. Shortly before landing in Brazil, the captives aboard the slaving ship *Santa Cruz* "were about to rise against their masters, but one of the negresses peached, in consequence of which there was a great flogging on board and seven of the Africans were [flogged] to death."[110] The crew landed hundreds of captives at Rio de Janeiro.[111] They smuggled the captives into slavery with the help of a judge and local people. The British ship *Cormorant* subsequently seized and burned the *Santa Cruz* inside Brazilian waters. Hudson knew that this seizure broke the law of nations that protected shipping in territorial waters in peacetime. He also knew that the *Santa Cruz* case had rare value. No longer could the Brazilian government claim that the illegal trade was a private enterprise beyond regulatory control. The *Santa Cruz* case revealed that the local free population and the judiciary supported illegal trafficking.

The rear admiral, Barrington Reynolds, had ordered the *Cormorant*'s captain to make no further captures within Brazilian waters lest he breach treaty and parliamentary law. The ubiquitous Hudson took a different view, wishing to use the case as a pressure point. Perhaps he was enraged by the murders committed by the crew of the *Santa Cruz*. Perhaps Hudson saw Brazilian parliamentary protests against the capture as a sign of weakness. He notified Palmerston that the Brazilian government was prepared to start negotiating a new anti-slave-trade treaty. Hudson encouraged Palmerston to replace cumbersome naval steamers with lighter Banshee vessels to increase the number of captures along the Brazilian coast.[112] On 20 February, Hudson sent the secret report of 1848 and information about the *Santa Cruz* case. The parallel was clear. In both instances, the Brazilian government was "exposing the lives and fortunes of Brazilians, and the very existence of the Empire, to the chances of anarchy, massacre, and ruin."[113] Hudson was a far more astute diplomat than Turnbull had been in Cuba. By sending the secret report in his regular dispatches, he knew that by custom Britain's Parliament would publish it, causing embarrassment for the Brazilian government. Hudson leaked the special commission's report at the exact moment when it would both distract from a British breach of international law *and* present the Brazilian government as incapable of protecting the public without a new anti-slave-trade law.

Hudson's fateful dispatch arrived on Palmerston's desk on 5 April, an opportune time in Whitehall. By early 1850, an influential parliamentary select committee into the efficacy of naval suppression had been in full swing for almost two years. It regularly heard evidence about the failings of abolition policies. One naval surgeon's account of his service in the 1840s declared naval suppression of the Brazilian slave trade a failure.[114] William Hutt, the committee's chair and an opponent of naval suppression, proposed a parliamentary motion to withdraw from treaty arrangements that obligated Britain to maintain the naval squadrons. Lord John Russell's Whig government presented the issue as a vote of confidence in his administration.[115] The government won the vote by 232 votes to 154, but the strength of opposition threatened to undermine the naval squadrons.[116] Following the crucial vote, Russell was under pressure to consolidate parliamentary and public support for the naval squadrons. The earl of Minto, a former first lord of the admiralty, held meetings with the celebrity naval officer Joseph Denman and a former naval officer turned Whig MP, Dudley Pelham. Minto confidentially reported to Russell that Denman and Pelham advocated "inshore instead of distant cruising," that is, more barracoon raids.[117] The joint plan, based on Denman's charts of slave-trading locales on the West African coast, clearly aimed at suppressing the Brazilian slave trade by cutting off supply on the other side of the Atlantic. His collaborator, Pelham, rubbed his hands at the prospect of a preemptive strike to "defeat the attacks of the *Huttites*."[118] Russell authorized British naval vessels to seize slave ships inside territorial waters.

On 22 April, the law officers vindicated the *Cormorant*'s capture of the *Santa Cruz* by issuing new advice to the Admiralty. Existing legislation contained "no Restrictions as to the limits within which the Search, Detention, and Capture of Slave Traders under the Brazilian flag, or without any Nationality, are to take place."[119] Such advice ignored customary international law that specified that waters up to three nautical miles from the coast were sovereign spaces. Upon receiving the new instructions on 22 June, Admiral Reynolds ordered naval captures inside Brazilian waters and ports. Subsequent cases of controversial seizure, including by the *Sharpshooter* at Macaé and the *Cormorant* at Paranaguá, sparked violent resistance by locals. A municipal judge at Paranaguá labeled British actions "verdadeira pirataria" (true piracy) and a breach of "direito internacional" (international law).[120] On 11 July, the Conselho do Estado, the highest executive body, which included the emperor and cabinet members, discussed possible responses to Britain. The following day, the government resumed a debate, in secret, in the Câmara on a bill that would strengthen criminal penalties against new importations of African captives.[121] The bill applied criminal punishments to slave-trading and increased the powers of authorities to investigate disembarkations. Unlike the Barbacena Bill, the new bill was silent about the status of Africans trafficked between 1831 and 1850, including those who constituted the vast majority of the enslaved workforce on coffee plantations in the southeast.[122]

Rumor was not only a subaltern political tool but also a way for elites to justify political action. Prominent among them was a man who, as chief of police in Rio in the 1830s, had been responsible for monitoring liberated Africans. Despite Eusébio de Queirós's position, the apprentice Claro had escaped from service to him. In 1848, Queirós became minister of justice. He devised the new anti-slave-trade law in 1850. Queirós later said that rumors of insurgency prompted landowners to change their mind about suppression: "some occurrences or rather symptoms of a most serious nature, which revealed themselves in Campos, in Espirito Santo, and in other places like in the important municipalities of Valença and Vassouras, produced a terror, that I shall call salutary, because they caused opinion against the traffic to develop and be acknowledged."[123] Regardless of whether Queirós was sincere, he revealed how rumors of insurgency shifted the terms of debate from complicity with the illegal trade to political action in favor of suppression. Hudson also used rumor, not only to cover British attacks on Brazilian sovereignty that breached international law but also to retain British pressure even after Queirós introduced the new law. Hudson reported Brazil's offer to negotiate a new treaty in exchange for revoking the naval instructions, but he also advised the British government to maintain the pressure. In October 1850, a British cruiser captured the slaver *Amelia* and transferred seventy-two liberated Africans to Jamaica.[124] As Brazil's enforcement of its domestic anti-slave-trade law improved, the British nexus of diplomats and naval officers shifted from coastal aggression to supplying intelligence to Brazil.

The new anti-slave-trade bill had profound consequences for both enslavers and the enslaved. For slave-owning proprietors, coffee production by slave labor would continue but with increased police powers to investigate trafficked African people on their land. Enslaved people would now live under an arbitrary legal division that separated those who were illegally trafficked between 1831 and 1850 from those who were illegally trafficked after 1850. State authorities would not intervene to liberate the former, yet they would seize the latter and declare them to be liberated Africans. Insurgent rumor compelled Brazilian politicians to replace the failed 1831 law and bilateral treaty with a stronger domestic anti-slave-trade law.

In the expanding plantation zones of the 1840s, insurgent politics produced intense battles about the ramifications of the anti-slave-trade legal regime for slave societies. In Cuba, Mauricio Reyes's actions demonstrated how a liberated African's legal status made him both a potential insurgent and a target for state suppression. The legal position of liberated Africans made insurgent plans more potent because they raised the prospect of assistance from British diplomats or international allies. Insurgent plans fanned out from rural Matanzas, based on harnessing African diasporic beliefs and the aid offered by Turnbull. Insurgents fought against both plantation labor and colonial military rule. In Brazil, rumors indicated that insurgents in the Vale do Paraíba and urban Rio forged an alliance by using Yoruba and Central African practices. If the insurgent plan did exist, it involved a network, allegedly including liberated Africans and hawkers, that would rise against the proprietors and the proslavery government. As insurgents, they aimed to dismantle the institutions that underpinned plantation production and the legal geography of racial slavery. They would then redistribute land and install their own political authorities. Diasporic beliefs and practices, which drew on liberated Africans' presence, helped create new cohesive popular movements. These beliefs and practices critiqued the individualism and incessant accumulation of a highly unequal world in which rulers' actions were guided by material acquisition. They also articulated a vision of justice that could not be achieved within the formal legal order of Brazil or colonial Cuba or by British gunboat imperialism. Even if the insurgency was no more than rumor, it provoked both counterinsurgent forces among political authorities and visions of freedom among African diasporic groups that would endure long thereafter.

Insurgent activities exposed the limitations of the anti-slave-trade legal regime, and their projects failed in the face of massive state counterinsurgencies. The counterinsurgencies strengthened state apparatus to confront both enslaved Africans and British agents. In both Brazil and Cuba, the counterinsurgencies involved the state applying criminal law to subjects who participated in the politics surrounding the continuing illegal trade. State authorities applied criminal law to abolitionist insurgents rather than to traffickers. The counterinsurgent actions of state authorities set a precedent for new measures beyond prize and treaty law in ending the largest slave-trading routes, which were protected by an influential elite.

Rumors began to affect the legal order of slave societies. Brazil's Conservative government and Cuba's colonial administration initially took different paths in devising their own anti-slave-trade measures after the high tide of insurgency. The Brazilian executive and legislature defined anti-slave-trade law to apply to future transoceanic voyages alone. They thereby avoided liberating any African people illegally trafficked before the new legislation came into force. Strengthened police and naval forces applied the law on ships, inside territorial waters, and on nearby plantations. State authorities hoped that they could make suppression safe for economic growth driven by plantation slavery. Unlike Brazil's new anti-slave-trade law, in Cuba the Ley Penal of 1845 ruled out official investigations on plantations in search of illegal landings. Instead, the Spanish colonial administration hoped to use the newly strengthened state apparatus to deter any threat to the resurgent slave trade. The trade would continue to provide the captive labor force for Cuba's export-led agriculture. The colonial authorities sought to manage the attendant risks of British intervention, insurgencies by enslaved and free people of color, US annexationism, and a nascent independence movement. The path taken by Brazilian authorities in 1850–51 would eventually be followed by Spanish colonial authorities over a decade later: to adopt slave-trade suppression as the only way to protect sovereignty and slave ownership. Such a path had the unintended consequence of sparking debates about property rights in slave societies.

CHAPTER SIX

The Rupture of Property Rights

LATER, CHIPIANDA REMEMBERED HOW MANY of her fellow captives had suffered from so long at sea and then so many days on the Cuban mountainside. On the beach below, the traffickers burned the slave ship to remove evidence of the illegal landing. They hid the captives up on the mountain. As Chipianda recalled, the captives had so little to eat that "for that reason many died, counting them on her fingers and toes two or three times, she said it was so."[1] Since 1817, enslavers had trafficked millions of African captives like Chipianda into Brazil and Cuba in breach of treaty and domestic law. A typical slaving ship was financed by a major merchant and landed at a secluded coastal site. The merchant's armed subordinates marched the captives inland to an estate. After a few days, the merchant approached a corrupt judge to authorize a register of the captives as his property or agreed to sell the captives to a counterpart. Many forms of historical slavery are based on the fiction that property in a person is lawful. As revealed by Chipianda's testimony to a domestic court, the tactics of an illegal slave trader, ranging from creating a mountainside hideout to fake paperwork, crafted an additional fiction: that a criminal act could be converted into a property right. In the 1850s and 1860s, how did such practices come to an end?

Chipianda testified within two powerful contexts: the trauma caused by being trafficked from sub-Saharan Africa to the Cuban mountainside and the power dynamics of the courtroom. Understanding her testimony requires a method that attends to the story that she told and its political implications. It means understanding the judge as somebody whose verdicts decided who was worthy of freedom, somebody whose words made law. In many different contexts, judges have possessed the discretionary power to construct meaning with their judgments, including about the worthiness of immigrant people's claims against deportation.[2] Many aspects of Chipianda's story remain unknown. She communicated through interpreters named Gonzalez and Mayoli; the fact that only their first names were recorded suggests that they were probably enslaved or free people, perhaps born in Africa. We cannot know whether any meaning was lost in interpretation.[3] A notary transcribed her testimony as part of creating a trial record. He did not describe Chipianda beyond her presumed age (twenty-two) or the layout of the courtroom. Most importantly, the notary did not record exactly how many people she counted.[4] But putting Chipianda's story into conversation with those of other deponents and official correspondence reveals something new: how the legal politics of property rights changed during final suppression.

Under pressure from British anti-slave-trade diplomats and naval officers, internal insurgents, and shifting international allegiances, new anti-slave-trade measures came into force in Brazil in the 1850s and Cuba in the 1860s. These measures resulted in the "sudden death" of the slave trade to Brazil in 1856, in the same decade when slavery in Brazil reached its peak. British anti-slave-trade actions have often taken the limelight in a vibrant scholarly debate.[5] The immediate trigger of British naval captures inside Brazilian waters in early 1850 aligned with British medium-term goals since the 1810s to suppress the trade and open Brazilian markets to manufactured goods. The Afro-Brazilian planned insurrection in 1848 and similar projects into the 1850s provided a radical rationale for stopping imports of more African captives and bolstering the policing of plantations.[6] Brazilian statesmen's concerns that trafficked Africans were causing new epidemics of yellow fever and their desire to use suppression to gain British neutrality to wage war in the Rio de la Plata provided additional causes for a new suppression law.[7] In truth, no single decisive cause could explain the thrust toward the specific anti-slave-trade regulation that emerged in Brazil. None of these actors would have thought that the new anti-slave-trade law and its effects were the most desirable way to pursue their divergent objectives. This chapter instead focuses on the new anti-slave-trade court's operations by investigating its most prominent effect. The court changed understandings of property rights in illegally trafficked Africans, with implications for property rights in a slave society overall.

In the late 1860s, over fifteen years after the new anti-slave-trade law came into force in Brazil, the slave trade to Cuba came to an end. Unlike Britain, the United States, and (to a lesser extent) Brazil, Cuba lacked representative institutions that could give a platform to abolitionist ideas and practices. The imperial regime refused to grant any such representative body. Consequently, historians have tended to look outside Cuba to explain the end of the illegal trade. Many scholars have concluded that the decision by the Lincoln administration during the Civil War to stop US participation in the slave trade was the most important factor.[8] In 1862, the administration agreed to a treaty with Britain for the mutual right of search on the high seas, which ended the use of the US flag by slavers to avoid searches by anti-slave-trade squadrons.[9] The United States' shift in favor of suppression was vital, but it alone situates the end of the trade too early in the 1860s.

Other scholars have focused on metropolitan policy at a time when slavery was in crisis in Cuba. In the early 1860s, captains general such as Domingo Dulce y Garay and Francisco Serrano y Domínguez requested from Madrid the authority to search estates for illegal landings, but were rebuffed.[10] In 1865–66, metropolitan policy began to shift toward suppression, as the administration could reallocate naval and military resources following the failed recolonization of the Dominican Republic. These newly available resources converged with pressure from Puerto Rico and Cuba for major reforms of colonial taxation and governance.[11] They dovetailed with efforts by captains general to stop illegal landings and the emergence of an abolitionist political movement in Spain. Even so, the Spanish authorities banned the captain general from recognizing a Cuba-based abolitionist association because it feared that it would extend its political activism beyond suppression.[12] The new imperial anti-slave-trade law of 1866 did not go as far as defining the slave trade as piracy. Scholars have proposed interactions between US, Spanish, diplomatic, and ideological factors in ending the slave trade to Cuba.[13] One version of this argument contends that the trade died a "market death" in which potential buyers were no longer prepared to pay the price required to cover the traders' costs for illegal trafficking.[14] The focus on a "market death" has directed attention to price and cost and obscured how far the law framed market conditions.

The application of the new anti-slave-trade laws revealed how enslavers tried to claim property rights in illegally trafficked people by moving them from landing sites to inland plantations. Enslavers fabricated an ultimately rootless title to property to make ownership of a person socially permissible. Enslavers made the title seem rooted through social performance: they carried paperwork, they managed their households, and they presented themselves in public as though the title was self-evident. Scholars have revealed that enslavers fabricated such titles to reenslave people who were emancipated in the Haitian Revolution and migrated to Cuba and Louisiana.[15] There were no standardized ways to recognize free status within and between polities. This absence provided a large threshold in which enslavers fabricated titles to property to reenslave free people. In the era of the illegal transoceanic trade, these attempts to devise rootless titles to property grew in scale and complexity. Enslavers moved newly trafficked people rapidly between plantations, forced them into agricultural work, and used paperwork and performance to present their fabricated property title to wider society. Every time state officials captured newly trafficked people on land in Brazil and Cuba, they exposed enslavers' attempts to create property rights in illegally trafficked captive people.

Brazilian and Spanish colonial courts turned to various sources of evidence to adjudicate cases. The courts heard testimony from liberated Africans, which formed a large documentary archive. In these records, liberated Africans explained that they had been illegally trafficked and wished to be free. The courts tested whether any of these liberated Africans spoke Spanish or Portuguese, which might indicate that they had spent significant time in Cuba or Brazil instead of being recent arrivals. Other evidentiary tests included physical examinations of brand marks, scarification, and the effects of disease prevalent aboard slaving ships. Cases of the illegal trade provide new insight about how liberated Africans' testimony to judges created a route out of illegal enslavement and toward nominal freedom. Corrupt participation in the illegal trade, often encouraged by the official hierarchy rather than punished as deviant behavior, became exposed to judicial and even public scrutiny.[16]

In these court proceedings, liberated Africans' testimony ruptured the default social assumption that an enslaver's claim to have property rights in illegally trafficked people was true. Their testimony exposed traffickers' actions to legal decision-making. It turned the illegal trade from an activity that was socially permissible to one that entailed too many political risks to continue. Liberated Africans' testimony began the slow process of rupturing the powerful assumption in a slave society that somebody who claimed a person of color as property in fact had this right. This rupture casts final suppression in Brazil and Cuba in a new light. The consequence of liberated Africans' testimony was that the new anti-slave-trade court in Brazil played a crucial role in the "sudden death" of the Brazilian trade. In Cuba, their testimony shifted the legal and political framework that made market conditions averse to the illegal trade. In both locales, the rupture of property rights in these domestic courts provoked widespread reflection on the future of slavery.

REMAKING SOVEREIGNTY IN A SLAVE SOCIETY

On 4 September 1850, Brazil's legislature passed Lei 581 abolishing the Brazilian trade in enslaved African people, the largest in the Atlantic world. To enforce the new anti-slave-trade law from October 1850 onward, the government issued Decreto 708, which authorized the Brazilian navy to seize suspected slave ships. The decree gave jurisdiction to a particular court, the Auditoria Geral da Marinha in Rio de Janeiro, to determine the legality of seizures. It also established provincial auditors in other port cities.[17] Everyone implicated in the struggle for abolition—British diplomats and naval officers, insurgents, the Conservative cabinet, abolitionist campaigners, slave-trading merchants, and captives on incoming ships—would now be assessing how far the new law would be enforced. The record was not promising: both the Liberal and Conservative parties rowed back from the first criminal law, the Lei Feijó, in the 1830s. Still, the month of September was pregnant with political transformation. Three days after Lei 581 became law, the Sociedade contra o tráfico dos africanos e promotora de civilização (Society against the traffic of Africans and for the promotion of civilization) was established. It campaigned for the abolition of slavery as well as of the trade and for European immigration to create new colonial settlements. Later in September, the legislature passed the Lei de Terras, which applied high taxes to the purchase of "vacant land" and declared fines and prison sentences for breaching the law.[18] The law excluded freedpeople, Indigenous people, and European immigrants from owning land. The government and legislature may have been willing to suppress the illegal trade, but the wealth of large landowners would be secure. Such security would be meaningless if Britain continued to attack property in Brazil. Unlike in 1831, Lei 581 as a criminal anti-slave-trade law was a precondition for the Lei de Terras and indeed for property rights overall. Lei 581 was a test of state sovereignty: a monopoly on legitimate violence over a defined population, which foreign powers respected.

Lei 581 applied to future slaving voyages rather than any illegal but unpunished voyages between the Treaty of 1817 and 1850. Article 4 of Lei 581 defined the importation of slaves as piracy, punishable with prison for three to nine years and fines of 200$000 reis per captive. Guilty parties would also bear the costs of reexporting the captives to Africa. The punishment referred to article 2 of the Lei Feijó of 1831, which itself cited article 179 of the Código Criminal for "reducing a free person to slavery." Such punishments could apply equally to the slave ship's crew and to the merchants who funded the voyage and those who were the principal purchasers of the captives. But in practice, it was hard to prove that merchants "knowingly" funded a voyage or bought or sold its cargo, as required by the Lei Feijó. The new criminal law in Brazil was tightly defined: the Auditoria had jurisdiction only to try and punish the slave ship's owner, captain, officers, and crew and those who helped with the disembarkation in Brazilian territory or who hid information about it from the authorities or prevented the seizure.[19] The previous criminal law of 1831 defined "importers" expansively to include land proprietors (*fazendeiros*) who knowingly purchased illegally trafficked slaves. From 1850, land proprietors and all other possible perpetrators were subject to a jury trial instead of Auditoria jurisdiction, which invariably resulted in acquittal.[20] Court procedures needed to distinguish between an illegal shipment after the new criminal law of 1850 and illegal shipment in the period 1817–50. It is tempting to argue that in making this distinction, Lei 581 was fatefully compromised. True, the courts rarely convicted the traffickers with the largest operations.[21] But this conclusion is too dismissive: as we shall see, in applying the new anti-slave-trade criminal law, the Auditoria became a site where property rights in slaves came under scrutiny. The Auditoria brought the widest range yet of participants to account. These included traffickers, slave-ship crews, and corrupt public officials. The Auditoria provided a deterrent against future slaving voyages.

The auditor's jurisdiction may have been limited, but he still had extensive powers. The auditor could appoint experts to examine the ship and any captives. He had authority to interrogate the crew and captives. When he declared a capture lawful, he could auction the vessel. The auditor could also authorize voyages to Africa for licit commerce, if such a voyage had the paperwork required by the Código Comercial. From the court's inception, the auditor in Rio was Jose Baptista Lisboa, a judge trained at São Paulo, the leading law school in Brazil. Lisboa previously served as the *curador* of liberated Africans in Rio, which involved monitoring the treatment of Africans liberated by British patrols, corresponding with British diplomats over their welfare, and resolving disputes between apprentices and their masters.[22] Liberated Africans' petitions to the authorities and escapes from service in urban Rio informed Queirós's and Lisboa's approach to captives released under Lei 581. They knew that liberated Africans' testimony in the Auditoria, and the unpredictable consequences it might generate, would be a major factor in how final suppression unfolded.

The most controversial case in the court involved two captures at Marambaia, southwest of urban Rio de Janeiro. Marambaia was the largest island in the archipelagic fiefdom of the slaving merchant and coffee plantation owner Joaquim José de Souza Breves. Along with his brother, Souza Breves was responsible for importing at least forty-three hundred African people into Brazil illegally after 1831. Using slave labor, they produced 1.5 percent of Brazil's total coffee exports in the 1860s.[23] Souza Breves, known as the "King of Coffee," achieved vertical integration of his enslaving business interests: he invested in slaving ships, landing sites, and plantations. The two captures in Marambaia were a direct result of British pressure.[24] In January 1851, the British minister in Rio, James Hudson, reauthorized the navy to capture ships in Brazilian waters.[25] Hudson justified his decision by claiming that Brazilian suppression was desultory. Paulino José Soares de Sousa, the minister of foreign affairs, had refused to order Brazilian officers to cooperate with any nearby British naval vessel when seizing a ship. "It was understood and agreed by your Excellency and by myself," Hudson wrote to Paulino, "that barracoons or depôts for the sale of Africans should be closed by the proper authorities." Yet depots existed at many locations, including the Armação plantation and Marambaia, which were connected to Souza Breves.[26]

On 1 February 1851, Rio's acting chief of police, Bernardo Augusto Nascentes d'Azambuja, apprehended 199 enslaved captives near the Armação plantation in multiple stages. The police captured 160 people early on, followed by another 16 in the morning and 23 in the afternoon. Although the crew had fled, the police found a gold watch, suspected to belong to Souza Breves, and clothing on the beach. From 5 February, the Brazilian authorities began to track the captives from another vessel that had run aground. Having received intelligence about this second ship, the Brazilian naval vessels *Andorinha*, *Bertioga*, and *Golfinho*—the latter a repurposed slaving ship—searched around Marambaia.[27] Suspecting that the crew had disembarked the captives onto smaller canoes under night cover, the naval officers arrested some local fishermen to question them. The *Golfinho* took on board two African people—perhaps captives from the first Marambaia landing—to help with the search. The municipal judge of Mangaratiba, in whose jurisdiction Marambaia was located, João José de Andrade Pinto, also boarded the naval vessel to assist the investigation. Municipal judges were elected and so depended on local patrons for support, making them vulnerable to the demands of powerful slave traders to protect their illegal activities.[28] Andrade Pinto's motivations in assisting the investigation are unknown. Perhaps he supported suppression or thought it was his professional duty to help. Perhaps he intended to report on the investigation to slave traders. Andrade Pinto—who would reappear in a later investigation—was perhaps unusual, having sought elected office several times in different districts of Rio de Janeiro in the 1840s.[29] Over the next ten days, the naval vessels recaptured 466 African captives and five slave-ship crewmembers.[30]

On 6 February, the auditor, Jose Baptista Lisboa, began his investigation into the first capture of 199 enslaved people. Lisboa decided to take testimony from some of the captives. This decision made the Auditoria unusual. The Ordenações Filipinas, the major source of civil law, stipulated that a slave had limited legal personality and, with some exceptions, was not allowed to testify in court.[31] Lisboa prioritized hearing testimony from Lusophone captives, which itself pointed to a central paradox: if enslaved people could explain in Portuguese how they had been illegally trafficked into Brazil, they were likely to arouse the auditor's suspicions that they might not be recent arrivals. But speaking exclusively African languages, which might prima facie demonstrate illegal importation, would present an obstacle to the auditor's understanding the testimony.

Notwithstanding this paradox, Lisboa questioned the captive Firmino. Was it his first time in the "terra dos brancos" (land of the white people)? Yes. Who were the owners of the gold watch and clothing found at the beach? "Senhor Joaquim" and the crew who had fled, respectively.[32] According to

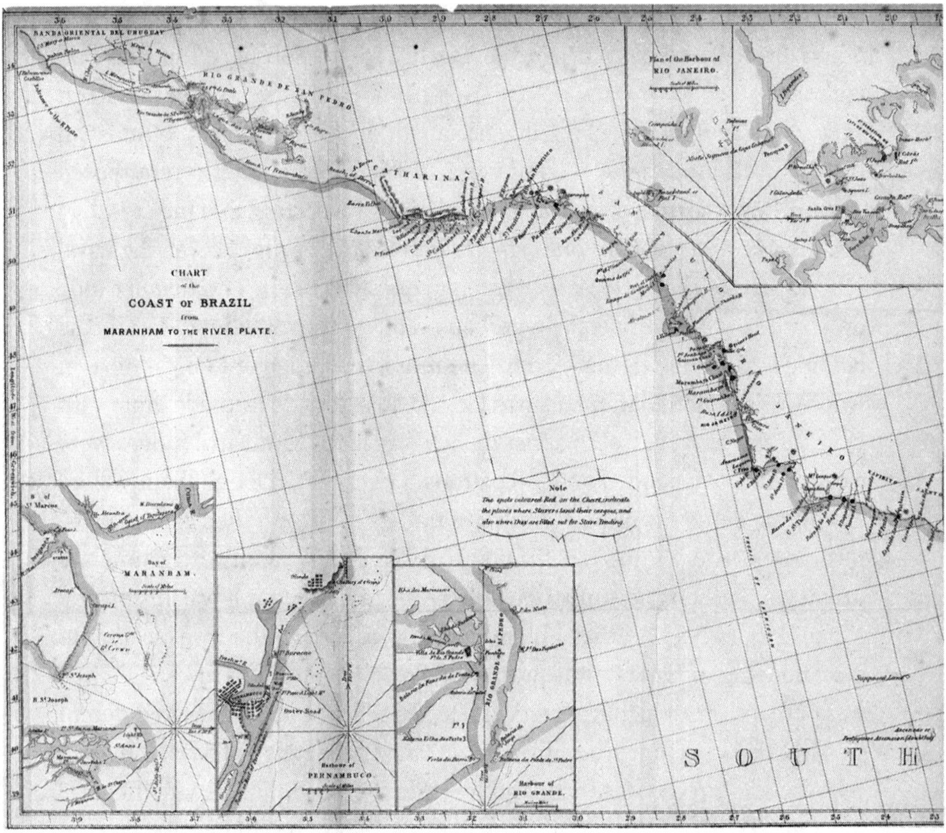

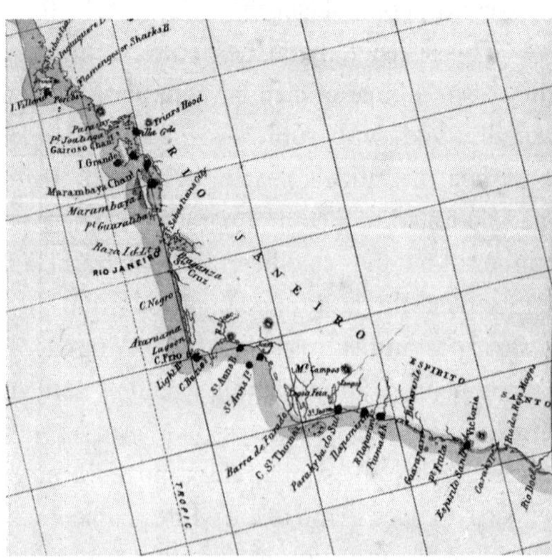

On John Arrowsmith's map of the Brazilian coast, produced for the select committee on the slave trade, the small dots indicate where slavers were fitted out and where they landed their human cargoes. There is a concentration of dots around Marambaia (see inset at left). (The Geography and Map Division, Library of Congress)

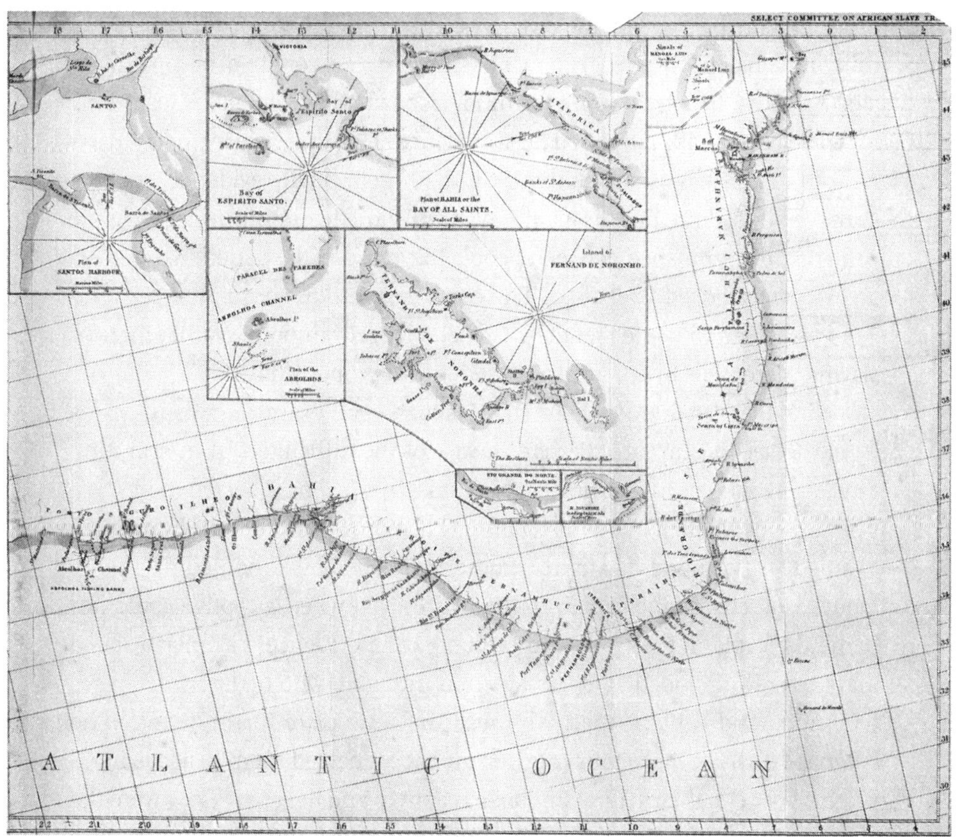

section 5 of article 33 of Decreto 708, evidence of the crew's flight constituted a "legal presumption" that the vessel was engaged in the slave trade. The auditor then asked the crucial question: Did any of the slaves *not* arrive with Firmino on the vessel? Firmino pointed at thirty-nine people.[33] At the time, Firmino did not know how his testimony would affect the lives of these thirty-nine alleged interlopers. But he must have known that the auditor was asking a question that could result in separating the thirty-nine people. The special treatment that he and the rest of the captive people had thus far received might no longer apply to them. The strange courtroom rituals, ranging from invasive bodily examinations to the judge's questions about a traumatic voyage, probably meant that Firmino felt obliged to identify potential interlopers. *How* Firmino did so is almost impossible to reconstruct. In the registration details, the thirty-nine people did not share any obvious common characteristic, though fifteen had brand marks described as *apagado* (faded).[34] Unlike the other 160 captives, Lisboa decided that these thirty-nine had not arrived on a recent ship and thus could not become liberated Africans. In interviewing Firmino, Lisboa had examined his testimony for consistency with the varied legal evidence. This evidence included material remains, such as the clothing on the beach; bodily evidence, such as brand marks; and linguistic ability. Firmino's testimony was how the Auditoria distinguished between people trafficked in the period 1831 to 1850 and those trafficked after 1850. The court imposed the burden of proof on Africans to demonstrate that they had been illegally imported rather than on slaving merchants to demonstrate their lawful property title.

Nine days later, on 15 February, Lisboa began examining the captives from the second capture. Perhaps aware of the difficulties in interpreting Firmino's evidence for the first capture, this time Lisboa collected more data. The captives Miguel, Lucas, Estanislão, Theolouco, Estacio, and Evaristo all testified in Portuguese. Miguel, Lucas, and Theolouco named Clemente Eleuterio Freire as the captain of the ship. Even when a captive could not name the captain, they provided corroborating evidence. Estanislão stated that the crew included "the captain, and the pilot, who he knew are [now] prisoners, and a black man who was the *dispenseiro* [pantryman]." The language skills of these four captives probably enabled them to act as interpreters between their fellow shipboard captives and the crew. They were the only captives allowed on deck. After capture, this privilege enabled them to identify the captain, officers, and seamen by sight and even by name. By contrast, non-Lusophone Estacio and Evaristo could not identify the crew because "they always traveled in the hold."[35] Unlike in Firmino's interrogation, the captive witnesses were unanimous in stating that they had been trafficked together to Brazil on the same ship. Despite differences in linguistic abilities and knowledge about the vessel due to differences in treatment on board, the six witnesses insisted that all the captives had arrived together. It was thus harder for the ship crew or Souza Breves to argue that some among the captured group had first arrived in Brazil between 1831 and 1850. These deponents' mutually corroborating testimonies ensured their status as liberated Africans and prevented any attempt by Souza Breves to claim a presumptive property right to them.

Such insistence added pressure on Lisboa in the second case at a time when news about Marambaia was spreading beyond the confines of the court. On 14 February, a dispute between the police chief Azambuja and the enslaver Souza Breves broke out in Rio's newspapers. Souza Breves wrote to the *Jornal do Commercio*, the newspaper with the widest circulation in Brazil, to recount the circumstances of the "horrific outrage" that Azambuja committed against his plantation. Artfully sidestepping the looming question of whether he had trafficked captives after Lei 581 came into force, Souza Breves insisted that Azambuja had exceeded his authority by entering his property. Indeed, the police used denunciations by various "country slaves" of further disembarkations as a reason for seizing slaves on other plantations, many leagues away from Souza Breves's property.[36] Souza Breves alleged that the police had seized perhaps as many as seventy ladino slaves whom he claimed to own and who had arrived prior to 1850.[37] Since the captives did not speak Portuguese, the police reasoned, they could not have spent much time in Brazil and so must be recently imported. But Souza Breves denied that linguistic ability was an accurate test of recent arrival: some slaves who spent years in Brazil lived among fellow African captives without ever needing to learn Portuguese, and others who had learned the language pretended that they had not, thereby tricking the police into seizing them.[38] Souza Breves even warned Azambuja at the time that his actions "caused anarchy on my *fazenda* and demoralized the slaves."[39] The choice of words was telling. Souza Breves saw the police presence on his plantation as giving other enslaved people, beyond those subject to naval capture, a reason to resist. He also saw the police as risking "demoralization," a term that combined the language of a master's paternalism with economic expectations of maximizing the productivity of labor power. Police hunts for newly imported captives, termed *boçal*, did not just affect Souza Breves's plantations but Brazil's entire slave society.

In reply, Azambuja argued that all 199 captives "are entirely and perfectly *boçaes*, and if among them exist three or four who can say something in Portuguese, they are called *linguas* who usually come on all vessels that transport Africans as contraband, and still they are as much *boçaes* as the others, as indicated in the [following] document." Azambuja enclosed a copy of a legal brief from the Auditoria, in which two "experts" had examined all 199 captive people. They had concluded that all of them had been imported after the 1831 law and that the vast majority did not understand Portuguese. Although five did speak Portuguese, "by their own declarations, and of those made through an interpreter, and other signs that they presented, it is evidently the case that all the said Africans 199 in number were recently imported."[40] The newspaper dispute meant that the Auditoria was no longer in full control of the adjudication process. The two Marambaia cases were now firmly embedded in Brazil's public sphere. Souza Breves was perceptive. In Brazil's public sphere and political circles, only one argument could trump the necessity of suppression for insulating Brazilian sovereignty from Britain. Suppression actions were self-defeating if they undermined the private property rights of slave-owning land proprietors that Brazilian sovereignty was supposed to protect.

The difference between Firmino's identification of thirty-nine interlopers and the unanimity of the six deponents from the second seizure led to an important divergence in the auditor's verdicts. On 18 March, Lisboa decided the first case, declaring the slaves as liberated Africans "minus those mentioned at folio 36 [i.e., the thirty-nine people identified by Firmino] . . . for not being recently disembarked."[41] He awarded prize money to the police and the naval vessels involved in the capture. On 20 March, Lisboa decided the second case, declaring all 450 captives who were still alive to be liberated Africans. Among other evidence, the testimony from the six established the "boçalidade dos Africanos." Lisboa stated, "although some speak the Portuguese language; still most know nothing of that language, and in general all of them came for the first time to this country, as slaves, and are recently imported and found in all the circumstances of the Law of 7 November 1831."[42] Lisboa's second verdict shifted the focus away from language as the evidence of *boçalidade* and toward the evidence of common arrival.

As well as declaring the capture lawful except for thirty-nine people, Lisboa applied criminal law against the traffickers. On 15 April, he punished the captain, Freire, and pilot, Jose Luiz da Silva, according to the maximum tariff applicable under Lei 581. Lisboa sentenced them to nine years in prison and a fine of 200$000 reis per captive whom they had imported. They were also liable for the costs of reexporting the captives to Africa. Lisboa sentenced four other crew members to the maximum according to article 35 of the Código Criminal—six years in prison with a fine—and one other crew-member, a minor, to four years in prison with a fine. The Tribunal da Relação rejected an appeal against the sentences.[43] Lisboa referred Souza Breves to a municipal judge for prosecution for slave-trading. In May, Souza Breves hired Augusto Teixeira de Freitas to mount his defense. Teixeira de Freitas was a conservative lawyer and the leading jurist behind the codification of Brazilian private law. He argued that "there is no objection to the apprehension made by the Chief of Police . . . of a portion of new Africans," but rather to the "violence" of "carrying off" forty-six *ladinos* during the seizure.[44] When facing the state, Souza Breves denied that he had any problem with the exercise of the police's powers of investigation on his estates. Instead, Teixeira de Freitas focused on circumscribing the geographic and temporal possibilities of one key aspect of Lei 581. Article 8 defined the jurisdiction of the Auditoria to be over "all captures of vessels . . . as well as the liberty of slaves apprehended on the high seas, or on the coast before disembarkation, in the act of disembarkation, or immediately afterward in warehouses, and deposit sites on the coast and ports." Teixeira de Freitas challenged article 8 in three important ways, extending arguments made by Souza Breves in his press campaign against Azambuja.

First, Teixeira de Freitas argued that Souza Breves could not reasonably be held accountable for disembarkations at different points on the island. Marambaia had a complex terrain. Some seizures had allegedly occurred eight leagues away from Souza Breves's *fazendas*. Second, Teixeira de Freitas argued that at least one *ladino*, Joaquim Cabinda, had disguised himself by replacing his clothes with "a loincloth" in order to join the newly imported slaves.[45] Joaquim Cabinda's actions meant that lawful state action against the slave trade had now unlawfully interfered with Souza Breves's private property rights. Third, and most importantly, Teixeira de Freitas made a deterrent argument. Despite superficially accepting police investigatory powers, Teixeira de Freitas warned of "imminent danger" if "the authorities invaded *fazendas* under arms." The Auditoria risked encouraging the police to undermine the "peace and tranquility of the Empire" by awarding prize money for apprehending newly imported captives.[46] Teixeira de Freitas claimed that the Auditoria had stimulated the police to engage in corruption by recruiting slaves as spies against their owners. By authorizing the baptism of captives, thereby changing the names associated with their bodily descriptions, Lisboa undermined property rights in ladino slaves. The Auditoria made it almost impossible for Souza Breves to identify the forty-six ladinos whom he claimed as his property. Teixeira de Freitas attacked the very logic of Auditoria jurisdiction.

Teixeira de Freitas's holy trinity—separating land ownership from complicity, blaming enslaved people for subversive behavior, and accusing the Auditoria of risking social disorder—was highly effective. He managed to cast the Auditoria as provoking conflict between slaving merchants, fugitive enslaved people, and state authorities. In July, the appeals court, the Tribunal da Relação, removed Souza Breves's name from the list of those who were guilty of slave-trading because it judged that disembarkations on his estate were "inconclusive" of guilt and because Firmino's testimony naming "Joaquim" as his master was "indeterminate."[47] Slave owners knew that they had often bought illegally trafficked captives and that this made them liable for prosecution as "importers" according to the expansive definition in the Lei Feijó and in Lei 581. Even with the likelihood of jury acquittal, major *fazendeiros* were loath to expend political and financial capital fighting criminal charges.

The flip side to rupturing Souza Breves's property rights in enslaved people who were recently trafficked was affirming those same rights in people trafficked in previous years. In August, the Conselho de Estado, the highest executive body, ruled that Firmino's testimony should result in the return of thirty-nine, rather than forty-six, enslaved people to Souza Breves. The Conselho rejected Teixeira de Freitas's argument that Souza Breves's proof of purchase of a *fazenda* (together with some Brazil-born enslaved people) constituted proof of ownership of all forty-six *ladinos*. Teixeira de Freitas's argument aligned with the implications of the Ordenações Filipinas, in which ownership flowed from possession. Once somebody possessed something, it was very difficult for any other body, including the state, to remove it.[48] There was a thread from Teixeira de Freitas's argument in the Marambaia case to his codification of civil law four years later. When he received the official commission in 1855, Teixeira de Freitas had opposed the incorporation of the law of slavery into the code. But he included his interpretation of slave law in the footnotes to a subsequent edition. According to him, the only limitation on an enslaver's right to property was the pursuit of the "public good" as defined in terms of defense, security, relief, or health.[49] This priority of state sovereignty over the private right to property was part of the logic behind the Conselho's affirmation of the Auditoria's verdict in declaring the Marambaia captures lawful. The Conselho also overturned the Auditoria's decision to award prize money to the police, arguing that only the navy was eligible for payment.

The most immediate consequence of the Marambaia case appeared to be the diminishing prospect of prosecuting slave traders. British diplomats lamented the result.[50] In 1859 and again in 1861, the emperor commuted the

Auditoria's sentences of four of the slave ship's crew, including captain Freire and pilot Silva.[51] José Maria da Silva Paranhos, the anonymous author of the popular "Cartas ao amigo ausente" ("Letters to the absent friend") published in the *Jornal do Commercio*, argued that it was unnecessary "in order to give proof of good faith to the foreigner, to take repression [of the slave trade] to the point of spreading terror through our plantations, putting at risk the life and property of their owners."[52] But a more significant long-term effect of the case was that testimony by Firmino, Miguel, Lucas, Estanislão, Theolouco, Estacio, and Evaristo propelled the Auditoria to assert its jurisdiction over slave traders. The newspaper debate between Azambuja and Souza Breves was the first time that suspected slave traders were open to public judgment in the Brazilian press. Such judgment meant that a wider reading public would weigh up the actions of suspects. The reading public might sympathize with suspects who suffered police investigations that disrupted plantation authority, or they might condemn them for risking British imperial violence. Despite the Conselho's refusal to award prize money to police officers who seized captives on land, Azambuja's actions marked a clear progression of activity by state agents. No longer was such action limited to the high seas, which had prevented the liberation of hundreds of thousands of illegally trafficked African people whom enslavers had brought into territorial waters. Suppression now firmly involved capturing vessels and cargoes in coastal waters, ports, and coastal land. The Brazilian police and navy replaced the British as the principal state agents capturing illegally trafficked captives inside Brazil's territorial waters, representing the gradual insulation of Brazilian sovereignty from British incursions.

AN EXPANSIVE ANTI-SLAVE-TRADE GEOGRAPHY

In late 1852, southwestern Rio de Janeiro was again alive with rumors of an attempted slaving voyage. Britain had sent the Brazilian government intelligence about a projected disembarkation of captives at Bracuhy, 120 kilometers southwest of Rio on the coast. Along with Marambaia, Bracuhy was part of Souza Breves's fiefdom. Brazil's minister of justice, Jose Ildefonso de Sousa Ramos, ordered a secret investigation. João José de Andrade Pinto, the same municipal judge who assisted the navy with the second capture at Marambaia in 1851, received Sousa Ramos's orders from the naval cruiser *Golfinho*. He had in fact carried out an investigation before receiving the order. Andrade Pinto found the rumor of an attempted landing to be unfounded. "I will not stop, however, taking the necessary care to gather and use whatever points of clarification that I may obtain by chance," he told Sousa Ramos in a letter published by the *Diário do Rio de Janeiro*.[53] Andrade Pinto must have known that the minister might decide to publish his letter. Perhaps he hoped that his resolute tone would deter prospective slave traders in the region. Sousa Ramos dismissed the British intelligence and moved the nearest ship, *Thetis*, from the region to cruise the northern coast between Alagoas and Recife instead.

Andrade Pinto was wrong: in December, the vessel *Camargo*, captained by the American Nathaniel Gordon, disembarked over five hundred captive people on the unguarded Bracuhy coast.[54] When the authorities received news of the landing, the police launched a three-month investigation. They searched the *fazendas* belonging to Souza Breves and a police chief suspected of slave-trading, Manuel de Aguiar Vallim. Some of the newly trafficked captives had escaped from the crew near Aguiar Vallim's *fazenda* Resgate. They "hid themselves in the neighboring scrubland," finding places between slave owners' plantations where establishing presumptive ownership would be difficult. A slave owner's guard managed to frustrate these illegally trafficked people's attempted flight. But the authorities had the area under investigation. On 16 January 1853, a soldier in disguise, a Permanentes da Corte (military police) dispatch, and a municipal judge managed to seize eight captive women and two men from the area.[55] The African captives' flight had created the conditions for anti-slave-trade seizure on a plantation.

Four days later, the authorities seized another thirty-three people in a small forest nearby. In total, the police seized around eighty enslaved people on various coffee-growing plantations.[56] British diplomats in Rio were predictably angry. On 13 January, William Jerningham drafted a report that accused Sousa Ramos of being compromised by his relationship with Souza Breves. According to Jerningham, "The family of this Breves has claims on Sr Sousa Ramos dating from the time when he was himself a needy lawyer, as well as a dealer in Slaves."[57] Unlike in January 1851, Britain did not renew naval operations in Brazilian waters. After the end of those operations in April 1852, Britain and Brazil reopened negotiations on a new anti-slave-trade treaty. Perhaps British diplomats in Rio wished to give those talks a chance to succeed. That same month, the Conselho de Estado supported Lisboa's expansive interpretation of article 8 over Teixeira de Freitas's restrictive reading. The Conselho defined the Auditoria's jurisdiction to apply to any captive person after disembarkation, in which the length of time or "any act" had not "occurred which could confound them with the slaves previously existing in Brazil. . . . The circumstance of the Africans having been found in hiding and wandering in the woods near to the place of landing, is only a proof of the precipitation with which it was endeavored to remove them from the reach of those who were seeking to capture them."[58]

The Brazilian government committed to the police investigation at Bracuhy, but it could have unexpected results beyond the control of any official. On 19 January, plantation owners complained to the Câmara Municipal of Bananal that enslaved people were using anti-slave-trade investigations in Bracuhy for their own insurgent projects. Five days later, the Câmara Municipal reported the complaint to Sousa Ramos. "Since this representation," the report stated, "the Câmara has seen that the general fear has increased, each time the spirit of insurrection develops in the *fazendas*, and it has not been possible for the plantation owners to contain the insubordination of some of the most audacious slaves; others are suffering the harm of repeated escapes of slaves of the greatest trustworthiness and who never used to flee." The plantation owners knew who to blame for insurrection talk and flight: "All these dangers, all this agitation seems to originate simply from the presence of forces in pursuit of apprehending Africans. The complaint of plantation owners against the means employed by the soldiers to find informers among all the slaves that they come across is widespread. Note that they do not limit themselves to inquiring simply about the existence of Africans, and they say that they employ all means of seduction and trickery. . . . Besides pecuniary rewards that they offer, note that they also assure liberty to the whistleblowers."[59] A month later, the minister of foreign affairs dismissed these complaints as a "great exaggeration."[60] However widespread the insurgent rumors and the complaints about them, both conveyed that enslaved people discussed how to leverage external anti-slave-trade forces for their own political projects of claiming freedom.

Unlike in the Marambaia case, the government made clear that local protests would not deter the police investigations at Bracuhy. In August 1852, a jury unanimously found Souza Breves innocent of importing captives. Still, the landing and criminal prosecution were widely reported in the press, breaking the silence that enabled the illegal trade to continue. Newspaper correspondents understood that opinion was shifting in favor of the expanded geographic application of anti-slave-trade criminal law. Even a defender of Souza Breves in a national newspaper felt compelled to start his letter by stating, "my intentions are not to throw scorn or censure on the proceedings of the authorities in this sad case, nor to defend those who are found to be involved."[61] Although the occasional provincial politician and newspaper correspondent criticized the prosecution of Souza Breves, no longer was it legitimate to protest outright against state anti-slave-trade investigations on *fazendas*.[62] Other newspapers warned that further importations risked a Haitian-style slave revolution. Souza Breves and other *fazendeiros* were required to disavow the illegal trade publicly.[63] Parallel to these land-based investigations under Lei 581, the police in São Paulo were investigating cases of illegal enslavement that enslaved African people brought to their attention. Luis Gama, the man who gained freedom from illegal enslavement in Lorena in 1848, masterminded these legal actions. Gama helped enslaved people gather evidence of illegal importation as grounds for freedom suits.[64] The investigations into illegal enslavement across southern Brazil indicated that the culture of public honor for slave traders was dying.

The multilevel implementation of Lei 58 stretched from police officers to municipal judges such as Andrade Pinto to the Auditoria Geral. This implementation transformed anti-slave-trade law into a potent manifestation of Brazilian sovereignty. When Sousa Ramos resigned as minister of justice in June 1853, his replacement, Luis Antonio Barbosa, promised to step down if a single enslaved person was trafficked into Brazil during his time in office.[65] In September, the cabinet sent to the Senate a project to extend the jurisdiction of the Auditoria Geral and regional auditors over Brazilian nationals indicted for participation in the slave trade. Those who were mainly involved in the Bracuhy case did not receive national honors, as the principal traffickers of previous generations had done. Where prosecutions failed, the Brazilian government made clear that suspected traffickers would no longer be considered worthy of honor.[66] Participation in the illegal trade became embedded in collective memory, as the descendants of enslaved people at Marambaia well knew. Some formed a *quilombo* there, where they sang, "the coffee plantation has already died," in *jongos* that alluded to Souza Breves as a coffee planter and enslaver.[67] The last known slaving ship to arrive in Brazil was the *Mary E. Smith* in 1856, but from 1853, the illegal trade no longer operated as a commercial system. Legal enforcement applied beyond the high seas. It encompassed a wide range of direct and indirect slave-trading activities. Enforcement imposed criminal punishments and ended a powerful honor culture. Liberated Africans' testimony to the new anti-slave-trade court disrupted the powerful assumption that somebody who claimed to own a person of color in fact had that property right—but only in cases of enslavement after 1850.

TESTIMONY AS SUPPRESSION IN CUBA

In November 1863, an illegally trafficked African man, recorded only by his Spanish name, Antonio, made a fateful journey across Cuba. Illegal traders had transported him, alongside over one thousand fellow captive people, on the *Ciceron*, a slaving steamer thought to be owned by the major trafficker Julián de Zulueta.[68] The crew landed the captives at Cienfuegos in southwestern Cuba and then marched the group northward to an estate owned by Zulueta in Colón. Like Souza Breves's operations in Marambaia, vertical integration characterized Zulueta's business. Forming a comprehensive anti-slave-trade law in Cuba thus required new criminal measures that would target operations that connected maritime slave-trading to plantation ownership. Only the captain general's authority was sufficient to enforce such new criminal laws. Such a legal regime would extend colonial sovereignty not only against the external threats of British maritime incursions and US filibustering but also over Cuba's slave society.

After the conclusive ending of the slave trade to Brazil through the Auditoria's reshaping of Brazilian sovereignty, the remaining destination in the Americas for the illegal trade was Cuba. High sugar prices and technological improvements in the 1850s meant that plantation owners wished to increase output by purchasing more captive laborers. The prospect of US annexation receded as US political divisions sharpened during the secession crisis over the future of slavery in the Southern states. Nonetheless, the Spanish colonial authorities knew that the situation in Cuba remained volatile. The loyalty of Cuba's influential white owners of the largest sugar estates was still conditional on official support for slavery. Metropolitan noninterference with the slave trade had been a mainstay of colonial policy since the first British-Spanish Treaty of 1817. Widespread trading networks and official collusion in the illegal trade produced a "distinct society" in Cuba, in which participation affected legal politics, administrative culture, and commercial life.[69] Deep-rooted collusion in the illegal trade developed alongside, and in tension with, the growing professionalization of the judicial system.[70] Domestic courts in Cuba were not independent of Spanish colonial interference. Still, by committing to the rule of law as a requirement of being a "civilized" imperial power, the colonial administration accepted that legal investigations into the slave trade would take place. Whether that commitment was sincere was beside the point; it introduced a set of conventions and a measure of behavior that required compliance with anti-slave-trade laws. The commitment shaped how liberated Africans, the captain general, and slave traders talked about the trade and property. Every illegal landing opened a potential rift in Cuba's legal fabric, which legalized the holding of people as property but outlawed the importation of new captives.

The Spanish colonial administration also supported landowners' attempts to secure alternative labor supplies to the slave trade. The recruitment of contract laborers from Yucatán (1849–50 and 1853–61) and China (1847–74) were particularly prominent. The Zulueta family firm transported the first group of Chinese laborers to Cuba, in a voyage approved by the Junta de Fomento, in 1847.[71] In 1854, Captain General José Guitérrez de la Concha responded to liberated Africans' demands for better regulation of apprenticeship by banning transfers of apprentices without his permission and by creating a general registry of *emancipados*.[72] By requiring masters to apply for a *cédula* (certificate) for each apprentice twice per year, Concha hoped to protect *emancipados* from reenslavement.[73] Another regulation of 1855 authorized public officials to enter estates to examine *cédulas* of enslaved people, with the authority to remove anybody suspected of being recently trafficked. Slave owners objected that state registration and investigations ran counter to the 1845 Ley Penal, which banned questions about the ownership and origins of slaves. Concha also investigated illegal landings on estates. By making enslavers answerable to a third party over such questions, state activities would undermine enslavers' authority over enslaved people. Underlying this objection was the concern that registration techniques would interfere with any attempt to purchase illegally trafficked people and present them as lawfully owned slaves. Proslavery opposition led to the withdrawal of the *cédula* system for slaves and Concha's removal in 1859.

In Cuba, the most important legal institutions for prosecuting illegal landings were first instance and appeals courts rather than a court established to apply anti-slave-trade law like the Auditoria in Brazil. As Zulueta's agents marched Antonio and over a thousand other captive people to Colón in late 1863, events took an unexpected turn. Unbeknownst to Zulueta's armed guards, the authorities had anticipated the landing. On 5 November, the Colón lieutenant governor, José Agustin Argüelles, instructed his secretary, Mariano Aguirre, to proceed to the coast to seize the disembarked captives. He warned Aguirre that the traffickers would try to bribe him. Aguirre should "appear to accept [the bribe] because to capture the expedition in the marshland would be difficult."[74] As the expedition entered the Sabana de Santa Rosa highway on 12 November, Aguirre captured the expedition in terms that projected Spanish colonial sovereignty. He announced, "This expedition of *bozales* is captured according to what the laws authorize, on the orders of the Lieutenant Governor of Colón and the authority of the Highest Civil Government of the Island, and therefore under the law I shall arrest anybody who is driving and guarding them."[75] After a commotion, the captors managed to seize some of the illegally trafficked captives. The captors transferred most of the recaptured Africans to Colón. Argüelles sent them by railroad from Colón to Captain General Domingo Dulce in Havana to be registered as *emancipados*.[76] Argüelles emphasized that the capturing force was too small to apprehend most of the guards and traffickers. Argüelles and Aguirre were vague about just how many captive people the force had rescued.[77] Sovereignty may have trumped the illegal traders' operations, but it did not necessarily liberate the captives.

Once the authorities had seized an African captive person under anti-slave-trade law, they should have recognized the person as a liberated African immediately and irrevocably, but they failed to do so. Dulce rewarded the captors with head money of twenty-five pesos per captive person.[78] He also agreed to Argüelles's request to assign some captives to the captors. Such assignments should have been for apprenticed labor, rather than the assignment of ownership in the trafficked African people. But Argüelles would later claim that Dulce "had gifted to [him] the black man Antonio, not as an *emancipado*, but as a slave."[79] Antonio now faced an uncertain future. On small farms and large sugar estates, Argüelles's officers sold hundreds of the reassigned recaptives into slavery across Cuba.[80] Argüelles himself was alleged to have sold 104 people. He sold four captives to Ramon Fernandez Criado, including Antonio and his partner, Fasilé.[81] Argüelles also assigned some recaptured people to the agents involved in the capture, including to Saturnino Santurio, a landowner and the senior lieutenant mayor of Colón's town council.[82] Argüelles later admitted that he knew that he should have distributed papers to the recaptured people to ensure their liberated African status but had failed to do so before leaving the colony.[83] Enforcing anti-slave-trade law had exposed the role of state officials in defining somebody's status. By failing to uphold the distinctions between being an illegally trafficked captive, a slave who could be legitimately sold, and a liberated African, state officials denied freedom to Antonio and many others.

The capture at Colón was the most controversial in Cuba because it revealed conflict between high-level colonial officers regarding the illegal trade. The case reached the international press and went through a lengthy appeal in the 1860s. It thus exposed the kind of arrangement that probably happened far more frequently without any criminal investigation throughout the 1840s and 1850s. By early 1864, Dulce had paid Argüelles some prize money, even though the legality of the capture had not yet been confirmed by a competent court. With Dulce's permission, Argüelles traveled to New York and used the money to purchase the Spanish-language newspaper *La Crónica*. Dulce then accused Argüelles of selling illegally trafficked *bozales* who had been delivered to the government. In newspaper articles and a short publication unambiguously titled *General Dulce and the Slave Traders*, Argüelles countered that Dulce had rewarded the captors with *bozales*.[84] Both Argüelles and Aguirre accused Dulce of ordering the release of Zulueta's agents from detention, enabling them to argue that they were not the importers but merely the *purchasers* of the captives on the coast, protected under article 9 of the Ley Penal of 1845.[85]

In early May 1864, two people suspected of being illegally trafficked *bozales* gave important statements to a hearing called by Luis Rodríguez, Argüelles's successor as the lieutenant governor of Colón. Their testimony revealed the extent of the sales conducted by corrupt public officials. One interpretation has emphasized that Spanish authorities rarely interviewed *bozales* to prevent news of their testimony leaking to other illegally trafficked people, but in this case, and in others, there were significant examples of such testimony.[86] In a case of disembarkation at Cochinos in 1854, liberated Africans testified to identify the crew of the slaving ship.[87] In other cases, the court examined the languages spoken by suspected *bozal* people and signs of disease as proof of recent transshipment.[88] Lieutenant Governor Rodríguez questioned Leopoldo Lucumí as part of a group of six African people whom district officers had found concealed in a wooden structure inside a guano hut on an estate in Roque.[89]

Leopoldo named six people, including Lieutenant Mayor Santurio, who had transferred him across different estates, which was a common tactic for illegal enslavers. Rapid transfers enabled traders to hide trafficked people among an inland estate's enslaved workforce, thereby re-presenting the trafficked captives as lawfully held slaves. Leopoldo said, "when they brought him to Macagua, there were fifty [captives in total and] that then only six came to punto del Roque."[90] The second witness, Mauricio Lucumí, corroborated Leopoldo's evidence. Mauricio stated that the traffickers "took him from Macagua to Colón and then to Roque and from there to where they are today, that Leopoldo Lucumí, Loreto Lucumí, Julio Lucumí, Saturnino Lucumí, and Petrona Lucumí accompanied him."[91] Leopoldo and Mauricio exposed the gap between the theoretical protection afforded to liberated Africans and Santurio's management of them. When state agents undermined liberated African status, presumptive property rights in the captives began to form.

Leopoldo focused attention onto the forty-plus other *emancipados* sold by Argüelles's group, and Mauricio named his shipmates to ensure the collective liberation of the six seized people. In trying to counter their claim that Santurio had intended to enslave them, Argüelles argued that the liberated Africans were merely in deposit with him. Santurio, Argüelles claimed, sent the Africans back to the local holding facility after they had tried to steal from him.[92] Yet the witnesses' account, rather than Argüelles's or Santurio's, most closely aligned with the documentary record: Santurio had never registered Leopoldo, Mauricio, and the others as slaves.[93] Leopoldo and Mauricio were aware that they had no documentary proof of illegal trafficking. On a plantation, the enslaver's performance of ownership rights would trump their claim to be *emancipados*. Leopoldo and Mauricio used their oral testimony to tell their story of trafficking, knowing that an official record would increase their chances of staying free. Liberated African testimony compelled courts to recognize shipmates as having a right to freedom rather than presuming them to be lawfully owned.

In the initial court case at the Real Audiencia in Havana, the prosecutor accused Zulueta, his subordinates, and public officials including Argüelles and Aguirre of *plagio de bozales*. *Plagio* was the crime of enslaving free people against their will, in the knowledge that they were free. Argüelles and others argued in their defense that the prosecution had not established "the indispensable antecedent for knowing if there was in reality a sale of slaves, or of free people."[94] Even if the indicted parties *had* sold free people, they alleged that the prosecution had not proved that they had done so with intent.

Argüelles, Aguirre, and other minor officials were found guilty and variously punished with prison sentences, exile, fines, and bans on political office; Zulueta was too powerful to convict.[95] The convicts appealed their sentence. In the original case, the guilt of public officials related to their failure to apprehend the traffickers rather than their complicity in selling free people. On appeal to the Supremo Tribunal de Justicia in Madrid in 1867, Argüelles's lengthy defense hinged on Dulce's responsibility for awarding property rights in people. He claimed that Dulce had awarded to him the recaptured people as slaves rather than as *emancipados*. In a letter from 6 April 1864, Dulce's secretary had stated to Argüelles that the captain general wanted to award some Black people to each captor as prizes.[96] The defense was adamant that Dulce had not made a "provisional declaration" that the people were *emancipados* during the investigation into the landing. The captain general had the authority to register the recaptured Africans as *emancipados*. He could decide whether to distribute them as apprentices and levy the fees to be paid by masters. The defense argued, "Not one of these requirements had been fulfilled, from when the capture was verified in November 1863 until 14 March 1864, when Argüelles was implicated in this case."[97] Dulce had failed to use his authority under anti-slave-trade criminal law to reclassify seized captives as liberated Africans rather than as slaves. In effect, Dulce created a rootless title to property in recaptured African people.

By confirming the original sentences, the Supremo Tribunal conceived anti-slave-trade criminal law to apply uniformly across Cuban territory and to demand compliance with it. Significant international changes made the strong application of criminal law against traffickers feasible. After the defeat of the Confederacy in 1865, Spain was the sole defender of the slave trade. This isolated position came under additional pressure with the formation of an abolitionist society in Spain. Criminal sentences included prison terms ranging between four and nineteen years, together with fines and the repayment of proceeds from the sale of *bozales*, including for Argüelles and Santurio.[98] Whether they served these sentences is unknown. What happened to people such as Antonio, who should have been *emancipados* but instead were sold as a reward for anti-slave-trade capture, also went unrecorded. Zulueta never stood trial for this case of trafficking. In March 1864, he used the *Ciceron* to traffic sixteen hundred captive people to his plantations.[99] Colonial administrators developed anti-slave-trade criminal law to include the capture of trafficked people in Cuba's coastal waters, landing sites, and estates *before* the metropolitan Cortes passed a new criminal law in 1866. But they could not encompass the most powerful traffickers within criminal jurisdiction. The testimony of liberated Africans like Leopoldo and Mauricio contributed to this gradual illegalization by exposing practices of transfer and concealment to judicial scrutiny. By the late 1860s, the patterns were well established: liberated African deponents presented scattered shipmates as part of the same landing, and judges held an ever-wider pool of people to account.

As the Colón case was awaiting the appeal, another criminal investigation extended these patterns in anti-slave-trade law that ruptured the default assumption of property rights in people of color. In March 1866, the naval cruiser *Neptuno* patrolled the waters south of the Cabo San Antonio. It was pursuing a tip-off from the superior civil government (the reformed name for the captain general's office). The crew spotted vessels burning on the beach, a telltale sign of slave traders trying to hide their tracks. The commander reported that it was "impossible that at the distance at which the fires were located that the [slaving] brig was not seen by the lighthouse keepers."[100] The *Neptuno*'s crew searched on the beaches and in the mountains for African captives. The commander reported, "as a consequence of the raid, on various points of the coast there appeared groups of black people shouting and acclaiming their happiness to see their saviors to the extreme degree . . . that some of them wanted to throw themselves into the water to reach the vessel."[101] For captive people at landing sites, the cruiser offered the prospect of rupturing enslavers' claims to property in them, producing a tantalizing possibility of claiming freedom.

The *Neptuno* could not safely dock at these rocky sites to take on board the land-based captives, but it did intervene several times in favor of freedom. With the assistance of a Black Lusophone interpreter known as Joaquín whom the naval commander had "caught in the expedition," the naval crew captured 278 people on land.[102] Joaquín's background was never fully explained. Perhaps he was a captive who had suffered recent disembarkation. Perhaps he had worked for the traffickers aboard the ship or during the march inland. In any case, he decided unequivocally to help the naval captors. The cruiser then spotted around a hundred Black people aboard a schooner in the Alacranes passage. The schooner was later identified as the *Matilde*, a vessel owned by the major slave trader Francisco Marty y Torrens. The *Neptuno*'s

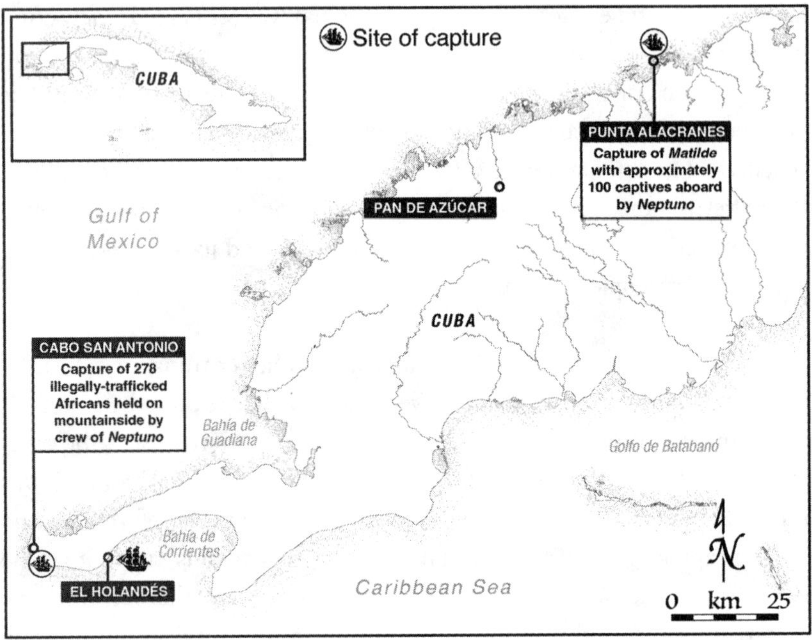

The patrol of *Neptuno*, 1866.

crew, "having passed by the ship with the black man Joaquín, who recognized thirty-eight of the people from the expedition," apprehended them.[103]

The suspects claimed that they held all the enslaved people as lawful property. The prominent slave owner and suspected trafficker José Ricardo O'Farrill y O'Farrill sought protection from the seizure of captives from the *Matilde* and from his sugar estate. He cited article 9 of the 1845 Ley Penal, which banned official investigations into the origins of enslaved people who were located on private estates.[104] O'Farrill claimed that the captives aboard the *Matilde* were "mostly criollos, wholly ladinos and accompanied with the corresponding passes." Two pieces of evidence contradicted O'Farrill's claim. The commander of the *Neptuno* stated that the passes were incomplete.[105] And Joaquín observed that the 278 people seized on land and the 100 people seized from the *Matilde* wore the same style of clothing.[106] O'Farrill's petition failed, and instead the investigating judge, Miguel Suarez Vigil, ordered him to appear before the Real Audiencia Pretorial in Havana.

If the Colón prosecutions proved that public officials would be held to account, Suarez Vigil's investigations applied the same logic to large-scale enslavers. The judge summoned Marty to ask if he had recently removed any enslaved people from one of his estates in Pinar del Río, Pan de Azucar. He replied that he had leased one hundred slaves to O'Farrill and sent them, with the requisite official passes, aboard the *Matilde* from Pinar del Río to Matanzas.[107] Marty insisted that all of them, whether born in Africa or Cuba, were of "old introduction." Yet copies of two passes dated 17 February 1866 for transferring thirty people contradicted Marty. They demonstrated that at least sixteen had been illegally imported after the 1835 treaty that outlawed the slave trade in the North and South Atlantic. A separate list of the one hundred people aboard the *Matilde* indicated that the majority were born in Africa, and most of them were also born after 1835.[108] Did Marty know anything about the illegal landing at Punta del Holandés? He confirmed that he had heard about it but knew no details.[109] O'Farrill insisted that the *Neptuno* "confused" the leased slaves aboard the *Matilde* with those from the expedition.[110] Of course, this explanation failed to refute Joaquín's observation about the captives' common clothing. A criminal court claimed jurisdiction to decide the legality of slave owners' decisions about the location and transfer of slaves between estates.

Suarez Vigil questioned twelve Africans liberated by the *Neptuno*, whose testimony revealed the traffickers' techniques for trying to create presumptive property rights in people by moving them inland. The deponents told of being born free or enslaved in sub-Saharan Africa. They spoke about suffering from warfare and kidnapping and the alienation of sale onto the "ship with two sails." The crossing was horrific. Upon landing, the traffickers smuggled many captives, including Chipianda, up to the mountains. One deponent, Bemba, said they spent forty days on the mountainside with little food.[111] Under guard at the hideout, Rufina knew that the crew "burned the vessel as she saw the fire during the night." Aquilino and Quisipo also witnessed the blaze.[112] At the hideout, Ynes noticed that "many of her *compañeros* [shipmates] were missing," and many others, including Pilar and Pinla, noticed that enslavers had taken people away.[113] As enslavers moved these people farther from the landing site, their presumptive property rights grew stronger. Perhaps the captives aboard the *Matilde* were the ones who had been removed from the mountainside. This separation would explain the common clothing that Joaquín had observed, but it was never verified. Some deponents also knew the first names of the ship's captain, senior crew, and the mountainside guards. Overall, their testimony corroborated the naval commander's claim that the lighthouse keepers' negligence facilitated the landing. The liberated African deponents insisted that those seized from the beach, mountainside, and elsewhere were all shipmates from the same illegal venture.

In May 1866, the mayor of Remates complied with Suarez Vigil's order to search all estates in his jurisdiction for any evidence of illegal trafficking.[114] Although he found no evidence, public officials obeyed a judicial order to trace illegally trafficked people on private lands despite the exclusion stipulated by the 1845 Ley Penal. This exclusion would only be formally modified by a royal order months later, in September 1866. From these searches on estates, the liberated African Cavé, given the Spanish name Bernardo, confirmed that "on the mountain there were eight whites who guarded them, and that if he sees these white people, he will recognize them."[115] When the traffickers moved the captives from the mountainside to try to sell them, according to Matunsi (also known as Catalina), "they tied handkerchiefs over their mouths and brought them to the beach where they put them on a boat, [then] they walked and walked to a house."[116] Throughout this testimony, the deponents confirmed that they were all shipmates. Based on the evidence of capture and the testimony, the public prosecutor indicted thirteen people for slave-trading. O'Farrill, the local lieutenant governor, Miguel Vilá, and the lighthouse keepers were all charged. Across Cuba, the testimony of liberated Africans was vital to identifying people subjected to recent illegal transshipment, breaking the chain of property ownership in them.

Several years later, after the investigation had been reopened, various defendants petitioned for absolution. O'Farrill played his final trick: he presented to the court a contract in which Marty *sold*, rather than leased, one hundred slaves to him. He brought proof of three payments to fulfill the contract. O'Farrill claimed that all the slaves were registered in the books of the Pan de Azucar estate with proof that they had departed for Matanzas on 16 February 1866. But here, he gave the game away. Although the judge did not seem to notice, Pinar del Río's lieutenant governor issued the passes on 17 February. If the *Matilde* had indeed set sail for Matanzas the day before, as O'Farrill claimed, it was an unauthorized interprovincial voyage.[117] Alongside testimony by captive people, the shift in contractual terms from leasing to sale and misdated passes revealed the truth behind the forged papers. Marty and O'Farrill planned to import African captives and move them between provinces to re-present them as legally owned slaves. No final verdict seems to have survived in the archives. The final two documents, from 1875, were a list of requests for absolution and a note on five defendants who had gone missing during the Ten Years' War (1868–78).[118] The investigation itself had a deterrent effect against trafficking, but its inconclusive end also reveals the judicial system's failure to liberate all people illegally trafficked into Punta del Holandés and punish all perpetrators.

Later in 1866, a new law devised in Madrid authorized colonial officials to enter estates to investigate landings. Zulueta had recently landed four hundred people at Yaguaramas in Cienfuegos. Like O'Farrill had done, Zulueta sought protection under the 1845 Ley Penal against an official investigation on his estates. The captain general, Francisco de Lersundi y Hormaechea, prevaricated in applying the new law. In response, the Sala Tercera de la Audiencia, and even the queen, commanded Lersundi's successor, Joaquín del Manzano, to investigate. He should determine whether illegally trafficked people were detained on plantations and indict Zulueta for the crime. According to the metropolitan authorities, the delays caused by Zulueta's opposition risked undermining political authority and its separation from the legal process.[119] They framed the application of anti-slave-trade criminal law as bolstering colonial sovereignty: "if [the wisdom of the Crown] judges that there is no danger to public order, nor to the country's institutions, in the strict application of the severe requirements of the new Law, and [the Crown's] worthy representative in this Island has made public his noble wishes in this regard . . . it would be best and suitable to apply it."[120] In June 1867, with evidence of scattered attempts to import further captives, Manzano made a significant decree. He declared, "The owners or tenants, and in their absence the Administrators, managers or those in charge of the estates on which a landing is verified or through which *bozales* are in transit, will be brought to this Capital on my orders, to be confined to whichever place I assign outside this Island."[121] If the landing succeeded, all regional government, military, naval, and judicial officers would be dismissed from office. The metropolitan law and the captain general's decree were the outgrowth of anti-slave-trade sovereignty, which colonial officials and slave traders had disputed at Colón.

The familiar claim that liberated Africans were in a limbo between fixed categories of slavery and freedom obscures the legal significance of their testimony for slave societies.[122] When liberated Africans such as Leopoldo

Lucumí, Rufina, and Matunsi testified in court, they narrowed the threshold where enslavers could successfully fabricate a rootless title to property in people. Throughout the Atlantic world after the Haitian Revolution, enslavers took advantage of the absence of standardized legal recognition of free status to fabricate a title to reenslave free people. But enslavers did not act alone. Each capture of an illegal landing exposed *the state* as a participant in these attempts to fabricate property titles. Eventually, the state stopped recognizing enslavers' presumed property rights, including those claimed by Argüelles, Zulueta, Marty, and O'Farrill. Liberated Africans' testimony generated debate about the legality of slave ownership that predated legislative changes in Brazil and Cuba in the 1870s. Laws that required enslavers to register enslaved people as their property and laws that freed children born to enslaved mothers, known as "free womb laws," changed the legal landscape for enslavers.[123] In response, enslavers made new attempts to perform ownership by registering illegally trafficked people and children as slaves. Before these laws came into force, liberated Africans exposed the corrupt actions of state officials and made it less likely that the state would permit property rights in illegally trafficked captives. Judges made discretionary judgments not only about captives' worthiness for freedom but also about official corruption and enslavers' presumed property rights. In court, liberated Africans ruptured the default social assumption that an enslaver's claim to property in illegally trafficked people was legitimate. Liberated African testimony was not sufficient to end the illegal trade or liberate people who had been historically trafficked, but it ruptured property rights in cases of illegal trafficking, which raised the general question of property rights in a slave society.

Contests over sovereignty and property rights explained the course of the final suppression of the illegal slave trade to Cuba and its aftermath. Certainly, the changing attitude of the US federal government mattered. Lincoln agreed to the mutual right of search in the 1862 treaty with Britain. He made a fateful decision in the case of a familiar figure: Nathaniel Gordon, the captain of the *Camargo* on its infamous voyage to Bracuhy. In 1861, Gordon had been found guilty of a federal charge of slave-trading. Lincoln refused to commute the death sentence. Gordon's execution in 1862 was a major deterrent to other slave traders. Yet, if prospective buyers were no longer prepared to pay a price that would cover the cost of trafficking enslaved people, this "market death" was not an inevitable outcome. Instead, it resulted from regulatory choices to hold more people responsible for breaking the law over a larger geographic area, as triggered by liberated African testimony.

As testimony from liberated Africans exposed illegal trafficking, it helped force a change in colonial policy in favor of suppression. Their participation in court cases contributed to pressure on metropolitan legislators who also faced a growing abolitionist movement. As a result, state practice shifted away from enabling enslavers to convert illegally trafficked people into legitimate property and toward punishing such behavior. The shift occurred even if the social attitudes of enslavers did not change. In 1867, this shift took shape when the captain general combined the threat of joint liability for illegal landings with a new registration exercise to record all people held in slavery in Cuba.[124] Such a registry would make it easier to spot subsequent illegal arrivals. The registry was also a way to monitor enslaved and free people of color to try to prevent their organized opposition to colonial slavery. These policies drew on the captain general's practices of the registration and maintenance of *emancipados.*

The rupture of property rights in domestic courts was double-edged. On the one hand, domestic courts presented liberated Africans with a new forum to testify about their common arrival in Brazil or Cuba. The liberty of all shipmates became possible. Liberated Africans seized the initiative. Estanislão, Evaristo, and Estacio from the second Marambaia landing emphasized their experiences of the same crossing. Bemba, Aquilino, and Quisipo explained how enslavers had smuggled them to a mountainside hideout in Cuba. On the other hand, the rupture did not liberate people illegally trafficked prior to Lei 581 in Brazil in 1850 or before new enforcement measures in Cuba in the mid-1860s. Indeed, these new measures strengthened state recognition of property rights in people who were illegally trafficked prior to these dates. State administrators and judges developed sovereignty over coastal waters and coastal land to project comprehensive power against the threat of foreign imperialism. They also demonstrated control over the internal population, including slave traders, enslaved people, and liberated Africans subjected to apprenticeship in state institutions. Authorities hoped that this combined projection would maintain a slave society, yet the contest between rival conceptions of legality opened debate over how far the state should protect a slavery-based social order.

That debate emerged even as the vast majority of people illegally trafficked to Brazil and Cuba between the treaty laws and the new criminal measures of the 1850s and 1860s saw little change to their lives. They remained enslaved until they died or until general emancipation in 1886 in Cuba or 1888 in Brazil. Probably included in their number were the thirty-nine people whom the Conselho de Estado returned to Souza Breves as slaves. In the short term, the major enslavers accepted increased state policing of coasts and plantations as the price for strengthening their hold over private property against domestic and foreign threats. But they were unable to predict the longer-term divergent consequences of the new anti-slave-trade laws in Brazil and Cuba. In Brazil, the law created predictable market conditions for the booming interprovincial slave trade from the declining economies of the Northeast to the coffee-growing South. By the late 1870s, the labor supply from the interprovincial trade faced a check from the Free Womb Law of 1871. In response, in 1878 the minister of agriculture, commerce, and public works convoked a Congresso Agrícola (Agricultural Congress) in Rio to consider the future of agricultural labor.[125] The Congresso included proposals for the indentured immigration of Chinese people.[126] The proposals failed, but the government experimented with schemes for the mass immigration of European contracted laborers to work on the plantations.[127] State sovereignty, strengthened by domestic anti-slave-trade law, shaped how the government and major landowners sought to expand the agricultural sector without creating a large enfranchised and propertied Afro-Brazilian population.

In Cuba, as captains general from Dulce to Manzano had hoped, suppression may have saved slavery from internal and external threats in the short term. But the birth rate among the enslaved population did not meet plantations' labor supply needs. Plantation owners demanded indentured labor, yet thousands of workers reported abuse to a commission in 1873. A year later, the Qing government prohibited indentured migration from China to Cuba.[128] The successful implementation of limited anti-slave-trade measures made it harder to gain political capital for further reform in Cuba. People such as Leopoldo O'Donnell, Dulce, and Serrano had served as captains general and were now prominent statesmen in Spain. When residents in Puerto Rico and Cuba asked for political and administrative reforms, such statesmen were in unfamiliar territory. The failure of a reform commission in 1866, combined with a new direct tax on income in the

Caribbean and a growing nationalist ideology, brought a militant anticolonial movement into being.[129] The year after Manzano commenced his registration exercise, enslaved and free people united in a multiracial alliance to wage a thirty-year war against colonial slavery. While political authorities used anti-slave-trade sovereignty to bolster racist policies and delay general emancipation, enslaved and free Black people and their allies never stopped fighting for freedom. The interactions between these rival visions would go on to shape imperial expansion and legal emancipation in the 1860s and beyond.

CHAPTER SEVEN

The Bonds of Freedom

THE PRIZE AUCTION IN FREETOWN was a spectacle. Every time the vice-admiralty court or Mixed Commission declared a capture to be lawful, the auction sprang into life: rum, coral, cotton, bread, cider, tea, the slaving ship's sails, the running rigging, and the foremast were among the most notable goods that went to the highest bidder. Profits from the auction went to the slave-ship captors or treaty parties. The successful bidders often sold the goods on for their own profit in Freetown's booming retail and wholesale sectors. Not every item from slaving ships was a desirable commodity; at one point, the stores of the anti-slave-trade courts were overflowing with over two hundred boilers and thirty-seven hundred shackles.[1] The administrators recommended that the boilers be auctioned and the shackles "be handed over to the Colonial Surveyor to be fabricated *either into agricultural tools for the model farm at Waterloo* or fetters for the use of the Gaol if required."[2] In the 1830s, some of the key bidders at auction were African people liberated from slaving ships. They resold the auction goods for profit and purchased land in Sierra Leone.[3] Liberated Africans were still active in 1862 at the auction of the fittings and cargo of the Dutch vessel *Jane*. Those who had been named after naval officers or abolitionists by colonial officials with surnames like Campbell, Lumpkin, Macaulay, Macfoy, and Shepherd were successful bidders.[4] Syble Boyle even ventured £22 10s on a chronometer, a device for measuring time and longitude at sea. Boyle, a prominent merchant, probably intended to use the chronometer on his extensive commercial voyages along the West African coast. Liberated Africans used prize auctions to purchase two ships, which they renamed *Wilberforce* and *Free Grace*, to engage in maritime commerce from Sierra Leone.[5]

Focusing on the trading diaspora from Sierra Leone to Lagos, an early paradigm viewed migrants like Boyle as the pioneers of a Christian, capitalist ethos of accumulation.[6] Subsequent research has situated the liberated Africans at Old Calabar as exponents of Afropolitanism: a view of African political community committed to mobility, small-scale autonomous trading, and advocating the emancipation of domestic slaves to create a supply of bonded labor for their own economic benefit.[7] These valuable insights apply to a small number of wealthy traders. Most liberated Africans, in a precarious position with few financial resources after the end of compulsory labor, had more urgent priorities than championing either capitalism or Afropolitanism. The patchwork of anti-slave-trade laws in the Atlantic world did not define the status of liberated Africans as the transatlantic slave trade came to an end in the 1860s. The treaties did not specify what should happen to them after they had completed their apprenticeships. The treaty between Britain and Brazil of 1826 made no mention of how compulsory labor should end. The treaty between Britain and Spain of 1835 contained regulations for the "good treatment" of liberated Africans, which aimed to provide protection of their liberty, their knowledge of Christianity, "their advancement in morality and civilization, and their sufficient instruction in the mechanical arts," but did not specify how the ending of apprenticeship would work.[8] In Brazil, an order in 1834 stipulated that liberated Africans should be deported, but neither federal nor provincial governments enacted such decrees at scale, probably because of the administrative cost involved.[9]

Treaty and domestic laws left many essential questions open: Did liberated Africans acquire rights to residency and property at the end of apprenticeship? What was the status of their children? Even British colonial Sierra Leone, which accommodated the largest number of liberated Africans, did not have a law for how to incorporate liberated Africans into the colonial structure of belonging. In other Crown colonies, political belonging depended on the attribution of imperial subjecthood.[10] Every liberated African faced the predicament of navigating an onward path without the protections afforded by citizenship or subjecthood.

To address these questions, liberated Africans and state officials developed contrasting visions of emancipation at the end of compulsory labor assignments. Officials in different Atlantic polities attempted to use liberated Africans as a precedent for various new policies. Officials used liberated Africans to settle newly conquered territories and to experiment with systems of control over laborers. Some liberated Africans assisted these projects, but most devised their own visions of freedom, drawing on their legal access and diasporic connections. These conflicting views of emancipation produced divergent trends in defining post-apprenticeship status, ranging from the recognition of imperial subjecthood to attempts to reestablish apprenticeship in new frontier zones. Having developed through assigning liberated Africans to compulsory labor, in the 1860s the authoritarian strategies that political authorities devised through anti-slave-trade law proliferated dramatically. The British, Brazilian, and Spanish Empires all sought to settle liberated Africans in frontier zones or in conquered territories, without anticipating that they would demand greater security for themselves and their communities.

The aftermaths of anti-slave-trade law in the Atlantic world throughout the 1860s were manifold. Liberated Africans generated a new diaspora from Sierra Leone to Lagos. Some lobbied for political rights in Sierra Leone. Those who settled in the Cape became part of the urban population of color. In Brazil, liberated Africans petitioned to end apprenticeship. They participated in the convergence of anti-slave-trade law with anticolonial insurgency in Cuba. Many scholars have shown that Black activists developed innovative visions of freedom even as state authorities sought to restrict them in the second half of the nineteenth century. These scholars have found reformulations of discriminatory laws and ideology, and the persistence of Black struggle against them, in places as varied as the Southern United States during Reconstruction, British colonial West Africa, and Cuba and Brazil before general legal emancipation in the 1880s.[11] Postemancipation political settlements could involve measures to exclude freedpeople, and particularly free Black women, from citizenship.[12]

Focusing on the political life of liberated Africans after the end of compulsory labor extends our insight into the legal struggles of nineteenth-century slaveholding and postemancipation societies. For most liberated Africans, there was no single vision of political belonging or economic life. Liberated Africans devised plural ideas and practices for their futures, which revolved around the single element that they had in common, the relationship formed between people who had arrived in a given society on the same slaving ship: the shipmate bond.[13] Alongside many forms of collective identity, such as ethnolinguistic community and religious affiliation, shipmate bonds were vital for freedpeople's visions of freedom. Sometimes, as with the *Amelia* rebels in Sierra Leone in 1811 or the people liberated from the *Relámpago* in Cuba in 1824, shipmate bonds reinforced family relationships that had existed prior to enslavement. At other times, people forged shipmate bonds with people whom they met for the first time in a barracoon or aboard a slaving vessel. Freedpeople used shipmate bonds to develop norms surrounding sex, marriage, and kinship; as kin, shipmates did not have sexual relations with each other.[14] Shipmates also collaborated to build credit networks and mutual-aid societies.

To remediate displacement, liberated Africans sought security not in territorial belonging or national allegiance but rather in the shipmate community. Something as quotidian as an auction revealed how liberated Africans used shipmate bonds to protect their property rights and social ties in the shadow of projects of imperial expansion. Liberated Africans were in a predicament of lacking paperwork about their arrival in a society that privileged written documents as legal evidence. Political authorities did not give them any guarantees about their future civil or political rights. In this precarious position, liberated Africans called on shipmates and their allies to gain standing as petitioners, residents, and property owners.

COLONIAL GOVERNANCE IN SUB-SAHARAN AFRICA

When liberated Africans like Syble Boyle set off on voyages from Sierra Leone to the Bight of Benin, shipmate communities and new modes of imperialism followed in their wake. The liberated Africans' purchases at the auction of the *Jane* in 1862 formed part of a decades-long pattern of using capital accumulated from auctions to help thousands of people migrate to Lagos and the surrounding region, where they became known as the "Saro" diaspora.[15] Liberated Africans and other freedpeople in Brazil and Cuba who accumulated capital through their daily wage work also financed voyages to Lagos, forming the "Aguda" and "Amaro" diaspora there.[16]

Lagos was both a refuge for freedpeople and an active slave-trading port, which produced debate among liberated Africans and British imperial officials about its future role in global trade. Prominent liberated African traders such as W. A. Savage, H. Pratt, and J. M. Turner saw Lagos as a new hub for shipping palm oil, which was much in demand in industrializing Europe as a machine lubricant, fuel for lighting, and ingredient in soap.[17] African American settlers also saw Lagos and inland towns as potential places to establish communities with an antislavery, and in some cases a Christian, ethos. Slaving raids often threatened these projects.[18] Foreign Office officials in London, especially Lord John Russell, wished to transform Lagos into a base for British mercantile shipping and access to the Niger Delta. The interests of elite liberated African traders and the ambitions of imperial officials converged in the British policy of promoting "legitimate commerce" in African exports of groundnuts, cotton, and palm oil rather than shipments of enslaved people—even though people held as slaves in Africa produced many of these goods.[19]

The most dramatic example of using anti-slave-trade law to justify imperial expansion was increasing British control over the independent kingdom of Lagos between 1851 and 1861. In 1851, Samuel Ajayi Crowther, a liberated African who became an Anglican minister, traveled to England to protest the mistreatment of missionaries by Kosoko, the *oba* of Lagos. Kosoko also supported slave-trading merchants who were based in the kingdom's port. Led by the British consul, John Beecroft, British forces used gunboats to replace Kosoko with his main rival, Akitoye. Freedpeople who had settled in the nearby town of Abeokuta and a faction in Badagry supported the British because they wished to reduce the regional power of Kosoko's principal ally, the slave-trading kingdom of Dahomey.[20] In 1861, the British went a step further, annexing Lagos as a colony. One prominent interpretation has argued that the main objective of annexation was to protect liberated Africans' claims to private property rights in Lagosian land.[21] Other scholars have suggested that the synergy between the consulate and the Foreign Office under Palmerston and his successor, Russell, caused annexation, though they have identified different intentions and justifications, ranging from implementing antislavery ideology to extending commercial interests.[22]

Britain's annexation of Lagos in fact had multiple causes. Although some liberated Africans favored annexation, others opposed colonial control. For instance, some liberated Africans in the Egba United Board of Management in Abeokuta emphasized their wish to remain independent of British imperial encroachment at Lagos.[23] Nor did the British bring private property rights to Lagos; the "White capped Chiefs . . . are the rightful possessors of the land upon which they depend for their subsistence whenever war breaks out."[24] These chiefs, who served alongside the *oba* prior to annexation, understood land rights to combine private property with elements of communal holding. In the crucial parliamentary papers relating to annexation, parliamentarians and the Foreign Office did not rely on either slave-trade prohibition or protection of private property alone to justify annexation. Instead, they cited the treaty that the British consul and naval commander had agreed with Akitoye following the British naval attack in 1851. The treaty declared a ban on the export of slaves from Lagos, a commitment to free trade between Indigenous people and British subjects, and protection for missionaries.[25] The parliamentary papers also reprinted the British consul's proposal for turning Lagos into a colony or protectorate in 1860, which reiterated these varied goals: annexation would end the slave trade, extend "Christian civilization" to the region, and protect private property.[26]

The first governor, H. Stanhope Freeman, appointed merchants as judges and liberated Africans and their descendants to many official positions.[27] In 1866, the Colonial Office decided to put Lagos under the general government of Sierra Leone. Implementing anti-slave-trade law provided commercial opportunities to the wealthiest liberated Africans and enabled British statesmen to justify a transformation from gunboat violence to colonial annexation. This new mode of empire was an incomplete reorientation of imperial sovereignty in West Africa rather than a culmination of antislavery ideology or the birth of a new capitalism driven by private property rights. The far-reaching effects of interactions between British imperial officials and liberated Africans within the empire foreshadowed later political developments across the globe.

The annexation of Lagos ran parallel to longer-term transitions in empire at the Cape. Administrators focused on governing liberated Africans as part of the urban workforce of color in a settler colony. Into the 1850s, colonial authorities promoted an assimilationist gradualism that conceived of freedpeople of color as capable of ascending to the same civilizational standard as white settlers through wage labor, conversion to Protestantism, and households structured by monogamy and patriarchy.[28] Liberated Africans were a crucial group for such an ideology. New waves of liberated Africans arrived in the Cape from unilateral maritime captures of slaving vessels primarily from Mozambique. These liberated Africans were apprenticed mainly in Cape Town, with smaller groups apprenticed elsewhere in the Western Cape. The magistracy was the primary jurisdiction involved in adjudicating labor relations between apprentices and masters. In 1844–46, 113 of 159 convictions (71 percent) in the Cape Town Magistrate's court were based solely on the master's testimony.[29] Common offenses included desertion, insolent conduct, and theft. These convictions laid the groundwork for unequal employment relations after the end of apprenticeship.

One rare case in which a liberated African was a complainant confirmed the constructed racial hierarchy. In Simon's Town, a naval base south of Cape Town where many liberated Africans had settled after arriving in port, George accused Peter Francis Hugo of "striking him a severe blow with a stick on the head in the public street" at the magistrate's court on 24 December 1844.[30] Two witnesses supported George's accusation, Komamadin and Sabadin, both designated by the court as "Malays." The court's clerk listed Hugo as a "Field Cornet." This was a civilian office with military and judicial powers who served under a *landdrost*, a rural judge appointed during the time when the Dutch East India Company ruled the Cape. Hugo brought two witnesses in defense, Prato and Kebo, "negro apprentices." The magistrate judged the case "not proved"—not strictly an option in English criminal law, even though similar cases required only *one* corroborating witness to secure convictions. It seems that Hugo was able to cancel out George's two witnesses by recruiting two of his own. Although the office of field cornet was defunct by 1844, it retained vestiges of honor for the magistrate in Simon's Town. The case reveals that there was no equality before the law in Simon's Town. Indeed, justice seemed similar to the previous Roman-Dutch system, in which the status of a party or witness helped determine the admissibility and value of their testimony. Although bonds of solidarity existed among liberated African and Malay workers, social norms could still favor the white employer in cases of labor dispute.

In Cape Town, the magistrate played a crucial role in the issues that affected assimilationist ideals. One major issue was sex work. In 1868, the medical inspector's report revealed that 20 of 213 sex workers in Cape Town were Mozambican, that is, liberated Africans from Mozambique.[31] Almost 80 percent of the sex workers had other occupations, including as domestic servants and washerwomen. The report revealed that 109 women had started "prostitution" by the time they were seventeen years old;

99 women had lost both parents.[32] The medical inspector concluded that domestic service and the death of both parents "in the late Epidemic" explained why many of the women had turned to sex work.[33] The inspector did not consider how men's behavior in buying sexual services affected women's options. Toward the late 1860s and early 1870s, the magistrate punished women suspected of sex work with increasing severity. The main offense was contravening the Contagious Diseases Act by refusing to attend the Old Somerset Hospital for medical inspection for sexually transmitted infections. The sworn testimony of the medical inspector was considered sufficient to convict the women to five days' hard labor.[34] The magistrates' treatment of sex workers speaks to a more general paradox in the legal status of people of color including liberated Africans in Cape Town. Despite the superficial color blindness of assimilationist gradualism, the magistrate contributed to stratifying Capetonian society by class, at a time when class was highly correlated to race.

For many liberated Africans, including those from Mozambique, Islam could help produce an alternative vision of freedom. As well as religious tenets, Islam provided social solidarity and trade relations with the Indian Ocean that were separate from the Protestantism of household masters and colonial officials. In 1808, the first British colonial governor of the Cape observed that trafficked slaves from Mozambique "for the most part embrace the Mahomedan faith."[35] Colonial officers who claimed authority under formal anti-slave-trade law perceived Islam to be a threat. So strong was the commitment of enslaved people to Islam that Petrus Borcherds, resident magistrate of Cape Town between 1828 and 1857, lamented that they were "exposed to the influence of Mohammedan priests, and liable to their perversion."[36] In the 1830s, some Muslims shifted from Sufi worship to institutionalization through mosques and schools. Tuan Guru, an exiled prince from the Ternate Islands (in present-day Indonesia), established a mosque on Dorp Street. He held the Jumu'ah prayers at a quarry in western Cape Town, the neighborhood for urban free people of color.[37] In 1828, the Commissioners of Inquiry found that free burghers expressed "jealousy and suspicion" of the social solidarity between Malay, free Black, and liberated African people. Islam "also accounts for that marked distinction observed in the exposure of the houses and persons of these classes to entry and arrest."[38] As late as 1861, a critical account noted this solidarity through Islam: "The term 'Malay' is . . . locally applied to all Mahometans. These include Arabs,

A multigenerational, multiracial procession in Cape Town celebrates, in the words of the artist George Duff, "slave liberation." By using this term rather than "emancipation," Duff raises the question of whether liberated Africans participated. (MuseumAfrica)

Mozambique prize-negroes, Hottentots, and Christian perverts,—too many of the last named pressed by poverty, and allured by Mahometan benevolence."[39] Charitable and educational activities and the mosques' clear office-holding structure provided order and value outside the formal law.

Islam also provided a structure for using shipmate bonds to claim freedom in ways that stretched into the Indian Ocean world. In 1860, the imperial government ended the transshipment of liberated Africans from Africa to the British Caribbean as indentured laborers. The policy suited wider imperial objectives. The illegal transatlantic trade was declining, and the need for naval patrols in African waters and the Indian Ocean increased with growing British imperial interests there. In October 1859, a British warship captured a vessel with Zanzibari merchants aboard. As one of the merchants, Mochamat Ali, later petitioned, "I together with 19 others, and our wives, 8 in number, were taken from [on] board a craft, on our way from Mombas[a] to Zanzibar, and placed on board a British Man-of-War [which] dispossessed us of all our valuable property, destroyed the craft, and brought us to Table Bay." Although the collector of customs, William Field, determined that the group "were not slaves," Ali continued, "no provision was . . . made for us, and we were obliged to go and work for our daily bread." Since they did not speak English or Afrikaans, they relied on "the kind assistance of a few Mahomdean friends" to get by.[40] The group petitioned Petrus de Roubaix, the consul general of the Ottoman Empire at the Cape. They asked de Roubaix to lobby the colonial government to restore their property and arrange their passage to Zanzibar.[41]

Even the sultan of Zanzibar wrote to the governor of the Cape to ask him "to send the people in question to Zanzibar and to do justice to the Captain who took them."[42] Only in November 1866 did the remaining twenty-two adults get their passage home, which de Roubaix paid for himself.[43] Colonial administrations excluded liberated Africans from imperial subjecthood along the intersection of race and religion, and so they found political community among urban laboring groups. This trend would continue among African people liberated from the Indian Ocean slave trades and settled at Durban in the later nineteenth century.[44] As British imperial officials devised new tools of governance over them, liberated Africans created a diasporic vision of freedom that emphasized solidarity between urban workers and a commitment to Islam.

SHIPMATE LIBERATION IN SIERRA LEONE AND BRAZIL

In 1861, the year before liberated Africans bought the goods from the slaving ship *Jane* at auction, a dispute broke out in a court in Sierra Leone. It concerned the financial credit organized by a group of shipmates. A mutual-aid society had lent one pound, five shillings, of "Company money" to John William. After a year, William had not repaid the loan. J. Thomas, the society's president, sued William in the Court for the Easy and Speedy Recovery of Small Debts.[45] Two company members corroborated Thomas's testimony. One deponent disputed William's claim that he had used the money for a funeral for one Betsy John because "the company had buried [her] before this" loan was agreed.[46] The court found for Thomas and ordered William to repay the loan plus court costs. Another case involved the Waterman's Society, which provided members with basic insurance that involved sending out recovery vessels if a member's vessel was cut adrift. The society had a clear internal order, with a king, judges, and rules that senior members read aloud to each prospective member.[47] The court heard many cases concerning mutual-aid societies, which provided members with financial credit, employment opportunities, and help with major life events such as funerals.[48] Although court cases were by nature about the breakdown of relations in a company, the frequency of cases over savings and small loans indicates that these associations were an attractive source of credit and that the court was an accessible forum for resolving disputes over debt.[49]

In March 1864, a case in the debt court revealed the wide-ranging role that shipmate societies could play in helping a member accumulate property. Phaelee Coker, the estranged wife of the recently deceased Jacob Coker, brought a case against M. A. Coker, Jacob's mistress. Phaelee sued for twelve pounds, five shillings, and sixpence regarding the ownership of Jacob's ginger farm. In Phaelee's testimony, she stated that M. A. Coker had lived on the farm, cooking for the farm laborers. Phaelee testified, "on one occasion I was passing I saw the Society my husband was belonging to in the farm working—the Society is called the 'Shipmates Society,' I was not present when the bargain was made between my husband, the Society, and the laborers about planting the ginger seed."[50] Jacob Coker and his fellow shipmates had endured captivity and maritime liberation from the same slaving ship. After they arrived in Sierra Leone, they began a society to extend credit, either in cash or in fellow shipmates' labor time, to each other. The society helped Coker start his farm. Shipmate societies also funded funeral expenses through joint payments—and in finding for Phaelee, the court deducted funeral costs from the settlement.[51] In seeking self-directed work, liberated Africans sought to own a stake in production, whether through bidding in prize auctions, selling services at markets and in the maritime economy, or growing food. By innovating with financial credit, liberated Africans turned shipmate bonds into long-term meaningful relationships to build livelihoods independent of the colonial state.

Alongside these private credit relationships, liberated Africans used shipmate bonds to claim political rights in Sierra Leone. In 1848, over one thousand residents petitioned the Colonial Office to remove the governor, Norman Macdonald. The petitioners alleged that Macdonald discriminated against all inhabitants of color, stating, "*I have no good to do for Blackmen.*"[52] Leading liberated Africans signed the petition. Signatories included John Macaulay, an elected "king" who resolved disputes between villages, and John Ezzidio, a prominent businessman. Indeed, Macaulay may have helped organize the petition; he was its first signatory. Residents of Sierra

Leone did not have the right to petition the metropolitan government. Liberated Africans' legal mobilization prompted Parliament to pass legislation in 1853 that recognized them as British subjects with this right and to create a local legislative council.[53] Soon, prominent liberated Africans were elected to serve on the Legislative Council.[54] Liberated Africans' demands for political rights in Sierra Leone and their efficacy as colonial administrators in Lagos converged with the metropolitan government's priority of cutting the cost of colonial rule. Together, these trends prompted a reimagining of the colonial constitution for the first time since the establishment of Crown rule in 1808. In 1865, a select committee recommended that the primary objective of colonial rule should be preparing West Africans for self-government, a transformation that remained unrealized for almost another century.[55] Liberated Africans in Sierra Leone developed a vision of political belonging rooted in the shipmate community rather than in a territory or nation.

As in Sierra Leone, liberated Africans in Brazil used shipmate bonds to claim freedom and establish post-apprenticeship livelihoods. These bonds were strengthened by the government's decision to assign apprentices to institutions rather than households. In Brazil's new anti-slave-trade law of 1850, Lei 581, the government stipulated that all African people liberated by the Brazilian navy would either be immediately deported or apprenticed in institutions "under the Government's guardianship."[56] Just as those who were apprenticed under treaty law and the 1818 Alvará, liberated Africans subjected to compulsory labor under Lei 581 contributed to state-building initiatives. Such state-building extended beyond Rio and the coast. Liberated Africans, including those rescued at Marambaia, were crucial to constructing the road Estrada da Marioridade between São Paulo and Santos. As they formed families and communities on such projects, liberated Africans in the 1850s made collective demands for better work conditions and group protection.[57] Liberated Africans also escaped from apprenticeship in the mining industry in Minas Gerais. Some apprentices had been transferred from the Casa de Correção in Rio to the Sociedade de Mineração de Minas Gerais. Their labor revealed how state-building now operated through agreements between public and private bodies. The state offered the mining company apprentices and guaranteed interest payments, tax exemptions, and a monopoly on mining in exchange for constructing roads and railways.[58] Such labor assignments revealed how the concept of "free labor" as antithetical to slavery contained elements of coercion that were developed through the management of liberated Africans. By 1865, 48 percent of liberated African apprentices were working in institutions, more than double the proportion before the new law came into force.[59] Collective petitioning and escapes from these institutions became a crucial strategy for freedom for liberated Africans across Brazil's territory and different economic sectors.

As well as treaty law and Lei 581, the key Brazilian law that authorized liberated Africans to petition to end apprenticeship was a decree in 1853. The decree applied to those who had served for fourteen years in private households. The petitioning process infamously involved twenty steps.[60] An apprentice usually began by asking a lawyer to write a petition.[61] The state authorities who processed the petition included the chiefs of police for the province and the city, the *curador* of liberated Africans, the Juiz d'Orfãos, and the Ministério da Justiça (Ministry of Justice).[62] After a liberated African had submitted the petition, they were required to move to the Casa de Correção until the minister approved or denied it. Many petitions were formulaic. They stated the petitioner's name, the vessel on which they had arrived in Brazil, and where the petitioner had served as an apprentice. The petitioner then appealed to the emperor's "justiça" or "humanidade" for a "carta de emancipação," a letter of irrevocable emancipation. The twentieth step involved the provincial chief of police handing over the letter of freedom and designating where the liberated African should now live.

Petitions from the 1850s and 1860s revealed how liberated Africans developed their visions of freedom in a context of tense political exchanges over the future of slavery in Brazil. These visions emphasized collective irrevocable liberation, protection of property, and secure residency. Liberated Africans emphasized that true emancipation included protection against reenslavement and unconditional freedom for their children.[63] One influential analysis has interpreted these petitioners as claiming "rights" and "autonomy" through petitioning, though the consequent emancipation was a "mirage" because state officials often moved liberated Africans to new settlements on Brazilian frontiers as a condition of their emancipation.[64] Although the language of rights and autonomy was important, liberated Africans made innovative claims in terms beyond this language, and the exact reasons for the deportation to the frontiers have remained obscure.

There were three possible outcomes of petitions: rejection, approval, or conditional approval. Between 1853 and 1859, the Ministério rejected many petitions because liberated Africans had not served the requisite fourteen years. Some petitioners had served some time in institutions rather than households. Others had—according to the master—displayed "bad behavior" during apprenticeship. Such behavior included absence from work, laziness, or drunkenness. A second outcome was for the master to renounce responsibility for the liberated Africans, allowing the petition to proceed unconditionally.[65] Third, the Ministério might approve the petition with a condition such as residency in a particular location or migration to Africa. Liberated Africans protested the residency clause in the 1853 decree.[66] For instance, Domingas contested a move to Vassouras because she owned a *casa de quitanda* (greengrocer's shop) in Rio. Her protest enabled her to stay in the city.[67] Liberated Africans like Domingas in Brazil used the legal process to turn the capital that they had earned during apprenticeship into private property that had official recognition.

In November 1859, the Conselho de Estado, the highest executive body, advised the emperor to make a comprehensive plan for the liberated Africans. The emperor should either award *cartas* to all of them or, if their numbers were too large, "disperse" them to various "colonies" on the Brazilian frontier. The Conselho concluded that "it is certain that, being free [*livres*], they cannot stay perpetually subject to an apprenticeship close to slavery, in the hope of a reexportation [to Africa] that is becoming truly a farce."[68] Faced with either the indiscriminate awarding of *cartas* or dispersal to frontiers, the Ministério opted for the latter. With the threat of dispersal hanging over liberated Africans, they urgently sought freedom letters. They knew the information required for petitioning: besides their memories, details like arrival dates were inscribed on metal tags that they wore around their necks.[69] Liberated Africans then needed to find supporters to petition. They could use the periodical *Almanak Laemmert* to find lawyers who advertised their services. Others may have passed messages to British diplomats. Continuing practices that they had established during apprenticeship, liberated Africans kept in touch with each other inside institutions, on the street, and in the Casa de Correção.

In the 1860s, these communication networks enabled collective petitioning to accelerate, at the same time as domestic and international tensions regarding liberated Africans and anti-slave-trade law were growing. From 1857, the influential Instituto de Advogados Brasileiros adopted a gradual abolitionist stance, favoring the view that a child born to a conditionally free mother should be considered legally free.[70] In an annual address to the Instituto, the abolitionist lawyer and former *curador* of liberated Africans Agostinho Perdigão Malheiro announced that slavery was the biggest problem for Brazilian law, because it created a contradiction between understanding a slave as legitimate property and as a person capable of acquiring and exercising rights.[71] Malheiro received support from the lawyer and former government minister Aureliano Tavares Bastos, who used his government and British contacts to pressurize the Brazilian government into emancipating liberated Africans from institutional apprenticeship.[72] British diplomats also insisted on the emancipation of all liberated Africans as part of a broad attack on Brazilian authorities. In 1862, William Christie, envoy extraordinary and minister plenipotentiary to Brazil, demanded Brazilian redress for the plundering of the *Prince of Wales*, a shipwrecked British ship. Christie sought compensation for goods seized from the vessel and the prosecution of the alleged murderers of the ship's crew. He also demanded restitution for the arrest of sailors from other British ships. He alleged that one man who plundered the *Prince of Wales* had fled to Uruguay at a time when Brazil frequently accused its southern neighbor of harboring fugitives from slavery. Uruguay conversely accused Brazilian enslavers of conducting illegal cross-border slaving raids.[73]

People born outside Brazil wished to know whether they could claim the constitutional protection of Brazilian citizenship against illegal enslavement. The imperial legation in Montevideo sent a request to the Conselho de Estado to clarify whether *libertos* who were born outside Brazil were Brazilian citizens. In 1859, the Conselho, including Eusébio de Queirós, produced a detailed analysis about the relationship between citizenship, slavery, and birthplace. The Constitution of 1824 granted citizenship to manumitted people born in Brazil and people born in Portuguese Africa. But illegally trafficked people and liberated Africans were excluded from citizenship: "if there were some illegal traffic, or if we imported some Africans from abroad, then this is so difficult to prove, and such a small matter in relation to the few freedpeople of this small number, that it is not possible to go into similar details" regarding their claim to citizenship.[74] Border disputes over Brazilian complaints about fugitivity and Uruguayan counterclaims of illegal enslavement were major causes of the bloodiest war in Latin American history: the War of the Triple Alliance (or Paraguayan War) of 1864–70.[75] The Constitution of 1824 denied liberated Africans citizenship in the Brazilian Empire, and by the 1860s, the outlook had worsened. Internal legal reasoning and international conflict forced liberated Africans to look beyond not only the rights framework of citizenship but also the prospect of protection by the Brazilian or British state. As political exclusion intensified, it narrowed the options about what post-apprenticeship legal status could be.

For Christie, the maritime disputes were a pretext for demanding the emancipation of the liberated Africans in a controversy that became known as the "Christie Question."[76] Prior to the American Civil War, the United States had been a prominent defender of slaveholding in Cuba, Puerto Rico, and Brazil, the last slave societies in the Western Hemisphere. But Lincoln's Emancipation Proclamation of 1863, which declared all slaves in the rebellious states to be free, threw into doubt US diplomatic protection for Brazilian slaveholding. Britain's government and Parliament took advantage of this vulnerability to increase pressure on Brazil.[77] Later that year, Britain's Parliament published separately, for the first time, correspondence between the two governments on liberated Africans.[78] Diplomatic pressure over liberated Africans served Britain's interests of ensuring access to Brazil's markets, but it also risked damaging relations that could disrupt economic activity. Brazil's government refused to meet Christie's demands to pay compensation or release liberated Africans from apprenticeship. In May 1863, Brazil broke off diplomatic relations with Britain amid renewed talk of war.[79] The ending of apprenticeship had become a political issue pincered between Brazilian abolitionist activism and the breakdown of diplomatic relations with Britain in a growing hemispheric crisis of slavery.

The diplomatic rupture created an urgent predicament for the liberated Africans, who could no longer rely on British diplomats to support their claims to freedom. In their petitions to the Ministério da Justiça, they developed a novel strategy of using shipmate bonds to provide evidence that they had finished apprenticeship. On 11 April 1864, the liberated African Porciano petitioned for a *carta*. After maritime capture, he had arrived in Brazil on the Brazilian naval cruiser *Affonso* and worked at the Santa Casa da Misericordia da Corte hospital as an apprentice. Porciano, "having served the time stipulated by the Decree No. 1303 of 28 December 1853, judges that he finds himself in the position of being able to obtain his letter of emancipation, [and] that he comes to implore his Imperial Majesty for clemency."[80] On the same day as Porciano's petition, Honorato and Gonsalo also submitted petitions. Honorato was apprenticed to the secretary of police, and Gonsalo was working in the monastic Ordem Terceira da Penitencia. Like Porciano, Honorato and Gonsalo had arrived in Brazil on the *Affonso*. It was not a coincidence that three people who had spent time on the same ship, dispersed around the city and province of Rio, petitioned on the same day. Honorato's petition echoed Porciano's: "having served the time stipulated by the Decree No. 1303 of 28 December 1853, judges that he finds himself in the position of being able to obtain his letter of emancipation, [and] that he comes to implore his Imperial Majesty."[81] Gonsalo, "having served the time stipulated by law, comes to implore his Imperial Majesty for clemency" in granting a *carta*.[82]

The phrasing of "judging to find oneself in a position to obtain a *carta*" and the emphasis on "clemency" were unusual. The conventional petitions emphasized the emperor's "humanidade" or "justiça." The invocation of the petitioner's "judgment" presented him as a legal subject with individual agency. These were not three individual petitions but rather three people collectively mobilizing for freedom as shipmates to maximize their chances of success.[83] In Bahia, in July 1864, the apprentice Joaquim successfully petitioned for a *carta* based on diligent service and the fact that "some of the *companheiros* of this African already are *emancipados*," that is, they possessed freedom letters.[84] To claim a *carta* was not simply to claim an individual's documentary proof of the end of apprenticeship. It was also a way to harness shipmate bonds to regularize the liberated Africans' legal status. Liberated Africans petitioned as shipmates to devise an alternative pathway to belonging and, beyond the law, to give their post-apprenticeship lives meaning.

Legal activism among liberated Africans involved petitioning to gain freedom for family members whose legal status was uncertain. Four liberated Africans, Deoclecianna, Umbelina, Henrique, and Joaquim, all petitioned for freedom on 10 June 1864.[85] Umbelina's petition states that she "comes to implore Your Imperial Majesty now to give her letter of emancipation to her; as well as a letter for her two small children, Manoel and Maria (both creoles)." The four adults had not disembarked from the same slaving ship, nor had they been apprenticed to the same private master or institution. Perhaps the lawyers who lodged the petitions arranged to submit them simultaneously, hoping that they would be mutually reinforcing. That said, even small groups of liberated Africans from different ships could form a community: around two hundred people from three different landings who settled in the city of Fortaleza in Ceará in northeastern Brazil formed a defined group called "Samangolês." The group, whose name was a contraction of the phrase "somos Angola" (we are Angolan), instituted legal proceedings against attempts to "reduce them to slavery."[86] However the petitioners in 1864 came together, their collective strategy worked: the clerk in the Ministry of Justice annotated each petition with, "a *carta* was sent." Simultaneous petitions gained irrevocable freedom for Umbelina and her two Brazil-born children, whose status had not been defined in treaty or domestic law.

These collective petitioning efforts pushed legislators to devise a solution to the flood of freedom claims. In September 1864, a decree emancipated all remaining apprentices. Shipmates developed vernacular understandings of how and when to petition, which they kept hidden from state authorities, household masters, and institutional bureaucrats. Their collective shipmate petitioning was an alternative to citizenship, which liberated Africans made visible only when shipmate bonds provided strong evidence for claiming letters of freedom. This hidden shipmate strategy of petitioning may have helped a claim for freedom from apprenticeship, but it also marked the liberated Africans as a potential risk to the institution of slavery. The language used by petitioners suggested that they threatened to create the precedent of an emancipatory group that was highly interconnected. Shipmate petitioning was a mechanism for collective freedom that risked providing further inspiration to enslaved people during an intensive period of risings: the Ministério da Justiça reported to the legislature that sedition and insurrection were two of the crimes that had increased most by incidence in the period 1860–64.[87] In response, the authorities began to deport liberated Africans to the frontiers.[88] Deportation cut the connective tissue between liberated Africans' petitioning, British diplomatic pressure, and the legal activism of the Instituto de Advogados Brasileiros. State officials turned to deportation to prevent an international alliance that could have formed an early broad-based abolitionist movement in Brazil.

In May 1865, the Visconde de Jequitinhonha, a member of the Instituto, presented the first general emancipation legislative project in Brazil to the Senate. His proposal aimed to emancipate all slaves in fifteen years' time. The proposal was one of three that he devised to reform the law of slavery. The emancipation bill would subject freedpeople to further measures regarding work and would not provide financial compensation to slave owners for emancipation. Enslaved people over the age of twenty-five would be freed first, after ten years' service to their enslavers. The Ministério da Justiça would have authority to review any proposed sale of these people before the ten-year deadline and to award manumission letters to them. All district centers would build workhouses for corralling "vagrants." The local *juiz de paz* and police chief would "promote and maintain" labor contracts between manumitted people and former enslavers.[89] The proposal envisaged strong public oversight of the emancipation process and penal powers to prevent freedpeople from leaving contracted agricultural work for itinerant independent ways of living.

In Jequitinhonha's speech to the Senate, he did not explain how he had formulated his plan, but his interactions with liberated Africans left a trail of clues. In 1848, before becoming a viscount, Francisco Gê Acaiaba de Montezuma participated in the secret commission that denounced the planned insurrection in the Vale do Paraíba. The commission accused liberated Africans of providing inspiration for the plan. In 1850, Montezuma joined the Conselho de Estado. The Conselho adjudicated cases of naval capture that were appealed from the Auditoria Geral da Marinha. Here, the Conselho prioritized the projection of state sovereignty over coastal waters and plantations over the enslaver's presumptive property right in illegally trafficked people. In the years before Jequitinhonha's proposal, liberated Africans such as Domingas and Honorato petitioned the Ministério da Justiça for freedom letters. Jequitinhonha probably heard about these collective shipmate petitions at the same time as news reached Brazil that one of the three remaining large slave societies in the Americas was crumbling.[90] In the months before his speech to the senate, Brazilian newspapers regularly reported Union victories against the proslavery Confederacy in the US Civil War, which provided fresh impetus to insurrections by enslaved people.[91] The war had diplomatic and economic ramifications for Brazil. Tensions between the Brazilian government and the Union arose over the Union capture of the Confederate warship *Florida* in the Brazilian port of Salvador.[92] The war dampened US demand for Brazilian coffee: exports to the United States almost halved between 1860 and 1864.[93] In confronting these rippling effects of militarization against slaveholding, Brazilian state authorities responded to liberated Africans' demands for freedom by increasing police surveillance and the Ministério da Justiça's efforts to control the emancipation process.

Francisco Gê Acaiaba de Montezuma, Visconde de Jequitinhonha, four years before his general emancipation proposal. (Sébastien Auguste Sisson, *Galeria dos Brasileiros Ilustres* [1861]. Biblioteca Brasiliana Guita and José Mindlin)

Now Jequitinhonha applied the anti-slave-trade framework of gradual emancipation for liberated Africans to Brazilian slave society. The three key planks of his proposal—compulsory service, freedom letters awarded by the Ministério da Justiça, and police surveillance of labor contracts—all drew on the regulation of liberated Africans. He sought to order postemancipation relations between freedpeople and former owners without redistributing property or allowing freedpeople to choose their work arrangements. Jequitinhonha's proposal went no further.[94] But it illuminated why the liberated Africans as a small population mattered. They demonstrated how freedpeople, when obliged to work under state supervision justified by the alleged need to protect public order, went to court to increase their range of action. The liberated Africans developed visions of freedom both earlier and in more radical ways than Jequitinhonha's postemancipation bill did.

This strategy of calling on shipmates to gain standing when petitioning the Ministério da Justiça became more urgent as the hemispheric patchwork of free soil was expanding. Diplomatic disputes with Britain, warfare on the southern border, and emancipation in the United States increased public talk of freedom for liberated Africans. But these developments also marked them out as a risk. Shipmate bonds were vital corroborating evidence that the petitioner was a liberated African rather than an enslaved person. The intensity of petitioning, with support from abolitionist lawyers, made it almost impossible for the Ministério to deny the validity of such corroborative testimony. These trends challenged the presumption that African birth and darker skin color indicated slave status. Collaborative petitioning by shipmates reinforced other evidence, such as faithful service as an apprentice and the accumulation of sufficient property, as grounds for receiving a freedom letter. In judging petitions, the Ministério prioritized an evaluation of whether the petitioner had served for the required length of time. Yet, for liberated Africans, petitioning served a wider objective: it strengthened social bonds between shipmates. Liberated Africans shaped the petitioning process by communicating with shipmates to make their case. They also used shipmate bonds as evidence for freedom. With lawyers' help, they cited key legislation. But their petitions were still constrained by a state that was committed to slave ownership. State officials imposed limitations on liberated Africans' residency and terms of labor. Their claims for freedom operated at multiple scales, from the Ministério da Justiça's processes to conflicts among polities. Consequently, liberated Africans and

Brazilian elites participated in a legal politics of emancipation that was simultaneously local and global.

ENDING COMPULSORY LABOR AMID INSURGENT WARFARE IN CUBA

In 1860, the notorious slave trader Manuel Basilio de Cunha Reis and his associates sent a plan to the captain general to ship African people to Cuba as "free colonists." The captain general tasked the Intendencia (the tax office) with holding a consultative vote on the proposal. The scheme was a thinly veiled slave-trading venture, and the Intendencia's officials were suspicious. The Intendencia considered reports from the Junta de Fomento, which favored the scheme, and the Real Universidad, which opposed it. The Intendencia quoted a proposal from the Junta's *fiscal* approvingly, which outlined a vision for the integral role of immigration in Cuba's agricultural growth. The state should distribute public land to cultivators and remove regulations on shipping and on building sugar mills. Liberated Africans should be apprenticed to cultivators for ten years, after which "they could contract themselves as workers to whomever it suited, or be expelled from the Island as vagabond and idle free people."[95] Neither the colonist immigration scheme nor the *fiscal*'s proposal would come to fruition. Nonetheless, as with Jequitinhonha's later proposal in Brazil, the Junta's plans to control liberated Africans to produce economic growth and racialized public order would endure. The policy of making liberated Africans subordinate to landowners as a model for Cuban slave society in transition would collide with liberated Africans' own visions of emancipation.

In the 1860s, dozens of landowners in eastern Cuba petitioned the government to receive ten liberated Africans each as laborers on their new cotton farms. They hoped to take advantage of falling US cotton output during the Civil War. Among the applicants was Carlos Manuel Céspedes, a slave owner in Manzanillo. In 1865, Céspedes received some of these laborers from a fellow farmer after an investigation had found that they were not engaged in cotton cultivation as required. Céspedes petitioned the lieutenant governor of Manzanillo "to exempt him for one year from paying the pension for the *emancipados* who were assigned to him."[96] Whether he received the exemption is unclear, but Céspedes's cotton farm revealed how landowning enslavers combined enslaved labor with the compulsory service of liberated Africans. Three years later, Céspedes freed the enslaved people whom he owned and declared the Grito de Yara, the armed struggle against Spanish colonial rule. Anti-slave-trade law and liberated Africans remained of enduring importance to both the colonial state and anticolonial fighters during the ensuing Ten Years' War (1868–78).

The revolutionary forces first mustered on plantations in eastern Cuba, which on average had smaller enslaved populations and were less technologically advanced than western plantations. Enslaved people on these plantations had formed communities that provided credit for manumission. They expected to have access to land for their postmanumission livelihoods. The encroaching sugar industry now threatened these two hard-won concessions, pushing people toward revolution.[97] The insurgents espoused an antiracist nationalist ethos, with a leadership committed to immediate emancipation without compensation for slave owners in the Constitution of Guáimaro in 1869. Slave owners successfully lobbied for a gradualist eradication of slavery enacted by imperial legislation instead.[98] The years 1867–69 were a transitional period in which maritime affairs remained integral to slave-trade suppression and both sides' war campaigns.[99] There were still rumors of disembarkations in the years leading up to 1868. State officials needed to contend with distributing prize money to Spanish captors.[100] During the war, the colonial authorities confiscated the property—including slaves—owned by suspected insurgents, a process through which influential plantation owners acquired new laborers.[101] Colonial state control of coastal land and of nearby islands such as the Isla de Pinos, which had been difficult to patrol for suppression, now became vital for deporting insurgents.[102] Significant problems had arisen during the implementation of anti-slave-trade law. These included the susceptibility of the legal system to political corruption, the bureaucratic incapacity to monitor enslaved people under the state's authority, and the failure to uphold a legal distinction between enslaved and freed people. Each problem reemerged in new arrangements in wartime, not least in relation to liberated Africans and their families. Some were now apprenticed in regions beyond Havana and Matanzas, including in the eastern jurisdiction where the armed struggle began. Both state officials and insurgents viewed the coastlines as spaces of slave-trade suppression and insurgency, where they might assert or contest colonial sovereignty. In the early war years, the legal politics surrounding suppression of the illegal trade remained dynamic, shaping the background to debates about the future of slavery.

By the end of 1866, the colonial government was working out how to implement the royal decree that brought the collective testimony of liberated Africans to its logical conclusion: the assumption would henceforth be that all individuals of color arriving in Cuban ports were of free rather than slave status. This presumption shifted the onus from the person held by an enslaver, who would formerly have needed to demonstrate a right to freedom, to the enslaver, who now needed to demonstrate legitimate title.[103] As in Brazil, the policy applied to *future* arrivals, rather than retrospectively to illegally trafficked people. If news of this dramatic policy shift spread among plantations, it probably inspired new liberation plans. At the first sign of any political dissent, the Spanish colonial government used its considerable powers to police the plantations and coasts. In May 1868, district officers investigated a conspiracy on an estate in eastern Cuba. The alleged conspirators had sought to take advantage of the festivals of San Juan and San Pedro the previous year. One woman testified that on San Juan's Day, she visited a neighbor and "saw a black man arrive, who expressed himself in insolent terms, talking about the equality of people of color," a commitment to racial equality that echoed Mauricio Reyes's opinions during the 1844 insurgency.[104] As in 1844, the conspiracy connected enslaved people with free people of color and white people. By the late 1860s, it was becoming ever harder for colonial authorities to police the mobility and speech of enslaved and freed people in their advocacy for ending slavery and colonial rule.

In at least one case, insurgents' recruitment of enslaved and freed people to their cause sparked an official investigation into the whereabouts of a liberated African. On 11 December 1868, over 150 insurgents marched on San Fernando plantation, whose owner was Fernando Pons. Armed with machetes and shotguns, the insurgents lined up all the enslaved people and chose thirty to join their cause.[105] Among the chosen was the liberated African Martín, who had been apprenticed to Pons. When the estate manager, Eugenio Soulé, appealed to the insurgents' commander to leave Martín, "because he was an *emancipado* . . . he replied: that is exactly why they were looking for him, and that if he [Soulé] did not shut up, something bad would happen to him."[106] The authorities struggled to discern what happened to Martín, using the terms "disappearance," "*plagio*" (kidnap), and "flight" over the course of the investigation in early 1869.[107] The first term refrained from allocating criminal responsibility for Martín's recruitment;

the second blamed the armed insurgents; and the third held Martín responsible. Despite continuing their investigation into April 1869, including a search of at least one other plantation, the authorities failed to find him; Martín had disappeared into the insurgents' fold.

Four years later, Captain General José de la Concha organized nine companies of liberated Africans, each with 150 men, to fight for the Spanish cause. After sending three companies to the front, the captain general was obliged "to recall them and send them to work because more than 40 individuals, almost all from Cinco Villas, had deserted with arms and munitions in the first two days of service, conduct that should not have been surprising, because it had already been made clear that if they were forced to take up arms they would almost certainly use them in favor of the insurrection."[108] Insurgents looked specifically for liberated Africans as potential mediators between enslaved people and colonial authorities, albeit on a smaller scale than they had done in 1844.

Spain desperately needed to reallocate resources to defeat the insurgency. It was becoming ever more difficult for colonial officials to stop liberated Africans from leaving compulsory labor assignments. In June 1870, five liberated Africans escaped from the sugar plantation Ingenio Espinola in Matanzas to complain about ill-treatment. As recorded in the Depósito de Cimarrones in Sabanilla, Narciso, Justo, Fausto, Aquilino, and Pedro "complain about the son of D. Federico, administrator of the estate, who punishes them with a stick and with leather, little food, and when they are in the infirmary he does not pay them 5 pesos per month."[109] The five men requested a transfer to a different master. Federico admitted to using corporal punishment, but the outcome of the complaint is unknown.[110] Liberated Africans continued to escape and complain to authorities to improve labor conditions.

Wartime pressures, combined with frequent claims by liberated Africans for freedom, probably explained the central government's decision to free *emancipados* from apprenticeship from July 1870 onward. By this time, the liberated Africans constituted less than 1 percent of the population in eastern Cuba.[111] The government could reduce the cost of monitoring liberated Africans by offering them the choice of receiving freedom papers or continuing to work for their masters as contracted laborers. Such was the keenness to reduce costs that the circular applied to all *emancipados* from selected captures, including the Colón expedition captured by Argüelles in

1863 and the landing at Punta del Holandes in 1866.[112] This decision meant that some apprentices served shorter terms than did people apprenticed under treaty law in the 1820s–1840s. A typical contract bound the employee to work for a number of years for a fixed salary, subsistence, clothing, medical care, and limited sick pay. The contract required the employee to deposit their freedom papers with the employer.[113] The government even authorized Jose Ricardo O'Farrill y O'Farrill to contract with some liberated Africans seized by the *Neptuno*—perhaps the very same captures for which he was indicted. Tiburcio, Silvio, Genoveva, and Lorenzo contracted to work for O'Farrill for six years.[114] Colony-wide apprenticeship for liberated Africans may have ended, but the obligation to work contractually, even for a slave owner, to avoid destitution continued.

Soon after the government circular in 1870, liberated Africans organized themselves as groups to choose their own work arrangements when possible. In November 1870, nine of twenty-three people apprenticed to Nicolas Valdivieso appeared before the governor of Matanzas to state that "they had refused to continue" to work for him. To exercise this choice, the apprentices needed to be both brave and persistent in leaving Valdivieso's estate and gaining an audience with the governor. Among them, Pio, Antonio, Petronilo, and Ysabel had endured the same transatlantic crossing and been recaptured at Santo Spiritus y Trinidad. As in Brazil, the shipmate bond helped them make a collective choice to leave Valdivieso's employ and search for a better future.[115] The governor sent them to the Central Deposit in Havana and their freedom papers to the central government.[116] Almost a year later, Toribio Congo, Anastacio Congo, and Cresenciano Lucumí fled from a plantation in Cuevitas (in Jovenallos, Matanzas) where they were contracted to work for Ramon Abreu. The rural police force detained them. In the municipal depot, they explained that "the reason for their escape is that their monthly allowance of nine pesos does not satisfy them, and that he forces them to work when they are sick with sores on their legs." A local officer organized medical care at the depot, but the official report to the governor of Matanzas does not state what happened to the men.[117] As in Sierra Leone and Brazil, the African workers for Valdivieso and Abreu made their legal claims as a group. They wished to protect the interests of fellow liberated Africans with whom they had formed relationships as shipmates or in the workplace. Liberated Africans' refusal to contract and persistence in lodging complaints were ways to demand justice when deciding labor arrangements, creating one pathway to postemancipation freedom in Cuba.

During the protracted ending of the illegal trade and compulsory labor, liberated Africans developed plural ideas and practices of political belonging and economic life that contributed to global emancipation politics. Scholars have demonstrated that emancipation was not a single event but rather constituted overlapping processes. Migrants brought ideas of freedom with them when they moved from one region of revolution and military occupation to another.[118] External powers declared legal emancipation in conquered territories, changing property rights in them.[119] In enforcing emancipation policies, these powers rejected freedpeople's demands for a more radical emancipation that would include redistributing land rights and declaring equal citizenship.[120] By making extensive connections between the North and South Atlantic, liberated Africans provided a different perspective on global emancipations. Scattered across different territories, liberated Africans developed convergent legal strategies. With scant documentary proof about their service as compulsory laborers, liberated Africans used shipmate bonds to prove their status and navigate a future path toward greater security.

By the 1860s, there was considerable divergence between the Cape, Sierra Leone, Brazil, and Cuba regarding the post-apprenticeship legal status of liberated Africans. In the Cape, the state classified liberated Africans as "Coloured" people who had access to the urban labor market but not the security of British subjecthood. In Sierra Leone, liberated Africans became British subjects in 1853, prompting them to use conventional methods of political representation, such as petitioning the monarch to change official policy. In Brazil, liberated Africans fought simply to stay in the places where they had built family lives and social capital during apprenticeship. They contended with a state that was determined to move them to frontier regions. In Cuba, liberated Africans sought to exit from compulsory labor arrangements by petitioning local political authorities and enlisted to fight principally on the side of the insurgents.

Alongside these divergent trajectories, liberated Africans found common meaning in diaspora by collaborating as shipmates. They were confronted with the lack of definition of post-apprenticeship status in the formal law. Liberated Africans resolved this predicament by registering their children as irrevocably free and pooling resources with shipmates to create new ventures. They formulated their own visions of freedom, demanding recognition of their associations, their private property rights, and their bonds with fellow liberated Africans and enslaved and free people of color. Liberated Africans made these demands even when state authorities refused to grant them the rights of freeborn white people. Liberated Africans' visions of freedom came into conflict with state officials' attempts to harness liberated Africans for their own projects of imperial expansion and the public control of freed populations. The shipmate bond provided the social and material basis for imagining a political community that valued reciprocity, which transcended empires' commitment to governing through inequality.

Liberated Africans focused on independent control of work conditions, protection of the property that they had worked so hard to accumulate, and security of their residency in a given society. These benefits were alternatives to citizenship but not equal to it. Most obviously, they never amounted to substantial individual civil or political rights. At best, these entitlements drew liberated Africans and state officials into bonds of obligation without creating predictable ways to enforce those bonds. For liberated Africans, establishing post-apprenticeship status was not just about eligibility or fair process. They used the law to make new social relations between shipmates long-lasting and meaningful.

Conclusion

THE MARITIME CAPTURE OF SLAVING ships formed a major part of the suppression of the transatlantic trade in enslaved African people during the nineteenth century. In port cities, courts adjudicated the legality of maritime captures and handed the rescued African people to host governments to bind them to compulsory labor according to the terms of treaties and domestic legislation. These governments decided on the ending of such labor arrangements. Maritime capture, court adjudication, compulsory labor, and the ending of compulsory labor formed the pathway of slave-trade suppression that brought liberated African legal status into being.

The pathway produced a layered and compromised anti-slave-trade legal regime. It did not fulfill the objectives of any party involved in suppression. Liberated African status did not apply retrospectively to the hundreds of thousands of people trafficked illegally into slavery. The rupture of property rights over illegally trafficked people exposed by liberated Africans' testimony in Brazilian and colonial Cuban courts was a hairline fracture rather than a dam breach. By tracing this pathway, we have seen that the course of suppression was so complex and multilateral that it is impossible to disentangle its causal threads. Rather than seeking any individual underlying cause, the approach taken has been to follow the top-down and bottom-up interactions in developing the pathway. The anti-slave-trade legal regime subjected liberated Africans to authoritarian control yet also provided them

The African-American spiritual "Deep River," arranged by British-Sierra Leonean composer Samuel Coleridge-Taylor and transcribed by Maud Powell. (Courtesy of Sibley Music Library, Eastman School of Music, University of Rochester)

with a domain to produce their own visions of freedom. The regime reshaped international law by consolidating the importance of treaties and freedom of navigation on the high seas yet also left scope for Britain to suppress the trade unilaterally. It provided for new labor migration policies in zones dominated by the production of slave-produced commodities. The regime shaped the market conditions for exchange. The authoritarian control and diasporic visions of freedom that emerged from the pathway shaped major processes in global history.

In the development of the anti-slave-trade legal regime, liberated Africans were not always the central actors. Naval and privateer patrols and vice-admiralty courts adapted prize law to early slave-trade suppression. In the system of bilateral treaties, the Mixed Commissions advocated for their jurisdiction over the legality of captures. Host governments, particularly those of slave societies, sought to limit the jurisdiction of the Mixed Commissions. Under both prize and treaty law, liberated Africans in the early nineteenth century were put in a subordinate position and struggled to advocate for their freedom. They owed a debt for their liberation and were subjected to high levels of official oversight. Liberated Africans released under prize and treaty law challenged their precarious position by escaping labor assignments and lodging legal complaints.

Liberated African legal activism took off in the late 1830s and early 1840s under various systems of compulsory labor in both sub-Saharan Africa and the Americas. Liberated Africans went forum shopping to gain greater freedom for themselves and to exit compulsory labor arrangements early. They demanded wages, days off to work on their own account, and benefits such as food and accommodation. By the 1840s, political authorities in slave societies perceived such activism as a major threat that was potentially connected to insurgent politics. In the 1850s and 1860s, liberated Africans became key drivers of change. They testified to domestic courts, which ruptured the powerful social assumption that somebody who claimed to have a property right in a Black person in the Americas possessed such a right. In the 1860s, as polities around the Atlantic devised new mechanisms to monitor or expel liberated Africans, they turned to shipmate bonds to defend their community from these discriminatory state practices.

Authoritarian mechanisms of control developed through anti-slave-trade law. Under prize law, liberated Africans were released from slaving ships into apprenticeships and enlistment that helped build British naval and armed forces. As bonded laborers, they built state infrastructure in the Caribbean, the Cape, and Sierra Leone. Under treaty law, liberated Africans in Brazil and Spanish colonial Cuba also participated in state-building. There was a liberation-to-prison pathway in which state authorities developed policing and carceral institutions to monitor liberated Africans during compulsory apprenticeship. Police forces and prison officials easily adapted such techniques to detecting and persecuting insurgents who had alleged links to liberated Africans. They later applied these techniques to the suppression of the slave trade in the 1850s and 1860s by detecting illegal landings on coastal plantations. By this time, authoritarian control expanded beyond the liberated Africans to embrace the sovereign protection of territorial waters and land, above all from the British Empire. In the 1860s, political authorities used mechanisms of slave-trade suppression and liberated African labor indenture to expand imperial territories and settlement.

Behind these intensifying coercive practices lay potential economic drivers such as the need for South Atlantic polities to find a place in a world that was increasingly dominated by industrial economies in North America and Britain. Industrialized economies provided manufactured goods and services worldwide. The comparative advantage for economies in sub-Saharan Africa and Latin America and the Caribbean lay in providing raw materials and cash crops for manufacturing processes and consumption. The political authorities of slave societies such as Brazil and Cuba wished to prolong commodity production by slaves for as long as possible. But these mechanisms of authoritarian control were not simply economically determined. After all, in none of these slave societies did authorities revert to the pre-nineteenth-century models of jurisdiction in which enslavers' power over the people on their estates was left largely untouched by the state. Instead, the contingent need to manage liberated Africans released throughout urban and rural areas meant that once policing and carceral methods had developed, they were not revoked.

In response to these authoritarian methods of control, liberated Africans devised their own diasporic visions of freedom. They deployed mechanisms available to them under the formal law, such as petitioning as shipmates. Successful petitioning needed to meet the conditions set by domestic or international laws. Legal institutions like British imperial commissions of inquiry and Brazil's Ministério da Justiça provided new fora for claimants to petition for freedom. They imposed their own conventions to which claimants were obliged to conform. Aware of these constraints, liberated Africans also turned away from formal anti-slave-trade laws to formulate their own ideas and practices of social regulation. Sometimes, they combined both strategies. Liberated Africans' diasporic visions of freedom illuminated how suppression did not have to take the authoritarian path that it so frequently did. Some captive people rose up on ships to create new insurgent communities at sea that endured on land in places like Congo Town. Others sought fugitive communities in urban Havana and Rio. Still others became adepts in Santería, Candomblé, and Islam. Liberated Africans' strategies to claim justice were neither necessarily emancipatory (a collective fight against slavery) nor abolitionist (a commitment to dismantling all forms of racist repression). But they did oppose the slave trade and slavery for people with liberated African status. They proposed solutions to a novel predicament not of their own making: transoceanic displacement, maritime capture, compulsory labor to repay the "debt" of capture, and official refusals to determine postlabor status. They created a precedent that enslaved people could use for their own projects. These strategies created something new: Afro-diasporic justice.

To challenge forced labor, liberated Africans refused not only the terms of apprenticeship but also the underlying assumption that they needed to be trained to be responsible with their freedom. They sought self-directed work, which did not depend on working for a wage or for an employer. Usually, liberated Africans sought to own a stake in production. They bought goods in prize auctions, sold services at markets and in the maritime economy, and engaged in subsistence agriculture. To resolve the ambiguity that political authorities constructed regarding post-apprenticeship status, liberated Africans went to the law for their own purposes. They registered their children as free and pooled resources with shipmates to create new ventures. To remediate displacement, liberated Africans sought security not in territorial belonging or national allegiance but rather in the shipmate community. The commitments of Afro-diasporic justice to independent work, reciprocity, security for their children, and shipmate community would endure in both local and global settings long after the final suppression of the illegal trade.

Understanding the anti-slave-trade legal regime's authoritarian and freedom-making aspects provides a new perspective on the transition from slavery to free labor in nineteenth-century global history. Liberated Africans made clear to political authorities that the end of the slave trade was possible. As their story shows, the problem of freedom emerged early. They made it visible in the era of slave societies long before emancipation policies in the British Caribbean in the 1830s or Cuba in the 1870s. A small number of liberated Africans indicated in every slave society from British Tortola and the Cape to Portuguese Brazil and Spanish colonial Cuba that the maritime ban on the slave trade could result in a widespread interpolity commitment to abolition. An effective ban would also mean that free African people such as liberated Africans would become a much larger population in the nineteenth century. They would become ever more influential as a source of labor and as a political constituency. Early petitioning by liberated Africans in all these societies revealed that they resisted the coercion that was inherent in anti-slave-trade law. Liberated Africans challenged the limited legal capacity to which they were subjected under each state's local legal system. The authoritarian control over liberated Africans set a compelling precedent for the transition to postslavery labor for statesmen such as Jequitinhonha and institutions such as the Spanish colonial Junta de Fomento. Gradualist, state-directed emancipation began with the liberated Africans.

The features that historians have often attributed to the problem of freedom—the continued commodification of Black people's labor, the expansion of carceral institutions, and the withholding of citizenship from free Black people—did not originate in late nineteenth-century legal emancipation but rather in the management of liberated Africans during the era of slave-trade suppression. Their paths toward freedom reveal neither a transition to free labor nor an expansion of unfree labor but rather the invention of "free labor" in the process of slave-trade suppression.[1] The interdiction of slave-trading vessels and assignment of liberated Africans into compulsory labor helped define free labor as the antithesis to slave labor. Each claim by liberated Africans to a contract, to days off, or to rights to health care created new labor norms. But as liberated Africans' escapes and shipmate communities remind us, free labor defined by contracts and wages was not an inevitable outcome.

Liberated Africans' claims reframe the historical development of the spectrum of statuses, with slavery at one end, full freedom at the other, and indenture and convict labor in between. Salaried contract work in the market is a familiar aspect of a definition of full freedom that emerged in the nineteenth century and persisted long thereafter. Its significance took shape not when societies passed emancipation legislation but rather when they began the process of ending the trade. For the first time, political authorities planned for demographic shifts in the labor supply and devised methods to manage liberated Africans. Indenture was not subsequent to slavery, nor was it geographically distinct from it. The migration of indentured laborers from China, the Indian subcontinent, and elsewhere overlapped with the indenture of liberated Africans in places as far-flung as Guyana, Cuba, KwaZulu-Natal, and Mauritius. Slave-trade suppression provided a precedent for the authoritarian aspects of indenture across the globe, including lengthening periods of service and the racialized management of laboring populations.[2] The spaces of alliance-building between liberated Africans, Indigenous people in Africa and in the Americas, and Asian indentured laborers await further study. Attending to the margins of the sources generated by the anti-slave-trade legal regime has produced vital new insight into histories of African diasporic revolutionary politics. Alliances between groups probably formed in ways that were also recorded on the margins of official archival sources. The significance of these alliances in part lay in creating alternatives to "free labor." Liberated Africans were a crucial group where free legal status, time-limited bonded service, and the political turn to immigration to fill the gaps in the supply of enslaved laborers converged.

These features were coconstitutive. Instead of a spectrum, there was a constellation of bonded labor statuses that emerged from slave-trade suppression, often separated by little more than how official documentation classified different laborers.

Sub-Saharan Africa's integration into a post-slave-trade global order extended beyond the overlapping waves of Asian and liberated African indenture. The suppression of the illegal trade and release of liberated Africans advanced the British imperial agenda, in which obtaining raw materials, controlling people, and colonizing lands were interrelated. This imperial turn occurred before the era of the "Scramble for Africa" in the 1880s. Maritime patrols advanced British imperial priorities on the high seas and in territorial waters, breaching the freedom of the former and the sovereignty of foreign polities over the latter. Patrols combined the rescue of captives with onshore invasions that linked land and sea. This pattern began with the earliest prize captures, such as in the case of the *Ysavel* in 1814. It continued in raids on the Upper Guinea Coast in the 1840s, which developed the act of state doctrine. And it was evident in the annexation of Lagos in 1861. Liberated Africans outside British jurisdictions in sub-Saharan Africa raised the question of British responsibilities to them and the purpose of an empire in Africa.

One possible solution was that British authorities should extend a free-soil policy to anybody who had set foot inside British jurisdiction. Free-soil freedom could have applied to all residents in territories, including those who subsequently emigrated. Free soil could have been grounds for extending British subjecthood to liberated Africans, but this rarely occurred. In the Cape after legal emancipation, liberated Africans gained freedom from reenslavement and access to the urban labor market but not formal inclusion as British subjects. Through forming relationships with Indigenous people, Cape Malay people, and immigrant workers and sailors, in the Western Cape, liberated Africans and their descendants formed part of the "Coloured" population (who are still known by this term), but their precise political participation has gone unrecorded. In the early 1900s, Coloured people exerted political influence, constituting 35 percent of the electorate in District Six in Cape Town. They also held the Stone Meetings, led by John Tobin, where they discussed the legacies of slavery and emancipation for residents of color.[3] British subjecthood for liberated Africans settled in Sierra Leone was unusual. The recognition of subjecthood corroborates the finding that Sierra Leone was the most secure site for liberated Africans. A focus on legal politics recasts the security of Sierra Leone as heavily circumscribed by pervasive precarity and sustained political subordination to an imperial authority.[4]

Instead of a free-soil commitment, the common British imperial policy was to delegalize slavery. Delegalization meant that British courts and political authorities would no longer recognize slavery as a legal status, but they placed the onus on an enslaved person to go to a British court to claim freedom. Enslavers reclassified enslaved concubines as wives under customary law to avoid manumitting them. For enslaved people, claiming freedom in court risked separation from their children, who belonged to the enslaver's kin lineage.[5] In agricultural areas, enslaved people knew that a freedom claim would probably result in the landowning enslaver removing them from their workplace, family home, and only source of subsistence.[6] In Lagos, the British recognized that any enslaved person who reached the colonial territory would be free there. But no official encouragement would be offered to slaves to travel to Lagos for freedom, nor would British protection of such freedom continue if the freedperson left the colony.[7] Delegalization ensured the continued export of slave-produced commodities right across sub-Saharan Africa, from Lagos to Zanzibar, without substantially increasing the financial and moral commitments of the imperial government toward enslaved people. Delegalization was the cheapest form of imperial governance before the Scramble.

The long-term legacy of liberated Africans' insecure rights can be seen in the unequal distribution of property, the racial wealth gap, and discriminatory policing practices throughout the Atlantic world. Liberated Africans were brave in advocating for their own visions of justice. They testified in court to puncture the performance of presumptive property rights that enslavers claimed in illegally trafficked people. Yet the rupture did not mean that liberated Africans could gain meaningful rights. In societies that privileged asset wealth, racialized white status, and paperwork, liberated Africans faced severe constraints. These three factors shaped free status, property rights, and citizenship. Polities denied that free people of color, including liberated Africans, along with Indigenous people and indentured immigrants, were as worthy as white colonists of these benefits. These legacies do not straightforwardly have their roots in slavery because during the era of colonial slavery, enslavers had jurisdiction over enslaved people on the estates that they owned. Instead, these legacies form part of the problem of slave-trade suppression because they emerged when state jurisdiction began to replace the private jurisdiction of slave owners. In Brazil, Luiz Felipe de Alencastro has powerfully argued that three social "deformities" were caused by slavery and were thus grounds for protecting quotas for Afro-Brazilian students in higher education: the inequality of free and enslaved people before the criminal law, the use of public terror to regulate the enslaved population in urban areas, and the discriminatory literacy test for citizenship.[8] We can extend this insight by positioning these problems as rooted in how state practices developed to manage liberated Africans under anti-slave-trade law. The Constitution of 1824 excluded African-born freedpeople from citizenship. Policing and carceral infrastructure, particularly the Casa de Correção, expanded to regulate liberated Africans' compulsory labor in the 1840s. The Ministério da Justiça refused to recognize emancipation petitions as grounds for formal property or residency rights in the 1860s. After the state denied liberated Africans formal free status, property rights, and citizenship, it became possible to imagine the same measures applying to all subsequent generations of Afro-Brazilian people.

State authority imposed its own jurisdiction to encompass private jurisdictions and thereby enforce anti-slave-trade measures across a territory. A major part of the imposition of state jurisdiction was the increasing importance of the magistrate in governing labor relations and resolving civic disputes across the British Empire. The magistrate replaced forms of dispute resolution that took place inside households or on plantations. Observing this transformation does not require nostalgia for the forms of legal pluralism that existed in the early-modern world. Such pluralism could result in greater repression just as easily as in greater choice.[9] Nor does the growth of state jurisdiction obscure how professional policing could draw on mob rule.[10] The growing role of the magistrate and carceral institutions in disciplining liberated African labor reveals the emerging power of the state in the nineteenth century. State authority often worked through racialized distinctions between people regarding access to land and political power. As the previous chapters have revealed, liberated Africans often contested discriminatory state practices. But they could also lapse into the divisions that state authorities had imposed. In Guyana, liberated Africans participated in riots attacking Portuguese-owned shops in 1856.[11] Two years later, in Sierra Leone, liberated Africans petitioned the governor to complain about the alleged corruption, mismanagement, and nepotism of colonial administrators from the Caribbean.[12] Neither the riots nor the petitions commanded unanimous support from liberated Africans, and they were ultimately protests about the lack of resources and political domination rather than nativist movements. But both examples revealed how liberated African politics could work to exclude rather than to build alliances between dispossessed groups. State power and the colonial magistracy developed through the management of liberated Africans and then encompassed all people swept up in the troubling transition from slavery to emancipation.

Both inside formal anti-slave-trade legal processes and outside them, diasporic visions of freedom emerged, producing different temporalities for justice from those that were imposed by the authoritarian pathway of liberation.[13] The commitments of Afro-diasporic justice to self-directed labor, reciprocity, security for one's children, and shipmate community stretched across imperial boundaries. They transcended a reliance on a monopoly of violence by the state. One prominent ideology that extended this vision was Pan-Africanism. Pan-Africanist political community existed beyond the level of the nation-state. In 1868, James Africanus Beale Horton, the son of liberated Africans, published a major text in the history of political thought that promoted Pan-Africanism. He aimed to refute the arguments of the Anthropological Society, which in the aftermath of the American Civil War had proposed that Black people were an inherently inferior race on the basis of pseudoscientific evidence. Horton, who was educated at a Church Missionary School and Fourah Bay College in Freetown, followed by medical training at King's College London and the University of Edinburgh, dismissed this racist argument. "It would have been sufficient to treat this with the contempt it deserves," he argued, "were it not that leading statesmen of the present day have shown themselves easily carried away by the malicious views of these negrophobists, to the great prejudice of that race."[14]

After an extensive refutation of these arguments, Horton turned to his second aim. He wished to build on the parliamentary select committee's recommendation in 1865 for self-government in the West African colonies. Horton envisaged a self-governing federation of West African polities within the British Empire that would benefit from Christian education and European technology. Horton participated in the intense political battles opened by the anti-slave-trade legal regime. His arguments helped lay the ground for the Pan-African Congresses, the first of which was held in

London in 1900. Among the delegates were W. E. B. Du Bois, author of one of the earliest studies of the United States and the suppression of the slave trade, and the composer Samuel Coleridge-Taylor, who arranged the music.[15] Horton wrote his text at a time when there were liberated Africans like Librada still serving as bonded laborers in Cuba, hoping to petition for freedom for themselves and their children. When Horton published and Librada petitioned, the authoritarian controls imposed by the anti-slave-trade legal regime constrained opportunities not only for freedpeople but for entire societies. Both Horton and Librada struggled for true freedom. The struggle is now ours.

NOTES

ABBREVIATIONS

AGCRJ: Arquivo Geral da Cidade do Rio de Janeiro
AHI: Arquivo Histórico do Itamaraty
AHN: Archivo Histórico Nacional, Spain
AHPM: Archivo Histórico Provincial de Matanzas (cited by series, legajo number, and document number)
ANC: Archivo Nacional de Cuba (cited by series, legajo number, and document number)

- AP: Asuntos Políticos
- CM: Comisión Militar
- GG: Gobierno General
- ME: Miscelánea de Expedientes
- GSC: Gobierno Superior Civil
- RCO: Reales Cédulas y Órdenes
- RCJF: Real Consulado y Junta de Fomento

ANRJ: Arquivo Nacional, Rio de Janeiro

- AGM: Auditoria Geral da Marinha

APEB: Arquivo Público do Estado da Bahia
AS: *Anais do Senado do Império do Brasil*
ASCBV: Archive of Santo Cristo Buen Viaje
BNJM: Biblioteca Nacional de Cuba José Martí

- CM: Colección Manuscrito

BNRJ: Biblioteca Nacional, Rio de Janeiro
C. (1st series): Command Paper (cited by year of parliamentary session, abbreviated title, and paper number)

EAP: Endangered Archives Programme, British Library
LADLB: Liberated African Department Letter Books, Public Archives of Sierra Leone
HCP: House of Commons Papers (cited by year of parliamentary session, abbreviated title, volume, and paper number)
HL: Houghton Library, Harvard University
EC: Escoto Collection, MS Span 52 (cited by identifier number and folder number)
PASL: Public Archives of Sierra Leone
PMCRB: Police Magistrate Court Record Book
UKNA: United Kingdom National Archives
ADM: Admiralty Records (cited by reference code)
CO: Colonial Office Records (cited by reference code; for governors' despatches, citation includes date of despatch; where more than one despatch has the same date, the despatch number is also supplied)
FO: Foreign Office Records (cited by reference code)
HCA: High Court of Admiralty Records (cited by reference code)
WCARS: Western Cape Archives and Records Service

INTRODUCTION

1. Petition of Librada, 30 September 1879, Emancipados 108/11338, AHPM, fol. 2r.
2. Petition of Librada, 3 November 1879, Emancipados 108/11338, AHPM, fol. 6v.
3. On the legal regime, see Edward Keene, "A Case Study of the Construction of International Hierarchy: British Treaty-Making against the Slave Trade in the Early Nineteenth Century," *International Organization* 61, no. 2 (2007): 311–39; Lauren A. Benton and Lisa Ford, *Rage for Order: The British Empire and the Origins of International Law, 1800–1850* (Cambridge, MA: Harvard University Press, 2016). On the scale of the illegal trade to Cuba and Brazil, see Laird W. Bergad, Fe Iglesias García, and María del Carmen Barcia, *The Cuban Slave Market, 1790–1880* (Cambridge: Cambridge University Press, 1995); Sidney Chalhoub, *A força da escravidão: Ilegalidade e costume no Brasil oitocentista* (São Paulo: Companhia das Letras, 2012); Daniel B. Domingues da Silva, *The Atlantic Slave Trade from West Central Africa, 1780–1867* (Cambridge: Cambridge University Press, 2017).
4. The Prize Papers Project will provide digital access to many materials from the vice-admiralty courts. For one study of the operations of the vice-admiralty court in Tortola, see Sean M. Kelley, "The 'Captured Negroes' of Tortola, 1807–22," in *Liberated Africans and the Abolition of the Slave Trade, 1807–1896*, ed. Richard Anderson and Henry B. Lovejoy (Rochester, NY: University of Rochester Press, 2020), 25–44. On the Mixed Commissions, see Leslie Bethell, "The Mixed Commissions for the Suppression of the Transatlantic Slave Trade in the Nineteenth Century," *Journal of African History* 7, no. 1 (1966): 79–93; Jennifer Nelson, "Liberated Africans in the Atlantic World: The Courts of Mixed Commission in Havana and Rio de Janeiro 1819–1871" (PhD diss., University of Leeds, 2015). The most recent comprehensive analysis of liberated Africans in

Sierra Leone is Richard Peter Anderson, *Abolition in Sierra Leone: Re-building Lives and Identities in Nineteenth-Century West Africa* (Cambridge: Cambridge University Press, 2020). For studies of domestic anti-slave-trade law in the era of the vast illegal slave trade to Cuba and Brazil, respectively, see Aisnara Perera Díaz and María de los Ángeles Meriño Fuentes, *Contrabando de bozales en Cuba: Perseguir el tráfico y mantener la esclavitud (1845–1866)* (Mayabeque: Ediciones Montecallado, 2015); Beatriz Mamigonian, *Africanos livres: A abolição do tráfico de escravos no Brasil* (São Paulo: Companhia das Letras, 2017).

5. For two important studies that have begun a trend toward the comparative global study of liberated Africans, see Anderson and Lovejoy, *Liberated Africans and the Abolition of the Slave Trade*; Maeve Ryan, *Humanitarian Governance and the British Antislavery World System* (New Haven, CT: Yale University Press, 2022).
6. Natalie Zemon Davis, "Judges, Masters, Diviners: Slaves' Experience of Criminal Justice in Colonial Suriname," *Law and History Review* 29, no. 4 (2011): 936–37.
7. The Voyages Database states that for the period 1808–66, 2.76 million people were embarked out of a total of 10.04 million (27.49 percent). See SlaveVoyages, "Trans-Atlantic Slave Trade—Database," accessed 17 April 2024, https://www.slavevoyages.org/voyages/xzEoQX3Y. The Estimates Database states 3.20 million people out of a total of 12.52 million (25.56 percent). See SlaveVoyages, "Trans-Atlantic Slave Trade—Estimates," accessed 17 April 2024, http://www.slavevoyages.org/estimates/bLovnIOs.
8. 80.5 percent of all estimated embarked captive people according to the Voyages Database: SlaveVoyages, "Trans-Atlantic Slave Trade—Database," accessed 28 July 2023, https://www.slavevoyages.org/voyages/zbPwtRwI; 81.3 percent of all estimated embarked African captive people according to the Estimates Database: SlaveVoyages, "Trans-Atlantic Slave Trade—Estimates," accessed 28 July 2023, http://www.slavevoyages.org/estimates/1g79jfPr.
9. In giving a comprehensive, but not exhaustive, account of the anti-slave-trade legal regime, the selection principle foregrounds the sites primarily involved in the suppression of the illegal trades to Brazil and Cuba. It does not cover the Indian Ocean world, for which see Matthew S. Hopper, *Slaves of One Master: Globalization and Slavery in Arabia in the Age of Empire* (New Haven, CT: Yale University Press, 2016). The regime's connections to the emerging field of conflict of laws, particularly between British and US jurisdictions, awaits further study. For three cases that provoked a long legal dispute that eventually resulted in the award of British compensation to US slavers by international arbitration, see *Message from the President of the United States, Communicating, in Compliance with a Resolution of the Senate, Copies of Correspondence in Relation to the Mutiny on Board the Brig Creole, and the Liberation of the Slaves Who Were Passengers in the Said Vessel. January 20, 1842. Read, and Referred to the Committee on Printing. January 21, 1842*, S. Doc. 51, 27th Cong., 2nd sess. (1842); United Nations, "Commission Established under the Convention Concluded between the United States of America and Great Britain on 8 February 1853: Case of the *Enterprise* v. Great Britain, Opinions of the Commissioners and Decision of the Umpire,

Mr. Bates, Dated 23 December 1854; Case of the *Hermosa* v. Great Britain, Decision of the Umpire, Mr. Bates; and Case of the *Creole* v. Great Britain, Decision of the Umpire, Mr. Bates," in *Reports of International Arbitral Awards*, vol. 29 (New York: United Nations, 2011), 9–56. On slavery in the jurisprudence of the conflict of laws, see Joseph Story, *Commentaries on the Conflict of Laws, Foreign and Domestic: In Regard to Contracts, Rights, and Remedies* (Boston: Hilliard, Gray, 1834), chap. 2, §§ 27–38.

10. This estimate relates to the approximately one hundred thousand people liberated at Sierra Leone, including those subsequently shipped to other territories, plus those liberated from slaving ships at various sites around the Atlantic world under domestic, treaty, or imperial law. It thus corresponds to the estimate provided in Daniel Domingues da Silva, David Eltis, Philip Misevich, and Olatunji Ojo, "The Diaspora of Africans Liberated from Slave Ships in the Nineteenth Century," *Journal of African History* 55, no. 3 (2014): 347–69, table A.1, 367. A more expansive definition, which relates to any African person liberated and relocated in the Atlantic or Indian Ocean, is used in the Liberated Africans Digital Project. This number increases to around seven hundred thousand if one takes into account the liberation of African people in the Indian Ocean world and within various empires' forms of antislavery legislation within African colonial territories including by British, French, and Portuguese authorities. See the Liberated Africans Digital Project: https://liberatedafricans.org/public/index.php. An even greater number of Africans liberated from slavery would emerge if all forms of legal release from slavery, such as from delegalization decrees in European colonies in Africa, were included.
11. Da Silva et al., "Diaspora of Africans Liberated from Slave Ships," table A.1, 367.
12. Leonardo Marques, *The United States and the Transatlantic Slave Trade to the Americas, 1776–1867* (New Haven, CT: Yale University Press, 2016); John Harris, *The Last Slave Ships: New York and the End of the Middle Passage* (New Haven, CT: Yale University Press, 2020).
13. Seymour Drescher, *The Mighty Experiment: Free Labor versus Slavery in British Emancipation* (New York: Oxford University Press, 2002), chap. 10.
14. My approach investigates the operations of the anti-slave-trade legal regime, rather than the causes of abolition and emancipation. On the debate about causation, see Eric Eustace Williams, *Capitalism and Slavery* (Chapel Hill: University of North Carolina Press, 1944); Seymour Drescher, *Econocide: British Slavery in the Era of Abolition* (Pittsburgh: University of Pittsburgh Press, 1977); Thomas L. Haskell, "Capitalism and the Origins of the Humanitarian Sensibility, Part 1," *American Historical Review* 90, no. 2 (1985): 339–61; Thomas L. Haskell, "Capitalism and the Origins of the Humanitarian Sensibility, Part 2," *American Historical Review* 90, no. 3 (1985): 547–66. The polycentric origins of antislavery movements and antislavery laws have a parallel in the polycentric origins of international human rights law. For this argument about human rights, see Philip Alston, "Does the Past Matter? On the Origins of Human Rights," *Harvard Law Review* 126 (2013): 2043–81.

15. Christopher Leslie Brown, *Moral Capital: Foundations of British Abolitionism* (Chapel Hill: Omohundro Institute of Early American History and Culture / University of North Carolina Press, 2006).
16. Robert Burroughs, "Eyes on the Prize: Journeys in Slave Ships Taken as Prizes by the Royal Navy," *Slavery and Abolition* 31, no. 1 (2010): 99–115; John Rankin, "British and African Health in the Anti-Slave-Trade Squadron," in *The Suppression of the Atlantic Slave Trade: British Policies, Practices and Representations of Naval Coercion*, ed. Robert M. Burroughs and Richard Huzzey (Manchester, UK: Manchester University Press, 2015), 95–121.
17. Seymour Drescher, "Emperors of the World: British Abolitionism and Imperialism," in *Abolitionism and Imperialism in Britain, Africa, and the Atlantic*, ed. Derek Peterson (Athens: Ohio University Press, 2010), 129–49; Robin Law, "Abolition and Imperialism: International Law and the British Suppression of the Atlantic Slave Trade," in Peterson, *Abolitionism and Imperialism*, 150–74; Richard Huzzey, *Freedom Burning: Anti-Slavery and Empire in Victorian Britain* (Ithaca, NY: Cornell University Press, 2012).
18. Johnson Uzoha Jonah Asiegbu, *Slavery and the Politics of Liberation, 1787–1861: A Study of Liberated African Emigration and British Anti-Slavery Policy* (London: Longmans, 1969); Monica Schuler, *"Alas, Alas, Kongo": A Social History of Indentured African Immigration into Jamaica, 1841–1865* (Baltimore: Johns Hopkins University Press, 1980); Christopher Saunders, "Between Slavery and Freedom: The Importation of Prize Negroes to the Cape in the Aftermath of Emancipation," *Kronos* 9 (1984): 36–43.
19. David Northrup, "Becoming African: Identity Formation among Liberated Slaves in Nineteenth-Century Sierra Leone," *Slavery & Abolition* 27, no. 1 (1 April 2006): 1–21; Rosanne Marion Adderley, *"New Negroes from Africa": Slave Trade Abolition and Free African Settlement in the Nineteenth-Century Caribbean* (Bloomington: Indiana University Press, 2006); Jofre Teófilo Vieira, "Os 'Samangolês': Africanos livres no Ceará (1835–1865)" (PhD diss., Universidade Federal do Ceará, 2017); Anderson, *Abolition in Sierra Leone*.
20. Inés Roldán de Montaud, "En los borrosos confines de la libertad: El caso de los negros emancipados en Cuba, 1817–1870," *Revista de Indias* 71, no. 251 (March 2011): 159–92; Samuël Coghe, "The Problem of Freedom in a Mid Nineteenth-Century Atlantic Slave Society: The Liberated Africans of the Anglo-Portuguese Mixed Commission in Luanda (1844–1870)," *Slavery & Abolition* 33, no. 3 (2012): 479–500.
21. Mamigonian, *Africanos livres*; Mariana P. Candido, *Wealth, Land, and Property in Angola: A History of Dispossession, Slavery, and Inequality* (Cambridge: Cambridge University Press, 2022), chap. 5.
22. The global management of liberated African labor bears resemblance to the authoritarian aspects of maintaining public order, for which see Lisa Ford, *The King's Peace: Law and Order in the British Empire* (Cambridge, MA: Harvard University Press, 2021); Monica Dantas and Roberto Saba, "Contestations and Exclusions," in *The Cambridge History of Latin American Law in Global Perspective*, ed. Thomas Duve and Tamar Herzog (Cambridge: Cambridge

University Press, 2024), 345–88. For later developments in Latin America, see Anthony W. Pereira, *Political (In)Justice: Authoritarianism and the Rule of Law in Brazil, Chile, and Argentina* (Pittsburgh: University of Pittsburgh Press, 2005).

23. For two significant interpretations in the debate about the origins of Candomblé, see James Lorand Matory, *Black Atlantic Religion: Tradition, Transnationalism, and Matriarchy in the Afro-Brazilian Candomblé* (Princeton, NJ: Princeton University Press, 2005); and Luis Nicolau Parés, *A formação do candomblé: História e ritual da nação jeje na Bahia* (Campinas: Editora Unicamp, 2006). For our purposes, what matters is the availability of these ideas and practices to liberated Africans.
24. Da Silva et al., "Diaspora of Africans Liberated from Slave Ships," 361, 365.
25. Padraic X. Scanlan, *Freedom's Debtors: British Antislavery in Sierra Leone in the Age of Revolution* (New Haven, CT: Yale University Press, 2017); Sharla M. Fett, *Recaptured Africans: Surviving Slave Ships, Detention, and Dislocation in the Final Years of the Slave Trade* (Chapel Hill: University of North Carolina Press, 2017); Ryan, *Humanitarian Governance.*
26. Jake Christopher Richards, "Anti-Slave-Trade Law, 'Liberated Africans' and the State in the South Atlantic World, c. 1839–1852," *Past & Present* 241, no. 1 (1 November 2018): 179–219. This clarification corrects the unfortunate misrepresentation of my argument in Beatriz G. Mamigonian, "The Rights of Liberated Africans in Nineteenth-Century Brazil," in *Current Trends in Slavery Studies in Brazil*, ed. Stephan Conermann, Mariana Dias Paes, Roberto Hofmeister Pich, and Paulo Cruz Terra (Berlin: De Gruyter, 2023), 73n5.
27. See the classic works by Bernard Bailyn and J. H. Elliott. Bernard Bailyn, *Atlantic History: Concept and Contours* (Cambridge, MA: Harvard University Press, 2005); J. H. Elliott, *Empires of the Atlantic World: Britain and Spain in America, 1492–1830* (New Haven, CT: Yale University Press, 2006). For an overview of Atlantic history as a field, see Jack D. Greene and Philip D. Morgan, *Atlantic History: A Critical Appraisal* (Oxford: Oxford University Press, 2009). A collection that pushes beyond the age of revolutions is Matthew Brown and Gabriel B. Paquette, eds., *Connections after Colonialism: Europe and Latin America in the 1820s* (Tuscaloosa: University of Alabama Press, 2013).
28. Michel-Rolph Trouillot, "North Atlantic Universals: Analytical Fictions, 1492–1945," *South Atlantic Quarterly* 101, no. 4 (2002): 839–58.
29. Roquinaldo Amaral Ferreira, *Cross-Cultural Exchange in the Atlantic World: Angola and Brazil during the Era of the Slave Trade* (New York: Cambridge University Press, 2012); Luiz Felipe de Alencastro, *O trato dos viventes: Formação do Brasil no Atlântico Sul, séculos XVI e XVII* (São Paulo: Companhia das Letras, 2006).
30. For different interpretations, see Paul Lovejoy, *Jihād in West Africa during the Age of Revolutions* (Athens: Ohio University Press, 2016); Akinwumi Ogundiran, *The Yorùbá: A New History* (Bloomington: Indiana University Press, 2020), chap. 9.
31. Toby Green, *A Fistful of Shells: West Africa from the Rise of the Slave Trade to the Age of Revolution* (London: Allen Lane, 2019).

32. Jean-François Bayart, "Africa in the World: A History of Extraversion," trans. Stephen Ellis, *African Affairs* 99, no. 395 (2000): 217–67.
33. Walter Rodney, *A History of the Upper Guinea Coast, 1545–1800* (Oxford: Oxford University Press, 1970); Paul E. Lovejoy, *Transformations in Slavery: A History of Slavery in Africa*, 3rd ed. (Cambridge: Cambridge University Press, 2011). This transformation was perhaps less true for Angola, for which see Jelmer Vos and Paulo Teodoro de Matos, "The Demography of Slavery in the Coffee Districts of Angola, c. 1800–70," *Journal of African History* 62, no. 2 (2021): 213–34.
34. Parliament, 1863, *Brazil. Correspondence respecting liberated slaves*, C. (1st series) 3189.
35. Walter Hawthorne, " 'Being Now, as It Were, One Family': Shipmate Bonding on the Slave Vessel *Emilia*, in Rio de Janeiro and throughout the Atlantic World," *Luso-Brazilian Review* 45, no. 1 (2008): 70.
36. Ada Ferrer, "Haiti, Free Soil, and Antislavery in the Revolutionary Atlantic," *American Historical Review* 117, no. 1 (2012): 40–66. For earlier Black abolitionist politics, see José Lingna Nafafé, *Lourenço da Silva Mendonça and the Black Atlantic Abolitionist Movement in the Seventeenth Century* (Cambridge: Cambridge University Press, 2022).
37. For contrasting views, see Jenny S. Martinez, *The Slave Trade and the Origins of International Human Rights Law* (Oxford: Oxford University Press, 2012); Benton and Ford, *Rage for Order*.
38. Robert W. Gordon, "Critical Legal Histories," *Stanford Law Review* 36, nos. 1–2 (1984): 57–125; Hendrik Hartog, "Pigs and Positivism," *Wisconsin Law Review* 4 (1985): 899–936.
39. Quotation from Jane Burbank and Frederick Cooper, *Empires in World History: Power and the Politics of Difference* (Princeton, NJ: Princeton University Press, 2010), 5. See also Lauren Benton, *Law and Colonial Cultures: Legal Regimes in World History, 1400–1900* (Cambridge: Cambridge University Press, 2002); Bianca Premo and Yanna Yannakakis, "A Court of Sticks and Branches: Indian Jurisdiction in Colonial Mexico and Beyond," *American Historical Review* 124, no. 1 (1 February 2019): 28–55. For an approach that emphasizes the role of hidden groups in navigating the multi-imperial Caribbean, see Tessa Murphy, *The Creole Archipelago: Race and Borders in the Colonial Caribbean* (Philadelphia: University of Pennsylvania Press, 2021).
40. Jean Comaroff and John L. Comaroff, eds., *Law and Disorder in the Postcolony* (Chicago: University of Chicago Press, 2006).
41. Rebecca J. Scott and Jean M. Hébrard, *Freedom Papers: An Atlantic Odyssey in the Age of Emancipation* (Cambridge, MA: Harvard University Press, 2012); Michelle A. McKinley, *Fractional Freedoms: Slavery, Intimacy, and Legal Mobilization in Colonial Lima, 1600–1700* (New York: Cambridge University Press, 2016); Martha S. Jones, *Birthright Citizens: A History of Race and Rights in Antebellum America* (Cambridge: Cambridge University Press, 2018); Kimberly M. Welch, *Black Litigants in the Antebellum American South* (Chapel Hill: University of North Carolina Press, 2018).

42. R. J. M. Blackett, *The Captive's Quest for Freedom: Fugitive Slaves, the 1850 Fugitive Slave Law, and the Politics of Slavery* (Cambridge: Cambridge University Press, 2018). For an instructive approach that places activism by African Americans and their allies at the center of the history of abolition in the United States, see Manisha Sinha, *The Slave's Cause: A History of Abolition* (New Haven, CT: Yale University Press, 2016).
43. Robert M. Cover, "Nomos and Narrative," *Harvard Law Review* 97, no. 4 (1982): 4–68. I have examined this "world-making" feature of law in historical and anthropological perspective regarding liberated Africans in Jake Subryan Richards, "The Adjudication of Slave Ship Captures, Coercive Intervention, and Value Exchange in Comparative Atlantic Perspective, ca. 1839–1870," *Comparative Studies in Society and History* 62, no. 4 (2020): 838–39.
44. James H. Sweet, *Domingos Álvares, African Healing, and the Intellectual History of the Atlantic World* (Chapel Hill: University of North Carolina Press, 2011).
45. Pioneering scholars who developed these insights include Zora Neale Hurston and Elsa Goveia. See Zora Neale Hurston, *Barracoon: The Story of the Last Slave* (1927; repr., London: HQ, 2018); Elsa V. Goveia, *Slave Society in the British Leeward Islands at the End of the Eighteenth Century* (New Haven, CT: Yale University Press, 1965). For examples of microhistory, see Robert W. Harms, *The* Diligent*: A Voyage through the Worlds of the Slave Trade* (New York: Basic Books, 2002); Flávio dos Santos Gomes, Marcus J. M. de Carvalho, and João José Reis, *O alufá Rufino: Tráfico, escravidão e liberdade no Atlântico negro (c. 1822–c. 1853)* (São Paulo: Companhia das Letras, 2010). An influential macrohistory of the Brazilian slave trade is Manolo Florentino, *Em costas negras: Uma história do tráfico atlântico de escravos entre a Africa e o Rio de Janeiro, séculos XVIII e XIX* (Rio de Janeiro: Arquivo Nacional, 1995).
46. Judith Ann Carney, *Black Rice: The African Origins of Rice Cultivation in the Americas* (Cambridge, MA: Harvard University Press, 2002); Jessica Marie Johnson, *Wicked Flesh: Black Women, Intimacy, and Freedom in the Atlantic World* (Philadelphia: University of Pennsylvania Press, 2020).
47. Yuko Miki, *Frontiers of Citizenship: A Black and Indigenous History of Postcolonial Brazil* (Cambridge: Cambridge University Press, 2018); Yesenia Barragan, *Freedom's Captives: Slavery and Gradual Emancipation on the Colombian Black Pacific* (Cambridge: Cambridge University Press, 2021).
48. The classic statement is Sidney Wilfred Mintz and Richard Price, *The Birth of African-American Culture: An Anthropological Perspective* (Boston: Beacon, 1992).
49. Marcus Rediker, *The Slave Ship: A Human History* (New York: Viking Penguin, 2007).
50. Unsigned minute on Emilio Caneja to Gobierno Civil de Matanzas, 1 May 1880, Emancipados 108/11338, AHPM, fol. 32r.
51. Natalie Zemon Davis, *Fiction in the Archives: Pardon Tales and Their Tellers in Sixteenth-Century France* (Stanford, CA: Stanford University Press, 1987); Welch, *Black Litigants in the Antebellum American South*; Richard L. Roberts and Kristin Mann, "Law in Colonial Africa," in *Law in Colonial Africa*, ed. Kristin Mann and Richard L. Roberts (Portsmouth, NH: Heinemann, 1991), 43, 46.

52. Richard Roberts, *Litigants and Households: African Disputes and Colonial Courts in the French Soudan, 1895–1912* (Portsmouth, NH: Heinemann, 2005), 18.
53. Thomas C. Holt, *The Problem of Freedom: Race, Labor, and Politics in Jamaica and Britain, 1832–1938* (Baltimore: Johns Hopkins University Press, 1992).
54. For Cuba, see Rebecca J. Scott, *Slave Emancipation in Cuba: The Transition to Free Labor, 1860–1899* (Pittsburgh: University of Pittsburgh Press, 1985); Adriana Chira, *Patchwork Freedoms: Law, Slavery, and Race beyond Cuba's Plantations* (Cambridge: Cambridge University Press, 2022). For Brazil, see Hebe Maria Mattos, *Das cores do silêncio: Os significados da liberdade no sudeste escravista, Brasil século XIX* (Rio de Janeiro: Arquivo Nacional, 1995). The environmental knowledge that enslaved and freedpeople used to develop their own economic practices is examined in Oscar de la Torre, *The People of the River: Nature and Identity in Black Amazonia, 1835–1945* (Chapel Hill: University of North Carolina Press, 2018).
55. On Cuba, see Lisa Yun, *The Coolie Speaks: Chinese Indentured Laborers and African Slaves in Cuba* (Philadelphia: Temple University Press, 2008). For approaches that distinguish between chronological periods of indenture and slavery, see Stanley L. Engerman, "Servants to Slaves to Servants: Contract Labour and European Expansion," in *Colonialism and Migration: Indentured Labour before and after Slavery*, ed. P. C. Emmer (Dordrecht: Martinus Nijhoff, 1986), 263–94; David Northrup, *Indentured Labor in the Age of Imperialism, 1838–1922* (Cambridge: Cambridge University Press, 1995). For more critical interpretations of indenture, see Madhavi Kale, *Fragments of Empire: Capital, Slavery, and Indian Indentured Labor Migration in the British Caribbean* (Philadelphia: University of Pennsylvania Press, 1998); Jonathan Connolly, "Indentured Labour Migration and the Meaning of Emancipation: Free Trade, Race, and Labour in British Public Debate, 1838–1860," *Past & Present* 238, no. 1 (1 February 2018): 85–119.

1. WAR'S CRUCIBLE

1. Olaudah Equiano, *The Interesting Narrative of the Life of Olaudah Equiano, or Gustavus Vassa, the African, Written by Himself*, 9th ed. (London: Printed for and sold by the author, 1794), 143–44.
2. Vincent Brown, *Tacky's Revolt: The Story of an Atlantic Slave War* (Cambridge, MA: Harvard University Press, 2020), 4.
3. Alexander Mikaberidze, *The Napoleonic Wars: A Global History* (New York: Oxford University Press, 2020), 626.
4. C. L. R. James, *The Black Jacobins: Toussaint L'Ouverture and the San Domingo Revolution* (London: Secker and Warburg, 1938; repr., Penguin Books, 2001); Sudhir Hazareesingh, *Black Spartacus: The Epic Life of Toussaint Louverture* (London: Allen Lane, 2020).
5. As well as prize jurisdiction, these admiralty courts had civil jurisdiction to adjudicate disputes between naval crewmembers. Edward Stanley Roscoe, *A History of the English Prize Court* (London: Lloyd's, 1924); J. R. Hill, *The Prizes of War: The Naval Prize System in the Napoleonic Wars, 1793–1815* (Portsmouth, UK: Royal

Naval Museum, 1998); Shavana Musa, "Tides and Tribulations: English Prize Law and the Law of Nations in the Seventeenth Century," *Journal of the History of International Law / Revue d'Histoire du Droit International* 17, no. 1 (2015): 47–82.

6. Stephen D. Behrendt, "Markets, Transaction Cycles, and Profits: Merchant Decision Making in the British Slave Trade," *William and Mary Quarterly* 58, no. 1 (2001): 178n27.
7. J. M. Fewster, "Prize-Money and the British Expedition to the West Indies of 1793–4," *Journal of Imperial and Commonwealth History* 12, no. 1 (October 1983): 1–28; Charles R. Foy, "Eighteenth Century 'Prize Negroes': From Britain to America," *Slavery & Abolition* 31, no. 3 (September 2010): 379–93. Unlike maritime prize, military prize proceedings were poorly regulated and slow. See Margot C. Finn, "Material Turns in British History: I. Loot," *Transactions of the Royal Historical Society* 28 (December 2018): 17, 21.
8. Lord Dunmore's Proclamation, 7 November 1775, Broadside 1775, V852 FF, Special Collections, Library of Virginia, Richmond, VA.
9. Parliament, HCP 1826–1827, *Sierra Leone. Report of the commissioners of inquiry into the state of the colony of Sierra Leone*, vol. 7, paper number 312, p. 9.
10. On the rising, see Ruma Chopra, *Almost Home: Maroons between Slavery and Freedom in Jamaica, Nova Scotia, and Sierra Leone* (New Haven, CT: Yale University Press, 2018), chap. 7. For the relevant background, see James W. St. G. Walker, *The Black Loyalists: The Search for a Promised Land in Nova Scotia and Sierra Leone, 1783–1870* (Toronto: University of Toronto Press, 1992); Cassandra Pybus, *Epic Journeys of Freedom: Runaway Slaves of the American Revolution and Their Global Quest for Liberty* (Boston: Beacon, 2006); Alexander X. Byrd, *Captives and Voyagers: Black Migrants across the Eighteenth-Century British Atlantic World* (Baton Rouge: Louisiana State University Press, 2008).
11. Parliament, HCP 1806, *Copy of an order of His Majesty in council, dated the 15th of August 1805; made for prohibiting the importation of slaves into any of the settlements* . . ., vol. 12, paper number 84.
12. On Crown power more generally, see Lauren Benton, "This Melancholy Labyrinth: The Trial of Arthur Hodge and the Boundaries of Imperial Law," *Alabama Law Review* 64, no. 1 (2013): 91–122; Lauren Benton and Lisa Ford, "Island Despotism: Trinidad, the British Imperial Constitution and Global Legal Order," *Journal of Imperial and Commonwealth History* 46, no. 1 (October 2018): 21–46. For similar cases of Spanish royal power to confiscate captive people from slaving ships, see RCJF 150/7406, ANC; and RCO, 54/74, ANC.
13. Ann M. Burton, "British Evangelicals, Economic Warfare and the Abolition of the Atlantic Slave Trade, 1794–1810," *Anglican and Episcopal History* 65, no. 2 (June 1996): 213.
14. 46 Geo. III c. 52, §§ 1–3.
15. Quotation from Kelley, " 'Captured Negroes' of Tortola," 27. On Philadelphia, see V. Chapman-Smith, "Philadelphia and the Slave Trade: The *Ganges* Africans," *Pennsylvania Legacies* 5, no. 2 (2005): 20.
16. Lauren Benton, "Abolition and Imperial Law, 1790–1820," *Journal of Imperial and Commonwealth History* 39, no. 3 (2011): 355–74.

17. James Stephen, *War in Disguise; or, the Frauds of the Neutral Flags* (London: C. Whittingham, 1806), 8, 11–13, 153–54, 174.
18. A Bill, intituled, An Act for the Abolition of the Slave Trade, printed 10 February 1807, § 2, 10 February 1807, House of Commons Sessional Papers, vol. 1, paper number 68, 41–45.
19. Bill, intituled, An Act for the Abolition of the Slave Trade, § 5.
20. An Act for the Abolition of the Slave Trade 1807, 47 Geo. 3 c. 36, § 7.
21. 47 Geo. 3 c. 36, § 7.
22. 47 Geo. 3 c. 36, § 16.
23. 47 Geo. 3 c. 36, §17. Black soldiers had protested discriminatory pension provision after serving in the American War of Independence. Mary Beth Norton, "The Fate of Some Black Loyalists of the American Revolution," *Journal of Negro History* 58, no. 4 (1973): 402–26.
24. 47 Geo. 3 c. 36, § 8.
25. 47 Geo. 3 c. 36, § 11.
26. On apprenticeship, see chapter 4. On the age of fourteen as typical for nonpauper apprenticeship, see Joan Lane, *Apprenticeship in England, 1600–1914* (London: UCL Press, 1996), 16.
27. Goveia, *Slave Society in the British Leeward Islands*, 108, 123.
28. Gardner & Dean expenses invoice submitted to Phillips & Gardner, 22 January 1806, and Gardner & Dean to Phillips & Gardner, 22 January 1806, in Slavery Collection, 1709–1864, Series II, Gardner and Dean, Subseries 2, Business papers, 1771, 1805–1807, and undated, New-York Historical Society; Phillips & Gardner to Gardner & Dean, 5 June 1807, in Subseries 1, Correspondence, 1804–1807, New-York Historical Society.
29. Examination of Joshua Viall, 4 November 1807, Tortola Prize Court proceedings, HCA 42/472, UKNA, 3.
30. Boubacar Barry, *Senegambia and the Atlantic Slave Trade* (New York: Cambridge University Press, 2002), chap. 8; David Richardson, "Shipboard Revolts, African Authority, and the Transatlantic Slave Trade," in *Fighting the Slave Trade: West African Strategies*, ed. Sylviane A. Diouf (Athens: Ohio University Press, 2003), 199–218.
31. Examination of Thomas Bartholomew, 6 November 1807, Tortola Prize Court proceedings, HCA 42/472, UKNA, 11.
32. Sworn statement of Joshua Viall, 6 November 1807, HCA 42/472, UKNA, 7.
33. Allegations by George Clarke Forbes, King's Counsel, 24 November 1807, HCA 42/472, UKNA, 24–28.
34. Claim and attestation of Joshua Viall, 17 November 1807, HCA 42/472, UKNA, 30.
35. Extract from the Registry of the Vice-Admiralty Court, 27 November 1807, HCA 42/472, UKNA, 47.
36. Examination of James Johnson, 28 December 1807, Tortola Prize Court proceedings, HCA 42/367, UKNA, 1.
37. Robertson also awarded $1,000 to the captor in lieu of head money for each liberated African, which was irregular. Extract from Registry of Vice-Admiralty Court, 10 February 1808, HCA 42/367, UKNA, 27.

38. *The Amedie* (1810), 12 Eng. Rep. 96; Jean Allain, "The Nineteenth Century Law of the Sea and the British Abolition of the Slave Trade," *British Yearbook of International Law* 78 (2007): 349.
39. *The Nancy* (1810), II Acton 4–5.
40. The order is copied in African Institution, *Fourth Report of the Directors of the African Institution: Read at the Annual General Meeting on the 28th of March, 1810. to Which Is Added, a List of Subscribers* (London: George Ellerton, 1810). See especially 64–65.
41. African Institution, *Fourth Report*, 55, 69.
42. Parliament, HCP 1825, *Papers relating to captured negroes*, vol. 25, paper number 114, p. 39.
43. It is not clear whether any of the thirty-two men enlisted in the Royal Navy as per Cochrane's original request. CO 318/82, UKNA, tables N and O.
44. "Northumberland & Good Hope, Trinidad," Legacies of British Slave-Ownership Database, accessed 5 August 2021, https://www.ucl.ac.uk/lbs/estate/view/3874.
45. Quotation from R. G. Thorne, "Cochrane (Afterwards Cochrane Johnstone), Hon. Andrew James (1767–1833), of 13 Alsop's Buildings, New Road, Marylebone, Mdx.," in *The History of Parliament: The House of Commons 1790–1820* (London: History of Parliament Trust, 1986). For Jervis's background, see Fewster, "Prize-Money and the British Expedition."
46. Nicholas Guyatt, *Bind Us Apart: How Enlightened Americans Invented Racial Segregation* (New York: Oxford University Press, 2016).
47. For various positions in the debate about the effect of maritime suppression on stopping the trade, see "Lord Denman and the Slave Trade," *The Times*, 16 October 1848; "Lord Denman and the Slave Trade," *The Times*, 24 October 1848; Thomas Denman, *A Letter from Lord Denman to Lord Brougham, on the Final Extinction of the Slave-Trade*, 2nd ed. (London: J. Hatchard and Son, 1848); A Barrister [Sir George Stephen], *Analysis of the Evidence Given before the Select Committee upon the Slave Trade* (London: Partridge and Oakey, 1850).
48. David Eltis, *Economic Growth and the Ending of the Transatlantic Slave Trade* (New York: Oxford University Press, 1987), chap. 8.
49. On disease and malnutrition, see Joseph Miller, "Mortality in the Atlantic Slave Trade: Statistical Evidence on Causality," *Journal of Interdisciplinary History* 11, no. 3 (1981): 385–423.
50. For voyage length and mortality aboard vessels captured and sent to Sierra Leone, see SlaveVoyages, "Trans-Atlantic Slave Trade—Database," 12 September 2024, https://www.slavevoyages.org/voyages/jg7vBWUZ. For voyage length and mortality aboard completed voyages, see SlaveVoyages, "Trans-Atlantic Slave Trade—Database," accessed 12 September 2024, https://www.slavevoyages.org/voyages/IhNU4Gie.
51. Database composed by author from returns in Parliamentary Papers; Colonial Office—Sierra Leone Original Correspondence (CO 267), UK National Archives; and records created by the Police Court, Liberated African Department Letter Books, and the Local Letter Books, all in the Public Archives, Sierra Leone.
52. Miller, "Mortality in the Atlantic Slave Trade"; Rediker, *Slave Ship*.

53. Stephanie E. Smallwood, *Saltwater Slavery: A Middle Passage from Africa to American Diaspora* (Cambridge, MA: Harvard University Press, 2007); Mintz and Price, *Birth of African-American Culture.*
54. Stephen D. Behrendt, David Eltis, and David Richardson, "The Costs of Coercion: African Agency in the Pre-Modern Atlantic World," *Economic History Review* 54, no. 3 (August 2001): 454–76; Richardson, "Shipboard Revolts."
55. Phyllis M. Martin, "Family Strategies in Nineteenth-Century Cabinda," *Journal of African History* 28, no. 1 (March 1987): 65–86; Joseph Calder Miller, *Way of Death: Merchant Capitalism and the Angolan Slave Trade, 1730–1830* (Madison: University of Wisconsin Press, 1988); Roquinaldo Ferreira, "The Suppression of the Slave Trade and Slave Departures from Angola, 1830s–1860s," *História Unisinos* 15, no. 1 (January 2011): 3–13; Mariana Candido, *An African Slaving Port and the Atlantic World: Benguela and Its Hinterland* (Cambridge: Cambridge University Press, 2013); Robert W. Slenes, "Metaphors to Live By in the Diaspora: Conceptual Tropes and Ontological Wordplay among Central Africans in the Middle Passage and Beyond," in *Tracing Language Movement in Africa*, ed. Ericka A. Albaugh and Kathryn Michelle De Luna (New York: Oxford University Press, 2018), 343–63.
56. Roquinaldo Amaral Ferreira, *Dos sertões ao Atlântico: Tráfico ilegal de escravos e comércio lícito em Angola 1830–1860* (Luanda: Kilombelombe, 2012), especially 31–33.
57. African Institution, *Sixth Report of the Directors of the African Institution: Read at the Annual General Meeting on the 25th of March, 1812* (London: Ellerton and Henderson, 1812), 39.
58. On elite people from Cabinda who sent their children to Brazil for education, see Martin, "Family Strategies in Nineteenth-Century Cabinda"; Ferreira, *Dos sertões ao Atlântico.*
59. African Institution, *Sixth Report*, 36–39. Francis Depau's copies of the relevant papers were sold to a private buyer at auction by Goldberg Auctions, as Lot 259 of Sale 64 in 2011, for a price of $13,750. See "Francis De Pau and the Slave Trade," *American Genealogy: Clues and Steps in the Ancestor Search* (blog), 8 October 2011, http://sksgenealogy.blogspot.com/2011/10/francis-de-pau-and-slave-trade.html; Goldberg Auctions, "Sale 64," accessed 24 January 2023, http://images.goldbergauctions.com/php/lot_auc.php?site=1&sale=64&lot=259.
60. T. de Mello to Alexandre Cambell [*sic*], Bahia, 24 October 1810, HCA 42/371/70, UKNA.
61. African Institution, *Sixth Report*, 38, 42; *The Philanthropist, or, Repository for Hints and Suggestions Calculated to Promote the Comfort and Happiness of Man*, vol. 2 (London: Richard Taylor, 1812), 51. The Liverpool intermediary was Dixon Lavater & Co. See J. W. Hemmerick to Alexander Campbell, 17 May 1810, HCA 42/371/70, UKNA.
62. African Institution, *Sixth Report*, 41.
63. African Institution, *Sixth Report*, 39. I have followed the transcription of Ned Brown's testimony in which he called the man Jack White; according to *The Philanthropist*, his actual name was Jack Watts (*Philanthropist*, 47).

64. Harms, *Diligent*, 311–15; Smallwood, *Saltwater Slavery*, chap. 5; Barbara Bush, " 'Daughters of Injur'd Africk': African Women and the Transatlantic Slave Trade," *Women's History Review* 17, no. 5 (December 2008): 673–98.
65. African Institution, *Sixth Report*, 40.
66. African Institution, *Sixth Report*, 40.
67. Note of sale of enslaved man to Jose Carlos de Almeida, no author, n.d. (document marked number 32), HCA 42/371/70, UKNA. On enslaved sailors aboard slaving ships to Brazil, see Jaime Rodrigues, *De costa a costa: Escravos, marinheiros e intermediários do tráfico negreiro de Angola ao Rio de Janeiro, 1780–1860* (São Paulo: Companhia das Letras, 2005). For a rare case of a freed African man who became a slave trader, see Luis Nicolau Parés, *Joaquim de Almeida: A história do africano traficado que se tornou traficante de africanos* (São Paulo: Companhia das Letras, 2023).
68. African Institution, *Sixth Report*, 40.
69. *Philanthropist*, 47.
70. Stephen D. Behrendt, "The Captains in the British Slave Trade from 1785 to 1807," *Historic Society of Lancashire & Cheshire* 140 (1990): 88, table 1.
71. Affidavit of John Roach, 12 November 1812, *The Amelia*, HCA 45/70/24, UKNA, fol. 311r.
72. *Philanthropist*, 48–49.
73. *Philanthropist*, 47.
74. SlaveVoyages, "Trans-Atlantic Slave Trade—Database," accessed 12 September 2024, Voyage ID 7659; Anderson, *Abolition in Sierra Leone*, 93.
75. On naming in a slave society, see Robert Carl-Heinz Shell, *Children of Bondage: A Social History of the Slave Society at the Cape of Good Hope, 1652–1838* (Hanover, NH: Wesleyan University Press / University Press of New England, 1994), 240–46.
76. On how scribal practices constitute legal procedure, see Bhavani Raman, *Document Raj: Writing and Scribes in Early Colonial South India* (Chicago: University of Chicago Press, 2012).
77. Liberated African Register [1808–1812], Liberated African Department, Sierra Leone Public Archives, digitized as Endangered Archives Programme EAP443/1/17/20, liberated Africans registered numbered 1552–1636, https://eap.bl.uk/archive-file/EAP443-1-17-20.
78. Corrie Decker, "A Feminist Methodology of Age-Grading and History in Africa," *American Historical Review* 125, no. 2 (1 April 2020): 418–26.
79. Michael Charles Reidy, "The Admission of Slaves and 'Prize Slaves' into the Cape Colony, 1797–1818" (MA thesis, University of Cape Town, 1997); Patrick Harries, "Mozambique Island, Cape Town and the Organisation of the Slave Trade in the South-West Indian Ocean, c. 1797–1807," *Journal of Southern African Studies* 42, no. 3 (2016): 409–27.
80. *The Amelia*, petition as to salvages, 1816, HCA 45/70/24, UKNA.
81. Decree of the Lords, 8 December 1814; sworn affidavit of Constance Roach, Liverpool, 4 September 1816, both in *The Amelia*, petition as to salvages, 1816, HCA 45/70/24, UKNA, fol. 312v.

82. Verdict, 3 April 1817, on N. Gostling, petition as to salvages, 28 May 1816, in *The Amelia*, HCA 45/70/24, UKNA, fol. 312v.
83. I use "settler" to refer to any non-Indigenous person who lived in Sierra Leone, rather than the more restrictive sense of referring to Nova Scotian and Maroon people in contradistinction to liberated Africans. Samuel Abraham Walker, *The Church of England Mission in Sierra Leone: Including an Introductory Account of That Colony, and a Comprehensive Sketch of the Niger Expedition in the Year 1841* (London: Seeley, Burnside and Seeley, 1847), 4, quoting the account of Edward Bickersteth. The name Congo Town remains to this day.
84. "Extract of a Letter from Mr. BROWN, to the COMMITTEE; Dated FREE TOWN, Feb. 4, 1817," *Wesleyan-Methodist Magazine*, May 1817.
85. Fett, *Recaptured Africans*.
86. Philip Misevich, *Abolition and the Transformation of Atlantic Commerce in Southern Sierra Leone, 1790s to 1860s* (Trenton, NJ: Africa World, 2019), chap. 2; Northrup, "Becoming African."
87. King Amra to Governor of Sierra Leone, 2 March 1814, enclosure in Maxwell to Bathurst, 1 May 1814, Despatch 52, CO 267/38, UKNA.
88. Maxwell to Bathurst, 1 May 1814, Despatch 52, CO 267/38, UKNA.
89. William Henry Gould Page, sworn statement, 28 March 1815, High Court of Appeals for Prizes, in Ysavel (master Felix de Pusadas), Prize Appeal, HCA 42/524/1299, UKNA.
90. Maxwell to Bathurst, 1 May 1814, Despatch 52, CO 267/38, UKNA.
91. Vessels, Cargoes & Slaves Proceeded Against in the Court of Vice Admiralty at Sierra Leone between June 1808 & March 1817, HCA 49/97, UKNA, fol. 23.
92. Robert Thorpe, *A Reply "Point by Point' to the Directors of the African Institution* (London: F. C. and J. Rivington, 1815), 65.
93. Robert Thorpe, *A Letter to William Wilberforce, Esq. M.P., Vice President of the African Institution &c. &c. &c.*, 3rd ed. (London: F. C. and J. Rivington, 1815), 20; Robert Thorpe, *Postscript to the Reply "Point to Point" Containing an Exposure of the Misrepresentation of the Treatment of the Captured Negroes at Sierra Leone, and Other Matters Arising from the Ninth Report of the African Institution* (London: F. C. and J. Rivington, 1815), 35–36. See also African Institution, *Special Report of the Directors of the African Institution: Made at the Annual General Meeting, on the 12th of April, 1815: Respecting the Allegations Contained in a Pamphlet Entitled "a Letter to William Wilberforce, Esq. &c. by R. Thorpe, Esq. &c."* (London: Ellerton and Henderson, 1815); Emma Christopher, *Freedom in White and Black: A Lost Story of the Illegal Slave Trade and Its Global Legacy* (Madison: University of Wisconsin Press, 2018).
94. Joseph Marryat, *More Thoughts Still on the State of the West India Colonies and the Proceedings of the African Institution with Observations on the Speech of James Stephen Esq.* (London: Richardson, Cornhill and Ridgways, 1818), 108.
95. Memorandum prepared by order of the plenipotentiaries . . ., n.d. [1816], FO 84/1, UKNA, fol. 222r–28v (quotations at 227r, 228r, 228v).
96. Robert Hagan, commander, aboard HM Hired Colonial Schooner *Queen Charlotte* at sea, to Governor MacCarthy, 11 March 1816, enclosed in MacCarthy to Bathurst, 20 March 1816, CO 267/42, UKNA.

97. For the vice-admiralty court, see Process, *Le Louis*, Sentence, 3 April 1816, HCA 17/127/1027, UKNA, fol. 51.
98. Lord Stowell's notebook I, HCA 30/1041, UKNA, fol. 305; Lord Stowell's notebook II, a copy made by William Rothery, HCA 30/1042, UKNA, fol. 327–28. Henry Bourguignon emphasized the importance of nationality in Scott's jurisprudence. See Henry J. Bourguignon, *Sir William Scott, Lord Stowell: Judge of the High Court of Admiralty, 1798–1828* (Cambridge: Cambridge University Press, 1987). More generally on civil law in England, see Peter Stein, "Continental Influences on English Legal Thought, 1600–1900," in *The Character and Influence of the Roman Civil Law* (Ronceverte, WV: Hambledon, 1988), 209–29. For an interpretation that stresses the pluralist and inclusive impulses in Scott's jurisprudence of global legal order, see Jennifer Pitts, "Empire and Legal Universalisms in the Eighteenth Century," *American Historical Review* 117, no. 1 (2012): 92–121.
99. Lord Stowell's notebook II, HCA 30/1042, UKNA, fol. 179. On the longer history of concepts of property and possession in common, rather than civil, law, see David J. Seipp, "The Concept of Property in the Early Common Law," *Law and History Review* 12, no. 1 (1994): 29–91; and Carol M. Rose, *Property and Persuasion: Essays on the History, Theory, and Rhetoric of Ownership* (Boulder, CO: Westview, 1994). On how rules create meaning in relation to property, see Georgy Kantor, Tom Lambert, and Hannah Skoda, eds., *Legalism: Property and Ownership* (Oxford: Oxford University Press, 2017).
100. Richard Dana argued that the *Amedie* and *Le Louis* rulings were consistent, because the former was a prize cause in wartime and the latter was a civil cause regarding the use of search on suspicion of slave-trading in peacetime; in neither case did the judge decide that the slave trade was illegal under the law of nations. Henry Wheaton, *Elements of International Law*, ed. Richard Henry Dana (Boston: Little, Brown, 1866), 208–11n86; Tara Helfman, "The Court of Vice Admiralty at Sierra Leone and the Abolition of the West African Slave Trade," *Yale Law Journal* 115, no. 5 (2006): 1151, arguing that by 1817 the Sierra Leone Vice-Admiralty Court had "set in motion the ultimate demise of the European trade in African slaves" before the *Le Louis* decision; Benton, "Abolition and Imperial Law"; Martinez, *Slave Trade and the Origins of International Human Rights Law*, 27–28, stressing that the *Le Louis* decision emphasized state sovereignty and the need for positive law to ban the slave trade.
101. John Dodson, *Reports of Cases Argued and Determined in the High Court of Admiralty; Commencing with the Judgments of the Right Hon. Sir William Scott (Lord Stowell), Trinity Term 1811*, vol. 2, *1815–1822* (London: A. Strahan, 1828), 257–58.
102. Oscar Zanetti and Alejandro García, *Sugar and Railroads: A Cuban History, 1837–1959*, trans. Franklin W. Knight and Mary Todd (Chapel Hill: University of North Carolina Press, 1998), 4.
103. Aviso of Real Consulado, 18 July 1816, and table of claims, n.d. [1817], RCJF 86/3506, ANC.

104. One Spanish American dollar was worth eight reales.
105. The High Court of Appeals cited the compensation payment as grounds to dismiss the owner's appeal to the court. High Court of Appeals for Prizes, *Ysavel*, Felix de Pusadas, Master, Case for motion on behalf of His Majesty, 1819, HCA 42/565/1, 2, UKNA.
106. Examples include the captures of *Maria Josefa, Nueva Paz, Dolores* (schooner, 1813), *Nuestra Santa del Carmen*, and *Dolores* (brigantine, 1814), table of claims, n.d. [1817], RCJF 86/3506, ANC.
107. Lisa Ford and Naomi Parkinson, "Legislating Liberty: Liberated Africans and the Abolition Act, 1806–1824," *Slavery & Abolition* 42, no. 4 (2021): 827–46.
108. Parliament, HCP 1826, *Cape of Good Hope, West Indies, and Sierra Leone. Copies of the instructions*, vol. 26, paper number 332, p. 4.
109. Parliament, HCP 1826, vol. 26, paper number 332, p. 6.
110. Parliament, HCP 1826, vol. 26, paper number 332, p. 17.
111. On Dougan, see Anita Rupprecht, " 'When He Gets among His Countrymen, They Tell Him That He Is Free': Slave Trade Abolition, Indentured Africans and a Royal Commission," *Slavery & Abolition* 33, no. 3 (2012): 440–41. On Gannon, see Gannon to R. J. Wilmot Horton, 8 December 1823, CO 318/83, UKNA.
112. Statement by Barrow, 3 November 1823, enclosed in Gannon to Wilmot Horton, 8 December 1823; Bowles to Wilmot Horton, 15 February 1824, CO 318/83, UKNA.
113. Parliament, HCP 1825, vol. 25, paper number 114, p. 42.
114. Table M, CO 318/82, UKNA.
115. Table M, CO 318/82, UKNA.
116. Goveia, *Slave Society in the British Leeward Islands*, 226.
117. Goveia, *Slave Society in the British Leeward Islands*, 230.
118. Rupprecht, "When He Gets among His Countrymen"; Isaac Dookhan, *A History of the British Virgin Islands, 1672 to 1970* (Epping, UK: Caribbean Universities Press in association with Bowker, 1975), 97–119; Jeppe Mulich, "Maritime Marronage in Colonial Borderlands," in *A World at Sea: Maritime Practices and Global History*, ed. Lauren A Benton and Nathan Perl-Rosenthal (Philadelphia: University of Pennsylvania Press, 2020), 133–48.
119. Jeppe Mulich, *In a Sea of Empires: Networks and Crossings in the Revolutionary Caribbean* (Cambridge: Cambridge University Press, 2020), 130–31.
120. On Tortola, see Plan of Kings-Town, the location of the liberated Africans in Tortola. Surveyed by order of the Collector of His Majesty's Customs in 1831 . . ., CO 700/Virgin Islands 6, UKNA; Plan of the African Settlement and Village of Kingstown [Tortola], 1844, CO 700/Virgin Islands 7, UKNA; Dookhan, *History of the British Virgin Islands*, 97–119.
121. Parliament, HCP 1826–1827, *Captured negroes at St. Christopher's, Nevis, and Tortola. Reports of Commissioners Bowles and Gannon*, vol. 22, paper number 463, p. 21.
122. For illustrative examples, see Frank S. McGlynn and Seymour Drescher, eds., *The Meaning of Freedom: Economics, Politics, and Culture after Slavery*

(Pittsburgh: University of Pittsburgh Press, 1992); Thavolia Glymph, *Out of the House of Bondage: The Transformation of the Plantation Household* (Cambridge: Cambridge University Press, 2008), chap. 6.

123. Tables N, O, and P, CO 318/82, UKNA.
124. Parliament, HCP 1825, vol. 25, paper number 114, p. 35. For the ban on agricultural work, see African Institution, *Fourth Report*, 65.
125. Commissioners of Enquiry into the state of Captured Negroes in the West Indies 1823 & 1824, Commissioners Bowles and Gannon, table, n.d., marked "Enclosure No. 3 in Mr Bowles," enclosed in Bowles to Wilmot Horton, 12 January 1824, CO 318/83, UKNA, n.p. [fol. 6v] (original emphasis).
126. Parliament, HCP 1826–1827, vol. 22, paper number 463, p. 35. See further cases on 26–35.
127. Schedules of Examinations of the Apprentices and Liberated Negroes in Demerara, as taken before the Commissioners for inquiring into the State and condition of Captured Africans, January 1827, CO 318/93, UKNA, fol. 6r.
128. Schedule, January 1827, CO 318/93, UKNA, fols. 6v and 7r.
129. Parliament, HCP 1826–1827, *Slaves, Cape of Good Hope: (prize slaves), Copy of the memorial of Mr. Lancelot Cooke . . .*, vol. 21, paper number 42. Kirsten McKenzie, *Imperial Underworld: An Escaped Convict and the Transformation of the British Colonial Order* (Cambridge: Cambridge University Press, 2016), chap. 4.
130. Parliament, HCP 1826–1827, vol. 21, paper number 42, p. 16.
131. Parliament, HCP 1826–1827, vol. 21, paper number 42, p. 169.
132. Parliament, HCP 1829, *Protectors of slaves reports*, vol. 25, paper number 335, p. 79. See also A. M. Rugarli, "Eyes on the Prize: The Story of the Prize Slave Present," *Quarterly Bulletin of the National Library of South Africa* 62, no. 4 (2008): 161–72.
133. Parliament, HCP 1826–1827, *Captured negroes at Demerara. Report of Commissioners Sir C. W. Burdett and Mr. Kinchela*, vol. 22, paper number 464, p. 18.
134. "Negroes attached to the Army as Military Laborers at the Fort at Brimstone Hill, St Christopher's . . .," CO 318/83, UKNA, fol. 3.
135. Max Mishler, " 'Improper and Almost Rebellious Conduct': Enslaved People's Legal Politics and Abolition in the British Empire," *American Historical Review* 128, no. 2 (1 June 2023): 648–84.
136. Sierra Leone Commissioners of Enquiry: Report and Appendix A, 1827, CO 267/91; Appendices B and C, 1827, CO 267/92, UKNA.
137. Sierra Leone Commissioners of Enquiry: Report, CO 267/91, 88, 104–11, UKNA.
138. Ford and Parkinson, "Legislating Liberty," 840.
139. Alvin O. Thompson, "African 'Recaptives' under Apprenticeship in the British West Indies 1807–1828," *Immigrants & Minorities* 9, no. 2 (1990): 138.
140. On habeas corpus, see Paul D. Halliday, *Habeas Corpus: From England to Empire* (Cambridge, MA: Harvard University Press, 2010). On repressive political measures in London, see Vic Gatrell, *Conspiracy on Cato Street: A Tale*

of Liberty and Revolution in Regency London (Cambridge: Cambridge University Press, 2022). The relationship between increasing repression in the metropole and the empire awaits further study. On the latter, see Ford, *The King's Peace.*

141. Leslie Stephen, "Stephen, Sir James (1789–1859)," in *Dictionary of National Biography*, ed. Sidney Lee, vol. 54 (London: Smith, Elder, 1898), 163.

142. Katherine Paugh, *The Politics of Reproduction: Race, Medicine, and Fertility in the Age of Abolition* (Oxford: Oxford University Press, 2017). Technologies of registration for liberated Africans set a precedent for registers of enslaved people as collateral in the Cape: Kate Ekama, "Bondsmen: Slave Collateral in the 19th-Century Cape Colony," *Journal of Southern African Studies* 47, no. 3 (4 May 2021): 437–53.

2. A NARROW WINDOW

1. Hayne and Cunningham to Castlereagh, 22 December 1819, enclosure in Parliament, HCP 1821, *Papers relative to the slave trade*, vol. 22, paper number 003, Class B, p. 101.

2. Walter de Mattos Lopes, " 'A Real Junta do Commercio, Agricultura, Fabricas e Navegação deste Estado do Brazil e Seus Domínios Ultramarinos': Um tribunal de antigo regime na corte de Dom João (1808–1821)" (master's thesis, Universidade Federal Fluminense, 2009), 13–17, 94–99; Carlos Guimarães, " 'Negócios de Corte': Os homens de negócios da Praça do Rio de Janeiro, o tráfico de pessoas escravizadas e os subsídios para a manutenção do Reino, c. 1808–c. 1821," *Almanack*, no. 33 (2023): 23.

3. *Manifesto dos naturais da Provincia da Bahia*, Impressão Nacional, n.d. [15 January 1822], https://digital.bbm.usp.br/handle/bbm/1555, accessed 10 May 2024; reprinted in Ignacio Accioli de Cerqueira e Silva, *Memorias historicas, e politicas de provincia da Bahia*, vol. 2 (Bahia: Typ. do Correio Mercantil, 1836), 97–98n42. Melo was still an interpreter in 1825: see *Império do Brasil: Diario Fluminense*, 29 March 1825, 275.

4. Adriane Sanctis de Brito, "Seeking Capture, Resisting Seizure: Legal Battles under the Anglo-Brazilian Treaty for the Suppression of Slave Trade (1826–1845)" (PhD diss., Universidade de São Paulo, 2018).

5. Nelson, "Liberated Africans in the Atlantic World."

6. Leslie Bethell, *The Abolition of the Brazilian Slave Trade: Britain, Brazil and the Slave Trade Question, 1807–1869* (Cambridge: Cambridge University Press, 1970), chap. 5; Luis Martínez-Fernández, *Fighting Slavery in the Caribbean: The Life and Times of a British Family in Nineteenth-Century Havana* (Armonk, NY: M. E. Sharpe, 1998), chap. 3; Farida Shaikh, "Judicial Diplomacy: British Officials and the Mixed Commission Courts," in *Slavery, Diplomacy and Empire: Britain and the Suppression of the Slave Trade, 1807–1975*, ed. Keith Hamilton and Patrick Salmon (Brighton, UK: Sussex Academic Press, 2009), 42–64.

7. João Pedro Marques, *Os sons do silêncio: O Portugal de Oitocentos e a abolição do tráfico de escravos* (Lisbon: Imprensa da Ciências Sociais, 1999).

8. *Diário de Sesiones*, Legislatura 1810–13, Cortes de Cádiz, No. 185, 2 April 1811, 811; Josep M. Fradera, "Moments in a Postponed Abolition," in *Slavery and*

Antislavery in Spain's Atlantic Empire, ed. Josep M. Fradera and Christopher Schmidt-Nowara (New York: Berghahn Books, 2013), 268–69.

9. Convention, Indemnity for Slave Captures, Signed at Vienna 21 January 1815, FO 93/77/10, UKNA.
10. Henry Wellesley to Castlereagh, 29 August 1817, FO 72/200, UKNA, fols. 50r–54r; Treaty between his Britannic Majesty and his Catholic Majesty, for preventing their subjects from engaging in any illicit traffic in slaves, Signed at Madrid the 23rd of September 1817, *Hansard Parliamentary Debates*, 1st series, 28 January 1818, vol. 37, columns 67–80.
11. The number of white immigrants never reached the same level as the number of African people illegally trafficked to Cuba. Franklin W. Knight, *Slave Society in Cuba during the Nineteenth Century* (Madison: University of Wisconsin Press, 1986), 114–15.
12. Emily Haslam, *The Slave Trade, Abolition and the Long History of International Criminal Law: The Recaptive and the Victim* (Abingdon, UK: Routledge, 2019), 45.
13. Leslie Bethell calculated 623 cases; the Voyages Database lists 624 cases. See Bethell, "Mixed Commissions," 84; SlaveVoyages, "Trans-Atlantic Slave Trade—Database," accessed 24 August 2023, https://www.slavevoyages.org/voyages/EEsRIeUb.
14. For estimates of the illegal trade, see SlaveVoyages, "Trans-Atlantic Slave Trade—Database," accessed 23 August 2023, https://www.slavevoyages.org/voyages/Ut8Bm2eC. For estimates of liberated Africans, see da Silva et al., "Diaspora of Africans Liberated from Slave Ships," table A.3, 369.
15. "Regulations for the Mixed Commissions, which are to reside on the Coast of Africa, in the Brazils, and at London," 28 July 1817, Article VII; "Regulations for the Mixed Commissions, which are to reside on the coast of Africa, and in a Colonial Possession of His Catholic Majesty," 23 September 1817, Article VII, in Lewis Hertslet, *A Complete Collection of the Treaties and Conventions, and Reciprocal Regulations at Present Subsisting between Great Britain and Foreign Powers . . . so Far as They Relate to Commerce and Navigation; and to the Repression and Abolition of the Slave Trade; and to the Privileges and Interests of the Subjects of the High Contracting Parties* (London: Henry Butterworth and James Bigg and Son, 1840), vol. 2, 111, 301.
16. Slave Trade Act 1843, 6 & 7 Vict. c. 98.
17. A. G. Hopkins, *Economic History of West Africa* (London: Longman, 1973), 125–35; Martin Lynn, "The West African Palm Oil Trade in the Nineteenth Century and the 'Crisis of Adaptation,' " in *From Slave Trade to "Legitimate" Commerce: The Commercial Transition in Nineteenth-Century West Africa*, ed. Robin Law (Cambridge: Cambridge University Press, 1995), 57–77.
18. 1&2 George IV, c. 99.
19. Slave Trade Act 1824, 5 Geo. 4 c. 113, Art. XXII.
20. Sanctis de Brito, "Seeking Capture, Resisting Seizure," 83–84.
21. 5 Geo 4 c. 113, Articles LXVIII and LXIX.

22. AHN, Ultramar, 4814, Expediente 2, No. 5. The Cédula is copied in Hertslet, *Complete Collection of the Treaties and Conventions*, 1841, vol. 3, 370–74.
23. AHN, Ultramar, 4814, Expediente 2, No. 5.
24. Partida V, Título V, Law XLV, in *Las siete partidas*, by Alfonso, trans. S. P. Scott, ed. Robert I. Burns, 5 vols. (Philadelphia: University of Pennsylvania Press, 2001), 4:1045.
25. Partida III, Título XXIX, Law XXIII and Partida IV, Título XXII, Law VII, in Alfonso, *Las siete partidas*, 3:847, 4:983.
26. María Elena Díaz, *The Virgin, the King, and the Royal Slaves of El Cobre: Negotiating Freedom in Colonial Cuba, 1670–1780* (Stanford, CA: Stanford University Press, 2000); Ada Ferrer, *Cuba: An American History* (New York: Scribner, 2021), chap. 3.
27. Alejandro de la Fuente, "Slaves and the Creation of Legal Rights in Cuba: Coartación and Papel," *Hispanic American Historical Review* 87, no. 4 (1 November 2007): 668–69.
28. On *Nuestra Señora del Carmen*, see RCJF 150/7406, ANC; on *Dos Hermanos*, see Aisnara Perera Díaz and María de los Ángeles Meriño Fuentes, "The African Women of the *Dos Hermanos* Slave Ship in Cuba: Slaves First, Mothers Second," *Women's History Review* 27, no. 6 (November 2018): 892–909.
29. See also the failed attempt in Spain's reconstituted Congress to strengthen protections for liberated Africans to guarantee their "absolute liberty": Article 9 of bill, *Diário de Sesiones*, Legislatura 1821, No. 36, 2 April 1821, 831.
30. *Collecção das leis do Brazil de 1818* (Rio de Janeiro: Imprensa Nacional, 1889), 7–11, §§ 1, 3, 5 (quotation).
31. Ilana Peliciari Rocha, " 'Escravos da Nação': O público e o privado na escravidão Brasileira, 1760–1876" (PhD diss., Universidade de São Paulo, 2012).
32. *Collecção das leis do Brazil de 1818*, 7–11, § 5.
33. Livro IV, Título 102, in *Codigo Philippino, ou, Ordenações e leis do reino de Portugal*, ed. Cândido Mendes de Almeida (Rio de Janeiro: Typographia do Insituto Philomathico, 1870), Livros IV e V, 994–95.
34. Alan Krebs Manchester, *British Preëminence in Brazil* (Chapel Hill: University of North Carolina Press, 1933), 181–83; Hawthorne, "Being Now, as It Were, One Family."
35. Hayne to Londonderry, 24 October 1821, FO 84/12, UKNA, fols. 180r–81v.
36. Hawthorne, "Being Now, as It Were, One Family," 64.
37. Mary C. Karasch, *Slave Life in Rio de Janeiro, 1808–1850* (Princeton, NJ: Princeton University Press, 1987), 58.
38. Karasch, *Slave Life in Rio de Janeiro*, 249; Juliana Barreto Farias, Flávio dos Santos Gomes, and Carlos Eugenio Libano Soares, *No labirinto das naçoes: Africanos e identidades no Rio de Janeiro, século XIX* (Rio de Janeiro: Arquivo Nacional, 2005), chap. 1.
39. Patricia Alves-Melo, "Trabalho e trabalhadores livres: Os índios no Arsenal de Marinha do Rio de Janeiro, século XIX," *Topoi (Rio de Janeiro)* 23, no. 50 (August 2022): 497–515.
40. Robinson to Londonderry, 5 December 1821, FO 83/2343, UKNA, fol. 68v.

41. Robinson to Londonderry, 5 December 1821, FO 83/2343, UKNA, fol. 69r.
42. FO 84/12, UKNA, fol. 141r.
43. Constituição Politica do Império do Brazil (de 25 de março de 1824), Título 2, Art. 6, § I, "Planalto: Presidência da República do Brasil," https://www.planalto.gov.br/ccivil_03/constituicao/constituicao24.htm, accessed 9 September 2024. Such citizenship included a Brazil-born person "even if their father is a foreigner, as long as he does not reside in Brazil in service of his Nation."
44. Tâmis Parron, "Escravidão e as fundações da ordem constitucional moderna: Representação, cidadania, soberania, c. 1780–c. 1830," *Topoi (Rio de Janeiro)* 23, no. 51 (September 2022): 730–31.
45. Miqueias Henrique Mugge, "Building an Empire in the Age of Revolutions: Independence and Immigration in the Brazilian Borderlands," *Topoi (Rio de Janeiro)* 23, no. 51 (September 2022): 890.
46. Hawthorne, "Being Now, as It Were, One Family," 68–70.
47. Papers relating to the capture of *Relámpago*, FO 313/42, UKNA, fol. 7.
48. Dale T. Graden, "Interpreters, Translators, and the Spoken Word in the Nineteenth-Century Transatlantic Slave Trade to Brazil and Cuba," *Ethnohistory* 58, no. 3 (2011): 393–419; Henry B. Lovejoy, "The Registers of Liberated Africans of the Havana Slave Trade Commission: Implementation and Policy, 1824–1841," *Slavery & Abolition* 37, no. 1 (2016): 23–44; Marcos Abreu Leitão de Almeida, "African Voices from the Congo Coast: Languages and the Politics of Identification in the Slave Ship *Jovem Maria* (1850)," *Journal of African History* 60, no. 2 (2019): 167–89.
49. Ira Berlin, "From Creole to African: Atlantic Creoles and the Origins of African-American Society in Mainland North America," *William and Mary Quarterly* 53, no. 2 (1996): 251–88; David Wheat, *Atlantic Africa and the Spanish Caribbean, 1570–1640* (Chapel Hill: Omohundro Institute of Early American History and Culture / University of North Carolina Press, 2016), chap. 6; João José Reis, *Divining Slavery and Freedom: The Story of Domingos Sodré, an African Priest in Nineteenth-Century Brazil*, trans. H. Sabrina Gledhill (New York: Cambridge University Press, 2015).
50. For the preponderance of urban-based over rural-based enslaved people in freedom suits, see Aisnara Perera Díaz and María de los Ángeles Meriño Fuentes, *Estrategias de libertad: Un acercamiento a las acciones legales de los esclavos en Cuba (1762–1872)*, vol. 1 (Havana: Editorial de Ciencias Sociales, 2015), 288.
51. Register "Negros de la Goleta Española Rélampago [*sic*]," FO 313/56, UKNA, fols. 3, 4–5. Cascales signed the final page of this register (fol. 166); the handwriting is consistent throughout.
52. A different rare document, an inventory from the Remire plantation in French Guiana, recorded that the plantation had at least two cases of enslaved people who had formed intimate relationships in Africa that they continued in the Americas in 1690. See John Thornton, *Africa and Africans in the Making of the Atlantic World, 1400–1800* (Cambridge: Cambridge University Press, 1998), 200.

53. Papers relating to the capture of *Mágico*, 1826, FO 313/42, UKNA, fol. 42r.
54. Notes for the formation of "Regulations to be observed with respect of Emancipated Slaves" and "Condiciones" related to the liberated Africans from the Relámpago, enclosures in Kilbee to Canning, 29 December 1824, Parliament, HCP 1825, *Class A. Correspondence with the British commissioners*, vol. 27, paper number 011, pp. 135–40.
55. In a small sample for the period 1822–40, at least twenty-six liberated Africans were baptized there. See Libro de Bautismos de Pardos y Morenos, vols. 31, 32, 33, 36, 40, ASCBV.
56. For Quebé's registration details, see "Negros de la Goleta Española Rélampago [*sic*]," FO 313/56, UKNA, fol. 2.
57. Libro de Bautismos de Pardos y Morenos, vol. 32, ASCBV, fol. 203r.
58. Libro de Bautismos de Pardos y Morenos, vol. 32, ASCBV, fols. 201v–2r.
59. Court of Mixed Commission Judges Fernandina and Macleay to Mariano Ricaforte, 8 August 1832, Papers relating to the capture of *Relámpago*, FO 313/42, UKNA, loose insert.
60. Kilbee to Canning, 30 December 1824, FO 84/29, UKNA, fol. 338r–v. On the Ayuntamiento of Havana, see David A. Sartorius, *Ever Faithful: Race, Loyalty, and the Ends of Empire in Spanish Cuba* (Durham, NC: Duke University Press, 2013), 52.
61. Kilbee to Canning, 10 May 1825, FO 313/9, UKNA, fol. 158.
62. For the wider context of forming property titles in Cuba, see Rebecca J. Scott, "Paper Thin: Freedom and Re-enslavement in the Diaspora of the Haitian Revolution," *Law and History Review* 29, no. 4 (2011): 1061–87; Rebecca J. Scott and Carlos Venegas Fornias, "María Coleta and the Capuchin Friar: Slavery, Salvation, and the Adjudication of Status," *William and Mary Quarterly* 76, no. 4 (2019): 727–62.
63. Kilbee to Canning, 4 September 1825, FO 313/9, UKNA, fol. 172.
64. Commissioner Hayne to Londonderry, 24 October 1824, FO 84/12, UKNA, fol. 180v.
65. Commissioners Jackson and Grigg to Palmerston, 27 July 1835, in Parliament, HCP 1836, *Class A. Correspondence with the British commissioners*, vol. 50, paper number 005, pp. 285–26; Hawthorne, "Being Now, as It Were, One Family," 65.
66. Petition of Casemiro, 10 June 1831, 6.1.23, AGCRJ, fol. 111–12.
67. Petition of Casemiro, 10 June 1831, 6.1.23, AGCRJ, fol. 111–12.
68. Hawthorne, "Being Now, as It Were, One Family'; Mamigonian, *Africanos livres*, 67–68.
69. Petition of Casemiro, Yannis, Alberto, and Manuel [?], 12 July 1831, 6.1.23, AGCRJ, fol. 109.
70. Jose Joaquim Pires, sworn statement, 23 September 1843, IJ6 471, ANRJ.
71. Jose Baptista Lisboa to Deocleciano Augusto Cezar do Amaral, 9 November 1843, IJ6 471, ANRJ.
72. Statement of Flor Emelianna de Souza Fausto, August 1844, IJ6 471, ANRJ.
73. On forced labor in service of the state, see chapter 4 for analysis of the Casa de Correção in Brazil and the Depósito de Cimarrones in Cuba.

74. On policing in urban Rio, see Thomas H. Holloway, *Policing Rio de Janeiro: Repression and Resistance in a Nineteenth-Century City* (Stanford, CA: Stanford University Press, 1993); Martine Jean, *Policing Freedom: Illegal Enslavement, Labor, and Citizenship in Nineteenth-Century Brazil* (Cambridge: Cambridge University Press, 2023). The broader circum-Atlantic development of official policing to discipline freed, rather than enslaved, people, awaits further study. Baltimore and Rio bore similarities in this regard. On Baltimore, see Adam Malka, *The Men of Mobtown: Policing Baltimore in the Age of Slavery and Emancipation* (Chapel Hill: University of North Carolina Press, 2018).
75. *Jornal do Commercio*, 11 May 1839, 4.
76. *Diário do Rio de Janeiro*, 28 September 1840, 4. The Free Africans of Brazil Database, under the direction of Daryle Williams, has compiled comprehensive data on such cases of disappearance and escape. On using newspaper advertisements to explore freedom-seeking in a different urban context, see Simon P. Newman, *Freedom Seekers: Escaping from Slavery in Restoration London* (London: Institute of Historical Research: University of London Press, 2022).
77. *Jornal do Commercio*, 8 March 1839, 3.
78. Karasch, *Slave Life in Rio de Janeiro*, 198.
79. *Diário do Rio de Janeiro*, 3 January 1839, 4; other advertisements appeared under the "Fugitive Slaves" section, e.g., case of Alexandre, *Jornal do Commercio*, 20 April 1842, 4. The routes of liberated Africans into Afro-Brazilian communities in urban areas is a rich topic for future research.
80. Flávio dos Santos Gomes, "Quilombos do Rio de Janeiro no século XIX," in *Liberdade por um fio: História dos Quilombos no Brasil*, ed. João José Reis and Flávio dos Santos Gomes (São Paulo: Companhia das Letras, 1996), 309–10.
81. David R. Murray, *Odious Commerce: Britain, Spain and the Abolition of the Cuban Slave Trade* (Cambridge: Cambridge University Press, 1980), 285; Oscar Grandio Moraguez, "Dobo: A Liberated African in Nineteenth-Century Havana," *Echoes: The SlaveVoyages Blog*, 2008, repr. March 14, 2024, https://www.slavevoyages.org/blog/dobo; Montaud, "En los borrosos confines de la libertad," 169; Joseph C. Dorsey, "Agency and Its Lack among Liberated Africans: The Case of Gavino the Waterboy," in *Breaking the Chains, Forging the Nation: The Afro-Cuban Fight for Freedom and Equality, 1812–1912*, ed. Aisha K. Finch, Fannie Rushing, and Gwendolyn Midlo Hall (Baton Rouge: Louisiana State University Press, 2019), 199–210.
82. Dobó, Christian name Gabino, registered as the eleventh liberated African in Register of "Negros de la Goleta española *Fingal*," FO 313/56, UKNA, fol. 33.
83. Petition of Gavino to Court of Mixed Commission, January 1841, enclosure in Commissioners Kennedy and Dalrymple to Palmerston, 22 January 1841, FO 84/348, UKNA, fol. 63r–65v.
84. Declaration, FO 84/359, UKNA, fol. 606r–v.
85. Alfonso, *Las siete partidas*, Title V, Law I.
86. Declaration, FO 84/359, UKNA, fol. 606v.
87. Gavino's expulsion and its aftermath draws on Dorsey, "Agency and Its Lack among Liberated Africans."

88. Ramon de la Sagra to the President and Members of the Junta de Inspección del Jardin Botáncio, 17 January 1828, RCJF 150/7441, ANC.
89. Henry B. Lovejoy, *Prieto: Yorùbá Kingship in Colonial Cuba during the Age of Revolutions* (Chapel Hill: University of North Carolina Press, 2018), 89; Guadalupe García, *Beyond the Walled City: Colonial Exclusion in Havana* (Oakland: University of California Press, 2016), 114. For the sake of consistency, all references to Yoruba divinities known in different languages as *òrìṣà, orixá,* and *oricha* have been standardized to *orisha.*
90. Minute of RCJF, 1 October 1828, RCJF 150/7441, ANC.
91. On the transfer of power from the Real Consulado to the Junta de Fomento, see Zanetti and García, *Sugar and Railroads,* 24.
92. O'Donnell to Presidente de la Real Junta de Fomento, 15 October 1844, RCJF 152/7656, ANC.
93. Francisco Oger to O'Donnell, 7 November 1844, RCJF 152/7656, ANC.
94. R. H. Coase, "The Nature of the Firm" (1937), in *The Firm, the Market, and the Law* (Chicago: University of Chicago Press, 1990), 33–56.
95. José Luciano Franco, *Comercio clandestino de esclavos* (Havana: Editorial de Ciencias Sociales, 1980), 124–273; Martín Rodrigo y Alharilla, "Cuatro capitanes negreros catalanes en tiempos de la trata ilegal: José Carbó, Pedro Manegat, Gaspar Roig y Esteban Gatell," in *Negreros y esclavos: Barcelona y la esclavitud atlántica (siglos XVI–XIX),* ed. Martín Rodrigo y Alharilla and Lizbeth J. Chaviano Pérez (Barcelona: Icaria Editorial, 2017), 101–30.
96. Harris, *Last Slave Ships.*
97. AS, segunda sessão da primeira legislativa, 16 June 1831, vol. 1, 379.
98. See, for instance, the speeches by Almeida e Albuquerque, AS, 15 June 1831, vol. 1, 366, and Rodrigues de Carvalho, AS, 16 June 1831, vol. 1, 378.
99. Câmara dos Deputados, Brazil, Lei de 7 de novembro de 1831, accessed 14 February 2024, https://www2.camara.leg.br/legin/fed/lei_sn/1824-1899/lei-37659-7-novembro-1831-564776-publicacaooriginal-88704-pl.html.
100. Christopher David Absell, "The Rise of Coffee in the Brazilian South-East: Tariffs and Foreign Market Potential, 1827–40," *Economic History Review* 73, no. 4 (2020): 970, 972. See also online appendix S1, "Additional Information on Sources and Methodology."
101. Richards, "Anti-Slave-Trade Law," 189.
102. Bethell, *Abolition of the Brazilian Slave Trade,* 83.
103. Ilmar Rohloff de Mattos, *O tempo Saquarema* (São Paulo: Hucitec, 1987); Tâmis Parron, "Política do tráfico negreiro: O Parlamento Imperial e a reabertura do comércio de escravos na década de 1830," *Estudos Afro-Asiáticos* 29, nos. 1/2/3 (2007): 91–121; Tâmis Parron, "A política da escravidão no império do Brasil, 1826–1865" (master's thesis, Universidade de Saõ Paulo, 2009); Chalhoub, *A força da escravidão.* In Minas Gerais, those who owned a small and middling number of slaves also supported the illegal trade. See Kelly Eleutério Machado Oliveira, "A Assembleia Provincial de Minas Gerais e o tráfico ilegal de escravizados (1839–1845)," *Almanack,* no. 32 (2022): 1–32.

104. Legal Statement of Francisco Pereira de Souza to his lawyer, João Álvares Portella as sent to Provincial President [1862?]; Matrícula No. 1169 of slaves owned by the priest Francisco Pereira de Souza, Rio de Janeiro, 20 November 1861, Seção de Arquivo Colonial e Provincial, Maço 2886, Governo da Província, Escravos—Assuntos, 1860–1874, APEB.
105. Treaty between His Majesty and the Queen Regent of Spain (during the minority of her daughter, Donna Isabella the IInd, Queen of Spain) for the abolition of the Slave Trade, 28 June 1835, Articles IV and X (Equipment clause), in Edward Hertslet, *Hertslet's Commercial Treaties: A Collection of Treaties and Conventions, between Great Britain and Foreign Powers, and of the Laws, Decrees, Orders in Council, Etc., Concerning the Same, So Far as They Relate to Commerce and Navigation, Slavery Extradition, Nationality, Copy Right, Postal Matter Etc. and to the Privileges and Interests of the Subjects of the High Contracting Parties*, vol. 4 (London: Henry Butterworth, 1835), 440.
106. Article II of the Treaty, in Hertslet, *Hertslet's Commercial Treaties*, vol. 4, 441.
107. Petition of the heirs of Francisco E. Plá, 10 September 1875, and Governor of Matanzas to the chief of police of Matanzas, 25 September 1875, Esclavos, 6/12, AHPM, fols. 9r, 12v.
108. Jane Landers, *Atlantic Creoles in the Age of Revolutions* (Cambridge, MA: Harvard University Press, 2010), chap. 6; Alejandro de la Fuente and Ariela J. Gross, *Becoming Free, Becoming Black: Race, Freedom, and the Law in Cuba, Virginia, and Louisiana* (New York: Cambridge University Press, 2020), chap. 4.
109. Treaty of 1835, Annex C, Regulations, Article III, in Hertslet, *Hertslet's Commercial Treaties*, 458.
110. For the transfer of 304 people from Havana to British Trinidad in 1835, see AP, 132/9, ANC; Schuler, *"Alas, Alas, Kongo"*; Adderley, *"New Negroes from Africa."*
111. Howard Johnson, "The Liberated Africans in the Bahamas, 1811–60," *Immigrants & Minorities* 7, no. 1 (March 1988): 24.
112. Jennifer Nelson, "Slavery, Race, and Conspiracy: The HMS *Romney* in Nineteenth-Century Cuba," *Atlantic Studies* 14, no. 2 (2017): 174–95.
113. Beatriz G. Mamigonian, "In the Name of Freedom: Slave Trade Abolition, the Law and the Brazilian Branch of the African Emigration Scheme (Brazil—British West Indies, 1830s–1850s)," *Slavery & Abolition* 30, no. 1 (2009): 41–66; Henrique Antonio Ré, "H.M.R.S. *Crescent*: Navio hospital e presiganga Britânica no porto do Rio de Janeiro, 1840–1854," *Revista de História (São Paulo)*, no. 182 (2023): 1–26.
114. Court Martial of Donald Stewart, 19 July 1837, War Office Records WO 71/299, UKNA, fol. 5.
115. Court Martial of Maurice Ogston, 25 July 1837, WO 71/299, UKNA, fol. 9.
116. Thomas August, "Rebels with a Cause: The St. Joseph Mutiny of 1837," *Slavery & Abolition* 12, no. 2 (September 1991): 79–81, 85.
117. John Saillant, "Dâaga the Rebel on Land and at Sea: An 1837 Mutiny in the First West India Regiment in Caribbean and Atlantic Contexts," *CLR James Journal* 25, no. 1 (2019): 165–94.

118. Hill to Glenelg, 10 November 1837, Despatch 75, CO 295/115, UKNA, fols. 260r–63v; David Lambert, " '[A] Mere Cloak for Their Proud Contempt and Antipathy towards the African Race': Imagining Britain's West India Regiments in the Caribbean, 1795–1838," *Journal of Imperial and Commonwealth History* 46, no. 4 (4 July 2018): 643.
119. Glenelg to Governors of Colonies in the West Indies, 15 May 1838, in Parliament, HCP 1840, *Liberated Africans. Correspondence respecting the treatment of liberated Africans*, vol. 34, paper number 224, p. 3.
120. Russell to Jeremie, 20 March 1841, in Parliament, HCP 1842, *Emigration. Return to an address of the Honourable the House of Commons, dated 9 March 1842*, vol. 31, paper number 301, p. 448.
121. Glenelg to Governors of Colonies in the West Indies, 31 August 1838, in Parliament, HCP 1840, vol. 40, paper number 224, p. 4.
122. Asiegbu, *Slavery and the Politics of Liberation*, 49–56.
123. For a historiographical overview, see Edward Bartlett Rugemer, *The Problem of Emancipation: The Caribbean Roots of the American Civil War* (Baton Rouge: Louisiana State University Press, 2008), 258–61.
124. James K. Polk, "Slaves and Slavery," *United States Magazine, and Democratic Review* 19 (1846): 251 (original emphasis).
125. Huzzey, *Freedom Burning*, 183.
126. Diana Paton, "The Flight from the Fields Reconsidered: Gender Ideologies and Women's Labor after Slavery in Jamaica," in *Reclaiming the Political in Latin American History: Essays from the North*, ed. Gilbert M. Joseph (Durham, NC: Duke University Press, 2001), 175–204; Drescher, *Mighty Experiment*, chap. 10.
127. On contract terms for liberated Africans, see Asiegbu, *Slavery and the Politics of Liberation*, 44, 154. For the increasingly restrictive terms of indenture across the British Empire, see Jonathan Connolly, *Worthy of Freedom: Indenture and Free Labor in the Era of Emancipation* (Chicago: University of Chicago Press, 2024).

3. GUNBOAT REGULATION IN ATLANTIC AFRICA

1. George E. Brooks, *Landlords and Strangers: Ecology, Society, and Trade in Western Africa, 1000–1630* (Boulder, CO: Westview, 1993), 38–39, 137.
2. Inge Van Hulle, *Britain and International Law in West Africa: The Practice of Empire* (Oxford: Oxford University Press, 2020), chap. 2.
3. John Gallagher and Ronald Robinson, "The Imperialism of Free Trade," *Economic History Review* 6, no. 1 (1953): 1–15; Kenneth Pomeranz, *The Great Divergence: China, Europe, and the Making of the Modern World Economy* (Princeton, NJ: Princeton University Press, 2000), 186–94.
4. Bethell, *Abolition of the Brazilian Slave Trade*, 161, 164; Richard Huzzey, "The Politics of Slave-Trade Suppression," in Burroughs and Huzzey, *Suppression of the Atlantic Slave Trade*, 17–52.
5. Cf. Allain, "Nineteenth Century Law of the Sea," 360, 366.
6. Higher figure from 5 Geo. IV c. 113 § 26; lower figure from 11 Geo IV and 1 Wm IV c. 55 § 1.

7. Leroy Vail and Landeg White, *Capitalism and Colonialism in Mozambique: A Study of Quelimane District* (London: Heinemann, 1980), 16–18; Malyn Newitt, *A History of Mozambique* (London: Hurst, 1995), 243–53; Patrick Harries, "Middle Passages of the Southwest Indian Ocean: A Century of Forced Immigration from Africa to the Cape of Good Hope," *Journal of African History* 55, no. 2 (2014): 173–90.
8. M. D. D. Newitt, "Drought in Mozambique 1823–1831," *Journal of Southern African Studies* 15, no. 1 (1988): 15–35; José Capela, "A captura de escravos no Sudoeste Africano para o tráfico a longa distância," *Africana Studia* 14 (2010): 39–51. Slave traders also trafficked people from Delagoa Bay to Bourbon Island (Réunion), for which see Linell Chewins and Peter Delius, "The Northeastern Factor in South African History: Reevaluating the Volume of the Slave Trade Out of Delagoa Bay and Its Impact on Its Hinterland in the Early Nineteenth Century," *Journal of African History* 61, no. 1 (2020): 89–110.
9. Capela, "A captura de escravos," 43.
10. Log of HMS *Cleopatra*, 12 April 1843, ADM 53/2195, UKNA.
11. On slave-trade prohibition and liberated Africans in the Cape, see Saunders, "Between Slavery and Freedom"; Christopher Saunders, " 'Free, yet Slaves': Prize Negroes at the Cape Revisited," in *Breaking the Chains: Slavery and Its Legacy in the Nineteenth-Century Cape Colony*, ed. Nigel Worden and Clifton Crais (Johannesburg: Witwatersrand University Press, 1994), 99–116; Patrick Harries, "The Hobgoblins of the Middle Passage: The Cape of Good Hope and the Trans-Atlantic Slave Trade," in *The End of Slavery in Africa and the Americas: A Comparative Approach*, ed. Ulrike Schmieder and Katja Füllberg-Stolberg (Berlin: LIT Verlag, 2011), 27–50; Sandra Rowoldt Shell, *Children of Hope: The Odyssey of the Oromo Slaves from Ethiopia to South Africa* (Athens: Ohio University Press, 2018); Richards, "Anti-Slave-Trade Law."
12. See Muster Roll of HMS *Cleopatra*, 1 April–30 June 1843, ADM 38/433, 38–39, UKNA.
13. John Forrest, M.D., report, n.d., Annexure 15 in Field to Napier, 12 January 1844, enclosure in Napier to Colonial Office, 15 March 1844, CO 48/239, UKNA, fol. 203r.
14. Parliament, 1845, *Class A. Correspondence with the British commissioners relating to the slave trade, 1844*, C. (1st series) 632, p. 331.
15. Pascoe Grenfell Hill, *Fifty Days on Board a Slave-Vessel in the Mozambique Channel, in April and May, 1843* (London: John Murray, 1844), 68, 69.
16. Hill to Admiralty, 4 February 1844; Admiralty to Secretary of State, 8 February 1844, Digest of Correspondence, section 95, ADM 12/432, UKNA.
17. Percy to Sidney Herbert, 11 May 1844, marked No. 60, ADM 1/5538, UKNA.
18. Alexander to Percy, 17 April 1844, enclosed in Percy to Sidney Herbert, 11 May 1844, ADM 1/5538, UKNA.
19. Wyill to Percy, 19 April 1844, enclosed in Percy to Sidney Herbert, 11 May 1844, ADM 1/5538, UKNA.
20. J. Kittle to Percy, 17 April 1844, enclosed in Percy to Sidney Herbert, 11 May 1844, ADM 1/5538, UKNA.

21. There was also one incident of a fight between the captives. Hill, *Fifty Days on Board a Slave-Vessel*, 79, 82.
22. Parliament, 1845, C. (1st series) 632, p. 322.
23. Parliament, 1845, C. (1st series) 632, p. 324.
24. Carneiro de Campos to Cândido Baptista de Oliveira, 29 April 1839, L52/2, AHI. See also SlaveVoyages, "Trans-Atlantic Slave Trade—Database," accessed 9 September 2024, Voyage ID: 1872.
25. The Twelve Judges were the judges of the common law courts of the King's Bench, the Common Pleas, and the Exchequer, who were called together to discuss a difficult procedure or point of law. R v. Serva and nine others (1845), 169 Eng. Rep. 169.
26. Benton and Ford, *Rage for Order*, 127–29.
27. Dodson to Palmerston, 26 September 1846, FO 83/2353, UKNA, fol. 175r. In 1865, the Foreign Office discussed a proposal to extend British criminal jurisdiction to the master and crew of slaving ships that were not entitled to the protection of the flag of any nation or state. The proposal went no further. Stephen Lushington et al. to Russell, 18 January 1865, FO 83/2360, UKNA.
28. For the Portuguese political context, see J. Marques, *Os sons do silêncio*.
29. Annex C, "Regulations in respect to the Treatment of liberated Negroes," Articles III and IV, in Lewis Hertslet, *A Complete Collection of the Treaties and Conventions, and Reciprocal Regulations at Present Subsisting between Great Britain and Foreign Powers . . . so Far as They Relate to Commerce and Navigation; and to the Repression and Abolition of the Slave Trade; and to the Privileges and Interests of the Subjects of the High Contracting Parties*, vol. 6 (London: Henry Butterworth and James Bigg and Son, 1845), 647–48.
30. On Hayne's proposal, see Ryan, *Humanitarian Governance*, chap. 5.
31. Hertslet, *Complete Collection of the Treaties and Conventions*, 1845, 649, Article V.
32. Coghe, "Problem of Freedom."
33. Candido, *Wealth, Land, and Property in Angola*, chap. 5. One study has found that smallholding rather than slave labor was crucial for the expansion in coffee production. Vos and Matos, "Demography of Slavery," 227.
34. Calculated from Richardson, "Shipboard Revolts," 204, table 12.1.
35. See the decline in captives purchased for the transatlantic trade: SlaveVoyages, "The Trans-Atlantic Slave Trade—Database," accessed 3 November 2020, http://slavevoyages.org/voyages/Zed7r2xr; Rodney, *History of the Upper Guinea Coast*; Lovejoy, *Transformations in Slavery*.
36. Rodney, *History of the Upper Guinea Coast*, 261.
37. Ismail Rashid, " 'A Devotion to the Idea of Liberty at Any Price': Rebellion and Antislavery in the Upper Guinea Coast in the Eighteenth and Nineteenth Centuries," in *Fighting the Slave Trade: West African Strategies*, ed. Sylviane A. Diouf (Athens: Ohio University Press, 2003), 139.
38. Thomas Masterman Winterbottom, *An Account of the Native Africans in the Neighbourhood of Sierra Leone: To Which Is Added an Account of the Present State of Medicine among Them* (London: C. Whittingham, 1803), 155, 157.
39. Rashid, "Devotion to the Idea of Liberty," 146.

40. Misevich, *Abolition and the Transformation of Atlantic Commerce,* chap. 3.
41. Richards, "Adjudication of Slave Ship Captures."
42. Jorge Felipe Gonzalez, "The Transatlantic Slave Trade and the Foundation of the Kingdom of Galinhas in Southern Sierra Leone, 1790–1820," *Journal of African History* 62, no. 3 (November 2021): 319–41.
43. King Siaka and the Rogers family to Doherty, n.d. [ca. Sept. 1840], encl. in Doherty to Russell, 7 December 1840, CO 267/160, UKNA.
44. Identified as "Try Norman" in some sources.
45. Fry Norman to Rosanna Gray, 8 September 1840; see also William Fergusson to Doherty, 9 October 1840; both enclosed in Doherty to Russell, 7 December 1840, CO 267/160, UKNA.
46. Fry Norman to Joseph Norman, 6 September 1840, enclosed in Doherty to Russell, 7 December 1840, CO 267/160, UKNA.
47. Henry James Matson, *Remarks on the Slave Trade and African Squadron,* 2nd ed. (London: James Ridgway, 1848), 40, 75, 89; Joseph Denman, *The African Squadron and Mr. Hutt's Committee,* 2nd ed. (London: John Mortimer, 1850), 35.
48. Van Hulle, *Britain and International Law in West Africa,* chaps. 1–2.
49. *Burón v. Denman* (1848), 154 Eng. Rep. 450, 2 Exch 167.
50. *Buron v. Denman* (1848), 154 Eng. Rep. 450, 2 Exch 167. See also Amanda Perreau-Saussine, "British Acts of State in English Courts," *British Year Book of International Law* 78, no. 1 (2008): 176–254; Charles Mitchell and Leslie Turano, "Burón v Denman (1848)," in *Landmark Cases in the Law of Tort,* ed. Charles Mitchell and Paul Mitchell (Oxford, UK: Hart, 2016), 33–68. The doctrine has been used to deny compensation claims by victims of rendition during the "War on Terror." See Rahmatullah (Respondent) v. Ministry of Defence and another (Appellants) [2017] UKSC 1, https://www.supremecourt.uk/cases/docs/uksc-2015-0002-judgment.pdf (accessed 22 December 2019), paragraphs 23–24, 26, 37, 65.
51. The reasons why a particular set of liberated Africans had been enslaved is discussed in P. E. H. Hair, "The Enslavement of Koelle's Informants," *Journal of African History* 6, no. 2 (1965): 193–203.
52. Lauren A. Benton, *They Called It Peace: Worlds of Imperial Violence* (Princeton, NJ: Princeton University Press, 2024), chap. 5.
53. Parliament, 1846, *Class A. Correspondence with the British commissioners relating to the slave trade. 1845,* C. (1st series) 723, pp. 34–37.
54. William Fergusson to Harry Tucker, Chief of Little Boom River, 28 December 1844, Local Letter Books, PASL.
55. Hamilton to Canning, 12 October 1826, first enclosure, Report of the Case of the Brazilian Brig "Perpetuo Defensor," in Parliament, HCP 1826–27, *Class A. Correspondence with the British commissioners,* vol. 26, paper number 010, pp. 64–65.
56. Parliament, 1846, C. (1st series) 723, pp. 34–37; Fergusson to Harry Tucker, 28 December 1844, PASL.
57. Rogers family to Jones, 26 January 1845; Prince Manna to Jones, 6 February 1845, in Parliament, 1846, C. (1st series) 723, pp. 40, 54.

58. Tucker to Jones, 3 February 1845, in Parliament, 1846, C. (1st series) 723, p. 40.
59. Prince Manna, Lusinia Rogers, J. S. Rogers, and James Weston to Jones, 14 February 1845, in Parliament, 1846, C. (1st series) 723, p. 50.
60. Fergusson to Chief Sy-Cummah, 27 March 1845; see also William Raymond to anonymous, 26 March 1845, both in Parliament, 1846, C. (1st series) 723, p. 82.
61. It was apparently never established whether Eastman had been pregnant and had miscarried. Jones's attention shifted to two other women who were subjects of Sierra Leone but resident in Gendema, who confirmed that they were not enslaved but rather there willingly as the wives of local men.
62. Elizabeth Helen Melville, *A Residence at Sierra Leone: Described from a Journal Kept on the Spot, and from Letters Written to Friends at Home* (London: John Murray, 1849), 190.
63. Dougan to Colonial Secretary, 12 June 1855, in Parliament, 1854–55, *Correspondence relative to the recent expeditions against the Moriah chiefs in the neighbourhood of Sierra Leone*, C. (1st series) 1992, pp. 16–19.
64. Parliament, 1856, *Further correspondence relative to the recent expeditions against the Moriah chiefs*, C. (1st series) 2111, pp. 52–54.
65. I have calculated this number from a close reading of the extant Local Letter Books, 1842–67, PASL.
66. Kenneth Little, "The Political Function of the Poro. Part I," *Africa: Journal of the International African Institute* 35, no. 4 (1965): 349–65; Kenneth Little, "The Political Function of the Poro. Part II," *Africa: Journal of the International African Institute* 36, no. 1 (1966): 62–72. On contemporary Sherbro uses of Poro, see Anaïs Ménard, "Poro Society, Migration, and Political Incorporation on the Freetown Peninsula, Sierra Leone," in *Politics and Policies in Upper Guinea Coast Societies: Change and Continuity*, ed. Christian Kordt Højbjerg, Jacqueline Knorr, and William P. Murphy (New York: Palgrave Macmillan, 2017), 29–51. On elite political authority in the Sierra Leone region, see Allen M. Howard and David E. Skinner, "Network Building and Political Power in Northwestern Sierra Leone, 1800–65," *Africa* 54, no. 2 (June 1984): 2–28.
67. F. Harrison Rankin, *The White Man's Grave*, vol. 2 (London: Richard Bentley, 1836), 220, 302.
68. Marilyn Strathern, *The Gender of the Gift: Problems with Women and Problems with Society in Melanesia* (Berkeley: University of California Press, 1990), 134; Charles Piot, "Of Slaves and the Gift: Kabre Sale of Kin during the Era of the Slave Trade," *Journal of African History* 37, no. 1 (1996): 31–49. On gifting and diplomacy in Sherbro, see Carol P. MacCormack, "Wono: Institutionalized Dependency in Sherbro Descent Groups (Sierra Leone)," in *Slavery in Africa: Historical and Anthropological Perspectives*, ed. Suzanne Miers and Igor Kopytoff (Madison: University of Wisconsin Press, 1977), 199.
69. Governor to Sanasee Famah, 14 January 1860 and 8 March 1860, PASL. The governor addresses Sanasee Famah as both "king" and "alimamy" and calls him "Fanah Sanassee" in the second letter, probably because the governor was not accustomed to writing metronyms, in this case either Mandinka or Temne. Note that *alimamy* denoted the ruler of an Islamic polity in West Africa (similar to

alikali, a compound of *al-qadi*). It seems likely that Sanasee Famah / Fanah Sanassee was the same person.

70. Keene, "Case Study of the Construction of International Hierarchy."
71. Christopher Fyfe, *A History of Sierra Leone* (London: Oxford University Press, 1962), 316.
72. Herbert Thompson to Reverend J. H. Dufort, 15 November 1865, Local Letter Books 1864–1867, PASL.

4. COMPULSORY LABOR

1. Holly Case, *The Age of Questions, or, a First Attempt at an Aggregate History of the Eastern, Social, Woman, American, Jewish, Polish, Bullion, Tuberculosis, and Many Other Questions over the Nineteenth Century, and Beyond* (Princeton, NJ: Princeton University Press, 2018), 73, 93–94.
2. Stephanie McCurry, *Confederate Reckoning: Power and Politics in the Civil War South* (Cambridge, MA: Harvard University Press, 2010), 220.
3. For press gang, see Aviso, 31 December 1841, IIIJ7 139, ANRJ; for trades and servant work, see Table of occupations, 16 February 1864, IIIJ7 127, ANRJ.
4. Representação dos presos existentes nos trabalhos da Casa da Correção e dos pretos africanos que trabalham nas obras publicas, II-34, 25, 11 (1841), BNJM.
5. Sherwin K. Bryant, *Rivers of Gold, Lives of Bondage: Governing through Slavery in Colonial Quito* (Chapel Hill: University of North Carolina Press, 2014); Elena A. Schneider, *The Occupation of Havana: War, Trade, and Slavery in the Atlantic World* (Chapel Hill: Omohundro Institute of Early American History and Culture / University of North Carolina Press, 2018).
6. Sartorius, *Ever Faithful*; Marcela Echeverri, *Indian and Slave Royalists in the Age of Revolution: Reform, Revolution, and Royalism in the Northern Andes, 1780–1825* (New York: Cambridge University Press, 2016).
7. Stephanie M. H. Camp, *Closer to Freedom: Enslaved Women and Everyday Resistance in the Plantation South* (Chapel Hill: University of North Carolina Press, 2004); Marisa J. Fuentes, *Dispossessed Lives: Enslaved Women, Violence, and the Archive* (Philadelphia: University of Pennsylvania Press, 2016); Sasha Turner, *Contested Bodies: Pregnancy, Childrearing, and Slavery in Jamaica* (Philadelphia: University of Pennsylvania Press, 2017); J. Johnson, *Wicked Flesh*; Jennifer L. Morgan, *Reckoning with Slavery: Gender, Kinship, and Capitalism in the Early Black Atlantic* (Durham, NC: Duke University Press, 2021); Diana Paton, "Gender History, Global History, and Atlantic Slavery: On Racial Capitalism and Social Reproduction," *American Historical Review* 127, no. 2 (1 June 2022): 726–54.
8. Ford and Parkinson, "Legislating Liberty"; Richard Anderson, "Abolition's Adolescence: Apprenticeship as 'Liberation' in Sierra Leone, 1808–1848," *English Historical Review* 137, no. 586 (1 June 2022): 763–93.
9. For liberated Africans in São Paulo's political economy, see Enidelce Bertin, "Os meia-cara: Africanos livres em São Paulo no século XIX" (PhD diss., Universidade de São Paulo, 2006). For studies of liberated Africans in

agricultural zones in the Caribbean, see Monica Schuler, "Liberated Central Africans in Nineteenth-Century Guyana," in *Central Africans and Cultural Transformations in the American Diaspora*, ed. Linda M. Heywood (Cambridge: Cambridge University Press, 2002); Monica Schuler, "Liberated Africans in Nineteenth-Century Guyana," in *Slavery, Freedom and Gender: The Dynamics of Caribbean Society*, ed. Brian L. Moore, B. W. Higman, Carl Campbell, and Patrick Bryan (Kingston, Jamaica: University of the West Indies Press, 2003), 133–57.

10. Margaret Gay Davies, *The Enforcement of English Apprenticeship: A Study in Applied Mercantilism, 1563–1642* (Cambridge, MA: Harvard University Press, 1956); Robert J. Steinfeld, *The Invention of Free Labor: The Employment Relation in English and American Law and Culture, 1350–1870* (Chapel Hill: University of North Carolina Press, 1991), 3–54; Lane, *Apprenticeship in England*; Michael Scott, introduction to *Apprenticeship Disputes in the Lord Mayor's Court of London, 1573–1723*, vol. 1, ed. Michael Scott (London: British Record Society, 2016), 1–36.
11. Statute of Artificers 1563, 5 Eliz. I c. 4.
12. Regulation of Servants an Apprentices Act, 1746, 20 Geo. II c. 19.
13. For the more recent approach, see Patrick Wallis, "Apprenticeship in England," in *Apprenticeship in Early Modern Europe*, ed. Maarten Prak and Patrick Wallis (Cambridge: Cambridge University Press, 2019), 247–81; Patrick Wallis, *The Market for Skill: Apprenticeship in England, 1500–1800* (Princeton, NJ: Princeton University Press, 2025).
14. Alysa Levene, "Parish Apprenticeship and the Old Poor Law in London," *Economic History Review* 63, no. 4 (1 November 2010): 915–41.
15. For analysis of the apprenticeship of formerly enslaved people in agricultural areas, see Nigel Worden, "Between Slavery and Freedom: The Apprenticeship Period, 1834 to 1838," in *Breaking the Chains*, ed. Nigel Worden and Clifton Crais (Johannesburg: Witwatersrand University Press, 1994), 117–44.
16. Scanlan, *Freedom's Debtors*, chap. 5; Anderson, *Abolition in Sierra Leone*.
17. Rodney, *History of the Upper Guinea Coast*, 226–27; Philip R. Misevich, "On the Frontier of 'Freedom': Abolition and the Transformation of Atlantic Commerce in Southern Sierra Leone, 1790s to 1860s" (PhD diss., Emory University, 2009).
18. Adderley, *"New Negroes from Africa"*; Richards, "Anti-Slave-Trade Law," 185.
19. Commissioner Dr Madden, Report on Sierra Leone, Second Part, CO 267/172, UKNA, fol. 38.
20. Dixon to Fergusson, 28 August 1844; for a similar case, see Terry to Vincent, 30 September 1843; both in LADLB, EAP 443/1/18/7.
21. I sampled the records of the Police Magistrate Court in the Public Archives of Sierra Leone by reading every other extant volume for the period 1840–71.
22. Sometimes Thomas's surname was spelled "MacFoy." Hannah Kilham, *Report on a Recent Visit to the Colony of Sierra Leone* (London: William Phillips, 1828), 7–8, 12–13, 15–16.
23. Parliament, HCP 1842, *Report from the Select Committee on the West Coast of Africa*, Part II, vol. 12, paper number 551-II, Appendix 19, p. 396; HCP 1852–53, *Class A. Correspondence with the British commissioners*, paper number 0.2, pp. 19–20.

24. C. H. Fyfe, "The Life and Times of John Ezzidio," *Sierra Leone Studies*, n.s., no. 4 (1955): 218.
25. Nemata Amelia Blyden, *West Indians in West Africa, 1808–1880: The African Diaspora in Reverse* (Rochester, NY: University of Rochester Press, 2000).
26. R v. Butcher, 19 June 1840, PMCRB: 13 January 1840–16 November 1840, PASL.
27. R v. Butcher, 19 June 1840, PMCRB, PASL. On magistrate records regarding sexual assault in a different colonial African context, see Elizabeth Thornberry, *Colonizing Consent: Rape and Governance in South Africa's Eastern Cape* (New York: Cambridge University Press, 2019).
28. R v. Langley, 6 July 1840, PMCRB: 13 January 1840–16 November 1840, PASL.
29. R v. Sawyer, 7 June 1841, PMCRB: 27 May 1841–December 1841, PASL. I am grateful to Padraic Scanlan for sharing photographs of the proceedings of this case with me.
30. "Bill for declaring certain supposed Apprenticeships within the Colony of Sierra Leone to be illegal, null and void," 15 August 1808, CO 270/10, UKNA, fols. 23v–25r. For voiding these apprenticeships and various other actions, the governor was recalled by the Colonial Office. See Castlereagh to Thompson, 3 April 1809, CO 268/6, UKNA, fols. 60–62; see also Bruce Mouser, "The Expulsion of Dala Modu," in *African Voices on Slavery and the Slave Trade*, ed. Sandra E. Greene, Martin A. Klein, and Alice Bellagamba (New York: Cambridge University Press, 2013), 334–41; Michael Turner, "The Limits of Abolition: Government, Saints and the 'African Question,' c. 1780–1820," *English Historical Review* 112, no. 446 (1997): 319–57; Scanlan, *Freedom's Debtors*, chap. 2.
31. See, for instance, Terry, circular letter, 24 November 1838, LADLB, EAP 443/1/18/6; Dixon to Crowley and Cummings, 4 January [1845], and Dixon to Cummings and Crowley, 19 April 1845, LADLB, EAP 443/1/18/7. On the analogy between apprenticeship and marriage in the assignment of liberated Africans by the colonial administration, see Maeve Ryan, " 'It Was Necessary to Do Something with Those Women': Colonial Governance and the 'Disposal' of Women and Girls in Early Nineteenth-Century Sierra Leone," *Gender & History* 35, no. 2 (July 2023): 491–510.
32. Melville, *Residence at Sierra Leone*, 199.
33. P. C. Lloyd, "Agnatic and Cognatic Descent among the Yoruba," *Man* 1, no. 4 (1966): 488–89.
34. Caree A. Banton, " 'More Auspicious Shores': Post-Emancipation Barbadian Emigrants in Pursuit of Freedom, Citizenship, and Nationhood in Liberia, 1834–1912" (PhD diss., Vanderbilt University, 2013), 185, 188, 218; Fett, *Recaptured Africans*, chap. 3.
35. R v. Sawyer, 7 June 1841, PMCRB, PASL.
36. Allen M. Howard, David E. Skinner, and Barbara E. Harrell-Bond, *Community Leadership and the Transformation of Freetown (1801–1976)* (The Hague: Mouton, 1978); Gibril Raschid Cole, *The Krio of West Africa: Islam, Culture, Creolization, and Colonialism in the Nineteenth Century* (Athens: Ohio University Press, 2013).
37. Bronwen Everill, *Abolition and Empire in Sierra Leone and Liberia* (Basingstoke, UK: Palgrave Macmillan, 2013); Anderson, *Abolition in Sierra Leone*.
38. Terry to Vincent, 26 May 1843, LADLB, EAP 443/1/18/7.

39. Dixon to Vincent, 3 June 1844, LADLB, EAP 443/1/18/7.
40. See the cases of police registration and inspection of Indigenous "alien children," Police Magistrate, February 1861–May 1861, PASL.
41. Ordinance No. 18, For amending and consolidating the Laws regulating the relative Rights and Duties of Masters, Servants, and Apprentices, Chapter II, Clauses II and V, first enclosure in Napier to Russell, 30 January 1840, Despatch 7, CO 48/207, UKNA.
42. Minute of the unofficial members of the Legislative Council, 13 January 1840, third enclosure in Napier to Russell, 30 January 1840, CO 48/207, UKNA.
43. Russell to Napier, 26 October 1840, CO 48/207, UKNA.
44. Memorial of the Inhabitants of the Cape of Good Hope, n.d. [1840–41], enclosed in Napier to Russell, 15 March 1841, Despatch 19, CO 48/211, UKNA.
45. Huzzey, *Freedom Burning*, 180.
46. Legislative Council, 26 March 1842, as reported by the *Cape Town Mail*, 2 April 1842; see also Napier to Stanley, 1 May 1842, Despatch 91, CO 48/219, UKNA.
47. Andrew Pearson, *Distant Freedom: St Helena and the Abolition of the Slave Trade, 1840–1872* (Liverpool: Liverpool University Press, 2016).
48. Trelawny to Napier, 3 February 1842, enclosed in Napier to Stanley, 18 March 1842, Despatch 63, CO 48/218, UKNA; letter by "Fair Play," *Cape Town Mail*, 19 March 1842.
49. James Stephen, minute, 3 June 1842, CO 48/218, UKNA, fol. 215v; Stanley to Napier, 18 June 1842, CO 48/218, UKNA, fol. 215r–16v.
50. Trelawny to Napier, 24 February 1842, enclosure in Napier to Colonial Office, 15 April 1842, Despatch 83, CO 48/218, UKNA (original emphasis).
51. A1939 4/4, Baptisms, WCARS.
52. Trelawny to Napier, 24 February 1842, enclosure in Napier to Colonial Office, 15 April 1842, CO 48/218, UKNA.
53. *South African Commercial Advertiser*, 25 January 1839. For the "Negro Fund," see William Field to Governor, 3 February 1847, Enclosures to Governor's Despatches, GH 28/36, WCARS. One newspaper criticized the scheme for enabling Field to assign laborers arbitrarily: *De Verzamelaar*, 30 May 1843.
54. Da Silva et al., "Diaspora of Africans Liberated from Slave Ships," table A.3, 369.
55. 1/CT 8/4, 8/5, 8/6 are the only extant summaries of cases against apprentices in the Western Cape Archives and Records Service.
56. Public Prosecutor v. Capitango, 20 August 1845, 1/CT 8/5, WCARS.
57. George Duff, *Procession on the Anniversary of the Slave Liberation, Cape Town*, watercolor, MA1971-534, Museum Africa.
58. CCT 382, Collector of Customs Registration Book, "Negroes 24 Oct '43 to 23 May '51," WCARS. Another official made a single entry about four liberated Africans seized by HMS *Rapid* in 1864.
59. Jake Christopher Subryan Richards, "Liberated Africans and Law in the South Atlantic, c. 1839–1871" (PhD diss., University of Cambridge, 2020), appendix. Liberated Africans in Durban in the 1870s earned more than Indian indentured laborers. See Preben Kaarsholm, "Indian Ocean Networks and the Transmutations of Servitude: The Protector of Indian Immigrants and the

Administration of Freed Slaves and Indentured Labourers in Durban in the 1870s," *Journal of Southern African Studies* 42, no. 3 (3 May 2016): 448. For a different interpretation of apprenticeship, see Craig Iannini, "Contracted Chattel: Indentured and Apprenticed Labor in Cape Town, c. 1808–1840" (master's thesis, University of Cape Town, 1995), 27–28.

60. Cape of Good Hope Legislative Council, *Cape of Good Hope Blue Books. Master and Servants, Squatters Bill Etc. Documents on the Working of the Order-in-Council* (Cape Town: Saul Solomon, 1849), 223.
61. Cape of Good Hope Legislative Council, *Cape of Good Hope Blue Books*, 224.
62. Cape of Good Hope Legislative Council, *Cape of Good Hope Blue Books*, 229.
63. Cape of Good Hope Legislative Council, *Cape of Good Hope Blue Books*, 232.
64. The Capetonian magistrate also recommended that the jurisdiction of the justice of the peace apply regarding agreeing to contracts and implementing punishments. Cape of Good Hope Legislative Council, *Cape of Good Hope Blue Books*, 236.
65. *Government Gazette*, 19 June 1840.
66. Richard Price, *Making Empire: Colonial Encounters and the Creation of Imperial Rule in Nineteenth-Century Africa* (Cambridge: Cambridge University Press, 2008), 210.
67. See Field to Governor, 3 February 1847 GH 28/36, WCARS.
68. Cape of Good Hope Army Burgher Force, *List of Persons Drawn for the Burgher Force of Cape Town and Green-Point on the 7th Day of March 1846, for the Defence of the Eastern Frontier* (Cape Town: J. S. de Lima, 1846); Cape of Good Hope Army Burgher Force, *List of Cape Town Burgher Force, Substitutes, Etc. Who Went to the Frontier and of the Persons Enrolled to Do Burgher Duty in Cape Town* (Cape Town: [J. S. de Lima] printed at the Gazette Office, 1846).
69. Field to Governor, 3 February 1847, GH 28/36, WCARS.
70. Vives to Junta de Fomento, 21 December 1824, RCJF 150/7431, ANC.
71. Junta de Fomento to Vives, 22 December 1824, RCJF 150/7431, ANC.
72. Vives to Junta, 2 May 1827, RCJF 150/7437, ANC; see also RCJF 150/7434, ANC, for a similar case involving the apprentice Saturnino.
73. Sarah L. Franklin, *Women and Slavery in Nineteenth-Century Colonial Cuba* (Rochester, NY: University of Rochester Press, 2012). On the household as the locus of enslavement, see Stephanie E. Jones-Rogers, *They Were Her Property: White Women as Slave Owners in the American South* (New Haven, CT: Yale University Press, 2019).
74. Minute of Junta de Fomento, 16 May 1827, RCJF 150/7437, ANC.
75. Captain general to Real Consulado, 21 February 1832, RCJF 150/7460, ANC.
76. Contract from 1854, GSC 1626/81970, ANC.
77. Cuaderno promovido con certificado de la Comisión Mixta . . . acerca de la obrado en el expediente relativo a la detencion que hizo Speedwell del bergantin Aguila con cargamento de bozales, AP 41/58, ANC; David Turnbull, *Travels in the West: With Notices of Porto Rico, and the Slave Trade* (London: Longman, Orne, Brown, Green, and Longmans, 1840), 162.
78. Turnbull, *Travels in the West*, 393–96.
79. Informe de Audiencia Pretorial de la Habana, 18 September 1841, CM, Informe 3, BNJM.

80. Informe de la Junta de Fomento, 28 September 1841, CM, Informe 3, BNJM.
81. For examples, see RCO 156/302, 156/370, 156/399, ANC; Adderley, *"New Negroes from Africa."*
82. Parliament, 1845, *Class A. Correspondence with the British commissioners relating to the slave trade, 1844*, C. (1st series) 632, p. 108.
83. Parliament, 1845, C. (1st series) 632, p. 109.
84. Parliament, 1845, C. (1st series) 632, pp. 147–48.
85. Dale W. Tomich, *Through the Prism of Slavery: Labor, Capital, and World Economy* (Lanham, MD: Rowman and Littlefield, 2004).
86. Crawford to Aberdeen, 29 June 1844, FO 84/520, UKNA, fol. 165v. On the forced movement of enslaved people across Cuba, see Camillia Cowling, "Teresa Mina's Journeys: 'Slave-Moving,' Mobility, and Gender in Mid-Nineteenth-Century Cuba," *Atlantic Studies* 18, no. 1 (2 January 2021): 7–30.
87. Possibly (but less likely) "Erigo."
88. O'Donnell to Junta de Fomento, 17 February 1844, RCJF 152/7626, ANC.
89. Oyer to O'Donnell, 6 March 1844, RCJF 152/7626, ANC.
90. Rebecca Scott, "Social Facts, Legal Fictions, and the Attribution of Slave Status: The Puzzle of Prescription," *Law and History Review* 35, no. 1 (2017): 9–30.
91. O'Donnell to Junta de Fomento, 14 March 1844, RCJF 152/7626, ANC.
92. Geronimo Valdes to Governor of the City of Matanzas, 26 January 1843, Emancipados 107/11288, AHPM, fol. 2r; see also the case of Homobono: Valdes to Governor of Matanzas, 8 May 1842, 107/11290, AHPM, fol. 1r.
93. Dictamen of the asesor general, Pedro Villaverde, 15 November 1843; minute of O'Donnell, 20 November 1843, AP 41/58, ANC.
94. Captain General to Superintendent, 11 September 1849, Intendencia, 1051/18, ANC.
95. Correa, internal memorandum, Real Hacienda, 13 September 1849, Intendencia, 1051/18, ANC.
96. Captain General to Superintendent, 26 September 1849, Intendencia, 1051/18, ANC; for a case of recontracting of apprentices in 1854, see also RCJF 152/7668, ANC.
97. For similar processes in the Intendencia de Ejército y Real Hacienda, see work by apprentices on barges: Intendencia, 1052/36, ANC; surveillance of apprentices: neighbourhood reports, 28 July 1845, Hacienda, 192/14860, AHPM, fols. 3r–9v; for census: Revista of July 1836, Hacienda, 192/14865, AHPM, fols. 7r–10v; and Revista of July 1851, Hacienda 192/14861, AHPM, fols. 17r–19r.
98. Beatriz Mamigonian, "Revisitando o problema da 'Transição para o trabalho livre': A experiência dos africanos livres," in *Tráfico, cativeiro e liberdade: (Rio de Janeiro, séculos XVII–XIX)*, ed. Manolo Florentino (Rio de Janeiro: Civilização Brasileira, 2005), 389–417; Andréa Lisly Gonçalves and Marileide Lázara Cassoli Meyer, "Nas fímbrias da liberdade: Agregados, índios, africanos livres e forros na Província de Minas Gerais (século XIX)," *Varia Historia* 27, no. 46 (December 2011): 645–63; Télio Cravo, "Estrutura e dinâmica do trabalho compulsório e livre na infraestrutura viária do Império do Brasil: Africanos livres, escravizados e livres (1854–1856)," *História (São Paulo)* 40 (2021), e2021060.

99. For raw data for these calculations, see Antonio Paulino Limpo de Abreu, *Relatório da Repartição dos negócios da Justiça apresentado à Assembléa Geral Legislativa na sessão ordinária de 1836, pelo respectivo ministro e secretario de estado* (Rio de Janeiro: Typographia Nacional, 1836), 28; Carlos Eduardo Moreira de Araújo, "Cárceres imperiais: A Casa de Correção do Rio de Janeiro. Seus detentos e o sistema prisional do Império, 1830–1861" (PhD diss., Unicamp, 2009), 216.
100. Jackson and Grigg to Palmerston, 10 December 1834, FO 129/5, UKNA, fol. 17 (handwritten pagination).
101. The Treasury included salaries as income even after the general emancipation of liberated Africans in 1864. See Jose Pedro Dias de Carvalho, "Orçamento da receita geral do Imperio para o exercicio de 1866–1867," in *Proposta e relatorio do Ministerio da Fazenda apresentados à Assembléa Geral Legislativa . . .* (Rio de Janeiro: Typographia Nacional, 1865), appendix, table 3.
102. Carlos A. Weyll to Paulo Jose de Mello Azevedo e Brito, 20 November 1840, Provincial, Série Viaçao, maço 4882, APEB.
103. Thomé Joaquim Torres to Limpo de Abreu, 28 October 1845, IJ7 10, Casa de Correção, Ofícios: Africanos, 1834–1848, ANRJ.
104. Antônio Paulino Limpo de Abreu (Minister of Justice) to Inspector of Works, 23 October 1845, IIIJ7 139, Obras da Casa de Correção, Avisos, 1841–1849, ANRJ.
105. Torres to Limpo de Abreu, 28 October 1845, IJ7 10, ANRJ.
106. "Tabella do fornecimento para os africanos q. existem na Caza de Correção," first enclosure in Torres to Abreu, 28 October 1845, IJ7 10, ANRJ.
107. Joaquim de Paula Guedes Alcoforado, "História sobre o infame negócio de africanos da África Oriental e Ocidental, com todas as ocorrências desde 1831 a 1853," manuscript copy in FO 128/48, UKNA.
108. Kaori Kodama, "Os debates pelo fim do tráfico no periódico *O Philantropo* (1849–1852) e a formação do povo: Doenças, raça e escravidão," *Revista Brasileira de História* 28 (2008): 407–30. On abolitionist rhetoric in the press, see Thiago Campos Pessoa, "Aristocracia negreira: A formação da nobreza imperial e o comércio clandestino de Africanos em meados do oitocentos," *Almanack* 35 (2023), ea01023.
109. "Africanos de Caza de Correcao [*sic*]" to Robert Hesketh, 9 August 1850, FO 131/7, part 2, UKNA, fol. 276.
110. African apprentices in Casa de Correção to Hesketh, 23 November 1850, FO 131/7, part 2, UKNA, fol. 276; Mamigonian, *Africanos livres*, 255–56.
111. *Umanidade* seems to have been a relatively rare term in contemporary print. For some illustrative examples in the press where *umanidade* refers to equity in the political process and to liberated Africans' treatment during apprenticeship, see, respectively, *Jornal do Commercio*, 25 August 1850, 1; and *O Republico*, 15 July 1853, 3.
112. Petition by Anna, n.d., with official minute dated 6 March 1843, Série Justiça, Polícia, Africanos, IJ6 471, ANRJ.

113. Keila Grinberg, *O fiador dos brasileiros: Cidadania, escravidão e direito civil no tempo de Antonio Pereira Rebouças* (Rio de Janeiro: Civilização Brasileira, 2002).
114. McKinley, *Fractional Freedoms*; Chira, *Patchwork Freedoms*.
115. E.g., Mappa [*sic*] dos africanos livres, cujos serviços forão confiados a Establecimentos de caridade, estações e obras públicas. . . ., 24 May 1860, I-48, 17, 36, No. 001, BNRJ; Relação dos africanos existentes no serviço das Obras Públicas da Província do Rio de Janeiro no mês de julho 1860, Niterói, 31 July 1860, I-48, 17, 36, n. 002, BNRJ.
116. Emancipados: Inclosure in Consul Hesketh's Letter of 30 September 1851 [to unnamed recipient], FO 131/7, part 2, UKNA, fols. 258r–303r. An edited version of the survey was eventually sent to the Foreign Office in Southern to Malmesbury, 14 July 1852, enclosure, in Parliament, HCP 1852–53, *Class B. Correspondence with British ministers and agents in foreign countries . . . relating to the slave trade*, paper number 0.5, pp. 136–50. Of 856 liberated Africans' details recorded in Hesketh's survey, 763 entries remain sufficiently legible to identify the person's name, sex, and occupation(s); 84 of 176 women had multiple occupations and/or were hired out on their own account. The same was true of 78 of 587 men.
117. Karasch, *Slave Life in Rio de Janeiro*, 209–10; see, more generally, Sandra Lauderdale Graham, *House and Street: The Domestic World of Servants and Masters in Nineteenth-Century Rio de Janeiro* (Cambridge: Cambridge University Press, 1988).
118. For wage rates, see Richards, "Liberated Africans and Law," appendix, 234–48. For Florencia, see Emancipados, FO 131/7, part 2, UKNA, fol. 289r.
119. Juiz d'Órfãos, ZN, 1862. Número 20, Caixa 3631, Castro, Leonarda Angelica de (falecido), Saião, Joaquim Alexandre (inventariante), ANRJ; Juiz d'Órfãos, ZL, 1881, Número 1951, Caixa 4166, Carvalho, José Pedro Dias de (falecido), Carvalho, Josefa Cecilia de Figueiredo (inventariante), ANRJ; Juiz d'Órfãos, ZL, 1860, Número 1396, Caixa 4139, Barbosa, Fortunato Mariano (inventariante), Conceição, Genoveva Maria da, Conceição, Rosa Angelica da, Barbosa, Silveiro Mariano (falecidos), ANRJ; Richards, "Liberated Africans and Law," appendix.
120. For the large numbers of women who owned food stalls, see "Demonstração estatística a freguesia de Santa Rita 1841," Fundo Câmara Municipal, Série Estatística, 43.1.42, AGCRJ. "Africanos" owned 166 of 4,734 businesses, according to a survey of Rio in 1843: "Estatística das casas de commercio, número de rezes. . . ." (1843), Fundo Câmara Municipal, Série Estatística, 43.1.43, AGCRJ.
121. Mappa [*sic*] dos africanos livres, cujos serviços forão confiados a Establecimentos de caridade, estações e obras públicas. . . ., 24 May 1860, I-48, 17, 36, No. 001, BNRJ.
122. Jonathan M. Bryant, *Dark Places of the Earth: The Voyage of the Slave Ship* Antelope (New York: Liveright, 2015), 159–69, 184–87.
123. Petition of Juan Congo and Coleto Lucumi, 11 August 1884, Hacienda 192/14862, fol. 16r, AHPM.

124. Nicolas Lopez de la Torres to President of Real Junta, 24 November 1853, RCJF 152/7667, ANC.
125. Lopez de la Torres to Real Junta, 10 January 1854[?], RCJF 152/7667, ANC.

5. INSURGENT ABOLITION

1. Manuel Moreno Fraginals, *El ingenio: El complejo económico cubano del azúcar* (1964; repr., Barcelona: Critica, 2001), 135–39; Reinaldo Funes Monzote, *From Rainforest to Cane Field in Cuba: An Environmental History since 1492*, trans. Alex Martin (Chapel Hill: University of North Carolina Press, 2008).
2. Moreno Fraginals, *El ingenio*, appendix 1.2, chart 1, p. 535; Knight, *Slave Society in Cuba*, chaps. 4–5.
3. Francisco Marotegui to Comandante de Armas de Yumurí, 26 March 1844, 715:25, EC, HL.
4. Mario Samper and Radin Fernando, "Appendix: Historical Statistics of Coffee Production and Trade from 1700 to 1960," in *The Global Coffee Economy in Africa, Asia and Latin America, 1500–1989*, ed. W. G. Clarence-Smith and Steven Topik (Cambridge: Cambridge University Press, 2003), 411–62, table A.5, 418, and table A.14, 432. Christopher David Absell and Antonio Tena-Junguito, "Brazilian Export Growth and Divergence in the Tropics during the Nineteenth Century," *Journal of Latin American Studies* 48, no. 4 (2016): 677–706, 700, figure 4.
5. For approaches that emphasize official paranoia, see Robert L Paquette, *Sugar Is Made with Blood: The Conspiracy of La Escalera and the Conflict between Empires over Slavery in Cuba* (Middletown, CT: Wesleyan University Press, 1988); Jeffrey D Needell, "The Abolition of the Brazilian Slave Trade in 1850: Historiography, Slave Agency and Statesmanship," *Journal of Latin American Studies* 33, no. 4 (2001): 681–711. For interpretations that emphasize radical antislavery, see Aisha K. Finch, *Rethinking Slave Rebellion in Cuba: La Escalera and the Insurgencies of 1841–1844* (Chapel Hill: University of North Carolina Press, 2015); Robert W. Slenes, " '*Malungo, ngoma* vem!': África coberta e descoberta no Brasil," *Revista USP*, February 1992, 48–67. Jason Sharples cautions that investigators applied their own cognitive frames to understanding enslaved people's politics. Although those frames mattered in shaping the inquisitorial process, they did not ipso facto restrict the politics of the enslaved to the community formation that Sharples emphasizes. The cognitive frames of investigators struggled to comprehend the worldviews of the enslaved, which should focus our attention on political actions that were illegible within those frames rather than assuming that such actions were fabricated by them. Jason T. Sharples, "Discovering Slave Conspiracies: New Fears of Rebellion and Old Paradigms of Plotting in Seventeenth-Century Barbados," *American Historical Review* 120, no. 3 (1 June 2015): 811–43.
6. Saidiya V. Hartman, *Lose Your Mother: A Journey along the Atlantic Slave Route* (New York: Farrar, Strauss and Giroux, 2007); Fuentes, *Dispossessed Lives*.
7. Ann Laura Stoler, *Along the Archival Grain: Epistemic Anxieties and Colonial Common Sense* (Princeton, NJ: Princeton University Press, 2009); Stephen Best

and Sharon Marcus, "Surface Reading: An Introduction," *Representations* 108, no. 1 (2009): 1–21.

8. Steven Hahn, " 'Extravagant Expectations' of Freedom: Rumour, Political Struggle, and the Christmas Insurrection Scare of 1865 in the American South," *Past & Present*, no. 157 (1997): 122–58. For an interpretation that emphasizes how resistance led to an entrenchment of slavery in South Carolina, in contrast to the amelioration and eventual abolition of slavery in the British Caribbean, see Edward B. Rugemer, *Slave Law and the Politics of Resistance in the Early Atlantic World* (Cambridge, MA: Harvard University Press, 2018), chap. 7.
9. Tomich, *Through the Prism of Slavery*.
10. Ada Ferrer, *Freedom's Mirror: Cuba and Haiti in the Age of Revolution* (New York: Cambridge University Press, 2014).
11. Bergad, Iglesias García, and Barcia, *Cuban Slave Market*.
12. Matt D. Childs, *The 1812 Aponte Rebellion in Cuba and the Struggle against Atlantic Slavery* (Chapel Hill: University of North Carolina Press, 2006); Ferrer, *Freedom's Mirror*, chap. 7; Greg L. Childs, "Conspiracies, Seditions, Rebellions: Concepts and Categories in the Study of Slave Resistance," in *New Perspectives on the Black Intellectual Tradition*, ed. Keisha N. Blain, Christopher Cameron, and Ashley D. Farmer (Evanston, IL: Northwestern University Press, 2018), 217–31; Schneider, *Occupation of Havana*, 303–9; Landers, *Atlantic Creoles in the Age of Revolutions*, chap. 6.
13. Manuel Barcia Paz, *West African Warfare in Bahia and Cuba: Soldier Slaves in the Atlantic World, 1807–1844* (Oxford: Oxford University Press, 2014).
14. Stephan Palmié, *Wizards and Scientists: Explorations in Afro-Cuban Modernity and Tradition* (Durham, NC: Duke University Press, 2002), chap. 2; Carrie Viarnés, "Cultural Memory in Afro-Cuban Possession: Problematizing Spiritual Categories, Resurfacing 'Other' Histories," *Western Folklore* 66, nos. 1–2 (2007): 127–59.
15. Stephan Palmié, "Ecue's Atlantic: An Essay in Methodology," *Journal of Religion in Africa* 37 (2007): 275–315.
16. Joaquín Llaverías, *La Comisión militar ejecutiva y permanente de la Isla de Cuba* (Havana: Imprenta "El Siglo XX," A. Muñez y hno., 1929).
17. Andrés Pletch, " 'Coercive Measures': Slave Rebellion, Torture, and Sovereignty in Cuba, 1812–1844," *Slavery & Abolition* 40, no. 2 (3 April 2019): 271–94; de la Fuente and Gross, *Becoming Free, Becoming Black*.
18. Gerónimo Valdés, *Bando de gobernación y policía de la isla de Cuba espedido por el escmo. sr. d. Geronimo Valdes, presidente, gobernador y capitan general* (Havana: Impr. del gobierno por S.M., 1842), Article 34.
19. Captain General of Cuba report, 30 September 1842; Ministro de la Guerra to Captain General, 22 December 1842, AHN, Ultramar, 4617, Exp. 6.
20. Note by the captain general's secretary, 24 December 1841, GSC 940/33156, ANC.
21. Note of Manuel Aroy, 20 January 1842, GSC 940/33156, ANC.
22. Sindico Procurador General en representación del negro Feliz [Lucumi] contra Diego Fernandez Herrera y Jose Joaquin Carrera sobre libertad de aquello, Escribanía de Barreto—Ordinarios, 147/6, ANC.

23. Hebe Mattos, "The Madness of Justina and Januàrio Mina," *Quaderni Storici* 148, no. 1 (April 2015): 180.
24. Aureliano de Sousa e Oliveira Coutinho, *Relatorio do presidente da provincia do Rio de Janeiro, o senador Aureliano de Souza e Oliveira Coutinho, na abertura da 1.a sessão da 7.a legislatura da Assembléa Provincial, no dia 1.o de abril de 1848 . . .* (Rio de Janeiro: Typographia do Diario, de N. L. Vianna, 1848), 23–24.
25. Stanley J. Stein, *Vassouras: A Brazilian Coffee Country, 1850–1900* (Cambridge, MA: Harvard University Press, 1957), 32–35.
26. Verena Stolcke, *Coffee Planters, Workers, and Wives: Class Conflict and Gender Relations on São Paulo Plantations, 1850–1980* (Basingstoke, UK: Macmillan in association with St. Antony's College Oxford, 1988), 6.
27. Renato Leite Marcondes, "Small and Medium Slaveholdings in the Coffee Economy of the Vale do Paraíba, Province of São Paulo," *Hispanic American Historical Review* 85, no. 2 (May 2005): 259–81.
28. Minister of Justice to Inspector of Public Works, Casa de Correção, 17 February 1845, IIIJ 7 139, ANRJ.
29. Michele Reid-Vazquez, *The Year of the Lash: Free People of Color in Cuba and the Nineteenth-Century Atlantic World* (Athens: University of Georgia Press, 2011); Finch, *Rethinking Slave Rebellion in Cuba.*
30. Cuba, *Colección de los fallos pronunciados por una sección de la Comisión Militar establecida en la ciudad de Matanzas, para conocer de la causa de conspiración de la gente de color* (Matanzas: Imprenta de Gobierno, 1844), Case 12a; Landers, *Atlantic Creoles in the Age of Revolutions*, 227.
31. Valdés, *Bando de gobernación y policía*, Instrucción de pedáneos, Article 14, 74–75.
32. José María Zamora y Coronado, *Biblioteca de legislación ultramarina en forma de diccionario alfabético*, vol. 2, *Letters B, C* (Madrid: Imp. de Alegria y Charlain, 1844), 310.
33. García Oña to O'Donnell, 2 February 1844, 715:1, EC, HL.
34. Rafael Mariscal del Hoyo to Governor of Matanzas, 28 February 1844, 715:4, EC, HL.
35. CM 63/5, 1844. Criminal Contra el moreno Mauricio García, Orre o Reyes, acusando de haber vertido palabras alarmantes respecto a los blancos de la ciudad de Matanzas, ANC, fol. 29v.
36. Tamar Herzog, *Defining Nations: Immigrants and Citizens in Early Modern Spain and Spanish America* (New Haven, CT: Yale University Press, 2003).
37. CM 63/5, ANC, fols. 41r–v.
38. Julius Scott, *The Common Wind: Afro-American Currents in the Age of the Haitian Revolution* (London: Verso, 2018); Rugemer, *Problem of Emancipation.*
39. CM 63/5, ANC, fol. 32r.
40. V. Brown, *Tacky's Revolt*; Christopher L. Tomlins, *In the Matter of Nat Turner: A Speculative History* (Princeton, NJ: Princeton University Press, 2020); Hazareesingh, *Black Spartacus.*
41. Cuba, *Colección de los fallos*, 19a. On the absence of freedom of speech in slave societies, see G. Childs, "Conspiracies, Seditions, Rebellions"; and Miles

Ogborn, *The Freedom of Speech: Talk and Slavery in the Anglo-Caribbean World* (Chicago: University of Chicago Press, 2019).

42. CM 63/5, ANC, fol. 30r.
43. Andrés Pletch, "Isle of Exceptions: Slavery, Law, and Counter-revolutionary Governance in Cuba, 1825–1856" (PhD diss., University of Michigan, 2017), 81.
44. CM 63/5, ANC, fols. 30r–31r.
45. CM 63/5, ANC, fols. 121v–22r.
46. CM 47/2, 1844, 1ª Pieza de los criminales seguidos contra los individuos que a continuación se espresan, acusados de complicación en la sublevación intentada por la gente de color, ANC; Jonathan Curry-Machado, "How Cuba Burned with the Ghosts of British Slavery: Race, Abolition and the Escalera," *Slavery & Abolition* 25, no. 1 (April 2004): 71–93.
47. Interrogation of Tomas Lucumi on the Ingenio Las Nunes, partido de Macuriges, 17 March 1844, in CM 33/4, Pieza de los Criminales Contra los autores y cómplices del Incendio occurido en el Ingenio Encanto, ANC, fols. 84v/44v–86v/46v.
48. Hurston, *Barracoon*; David Westerlund, *African Indigenous Religions and Disease Causation: From Spiritual Beings to Living Humans* (Leiden: Brill, 2006), chap. 8; Sweet, *Domingos Álvares.*
49. Jacqueline Grant, "Leopard Men: Manhood and Power in Mid-Nineteenth-Century Cuba," in Finch, Rushing, and Hall, *Breaking the Chains, Forging the Nation*, 178–98.
50. Sherry B. Ortner, "Resistance and the Problem of Ethnographic Refusal," *Comparative Studies in Society and History* 37, no. 1 (1995): 173–93; V. Brown, *Tacky's Revolt.*
51. For contemporary travel writing about Catholic worship by enslaved people, see Richard B. Kimball, *Cuba, and the Cubans; Comprising a History of the Island of Cuba, Its Present Social, Political, and Domestic Condition; Also, Its Relation to England and the United States* (New York: Samuel Hueston, 1850), 153–54; Richard Henry Dana, *To Cuba and Back, a Vacation Voyage* (Boston: Ticknor, 1859), 251.
52. Cuba, *Colección de los fallos*, Case 29a.
53. Interrogation of Tomas Lucumi, CM 33/4, ANC, fol. 87r/47r.
54. Carlos Ghersi to García Oña, 30 March 1844, 715:3, EC, HL.
55. Esclavos (Bozales) 21/28, AHPM.
56. Nelson, "Slavery, Race, and Conspiracy."
57. John G. Wurdemann, *Notes on Cuba: Containing an Account of Its Discovery and Early History: A Description of the Face of the Country, Its Population, Resources, and Wealth: Its Institutions, and the Manners and Customs of Its Inhabitants: With Directions to Travellers Visiting the Island* (Boston: James Munroe, 1844), 271–72.
58. Murray, *Odious Commerce*; Paquette, *Sugar Is Made with Blood*; Curry-Machado, "How Cuba Burned with the Ghosts of British Slavery."
59. Finch, *Rethinking Slave Rebellion in Cuba*, 158–64.
60. Carlos de Castro and Miguel Pagem investigation, 30 March 1844, 715:25, EC, HL. See also folders 25–30.

61. Capítan pedaneo de Camarioca, undated report enclosed in Bernardo Mancebo to Governor of Matanzas, 3 April 1844, 715:26, EC, HL.
62. Cuba, *Colección de los fallos*, Cases 11a, 33a, 34a.
63. Cuba, *Colección de los fallos*, 25a.
64. Cuba, *Colección de los fallos*, Case 15a.
65. A claim most explicitly made by Knight, *Slave Society in Cuba*, 96; see, more generally, Reid-Vazquez, *Year of the Lash*, chap. 2; Landers, *Atlantic Creoles in the Age of Revolutions*, chap. 6; de la Fuente and Gross, *Becoming Free, Becoming Black*, chap. 4.
66. Paquette, *Sugar Is Made with Blood*, 229.
67. Stuart B. Schwartz, *Sea of Storms: A History of Hurricanes in the Greater Caribbean from Columbus to Katrina* (Princeton, NJ: Princeton University Press, 2015), 151. For hurricane-related repairs organized by the Junta de Fomento, see Resolution, 24 April 1845, RCJF 152/7655, ANC.
68. Louis A. Pérez, *Winds of Change: Hurricanes and the Transformation of Nineteenth-Century Cuba* (Chapel Hill: University of North Carolina Press, 2001).
69. SlaveVoyages, "Trans-Atlantic Slave Trade—Database," accessed 13 August 2020, https://www.slavevoyages.org/voyages/jPifCYni.
70. Bergad, Iglesias García, and Barcia, *Cuban Slave Market*, 61, figure 4.8.
71. Juan Luis Bachero Bachero, "La ley penal de 1845 en Cuba: Procesos de negociación, propuestas, contrapropuestas y resultado," *Anuario de Estudios Americanos* 80, no. 1 (January 2023): 285–309.
72. CM, Act No. 1: Acta de la reunion celebrada por los Sres que constituyen la junta creada para informar acerca de la ley penal, 1844, BNJM, fol. 4r. See also Perera Díaz and Meriño Fuentes, *Contrabando de bozales en Cuba*.
73. Reglamento de cimarrones, reformado por la Real Junta de Fomento, 1846, Part I, Articles 2, 3, 5; Part II, Article 48, Gobierno Provincial, Orden Publico, Cimarrones, 13/17, AHPM.
74. On the Junta's proposal and the captain general's response, see Jean-Pierre Tardieu, *"Morir o dominar": En torno al reglamento de esclavos de Cuba (1841–1866)* (Madrid: Iberoamericana; Frankfurt am Main: Vervuert, 2003), 192, 194.
75. Manoel de Jesus Valdetaro, "Relatório com que o Desembargardor Manoel de Jesus Valdetaro entregou a administração da Provincia do Rio de Janeiro ao seu sucessor o Visconde de Barbacena em 7 de junho de 1848 (manuscrito)" (Rio de Janeiro, 1848), 2.
76. Relatório Reservado, Special Commission of the Provincial Assembly of Rio de Janeiro, 8 July 1848, enclosed in Hudson to Palmerston, 20 February 1850, FO 84/802, UKNA, fol. 328v–29r.
77. Robert W. Slenes, "L'arbre nsanda replanté: Cultes d'affliction kongo et identité des esclaves de plantation dans le brésil du sud-est (1810–1888)," *Cahiers du Brésil Contemporain*, no. 67/68, part 2 (2007): 217–313.
78. FO 84/802, UKNA, fol. 330r.
79. FO 84/802, UKNA, fol. 331v.
80. Wyatt MacGaffey, "Constructing a Kongo Identity: Scholarship and Mythopoesis," *Comparative Studies in Society and History* 58, no. 1 (2016): 177.

81. Wyatt MacGaffey, "Fetishism Revisited: Kongo 'Nkisi' in Sociological Perspective," *Africa: Journal of the International African Institute* 47, no. 2 (1977): 172–84.
82. Robert Farris Thompson, *Flash of the Spirit: African and Afro-American Art and Philosophy* (New York: Vintage Books, 1984), 52–57, 113–16; Len Pole, *Iwa L'ẹwa: (Yoruba Saying, Meaning "Character Is Beauty"): Yoruba and Benin Collections in the Royal Albert Memorial Museum, Exeter* (Exeter, UK: Exeter City Museums, 1999), 25–26.
83. Paulo Roberto Staudt Moreira, "Escravidão, família e compadrio: A comunidade escrava no processo de ilegalidade do tráfico internacional de escravos (1831–1850)," *História Unisinos* 18, no. 2 (May 2014): 331. On Njinga's resistance to the Portuguese and her slave-trading activities, see Linda Marinda Heywood, *Njinga of Angola: Africa's Warrior Queen* (Cambridge, MA: Harvard University Press, 2017).
84. Ofício dirigido ao Vice-Presidente da Província pelo Juiz Municipal de Lorena, 11 April 1848, Arquivo Público do Estado de São Paulo, CJ48.7.8, in Marcos Couto Gonçalves, "A insurreição dos escravos no Vale do Paraíba," *Acervo Histórico*, no. 3 (2005): 54–70, annex, 68.
85. Ofício do Juiz de Guaratinguetá ao Presidente da Província, 8 June 1848, Arquivo Público do Estado de São Paulo, CJ48.7.14, in Gonçalves, "A insurreição dos escravos," annex, 70.
86. Gonçalves, "A insurreição dos escravos," 63.
87. See the liberated Africans David, numbered 84, Ginomma(?), numbered 138, and Honorio, numbered 154, in loose table of apprentices, n.d., IJ6 471, Polícia, Africanos, ANRJ.
88. Jaime Rodrigues, "Ferro, trabalho e conflito: Os Africanos livres na fábrica de Ipanema," *História Social* 4/5 (1997): 29–42.
89. AS, quinta legislatura, 25 April 1843, vol. 4, 346.
90. Código Criminal do Império do Brasil, Lei de 16 de dezembro de 1830, Título IV, Capitulo IV: Insurreição, accessed 7 May 2021, "Planalto," http://www.planalto.gov.br/ccivil_03/leis/lim/lim-16-12-1830.htm.
91. Carlos Augusto Taunay with L. Riedel, *Manual do agricultor Brazileiro*, 2nd ed. (Rio de Janeiro: Typographia Imperial e Constitucional de J. Villeneuve e Comp., 1839), 4; Rafael de Bivar Marquese, *Feitores do corpo, missionários da mente: Senhores, letrados e o controle dos escravos nas Américas, 1660–1860* (São Paulo: Companhia das Letras, 2004), 271.
92. Aureliano Coutinho, *Relatorio do presidente da provincia do Rio de Janeiro . . . no dia 1.o de abril de 1848*, 6; Roderick J. Barman, *Citizen Emperor: Pedro II and the Making of Brazil, 1825–1891* (Stanford, CA: Stanford University Press, 2001), 121.
93. Slenes, "*Malungo, ngoma* vem"; Mamigonian, *Africanos livres*; Miki, *Frontiers of Citizenship*, chap. 2; Hendrick Kraay, "Black Kings, Cabanos, and the Guarda Negra: Reflections on Popular Royalism in Nineteenth-Century Brazil," *Varia História* 35, no. 67 (January 2019): 141–75; João José Reis and Flávio dos Santos Gomes, "Introdução: Um guia para a revolta escrava," in *Revoltas escravas no Brasil*, ed. João José Reis and Flávio dos Santos Gomes (São Paulo: Companhia das Letras, 2021). The most comprehensive study of the formation of Palmares, the largest and longest-lasting settlement of self-liberated people, is Silvia Hunold Lara, *Palmares & Cucaú: O aprendizado da dominação* (São Paulo: Edusp, 2021).

94. FO 84/802, UKNA, fols. 326v–27r.
95. Francisco (no. 127), Luzia (no. 466), and Pedro (no. 469), in Survey of "Emancipados," enclosed in Hesketh to Palmerston[?], 30 September 1851, FO 131/7, part 2, UKNA, fols. 267v–68r, 282r.
96. Generosa (no. 133), in FO 131/7, part 2, UKNA, fol. 268r.
97. FO 84/802, UKNA, fol. 331r.
98. Demonstração das casas de negócio e oficinas existentes no município desta cidade . . ., compiled by Gabriel Getulio Monteiro de Mendonça, 30 January 1844, Série Estatística, 43.1.43, AGCRJ. More generally, see Sandra Lauderdale Graham, "Writing from the Margins: Brazilian Slaves and Written Culture," *Comparative Studies in Society and History* 49, no. 3 (2007): 611–36.
99. Aureliano Coutinho, *Relatorio do presidente da provincia do Rio de Janeiro, o senador Aureliano de Souza e Oliveira Coutinho, na abertura da Assembléa Legislativa Provincial no 1.o de março de 1846, acompanhado do orçamento da receita e despeza para o anno financeiro de 1846 a 1847*, 2nd ed. (Rio de Janeiro: Typographia de Amaral e Irmão, 1853), table 7, "Orçamento—Ensino mútuo e individual."
100. *Diário do Rio de Janeiro*, 10 January 1840, 2.
101. Thomas Flory, *Judge and Jury in Imperial Brazil, 1808–1871: Social Control and Political Stability in the New State* (Austin: University of Texas Press, 1981), 59.
102. *Diário do Rio de Janeiro*, 15 June 1848, 1.
103. FO 84/802, UKNA, fol. 331r.
104. For example, on the republican revolution in France, see *Jornal do Commercio*, 13 April 1848.
105. Aureliano Coutinho, *Relatorio do presidente da provincia do Rio de Janeiro . . . no dia 1.o de abril de 1848*, 9.
106. FO 84/802, UKNA, fol. 332r.
107. *Diário do Rio de Janeiro*, 17 July 1848, 1–2; 18 July 1848, 1.
108. FO 84/802, UKNA, fol. 339v.
109. S. Stein, *Vassouras*, 134. For the terminology of enmity in colonial Saint Domingue, see Malick W. Ghachem, *The Old Regime and the Haitian Revolution* (Cambridge: Cambridge University Press, 2012), chap. 1.
110. Jose Joaquim dos Santos to Leopoldo Augusto da Câmara Lima, 6 January 1850, enclosed in Hudson to Palmerston, 20 February 1850, *Correspondence Respecting the Slave Trade of Brazil. Confidential Print*, FO 467/13, UKNA, 49. A subsequent report by a British naval commander stated that ten captive people had died from flogging. Luckraft to Reynolds, 17 April 1851, enclosed in Hudson to Palmerston, 12 May 1851, in Parliament, HCP 1852–53, *Class B. Correspondence with British ministers and agents in foreign countries relating to the slave trade*, paper number 0.3, p. 174.
111. Hudson to Palmerston, 20 February 1850, in Parliament, 1851, *Class B. Correspondence with British ministers and agents in foreign countries relating to the slave trade*, C. (1st series) 1424-II, pp. 54–56.
112. Hudson to Palmerston (confidential), 3 February 1850, FO 84/801, UKNA, fols. 164–75.

113. Hudson to Palmerston, 20 February 1850, FO 84/802, UKNA, fols. 140r–v.
114. T. Nelson, *Remarks on the Slavery and Slave Trade of The Brazils* (London: J. Hatchard and Son, 1846), 74.
115. Huzzey, *Freedom Burning*, 112–14, 120–22.
116. *Hansard Parliamentary Debates*, 3rd series, 19 March 1850, vol. 109, column 1184.
117. Minto was also Russell's father-in-law. Minto to Russell, 25 March 1850, Domestic Records of the Public Record Office, Gifts, Deposits, Notes and Transcripts, PRO 30/22/8D, UKNA, fol. 124A.
118. Pelham to Minto, 25 March 1850 (original emphasis), enclosed in Minto to Russell, 25 March 1850, PRO 30/22/8D, UKNA, fol. 127v. Francis Baring warned Russell that he risked "getting into a squabble with the Brazils." Baring to Russell, 30 March 1850, PRO 30/22/8D, UKNA, fol. 140v.
119. Eddisbury to Hamilton, 22 April 1850, FO 84/823, UKNA, fol. 95–96; Benton and Ford, *Rage for Order*, 130.
120. Filastrio Nunes Pires to Schomberg, 30 June 1850, FO 84/804, UKNA, fols. 206v, 207r.
121. Câmara dos Deputados, Brazil, Lei 581, de 4 de setembro de 1850, accessed 13 December 2019, https://www2.camara.leg.br/legin/fed/leimp/1824-1899/lei-581-4-setembro-1850-559820-publicacaooriginal-82230-pl.html. See also Needell, "Abolition of the Brazilian Slave Trade in 1850," especially 707–11; Parron, "A política da escravidão no império do Brasil," 187.
122. Parliament, 1851, *Class B. Correspondence*, C. (1st series) 1424-II, p. 225.
123. Speech of Queirós, 16 July 1852, *Anais da Câmara da oitava legislatura, Sessão de 1852* (Rio de Janeiro: Typographia de H. J. Pinto, 1877), vol. 2, 249.
124. Parliament, 1851, *Class B. Correspondence*, C. (1st series) 1424-II, p. 301.

6 THE RUPTURE OF PROPERTY RIGHTS

1. Testimony of Chipianda (known also by her birthplace name Nonbiranda), ME 3383/A: 2ª Pieza, Real Audiencia Pretorial, Criminales sobre alijo de bozales en la punta del Holandés, prócsima al Cabo de Sn Antonio, Real Sala Primera, ANC, 264v.
2. Robert M. Cover, "Violence and the Word," *Yale Law Journal* 95, no. 8 (1986): 1601–29. For two empirical examples, see Dylan Farrell-Bryan, "Relief or Removal: State Logics of Deservingness and Masculinity for Immigrant Men in Removal Proceedings," *Law & Society Review* 56, no. 2 (2022): 167–87; Lili Dao, "Hollow Law and Utilitarian Law: The Devaluing of Deportation Hearings in New York City and Paris," *Law & Society Review* 57, no. 3 (2023): 317–39.
3. Research based on normalization process theory has found that interpreters can often present an obstacle to the reliable transmission of vulnerable displaced people's testimony by reframing questions and projecting their own biases, among other issues. A study of interpreters in the German asylum system found a failure to follow best practice regarding recruitment, training, quality control, and pay. Anne MacFarlane, Susann Huschke, Kevin Pottie, Fern R. Hauck, Kim Griswold, and Mark F. Harris, "Barriers to the Use of Trained Interpreters in

Consultations with Refugees in Four Resettlement Countries: A Qualitative Analysis Using Normalisation Process Theory," *BMC Family Practice* 21, no. 1 (5 December 2020): art. 259; Elke Cases Berbel, "Challenges and Difficulties of Translation and Interpreting in the Migration and Refugee Crisis in Germany," *Open Linguistics* 6, no. 1 (2020): 162–70.

4. On the notary's role in constructing archival knowledge, see Kathryn Burns, *Into the Archive: Writing and Power in Colonial Peru* (Durham, NC: Duke University Press, 2010).
5. Bethell, *Abolition of the Brazilian Slave Trade.*
6. Slenes, "*Malungo, ngoma* vem"; D. T. Graden, "Slave Resistance and the Abolition of the Trans-Atlantic Slave Trade to Brazil in 1850," *História Unisinos* 14, no. 3 (2010): 282–93.
7. Sidney Chalhoub, *Cidade febril: Cortiços e epidemias na corte imperial,* 2nd ed. (São Paulo: Companhia das Letras, 2017); Needell, "Abolition of the Brazilian Slave Trade in 1850"; Sidney Chalhoub, "Os conservadores no Brasil império," *Afro-Ásia* 35 (2007): 317–26.
8. Murray, *Odious Commerce,* chap. 14; L. Marques, *United States and the Transatlantic Slave Trade to the Americas;* Harris, *Last Slave Ships.*
9. Richard W. Van Alstyne, "The British Right of Search and the African Slave Trade," *Journal of Modern History* 2, no. 1 (March 1930): 37–47.
10. Arthur F. Corwin, *Spain and the Abolition of Slavery in Cuba, 1817–1886* (Austin: Institute of Latin American Studies / University of Texas Press, 1967); Julián Moreno García, "El cambio de actitud de la administración española frente al contrabando negrero en Cuba (1860–1866)," *Estudios de Historia Social,* nos. 1–4 (January 1988): 271–84.
11. Christopher Schmidt-Nowara, *Empire and Antislavery: Spain, Cuba, and Puerto Rico, 1833–1874* (Pittsburgh: University of Pittsburgh Press, 1999).
12. On the Cuban abolitionist association, see Murray, *Odious Commerce,* 318–19.
13. The most recent comprehensive synthesis is Jesús Sanjurjo, *In the Blood of Our Brothers: Abolitionism and the End of the Slave Trade in Spain's Atlantic Empire, 1800–1870* (Tuscaloosa: University of Alabama Press, 2021).
14. Eltis, *Economic Growth,* 219; Harris, *Last Slave Ships,* conclusion.
15. R. Scott, "Paper Thin"; Scott and Fornias, "María Coleta and the Capuchin Friar"; Andrew J. Walker, Ana María Silva Campo, Jane Manners, Jean M. Hébrard, and Rebecca J. Scott, "Impunity for Acts of Peremptory Enslavement: James Madison, the U.S. Congress, and the Saint-Domingue Refugees," *William and Mary Quarterly* 79, no. 3 (2022): 425–52; Emily A. Owens, *Consent in the Presence of Force: Sexual Violence and Black Women's Survival in Antebellum New Orleans* (Chapel Hill: University of North Carolina Press, 2023), chap. 1.
16. On problems with the paradigm of the "failure" of the rule of law in Latin America, see Ricardo Donato Salvatore, Carlos Aguirre, and Gilbert M. Joseph, eds., *Crime and Punishment in Latin America: Law and Society since Late Colonial Times* (Durham, NC: Duke University Press, 2001); Jorge L. Esquirol, *Ruling the Law: Legitimacy and Failure in Latin American Legal Systems* (New York: Cambridge University Press, 2019).

17. Câmara dos Deputados, Brazil, Decreto 708, de 14 de Outubro de 1850, accessed 10 April 2019, https://www2.camara.leg.br/legin/fed/decret/1824-1899/decreto-708-14-outubro-1850-560104-publicacaooriginal-82681-pe.html. On the provincial auditor in Bahia, see Jake Subryan Richards, "Jurisdiction and Afro-Brazilian Legal Politics from Colonialism to Early Independence," in "Ordering the Oceans, Ordering the World," *Past and Present*, supp. 17 (November 2024): 139–68.
18. Câmara dos Deputados, Brazil, Lei 601, de 18 de setembro de 1850, accessed 19 September 2024, https://www2.camara.leg.br/legin/fed/leimp/1824-1899/lei-601-18-setembro-1850-559842-publicacaooriginal-82254-pl.html.
19. Câmara dos Deputados, Brazil, Lei 581, de 4 de setembro de 1850, accessed 13 December 2019, https://www2.camara.leg.br/legin/fed/leimp/1824-1899/lei-581-4-setembro-1850-559820-publicacaooriginal-82230-pl.html, Articles 3 and 9.
20. Bethell, *Abolition of the Brazilian Slave Trade*, 371–72.
21. Chalhoub, *A força da escravidão*, chap. 5.
22. On Lisboa, see chapter 2. See also Parliament, 1844, *Class A. Correspondence with the British commissioners relating to the slave trade. 1843*, C. (1st series) 573, pp. 209–10; Parliament, 1846, *Class B. Correspondence on the slave trade with foreign powers*, C. (1st series) 724, p. 314.
23. Thiago Campos Pessoa, "O comércio negreiro na clandestinidade: As fazendas de recepção de Africanos da família Souza Breves e seus cativos," *Afro-Ásia*, no. 47 (2013): 44, 55.
24. On the controversies at Marambaia in relation to defining *boçalidade*, see Chalhoub, *A força da escravidão*, 133–38; Mamigonian, *Africanos livres*, 287–91.
25. Parliament, 1851, *Class B. Correspondence with British ministers and agents in foreign countries relating to the slave trade*, C. (1st series) 1424-II, pp. 387–90.
26. Hudson to Paulino, 11 January 1851, enclosed in Hudson to Palmerston, 11 January 1851, *Slave Trade of Brazil. Confidential Print*, FO 467/13, 374, UKNA.
27. On *Golfinho*, see Nilma Teixeira Accioli, *José Gonçalves da Silva à Nação Brasileira: O tráfico ilegal de escravos no antigo Cabo Frio* (Niterói: FUNARJ, 2012), 54–55.
28. Flory, *Judge and Jury in Imperial Brazil*, 99.
29. *Diário do Rio de Janeiro*, 3 December 1849, 4; 5 December 1849, 4; 7 December 1849, 4.
30. José Joaquim de Oliveira report, 16 February 1851, in Apreensão de um patacho encalhado na Ilha de Marambaia com mais de 450 africanos e outros objetos 0B.23, AGM, ANRJ, fols. 98r–v.
31. Cândido Mendes, ed., *Ordenações Filipinas* (Lisbon: Fundação Calouste Gulbenkian, 1985), Livro III, título LVI s.3. More generally, see Lenine Nequete, *O escravo na jurisprudência brasileira: Magistratura & ideologia no 2o. reinado* (Porto Alegre: Tribunal da Justiça, 1988); Mariana Armond Dias Paes, "Sujeitos da história, sujeitos de direitos: Personalidade jurídica no Brasil escravista (1860–1888)" (PhD diss., Universidade de Saõ Paulo, 2014).
32. Processo de presa de 199 Africanos na ilha de Marambaia . . . (1851), 0B.07.1, AGM, ANRJ, fols. 34–37.

33. It is unclear whether these thirty-nine enslaved people were the same as the thirty-nine apprehended in the morning and afternoon separately from the 160 enslaved people.
34. See "Relação dos Africanos apreendidos na ilha da Marambaia . . .," in 0B.07.1, AGM, ANRJ, fols. 28r–33v.
35. 0B.23, AGM, ANRJ, fol. 39r.
36. *Jornal do Commercio*, 14 February 1851, 1
37. *Jornal do Commercio*, 21 February 1851, 2.
38. Daniela Paiva Yabeta de Moraes, "A capital do comendador: A Auditoria Geral da Marinha no julgamento sobre a liberdade dos africanos apreendidos na ilha da Marambaia (1851)" (master's thesis, Unirio, 2009), 39.
39. Souza Breves to Editor, 7 February 1851, *Jornal do Commercio*, 14 February 1851, 2.
40. Azambuja to Editor, 20 February 1851, *Jornal do Commercio*, 21 February 1851, 1–2.
41. 0B.07.1, AGM, ANRJ, fols. 68r–v.
42. 0B.23, AGM, ANRJ, fol. 160v [archivist pagination].
43. Translado da sentença do processo contra um patacho com o carregamento de africanos que encalharam nas costas da Ilha da Marambaia, 0B.07.2, AGM, ANRJ, fol. 19r.
44. 0B.07.1, AGM, ANRJ, fol. 80r [archivist pagination].
45. 0B.7.1, AGM, ANRJ, fol. 80v [archivist pagination]; Chalhoub, *A força da escravidão*, 137.
46. 0B.07.1, AGM, ANRJ, fol. 81v.
47. *Jornal do Commercio*, 31 July 1851, 3.
48. Mendes, *Ordenações Filipinas*, Livro III, título XL, and Livro IV, título X; Thiago Campos Pessoa, "A indiscrição como ofício: O complexo cafeeiro revisitado" (PhD diss., Universidade Federal Fluminense, 2015), 280–82.
49. Augusto Teixeira de Freitas, *Consolidação das leis civis* (Brasília: Senado Federal: Superior Tribunal de Justiça, 2003), vol. 1, article 63, and footnote 41. For conditional liberty, see vol. 1, article 42, and footnote 1.
50. Parliament, HCP 1852–53, *Class B. Correspondence with British ministers and agents in foreign countries relating to the slave trade*, paper number 0.3, p. 267.
51. 0B.07.2, AGM, ANRJ, fols. 47–54. On pardons for slave-ship crewmembers more generally, see Jaime Rodrigues, *O infame comércio: Propostas e experiências no final do tráfico de africanos para o Brasil, 1800–1850* (Campinas: Editora da Unicamp, 2000), 140.
52. *Jornal do Commercio*, 11 May 1851, 3.
53. *Diário do Rio de Janeiro*, 11 December 1852, 4.
54. Total figure from Mamigonian, *Africanos livres*, 587. See also SlaveVoyages, "Trans-Atlantic Slave Trade—Database," accessed 12 September 2024, Voyage ID 4154.
55. *Jornal do Commercio*, 19 May 1853, 1.
56. *Jornal do Commercio*, 19 May 1853.

57. The report did not specify what Sousa Ramos owed Souza Breves. Jerningham[?] to Malmesbury, draft confidential despatch, 13 January 1853, FO 128/48, UKNA.
58. Parliament, HCP 1852–53, paper number 0.3, p. 187.
59. *Diário do Rio de Janeiro*, 18 February 1853, 3. The representation was reported in Jerningham to Russell, 4 March 1853, Despatch 7, draft, FO 128/48, UKNA.
60. Jerningham to Russell, 2 April 1853, draft confidential despatch, FO 128/48, UKNA.
61. *Jornal do Commercio*, 28 January 1853, 2.
62. Proceedings of Assembléa Legislativa Provincial, 25 August 1853, printed in *Diário do Rio de Janeiro*, 6 September 1853, 3; *Jornal do Commercio*, 7 September 1853, 1.
63. Martha Abreu, "O caso Bracuhy," in *Resgate: Uma janela para o oitocentos*, ed. Hebe Maria Mattos and Eduardo Schnoor (Rio de Janeiro: Topbooks, 1995), 173, 185.
64. Elciene Azevedo, *Orfeu de carapinha: A trajetoria de Luiz Gama na imperial cidade de São Paulo* (Campinas: Editora da Unicamp e CECULT, 1999); Elciene Azevedo, *O direito dos escravos: Lutas jurídicas e abolicionismo na província de São Paulo* (Campinas: Editora da Unicamp, 2010), chap. 2. Bruno Lima has written the most comprehensive analysis of Gama's legal thought: Bruno Rodrigues de Lima, *Luiz Gama contra o império* (São Paulo: Editora Contracorrente, 2024).
65. Jerningham to Clarendon, 27 June 1853, FO 128/48, UKNA.
66. Kwame Anthony Appiah, *The Honor Code: How Moral Revolutions Happen* (New York: Norton, 2010).
67. Hebe Maria Mattos and Martha Abreu, "Jongo, registros de uma história," in *Memória do jongo: As gravações históricas de Stanley J. Stein, Vassouras, 1949*, ed. Silvia Hunold Lara and Gustavo Pacheco (Campinas: CECULT, 2007), 100–102; "As gravações de Stanley J. Stein—Transcrição," in Lara and Pacheco, *Memória do jongo*, 180–81.
68. On Zulueta and other major traffickers, see Franco, *Comercio clandestino de esclavos*, 124–78.
69. María del Carmen Barcia, ed., *Una sociedad distinta: Espacios del comercio negrero en el occidente de Cuba (1836–1866)* (Havana: Editorial UH, 2017); Oilda Hevia Lanier, "La conspiración del silencio: Tráfico, complicidad e impunidad entre Yaguaramas y Colón," in *Sometidos a esclavitud: los africanos y sus descendientes en el Caribe Hispano*, ed. Consuelo Naranjo Orovio (Santa Marta, Colombia: Editorial Unimagdalena, 2021), 333–71
70. Perera Díaz and Meriño Fuentes, *Estrategias de libertad*, vol. 1, 117–257.
71. Yun, *Coolie Speaks*, 15; Eduardo Marrero Cruz, *Julián de Zulueta y Amondo: Promotor del capitalismo en Cuba* (Havana: Ediciones Unión, 2006), 55; Evelyn Hu-DeHart, "Chinese Contract Labor in the Wake of the Abolition of Slavery in the Americas: A New Form of Slavery or Transition to Free Labor in the Case of Cuba?," *Amerasia Journal* 45, no. 1 (April 2019): 6–26.
72. José Gutierrez de la Concha y de Irigoyen Habana, *Memoria sobre el ramo de emancipados de la isla de Cuba, formada con motivo de la entrega del mando de la*

misma al Excmo. Sr. D. Francisco Serrano . . . (Madrid: Imprenta de la América, á cargo de M. Moreno Fernandez, 1861), 5–10.

73. For examples, see Emancipados, 107/11249, AHPM.
74. 1864, Alcaldía mayor de sala segunda de justicia de la Real Audiencia Pretorial. Criminales formados para tratar del plagio de negros correspondientes a la expedición introducida por Cienfuegos y Colón, ME 3381/L, ANC, fol. 58r.
75. ME 3381/L, ANC, fol. 64r.
76. Statement of Aguirre, 30 April 1864, enclosed in Crawford to Russell, 10 May 1864, in Parliament, 1865, *Class B. Correspondence with British ministers and agents in foreign countries*, C. (1st series) 3503-I, p. 249.
77. ME 3381/L, ANC, fols. 2r–v, 65v.
78. Statement of Aguirre, 30 April 1864, in Parliament, 1865, *Class B. Correspondence*, C. (1st series) 3503-I, p. 253. NB: this source gives the unit as dollars rather than pesos.
79. José María Fernandez de la Hoz, *Defensa del señor don José Agustin Argüelles en la causa de supuesto plagio de bozales pertenecientes á la gran espedición apresada por el mismo en la isla de Cuba: Como teniente gobernador del distrito de Colon, hecha por el excelentisimo señor Don José María Fernandez de la Hoz para ante la Sala Segunda y de Indias de S. A. el Supremo Tribunal de Justicia* (Madrid: Imp. de Frias y Ca. Misericordia, 1867), 42–43.
80. Fernandez de la Hoz, *Defensa del señor don José Agustin Argüelles*, 62.
81. Fernandez de la Hoz, *Defensa del señor don José Agustin Argüelles*, 55–56.
82. Testimonio de criminales mandados formar para tratar del plagio de negros de la espedicion introducida en Cienfuegos y Colon (Escribano Jose Soroa), 1864, ME 3404/K, ANC, fols. 1335v–36r, 1341v.
83. ME 3404/K, ANC, fol. 1345r.
84. José Agustin Argüelles, *General Dulce y los negreros* (New York: n.p., 1864). A copy is enclosed in Crawford to Russell (separate), 10 May 1864, FO 84/1218, UKNA, fols. 144r–45v.
85. Aguirre statement, 30 April 1864, in Parliament, 1865, *Class B. Correspondence*, C. (1st series) 3503-I, p. 250; Crawford to Russell, 10 May 1864, FO 84/1218, UKNA, fol. 134r.
86. María del Carmen Barcia Zequeira, "Caracterizando los alijos en tierra," in Barcia Zequeira, *Una sociedad distinta*, 31–66.
87. Cienfuegos. Criminales Contra los que resulten reos en el trato ilisito de negros bozales y desembarco verificado estos la caleta del Rosario en la costa del sur, 1854, ME, 336/AY, ANC, fols. 177r–85v.
88. Expediente formado para averiguar si en las costas del Marial y Bahia Honda se efectuó desembarco de negros bozales, acusandose como reos à Jacinto Derizans y Manuel Alvarez, capitan y contramaestre, 1853, ME, 3383/W, ANC, fols. 52v–53r.
89. ME 3404/K, ANC, fol. 1139v.
90. ME 3404/K, ANC, fol. 1148v.
91. ME 3404/K, ANC, fol. 1150r.
92. ME 3404/K, ANC, fols. 1341v–42r.
93. ME 3404/K, ANC, fols. 1153r.

94. Alcaldía Mayor de Sala Segunda de Justicia de la Real Audiencia Pretoria. Testimonio de los Criminales mandado formar para tratar del plagio de negros de la especidion introducida en Cienfuegos y Colon, 1864, ME 3382/A, ANC, fols. 2491v–92r.
95. For the punishments sought by the prosecution, see ME 3382/A, ANC, fol. 2642v. For Argüelles's punishment for failing to keep suspects in custody, see *Código penal de España* (Madrid: Imprenta Nacional, 1850), Libro II, Título VIII, Capítulo II, Artigo 276, s. 2.
96. Fernandez de la Hoz, *Defensa del señor don José Agustin Argüelles*, 39–40.
97. Fernandez de la Hoz, *Defensa del señor don José Agustin Argüelles*, 41.
98. Oilda Hevia Lanier, "El tráfico ilegal de bozales entre Cienfuegos y Colón: La inusual historia del Agüica (1863–1866)," in Barcia Zequeira, *Una sociedad distinta*, 351.
99. Crawford reported that Zulueta had also been detained during the capture, but neither Argüelles nor Aguirre claimed to have detained him. At most, he may have been subsequently detained by the *oidor* of Havana on a technicality. Crawford to Russell, 10 May 1864, in Parliament, 1865, *Class B. Correspondence*, C. (1st series) 3503-I, p. 240.
100. Diaz de Herrera to Gobierno Superior Civil, 10 March 1866, GG 439/21268, ANC.
101. Diaz de Herrera to Gobierno Superior Civil, 10 March 1866, GG 439/21268, ANC.
102. The figure of 278 people comes from the Report with the declaration of the second lieutenant Enrique Sautaló, 10 March 1866, GG 439/21268, ANC. Diaz de Herrera identifies the witness as "the black Portuguese interpreter that I caught in the expedition" in his letter to Gobierno Superior Civil, 10 March 1866, GG 439/21268, ANC. He is named as "Joaquín," which may be a Hispanicization of "Joaquim," in Segundo apuntamiento de la causa sobre alijo de bozales por la Punta del Holandés continuada en el Juzgado de Pinar del Rio, 1875, ME 3404/B, ANC, fol. No.0860.039r. On how maritime patrols can shape the legal imagination of migrants and the spatial organization of jurisdiction by imperial authorities, see Jeffrey S. Kahn, *Islands of Sovereignty: Haitian Migration and the Borders of Empire* (Chicago: University of Chicago Press, 2019), chap. 6.
103. ME 3404/B, ANC, fol. No.0860.039r.
104. Telegram of O'Farrill y O'Farrill to the Governor of Matanzas and to the Lieutenant Governor of Guïnes, 23 March 1866, GG 439/21268, ANC.
105. Petition of O'Farrill y O'Farrill to the Captain General, 23 March 1866, GG 439/21268, ANC; Diaz de Herrera to Gobierno Superior Civil, 10 March 1866, GG 439/21268, ANC.
106. ME 3404/B, ANC, fol. No.0860.039r.
107. ME 3383/A, ANC, fols. 238v–39r.
108. ME 3383/A, ANC, fol. 240v (quotation), 231r and 232r (passes), 248 (table).
109. ME 3383/A, ANC, fols. 240v–41r.
110. ME 3383/A, ANC, fol. 243r.

111. "Bemba" is an offensive term in present-day Cuba, but it is how the witness stated her name, and the Spanish name assigned to her by the colonial authorities is illegible in the archival document. ME 3383/A, ANC, fol. 265r.
112. ME 3383/A, ANC, fols. 268v, 269v.
113. ME 3383/A, ANC, fols. 263r (quotation), 266r–v, 268r.
114. 5ª Pieza, Criminales, Sobre alijo de bozales en la Punta del Holandés prócsimo al cabo de S. Antonio, 1866, ME, 3380/J, ANC, fols. 812v–14v.
115. ME 3380/J, ANC, fol. 893r.
116. ME 3380/J, ANC, fol. 894v.
117. ME 3404/B, ANC, fols. N.1889.717v–18v.
118. ME 3404/B, ANC, fols. N.1889.719v–20r.
119. Queen's opinion to Gobernador Superior Civil, 27 November 1866, GG 439/21267, ANC.
120. Francisco Uvalde (Real Sala Tercera de la Audiencia) to Gobernador Superior Civil, 14 December 1866, GG 439/21267, ANC.
121. Manzano decree, 6 June 1867, GG 439/21261, ANC. The decree was published in *Gaceta de la Habana*, 7 June 1867, 1.
122. For limbo-type analyses, see Robert Conrad, "Neither Slave nor Free: The *Emancipados* of Brazil, 1818–1868," *Hispanic American Historical Review* 53, no. 1 (1973): 50–70; Martínez-Fernández, *Fighting Slavery in the Caribbean*.
123. Camillia Cowling, *Conceiving Freedom: Women of Color, Gender, and the Abolition of Slavery in Havana and Rio De Janeiro* (Chapel Hill: University of North Carolina Press, 2013).
124. *Havana Gazette*, 15 September 1867, enclosure in Crawford to Stanley, 30 September 1867, in Parliament, 1867–68, *Class A. Correspondence with the British commissioners*, C. (1st series) 4000, p. 7.
125. Announcement of Sinimbú, Congressos Agricolas, 12 June 1878, printed in *O Auxiliador da Industria Nacional*, No. 6, June 1878, 137–38. In Vassouras, enslavers had already reallocated enslaved women's labor from domestic work to agricultural labor. See Iamara da Silva Viana, " 'Tríplice utilização' dos corpos negros femininos: Gênero, raça, sevícias e escravidão—Rio de Janeiro, século XIX," *Tempo* 29 (2023), tables 1 and 2, 286–87.
126. Rodrigo Goyena Soares, "Racionalidade econômica, transição para o trabalho livre e economia política da abolição: A estratégia campineira (1870–1889)," *História (São Paulo)* 39 (2020): 10–12.
127. George Reid Andrews, *Afro-Latin America, 1800–2000* (Oxford: Oxford University Press, 2004). For an approach that presents the Lei de Terras, gradual abolition, and immigration as parts of the same transition to wage labor at minimal cost to the largest landowners, see Rafaela Domingos Lago, "Demografia escrava e o impacto das leis abolicionistas no Espírito Santo (1850–1888)," *Almanack*, no. 19 (August 2018): 119–66.
128. Yun, *Coolie Speaks*.
129. R. Scott, *Slave Emancipation in Cuba*, 40–41; Ada Ferrer, *Insurgent Cuba: Race, Nation, and Revolution, 1868–1898* (Chapel Hill: University of North Carolina Press, 1999).

7. THE BONDS OF FREEDOM

1. W. G. Terry (writer) to Michael Melville (Commissary Judge), 1 September 1842, LADLB, EAP 443/1/18/7.
2. Terry to George MacDonald, 1 September 1842, LADLB, EAP 443/1/18/7 (original emphasis).
3. Christopher Fyfe, "Four Sierra Leone Recaptives," *Journal of African History* 2, no. 1 (1961): 81.
4. See "Account sales" of the *Jane*, signed A. Pike, Commissioner of Appraisement and Sale, 7 September 1863, Sierra Leone, Parliament, 1864, *Class A. Correspondence with the British commissioners*, C. (1st series) 3339, pp. 22–25. I identified these names as liberated Africans by excluding all cases of naval officers' purchasing goods (listed as "Captains") and by comparing surnames to petitions in CO 267, which had representatives from the National Society of Liberated Africans, as well as secondary literature. Only two lots (of around two hundred) were bought by an identifiable woman: Emily Caille. I erred on the side of caution; in reality, the consortia may have been larger. The judge thought that the *Jane* was a Confederate slaver under the cover of the Dutch flag: Skelton to Russell, 30 September 1863, Parliament, 1864, C. (1st series) 3339, p. 34. On Boyle, see "Death of the Hon. Syble Boyle," *Sierra Leone Weekly News*, 23 May 1896. On Lumpkin, see Dee Tee, "Honourable Henry Lumpkin," *Sierra Leone Weekly News*, 17 June 1899, 2.
5. Arthur T. Porter, *Creoledom: A Study of the Development of Freetown Society* (London: Oxford University Press, 1963), 45.
6. Fyfe, "Four Sierra Leone Recaptives."
7. Ndubueze L. Mbah, "The Black Englishmen of Old Calabar: Freedom and Mobility in the Age of Abolition in West Africa," *Radical History Review* 2022, no. 144 (1 October 2022): 45–75.
8. See Parliament, 1844, *Instructions for the guidance of Her Majesty's naval officers employed in the suppression of the slave trade*, C. (1st series) 577, pp. 217–32, for the treaty between Britain and Brazil, and p. 284, for article 4 of the "Regulations" annexed to the treaty between Britain and Spain.
9. See clause 6 of the instructions accompanying the Aviso of 29 October 1834: *Colecção das decisões do governo do Imperio do Brasil* (Rio de Janeiro: Typographia Nacional, 1866), 280.
10. Hannah Weiss Muller, *Subjects and Sovereign: Bonds of Belonging in the Eighteenth-Century British Empire* (New York: Oxford University Press, 2017).
11. Eric Foner, *Reconstruction: America's Unfinished Revolution, 1863–1877*, updated ed. (New York: HarperPerennial, 2014); Maria Helena Pereira Toledo Machado, *O plano e o pânico: Os movimentos sociais na década da abolição* (Rio de Janeiro: Editora UFRJ, 1994); Frederick Cooper, Thomas C. Holt, and Rebecca J. Scott, *Beyond Slavery: Explorations of Race, Labor, and Citizenship in Postemancipation Societies* (Chapel Hill: University of North Carolina Press, 2000); Wlamyra R. de Albuquerque, *O jogo da dissimulação: Abolição e cidadania negra no Brasil* (São Paulo: Companhia das Letras, 2009); Carina Ray, *Crossing the Color Line: Race, Sex, and the Contested Politics of Colonialism in Ghana* (Athens: Ohio University

Press, 2015); Lisa A. Lindsay, *Atlantic Bonds: A Nineteenth-Century Odyssey from America to Africa* (Chapel Hill: University of North Carolina Press, 2017).

12. Pamela Scully and Diana Paton, eds., *Gender and Slave Emancipation in the Atlantic World* (Durham, NC: Duke University Press, 2005); Sarah J. Zimmerman, "The Gendered Consequences of Abolition and Citizenship on Nineteenth-Century Gorée Island," *Journal of Women's History* 35, no. 3 (2023): 19–38.
13. Mintz and Price, *Birth of African-American Culture.*
14. Jean Besson, *Martha Brae's Two Histories: European Expansion and Caribbean Culture-Building in Jamaica* (Chapel Hill: University of North Carolina Press, 2002), 27–28.
15. Jean Herskovits Kopytoff, *A Preface to Modern Nigeria: The "Sierra Leonians" in Yoruba, 1830–1890* (Madison: University of Wisconsin Press, 1965); Martin Lynn, "Technology, Trade and 'A Race of Native Capitalists': The Krio Diaspora of West Africa and the Steamship, 1852–95," *Journal of African History* 33, no. 3 (1992): 421–40.
16. Hawthorne, "Being Now, as It Were, One Family." For an example of freedpeople who wished to travel to Ambriz rather than Lagos, see Joaquim Nicolão de Brito et al. to James Hudson, 15 January 1851, enclosed in Hudson to Palmerston, 11 February 1851, FO 420/11, UKNA, p. 379. For an overview of movements to different parts of West Africa, see Andrew E. Barnes, " 'The Hand of God Was upon Them': Emigration, Diaspora Formation, and Christian Evangelization across the Black Atlantic," in *Migration and Diaspora Formation*, ed. Ciprian Burlăcioiu (Berlin: De Gruyter, 2022), 221–59.
17. Report by Consul Brand on the Trade of Lagos for the year 1859, FO 881/3621, UKNA, p. 3.
18. Lindsay, *Atlantic Bonds.* For an approach focused on Sierra Leone and Liberia, see Nemata Amelia Ibitayo Blyden, *African Americans and Africa: A New History* (New Haven, CT: Yale University Press, 2019).
19. Hopkins, *Economic History of West Africa*, 125–35; Lynn, "West African Palm Oil Trade."
20. Robert Sydney Smith, *The Lagos Consulate, 1851–1861* (Berkeley: University of California Press, 1979), 18–33; Martin Lynn, "Consul and Kings: British Policy, 'the Man on the Spot'; and the Seizure of Lagos, 1851," *Journal of Imperial & Commonwealth History* 10, no. 2 (January 1982): 150–67; Kristin Mann, *Slavery and the Birth of an African City: Lagos, 1760–1900* (Bloomington: Indiana University Press, 2007).
21. Antony G. Hopkins, "Property Rights and Empire Building: Britain's Annexation of Lagos, 1861," *Journal of Economic History* 40, no. 4 (1980): 777–98. For subsequent developments, see Lanre Davies, "Colonial Land Policies in Lagos," *Lagos Historical Review* 16, no. 1 (January 2016): 43–68.
22. Huzzey, *Freedom Burning*, 146; Olasupo Shasore, *Possessed: A History of Law and Justice in the Crown Colony of Lagos, 1861–1906* (Lagos: CLRN, 2014), 173–74. For the role of palm oil traders in demanding British protection for their commercial interests, see J. F. Ade Ajayi, "The Aftermath of the Fall of Old Ọyọ," in *History of West Africa*, ed. J. F. Ade Ajayi and Michael Crowder, vol. 2 (London: Longman, 1985), 205.

23. Kopytoff, *Preface to Modern Nigeria*, 276–77.
24. Freeman to Russell, 5 March 1862, enclosed in Freeman to Newcastle, 8 March 1862, Despatch 6, CO 147/1, UKNA.
25. Treaty with the King and Chiefs of Lagos, 1 January 1852 in Parliament, 1862, *Lagos. Additional papers relating to the occupation of Lagos*, C. (1st series) 2982 3003, pp. 1–2.
26. Brand to Russell, 9 April 1860, in Parliament, 1862, C. (1st series), 2982 3003, pp. 4–5. See also Brand to Wylde, 2 April 1860, WYL/23/5-12, Wylde Papers, Durham University Special Collections, United Kingdom.
27. Monday B. Abasiattai, "Sierra Leone and Liberia in the Nineteenth Century," in Ajayi and Crowder, *History of West Africa*, 329–30.
28. Stanley Trapido, " 'The Friends of the Natives': Merchants, Peasants and the Political and Ideological Structure of Liberalism in the Cape, 1854–1910," in *Economy and Society in Pre-Industrial South Africa*, ed. Shula Marks and Anthony Atmore (London: Longman, 1980), 247–74; Pamela Scully, *Liberating the Family? Gender and British Slave Emancipation in the Rural Western Cape, South Africa, 1823–1853* (Oxford: James Currey, 1997).
29. Based on a total of 167 cases involving apprentices brought by the public prosecutor. Police Court Records, 1/CT 8/4, 1/CT 8/5, and 1/CT 8/6, WCARS.
30. Public Prosecutor v. Peter Francis Hugo, Case 1154, 27 December 1844, 1/SMT 2/10, Police Court, 1844, WCARS.
31. Elizabeth van Heyningen, "Public Health and Society in Cape Town 1880–1910" (PhD diss., University of Cape Town, 1989), 373; Patrick Harries, "Cultural Diasporas and Colonial Classification: A History of the Mozbieker Community at the Cape," *Social Dynamics* 96, no. 2 (2000): 51n35.
32. Abstract of a register under the Contagious Diseases Prevention Act 25 of 1868, October 1868, in Letters received by the Colonial Office, 1868, CO 888, WCARS.
33. Memorandum by Inspector, 11 November 1868, CO 888, 1868, WCARS.
34. R v. Elizabeth Herring, Raben Abdol, Caroline Samodien, 31 December 1870, 1/CT 6/48, WCARS.
35. Caledon to Castelreagh, 4 February 1808, in *Records of the Cape Colony*, ed. G. M. Theal (London: William Clowes and Sons, 1904), vol. 6, 271.
36. Petrus Borcherds, *An Autobiographical Memoir of Petrus Borchardus Borcherds, Esq., Late Civil Commissioner of Cape Division and Resident Magistrate for Cape Town and District Thereof, and Cape District. Being a Plain Narrative of Occurrences from Early Life to Advanced Age* (1861; repr., Cape Town: Africana Connoisseurs, 1963), 143.
37. Muhammad 'Adil Bradlow, "Imperialism, State Formation and the Establishment of a Muslim Community at the Cape of Good Hope, 1770–1840: A Study in Urban Resistance" (master's thesis, University of Cape Town, 1988), 148n40.
38. Report of Commissioners of Inquiry on the Police of the Cape of Good Hope, 10 May 1828, in Theal, *Records of the Cape Colony*, vol. 35 (London: William Clowes and Sons, 1905), 138; Bradlow, "Imperialism," 179.

39. John Schofield Mayson, *The Malays of Cape Town* (Manchester, UK: John Galt, 1861), 15.
40. Mochamat Ali et al., petition to Petrus de Roubaix, 24 August 1864, Papers received from Foreign and Colonial Governments, GH 13/12, WCARS.
41. See also Hopper, *Slaves of One Master*, 162–64; Michael Francis Laffan, *Under Empire: Muslim Lives and Loyalties across the Indian Ocean World, 1775–1945* (New York: Columbia University Press, 2022), chap. 7.
42. Sultan Majid bin Sa'eed to Governor P. E. Wodehouse, 18 January 1866, enclosed in Lt.-Col. R. L. Playfair (consul and political agent, Zanzibar) to Wodehouse, 18 January 1866, Papers received from Foreign Consuls and Colonial Governments, 18 January 1866–20 July 1876, GH 13/13, WCARS.
43. De Roubaix to John Pakington, 16 November 1866, GH 13/13, WCARS.
44. Preben Kaarsholm, "Zanzibaris or Amakhuwa? Sufi Networks in South Africa, Mozambique, and the Indian Ocean," *Journal of African History* 55, no. 2 (2014): 191–210; Kaarsholm, "Indian Ocean Networks and the Transmutations of Servitude."
45. J. Thomas vs John William, 22 June 1861, Court for the Easy and Speedy Recovery of Small Debts, Case Book, June to September 1861, PASL.
46. Thomas vs William, 22 June 1861.
47. John Alex Wise vs James Richard, 6 July 1861, Court for the Easy and Speedy Recovery of Small Debts, Case Book, June to September 1861, PASL.
48. This court was established in 1800. Claude George, *The Rise of British West Africa: Comprising the Early History of the Colony of Sierra Leone, the Gambia, Lagos, Gold Coast, Etc. with a Brief Account of Climate, the Growth of Education, Commerce, and Religion, and a Comprehensive History of the Bananas and Bance Islands: And Sketches of the Constitution. New Impr.* (London: Houlston and Sons, 1903), 145. For company formation more generally, see David Northrup, "Identity among Liberated Africans in Sierra Leone," in *The Black Urban Atlantic in the Age of the Slave Trade*, ed. Jorge Cañizares-Esguerra, Matt D. Childs, and James Sidbury (Philadelphia: University of Pennsylvania Press, 2013), 21–41.
49. For instance, see Bucknor vs Williams, 10 August 1861, Court for the Easy and Speedy Recovery of Small Debts, Case Book, June to September 1861, PASL.
50. Phaelee Coker vs M. A. Coker, 5 March 1864, Court for the Easy and Speedy Recovery of Small Debts, Case Book, January to December 1864, PASL, fol. 58.
51. Phaelee Coker vs M. A. Coker, 5 March 1864, fol. 68. On funeral care by a mutual-aid society in Jamaica, see Besson, *Martha Brae's Two Histories*, 231–38.
52. Petition to Earl Grey, 19 September 1848, duplicate in CO 267/203, UKNA (original emphasis).
53. 16 & 17 Vict. 86.
54. Fyfe, *History of Sierra Leone*, 331; Bronwen Everill, "Experiments in Colonial Citizenship in Sierra Leone and Liberia," in *New Directions in the Study of African American Recolonization*, ed. Beverly C. Tomek and Matthew J. Hetrick, Southern Dissent (Gainesville: University Press of Florida, 2017), 185–205.
55. Parliament, HCP 1865, *Select Committee on State of British Settlements on W. Coast of Africa*, vol. 5, paper number 412, p. iii.

56. Article 6, Lei no. 581, 4 September 1850.
57. Mariana Alice Pereira Schatzer Ribeiro, "Trabalho e cotidiano dos africanos livres na Estrada da Maioridade–São Paulo–Santos (1840–1864)" (PhD diss., Universidade Estadual Paulista, 2019).
58. Zilda Alves de Moura, "Dos sertões da África para os do Brasil: Os africanos livres da Sociedade de Mineração de Mato Grosso (Alto Paraguai-Diamantino, 1851–1865)" (PhD diss., Universidade Federal de Santa Catarina, 2014), 55, 97–98, 203–11.
59. This is an underestimation, as the survey listed 396 apprentices in Bahia, without specifying where they worked. They are included in the total assuming that none of them worked in institutions, which was highly unlikely. Hunt to Russell, 22 March 1865, FO 84/1244, UKNA. Hesketh's survey, completed in 1851, found that 203 of 856 apprentices (23.7 percent) were working in institutions. FO 131/7, part 2, "Emancipados," UKNA, fols. 258r–303r.
60. *Diário do Rio de Janeiro*, 2 April 1863, 1–2.
61. One scholar has found that only 4 of 262 petitions in a sample were either written or signed by liberated Africans. Mamigonian, *Africanos livres*, 332.
62. William Dougal Christie, *Notes on Brazilian Questions* (London: Macmillan, 1865), 4–5.
63. Daryle Williams, " 'A necessária distinção entre liberdade e emancipação': Noções africana, inglesa e brasileira do que é ser emancipado," in *Instituições nefandas: O fim da escravidão e da servidão no Brasil, nos Estados Unidos e na Rússia* (Rio de Janeiro: Fundação Casa de Rui Barbosa, 2018), 151–70. Williams has argued that only Africans liberated under treaty law made such demands, whereas my analysis suggests broad continuity between those who were liberated under treaty law and those who were liberated under Brazilian domestic law (such as Lei 581).
64. Mamigonian, *Africanos livres*, 326, 343–59.
65. This is true for fifteen of forty-nine cases in GIFI 6D 136, ANRJ.
66. Beatriz Gallotti Mamigonian, "Do que 'o preto mina' é capaz: Etnia e resistência entre africanos livres," *Afro-Ásia* 24 (2000): 71–95.
67. Domingas petition, 6 December 1860, IJ6 525, ANRJ, fol. 32.
68. José Prospero Jehovah da Silva Caroatá and Bellarmino Brasiliense Pessoa de Mello, *Imperiaes resoluções tomadas sobre consultas da Secção de Justicça do Conselho de Estado desde o anno de 1842, em que começou a funccionar o mesmo Conselho, até hoje*, vol. 1 (Rio de Janeiro: B. L. Garnier, 1884), 843.
69. On the *Almanak Laemmert*, see Mamigonian, *Africanos livres*, 332. On metal tags, see Jose Pereira da Sa Moraes, Department of Bahia Police, to Antônio da Costa Pinto, President of the Province, 5 April 1861, IJ6 525, ANRJ.
70. Eduardo Spiller Pena, *Pajens da casa imperial: Jurisconsultos, escravidão e a lei de 1871* (Campinas: Editora da Unicamp and CECULT, 2001); Pedro Jimenez Cantisano and Mariana Armond Dias Paes, "Legal Reasoning in a Slave Society (Brazil, 1860–88)," *Law and History Review* 36, no. 3 (2018): 496.
71. Agostinho Perdigão Malheiro, *Correio Mercantil* [?], 7 September 1863, in Aureliano Tavares Bastos papers, MS-571 (03), Notas sobre escravidão, BNRJ.

72. Aureliano Tavares Bastos papers, MS-571 (05), 11,1,024, "Africanos livres e escravos de Ipanema," BNRJ; Christie, *Notes on Brazilian Questions*, xvii–xx; Mamigonian, *Africanos livres*, 366–67.
73. Christie, *Notes on Brazilian Questions*, 172.
74. L342/1/15, Conselho de Estado, Parecer sobre si são cidadãos Brasileiros os libertos no Brazil, nascidos fora d'elle (1859), AHI.
75. Keila Grinberg, "The Two Enslavements of Rufina: Slavery and International Relations on the Southern Border of Nineteenth-Century Brazil," *Hispanic American Historical Review* 96, no. 2 (2016): 259–90; Keila Grinberg, "Illegal Enslavement, International Relations, and International Law on the Southern Border of Brazil," *Law and History Review* 35, no. 1 (2017): 31–52.
76. Christie, *Notes on Brazilian Questions*.
77. Alain El Youssef, "Questão Christie em perspectiva global: Pressão britânica, guerra civil norte-americana e o início da crise da escravidão brasileira (1860–1864)," *Revista de História (São Paulo)*, no. 177 (2018): 1–26.
78. Parliament, 1863, *Brazil. Correspondence respecting liberated slaves*, C. (1st series) 3189.
79. Commentary on "Questão dos Africanos livres no Império," October 1864, L239, m1, AHI.
80. Porciano petition, 11 April 1864, IJ6 523, ANRJ.
81. Honorato petition, 11 April 1864, IJ6 523, ANRJ.
82. Gonsalo petition, 11 April 1864, IJ6 523, ANRJ.
83. See the petitions by João, Rufino, Hilario, and Benedito, who were apprenticed in different institutions: 11 May 1864, IJ6 523, ANRJ.
84. Jose Bernardo de Figueiredo to Minister of Justice, 6 July 1864, IJ6 523, ANRJ.
85. Deoclecianna petition, Umbelina petition, Henrique petition, and Joaquim petition, all 10 June 1864, IJ6 523, ANRJ.
86. Vieira, "Os 'Samangolês."
87. Francisco José Furtado, *Relatorio do Ministerio da Justiça apresentado á assembléa geral legislativa na terceira sessão da decima segunda legislatura* (Rio de Janeiro: Typographia Nacional, 1865), 29.
88. For the movement of liberated Africans to the Brazilian frontier, see IJ6 15 and IJ6 16, ANRJ.
89. Visconde de Jequitinhonha, Session of 17 May 1865, proposal for general emancipation, Articles 4, 6, and 7, *Anais do Senado* (Rio de Janeiro: Typ. do Correio Mercantil, 1865), 15–16; Pena, *Pajens da casa imperial*, 50–51.
90. On the effect of the American Civil War on Brazil and Cuba, see Samantha Payne, " 'A General Insurrection in the Countries with Slaves': The US Civil War and the Origins of an Atlantic Revolution, 1861–1866," *Past & Present* 257, no. 1 (2022): 248–79. Puerto Rico's population also included enslaved people and liberated Africans.
91. For instance, see the *Jornal do Commercio*, 18 January 1865, 1 (reporting on the Union advance on Georgia); 17–18 April 1865, 1 (on Lincoln's war aims); Isadora Moura Mota, "Other Geographies of Struggle: Afro-Brazilians and the American Civil War," *Hispanic American Historical Review* 100, no. 1 (February 2020): 35–62.

92. *Jornal do Commercio*, 9 March 1865, supplement, 2; 28 April 1865, 1.
93. *Jornal do Commercio*, 3 May 1865, 1.
94. On gradual emancipation law and ideology in Brazil, see H. Mattos, *Das cores do silêncio*; Roberto Saba, *American Mirror: The United States and Brazil in the Age of Emancipation* (Princeton, NJ: Princeton University Press, 2021).
95. Superintendent's report, 1 September 1860, Voto consultivo acerca del proyecto de Jose Suarez Argudin para introducir en esta Isla 40 000 negros libres en clase de aprendices, Intendencia, 929/42, ANC.
96. Averiguación del Gobierno del Departamiento Oriental, 7 April 1865, in Expediente promovido por el Teniente Gobernador de Manzanillo para averiguar la explicación que se dá a los negros emancipados concedidos por el Gobierno a los cultivadores de algodón, GSC 1581/81411, ANC.
97. María Dolores Domingo Acebrón, "Los hacendados cubanos ante La Guerra de los Diez Años (1868–1878)," *Revista de Indias* 43, no. 172 (May 1983): 707–27; R. Scott, *Slave Emancipation in Cuba*; Chira, *Patchwork Freedoms*.
98. Karen Robert, "Slavery and Freedom in the Ten Years' War, Cuba, 1868–1878," *Slavery & Abolition* 13, no. 3 (December 1992): 181–200; Ferrer, *Insurgent Cuba*; Teresa Prados-Torreira, *Mambisas: Rebel Women in Nineteenth-Century Cuba* (Gainesville: University Press of Florida, 2005); María del Carmen Barcia, "¿Una contradicción antagónica? Integristas y reformistas ante la abolición de la esclavitud," in *La revolución de 1868. Estudios históricos*, ed. Oscar Zanetti Lecuona (Havana: Ediciones Boloña Imagen Contemporánea Ediciones Demajagua, 2020), 467–503.
99. One key study of naval strategy makes no mention of possible connections between Spanish colonial forces' participation in slave-trade suppression and in counterrevolutionary coastal policing: Gustavo Placer Cervera, "La Guerra de los Diez Años: Sus aspectos navales," in Zanetti Lecuona, *La revolución de 1868*, 105–26.
100. For example, see petition of Francisco Lopez Martin to captain general, 5 December 1870, in Expediente promovido por Comandante General de Marina en solicitud que se le expida una certificacion que acredite haberse declarado emancipados los 281 bozales aprehendidos en Cayo Judio por el Vapor *Fernandito*, GSC 349/16844, ANC.
101. María Elena Meneses Muro, *El embargo de los esclavos: Movilidad, espacios y trabajo durante La Guerra de los Diez Años en Cuba* (Santa Marta, Colombia: Editorial Unimagdalena, 2021).
102. On deportation, see Juan Luis Bachero Bachero, "La deportación en La Guerra Cubana de los Diez Años (1868–1878)," *Cuban Studies* 50 (January 2021): 1–24.
103. Expediente relativo al Real Decreto de 29 de Septiembre de 1866, para que todo individuo de color, sujeto a servidumbre, que vaya a la península é Islas adyacentes, se repute emancipado, AP 228/6, ANC.
104. *Fiscal* report, 11 May 1868, in Documentos relacionados con la causa criminal por conspiración para cometer el delito de rebelión, fraguada por negros esclavos, AP 56/8, ANC, fol. 3v.

105. See statements of Juan Lousan and Fernando, Diligencias formadas para averiguar si es cierto que una partida de insurrectos se llevaron junto con los esclavos de la Hacienda San Fernando del Dr Fernando Pons el negro emancipado nombrado Martín, AP 57/18, ANC, fols. 6v–7r, 7v. For a criminal prosecution of an alleged insurgent for recruiting an enslaved man called Rafael, see Criminal de oficio por extracción de un esclavo del poder de un dueño y amenazas de fusilamiento si no lo entregaba (Político) por León Soublet, natural de Nueva Orleans, AP 58/18, ANC.
106. Statement of Eugenio Soulé, in AP 57/18, ANC, fols. 21v–22r.
107. AP 57/18, ANC, fols. 11r, 13r–v, 15.
108. Francisco de Acosta y Albear, *Compendio histórico del pasado y presente de Cuba y de su guerra insurreccional hasta el 11 de Marzo de 1875, con algunas apreciaciones relativas a su porvenir* (Madrid: Imp. a cargo de Juan José de las Heras, 1875), 44.
109. The file lists the following names by each liberated African—these were perhaps alternative names for each person or interpreters who helped them with their complaint: Enrique, Cirilo Congo, Mateo, Milano, and Tomas, respectively. Emancipados, 108/11327, AHPM, fol. 12r.
110. Emancipados, 108/11327, AHPM, fols. 6r, 7r.
111. For the five eastern jurisdictions, see Ferrer, *Insurgent Cuba*, tables 1.1 and 2.1.
112. Emancipados, 107/11290, AHPM.
113. For example, the eight contracts of Ignacio de Cárdenas with Remigio, Daniel, Julian, Simon, Plácido, Teresa, Felipa, Dolores, respectively, all 3 October 1870, Emancipados, 107/11265, AHPM, fols. 16–33.
114. Note of Gobierno Superior Político, 11 August 1871, Emancipados, 107/11244, AHPM, fol. 28r.
115. Unsigned table, 15 April [1871], in Emancipados, 107/11266, AHPM, fol. 3r.
116. Note by governor, 23 November 1870, Emancipados, 107/11266, AHPM, fol. 4v.
117. Enrique Rosales to the Brigadier Civil Governor of Matanzas, 16 June 1871, Emancipados, 107/11244, AHPM, fol. 26r. The men's demands for both medical care and freedom from compulsory labor bore resemblances to the "embodied self-sovereignty" emphasized by Anglo-American abolitionists. See Kathleen M. Brown, *Undoing Slavery: Bodies, Race, and Rights in the Age of Abolition* (Philadelphia: University of Pennsylvania Press, 2023).
118. Rebecca J. Scott, *Degrees of Freedom: Louisiana and Cuba after Slavery* (Cambridge, MA: Harvard University Press, 2005).
119. Dylan Penningroth, "The Claims of Slaves and Ex-Slaves to Family and Property: A Transatlantic Comparison," *American Historical Review* 112, no. 4 (2007): 1039–69.
120. Foner, *Reconstruction*, 104–5; Holt, *Problem of Freedom*.

CONCLUSION

1. On transitions to free labor, see Holt, *Problem of Freedom*; R. Scott, *Slave Emancipation in Cuba*; Cooper, Holt, and Scott, *Beyond Slavery*. On the expansion of unfree labor in Brazil, see Mamigonian, "Revisitando o problema da 'Transição para o trabalho livre.' "

2. On the carceral dimensions of indenture, see Marina Carter, V. Govinden, and S. Peerthum, *The Last Slaves: Liberated Africans in 19th Century Mauritius* (Port Louis, Mauritius: Center for Research on Indian Ocean Societies, 2003); Clare Anderson, "Convicts and Coolies: Rethinking Indentured Labour in the Nineteenth Century," *Slavery & Abolition* 30, no. 1 (1 March 2009): 93–109.
3. Gavin Lewis, *Between the Wire and the Wall: A History of South African "Coloured" Politics* (Cape Town: David Philip, 1987), 21, 24–25.
4. Da Silva et al., "Diaspora of Africans Liberated from Slave Ships."
5. Emmanuel Akyeampong and Hippolyte Fofack, "The Contribution of African Women to Economic Growth and Development in the Pre-Colonial and Colonial Periods: Historical Perspectives and Policy Implications," *Economic History of Developing Regions* 29, no. 1 (June 2014): 42–73.
6. Frederick Cooper, *From Slaves to Squatters: Plantation Labor and Agriculture in Zanzibar and Coastal Kenya, 1890–1925* (New Haven, CT: Yale University Press, 1980); Huzzey, *Freedom Burning.*
7. Mann, *Slavery and the Birth of an African City*, 191.
8. Luiz Felipe de Alencastro, "Parecer sobre a Arguição de Descumprimento de Preceito Fundamental, ADPF/186, apresentada ao Supremo Tribunal Federal," Audiência pública sobre Políticas de Ação Afirmativa de Reserva de Vagas no Ensino Superior, 4 March 2010, transcript available in *Anais do XXVI Simpósio Nacional de História—ANPUH*, 2011, http://www.snh2011.anpuh.org/resources/anais/14/1300915614_ARQUIVO_parecerSTFalencastro.pdf. On elites' use of racial domination to capture state power for economic growth that favored their own interests, see Anthony W. Marx, *Making Race and Nation: A Comparison of South Africa, the United States, and Brazil* (Cambridge: Cambridge University Press, 1998), 178–90.
9. Paul D. Halliday, "Laws' Histories: Pluralisms, Pluralities, Diversity," in *Legal Pluralism and Empires, 1500–1850*, ed. Lauren Benton and Richard J. Ross (New York: New York University Press, 2013), 261–77.
10. Malka, *Men of Mobtown*, 80–84.
11. Schuler, "Liberated Africans in Nineteenth-Century Guyana."
12. Blyden, *West Indians in West Africa*, chap. 5.
13. On temporalities of justice, Steven Feierman, *Peasant Intellectuals: Anthropology and History in Tanzania* (Madison: University of Wisconsin Press, 1990), chap. 3.
14. James Africanus Beale Horton, *West African Countries and Peoples, British and Native: And a Vindication of the African Race* (London: W. J. Johnson, 1868), i. Pan-Africanist thinkers differed over whether the imperial ideology of a civilizational hierarchy offered a template for political progress or weakened unity among people of the African diaspora, for which see Philip Janzen, "Tensions on the Railway: West Indians, Colonial Hierarchies, and the Language of Racial Unity in West Africa," *Journal of African History* 64, no. 3 (2023): 388–405.
15. W. E. B. Du Bois, *The Suppression of the African Slave-Trade to the United States of America, 1638–1870* (New York: Longmans, Green, 1896); Paul Richards, "A Pan-African Composer? Coleridge-Taylor and Africa," *Black Music Research Journal* 21, no. 2 (2001): 235–60, 240, figure 1.

INDEX